PROBABILITY
FOR
RISK MANAGEMENT

by

Matthew J. Hassett, ASA, Ph.D.

and

Donald G. Stewart, Ph.D.

Department of Mathematics and Statistics
Arizona State University

ACTEX Publications, Inc.
Winsted, Connecticut

Requests for permission should be addressed to
        ACTEX Publications, Inc.
        P.O. Box 974
        Winsted, CT 06098

Manufactured in the United States of America

10 9 8 7 6 5 4 3 2

Cover design by Christine Phelps

Library of Congress Cataloging-in-Publication Data

Hassett, Matthew J.
    Probability for risk management / by Matthew J. Hassett and Donald
G. Stewart. -- 2nd ed.
        p. cm.
    Includes bibliographical references and index.
    ISBN-13: 978-1-56698-583-3 (pbk. : alk. paper)
    ISBN-10: 1-56698-548-X (alk. paper)
  1. Risk management--Statistical methods. 2. Risk (Insurance)--
Statistical methods. 3. Probabilities. I. Stewart, Donald, 1933- II. Title.

    HD61.H35 2006
    658.15'5--dc22

                                                        2006021589

ISBN-13: 978-1-56698-583-3
ISBN-10: 1-56698-548-X

Preface
to the Second Edition

The major change in this new edition is an increase in the number of challenging problems. This was requested by our readers. Since the actuarial examinations are an excellent source of challenging problems, we have added 109 sample exam problems to our exercise sections. (Detailed solutions can be found in the solutions manual). We thank the Society of Actuaries for permission to use these problems.

We have added three new sections which cover the bivariate normal distribution, joint moment generating functions and the multinomial distribution.

The authors would like to thank the second edition review team: Leonard A. Asimow, ASA, Ph.D. Robert Morris University, and Krupa S. Viswanathan, ASA, Ph.D., Temple University.

Finally we would like to thank Gail Hall for her editorial work on the text and Marilyn Baleshiski for putting the book together.

Matt Hassett
Don Stewart

Tempe, Arizona
June, 2006

Preface

This text provides a first course in probability for students with a basic calculus background. It has been designed for students who are mostly interested in the applications of probability to risk management in vital modern areas such as insurance, finance, economics, and health sciences. The text has many features which are tailored for those students.

Integration of applications and theory. Much of modern probability theory was developed for the analysis of important risk management problems. The student will see here that each concept or technique applies not only to the standard card or dice problems, but also to the analysis of insurance premiums, unemployment durations, and lives of mortgages. Applications are not separated as if they were an afterthought to the theory. The concept of pure premium for an insurance is introduced in a section on expected value because the pure premium is an expected value.

Relevant applications. Applications will be taken from texts, published studies, and practical experience in actuarial science, finance, and economics.

Development of key ideas through well-chosen examples. The text is not abstract, axiomatic or proof-oriented. Rather, it shows the student how to use probability theory to solve practical problems. The student will be introduced to Bayes' Theorem with practical examples using trees and then shown the relevant formula. Expected values of distributions such as the gamma will be presented as useful facts, with proof left as an honors exercise. The student will focus on applying Bayes' Theorem to disease testing or using the gamma distribution to model claim severity.

Emphasis on intuitive understanding. Lack of formal proofs does not correspond to a lack of basic understanding. A well-chosen tree example shows most students what Bayes' Theorem is really doing. A simple expected value calculation for the exponential distribution or a polynomial density function demonstrates how expectations are found. The student should feel that he or she understands each concept. The words "beyond the scope of this text" will be avoided.

Organization as a useful future reference. The text will present key formulas and concepts in clearly identified formula boxes and provide useful summary tables. For example, Appendix B will list all major distributions covered, along with the density function, mean, variance, and moment generating function of each.

Use of technology. Modern technology now enables most students to solve practical problems which were once thought to be too involved. Thus students might once have integrated to calculate probabilities for an exponential distribution, but avoided the same problem for a gamma distribution with $\alpha = 5$ and $\beta = 3$. Today any student with a TI-83 calculator or a personal computer version of MATLAB or Maple or Mathematica can calculate probabilities for the latter distribution. The text will contain boxed Technology Notes which show what can be done with modern calculating tools. These sections can be omitted by students or teachers who do not have access to this technology, or required for classes in which the technology is available.

The practical and intuitive style of the text will make it useful for a number of different course objectives.

A first course in probability for undergraduate mathematics majors. This course would enable sophomores to see the power and excitement of applied probability early in their programs, and provide an incentive to take further probability courses at higher levels. It would be especially useful for mathematics majors who are considering careers in actuarial science.

An incentive course for talented business majors. The probability methods contained here are used on Wall Street, but they are not generally required of business students. There is a large untapped pool of mathematically-talented business students who could use this course experience as a base for a career as a "rocket scientist" in finance or as a mathematical economist.

An applied review course for theoretically-oriented students. Many mathematics majors in the United States take only an advanced, proof-oriented course in probability. This text can be used for a review of basic material in an understandable applied context. Such a review may be particularly helpful to mathematics students who decide late in their programs to focus on actuarial careers.

The text has been class-tested twice at Arizona State University. Each class had a mixed group of actuarial students, mathematically- talented students from other areas such as economics, and interested mathematics majors. The material covered in one semester was Chapters 1-7, Sections 8.1-8.5, Sections 9.1-9.4, Chapter 10 and Sections 11.1-11.4. The text is also suitable for a pre-calculus introduction to probability using Chapters 1-6, or a two-semester course which covers the entire text. As always, the amount of material covered will depend heavily on the preferences of the instructor.

The authors would like to thank the following members of a review team which worked carefully through two draft versions of this text:

> Sam Broverman, ASA, Ph.D., University of Toronto
> Sheldon Eisenberg, Ph.D., University of Hartford
> Bryan Hearsey, ASA, Ph.D., Lebanon Valley College
> Tom Herzog, ASA, Ph.D., Department of HUD
> Eugene Spiegel, Ph.D., University of Connecticut

The review team made many valuable suggestions for improvement and corrected many errors. Any errors which remain are the responsibility of the authors.

A second group of actuaries reviewed the text from the point of view of the actuary working in industry. We would like to thank William Gundberg, EA, Brian Januzik, ASA, and Andy Ribaudo, ASA, ACAS, FCAS, for valuable discussions on the relation of the text material to the day-to-day work of actuarial science.

Special thanks are due to others. Dr. Neil Weiss of Arizona State University was always available for extremely helpful discussions concerning subtle technical issues. Dr. Michael Ratliff, ASA, of Northern Arizona University and Dr. Stuart Klugman, FSA, of Drake University read the entire text and made extremely helpful suggestions.

Thanks are also due to family members. Peggy Craig-Hassett provided warm and caring support throughout the entire process of creating this text. John, Thia, Breanna, JJ, Laini, Ben, Flint, Elle and Sabrina all enriched our lives, and also provided motivation for some of our examples.

We would like to thank the ACTEX team which turned the idea for this text into a published work. Richard (Dick) London, FSA, first proposed the creation of this text to the authors and has provided editorial guidance through every step of the project. Denise Rosengrant did the daily work of turning our copy into an actual book.

Finally a word of thanks for our students. Thank you for working with us through two semesters of class-testing, and thank you for your positive and cooperative spirit throughout. In the end, this text is not ours. It is yours because it will only achieve its goals if it works for you.

May, 1999   Matthew J. Hassett
Tempe, Arizona   Donald G. Stewart

Table of Contents

Chapter 3: Elements of Probability 45

Chapter 4: Discrete Random Variables 83

Chapter 5: Commonly Used Discrete Distributions 113

Chapter 6: Applications for Discrete Random Variables 149

Chapter 12: Stochastic Processes 373

To Breanna and JJ,
Ty and Jake,
Flint,
Xochil

Chapter 1
Probability: A Tool for
Risk Management

1.1   Who Uses Probability?

Probability theory is used for decision-making and risk management throughout modern civilization. Individuals use probability daily, whether or not they know the mathematical theory in this text. If a weather forecaster says that there is a 90% chance of rain, people carry umbrellas. The "90% chance of rain" is a statement of a probability. If a doctor tells a patient that a surgery has a 50% chance of an unpleasant side effect, the patient may want to look at other possible forms of treatment. If a famous stock market analyst states that there is a 90% chance of a severe drop in the stock market, people sell stocks. All of us make decisions about the weather, our finances and our health based on percentage statements which are really probability statements.

Because probabilities are so important in our analysis of risk, professionals in a wide range of specialties study probability. Weather experts use probability to derive the percentages given in their forecasts. Medical researchers use probability theory in their study of the effectiveness of new drugs and surgeries. Wall Street firms hire mathematicians to apply probability in the study of investments.

The insurance industry has a long tradition of using probability to manage its risks. If you want to buy car insurance, the price you will pay is based on the probability that you will have an accident. (This price is called a **premium**.) Life insurance becomes more expensive to purchase as you get older, because there is a higher probability that you will die. Group health insurance rates are based on the study of the probability that the group will have a certain level of claims.

The professionals who are responsible for the risk management and premium calculation in insurance companies are called actuaries. Actuaries take a long series of exams to be certified, and those exams emphasize mathematical probability because of its importance in insurance risk management. Probability is also used extensively in investment analysis, banking and corporate finance. To illustrate the application of probability in financial risk management, the next section gives a simplified example of how an insurance rate might be set using probabilities.

1.2   An Example from Insurance

In 2002 deaths from motor vehicle accidents occurred at a rate of 15.5 per 100,000 population.[1] This is really a statement of a probability. A mathematician would say that the probability of death from a motor vehicle accident in the next year is $15.5/100,000 = .000155$.

Suppose that you decide to sell insurance and offer to pay $10,000 if an insured person dies in a motor vehicle accident. (The money will go to a beneficiary who is named in the policy — perhaps a spouse, a close friend, or the actuarial program at your alma mater.) Your idea is to charge for the insurance and use the money obtained to pay off any claims that may occur. The tricky question is what to charge.

You are optimistic and plan to sell 1,000,000 policies. If you believe the rate of 15.5 deaths from motor vehicles per 100,000 population still holds today, you would expect to have to pay 155 claims on your 1,000,000 policies. You will need $155(10,000) = \$1,550,000$ to pay those claims. Since you have 1,000,000 policyholders, you can charge each one a premium of $1.55. The charge is small, but $1.55(1,000,000) = \$1,550,000$ gives you the money you will need to pay claims.

This example is oversimplified. In the real insurance business you would earn interest on the premiums until the claims had to be paid. There are other more serious questions. Should you expect exactly 155 claims from your 1,000,000 clients just because the national rate is 15.5 claims in 100,000? Does the 2002 rate still apply? How can you pay expenses and make a profit in addition to paying claims? To answer these questions requires more knowledge of probability, and that is why

---

[1] *Statistical Abstract of the United States*, 1996. Table No. 138, page 101.

this text does not end here. However, the oversimplified example makes a point. Knowledge of probability can be used to pool risks and provide useful goods like insurance. The remainder of this text will be devoted to teaching the basics of probability to students who wish to apply it in areas such as insurance, investments, finance and medicine.

1.3   Probability and Statistics

Statistics is a discipline which is based on probability but goes beyond probability to solve problems involving inferences based on sample data. For example, statisticians are responsible for the opinion polls which appear almost every day in the news. In such polls, a sample of a few thousand voters are asked to answer a question such as "Do you think the president is doing a good job?" The results of this sample survey are used to make an inference about the percentage of all voters who think that the president is doing a good job. The insurance problem in Section 1.2 requires use of both probability and statistics. In this text, we will not attempt to teach statistical methods, but we will discuss a great deal of probability theory that is useful in statistics. It is best to defer a detailed discussion of the difference between probability and statistics until the student has studied both areas. It is useful to keep in mind that the disciplines of probability and statistics are related, but not exactly the same.

1.4   Some History

The origins of probability are a piece of everyday life; the subject was developed by people who wished to gamble intelligently. Although games of chance have been played for thousands of years, the development of a systematic mathematics of probability is more recent. Mathematical treatments of probability appear to have begun in Italy in the latter part of the fifteenth century. A gambler's manual which considered interesting problems in probability was written by Cardano (1500-1572).

The major advance which led to the modern science of probability was the work of the French mathematician Blaise Pascal. In 1654 Pascal was given a gaming problem by the gambler Chevalier de Mere. The problem of points dealt with the division of proceeds of an interrupted game. Pascal entered into correspondence with another French mathematician, Pierre de Fermat. The problem was solved in this correspondence, and this work is regarded as the starting point for modern probability.

It is important to note that within twenty years of Pascal's work, differential and integral calculus was being developed (independently) by Newton and Leibniz. The subsequent development of probability theory relied heavily on calculus.

Probability theory developed at a steady pace during the eighteenth and nineteenth centuries. Contributions were made by leading scientists such as James Bernoulli, de Moivre, Legendre, Gauss and Poisson. Their contributions paved the way for very rapid growth in the twentieth century.

Probability is of more recent origin than most of the mathematics covered in university courses. The computational methods of freshman calculus were known in the early 1700's, but many of the probability distributions in this text were not studied until the 1900's. The applications of probability in risk management are even more recent. For example, the foundations of modern portfolio theory were developed by Harry Markowitz [11] in 1952. The probabilistic study of mortgage prepayments was developed in the late 1980's to study financial instruments which were first created in the 1970's and early 1980's.

It would appear that actuaries have a longer tradition of use of probability; a text on life contingencies was published in 1771.[2] However, modern stochastic probability models did not seriously influence the actuarial profession until the 1970's, and actuarial researchers are now actively working with the new methods developed for use in modern finance. The July 2005 copy of the North American Actuarial Journal that is sitting on my desk has articles with titles like "Minimizing the Probability of Ruin When Claims Follow Brownian Motion With Drift." You can't read this article unless you know the basics contained in this book and some more advanced topics in probability.

Probability is a young area, with most of its growth in the twentieth century. It is still developing rapidly and being applied in a wide range of practical areas. The history is of interest, but the future will be much more interesting.

---

[2] See the section on Historical Background in the 1999 Society of Actuaries Yearbook, page 5.

1.5   Computing Technology

Modern computing technology has made some practical problems easier to solve. Many probability calculations involve rather difficult integrals; we can now compute these numerically using computers or modern calculators. Some problems are difficult to solve analytically but can be studied using computer simulation. In this text we will give examples of the use of technology in most sections. We will refer to results obtained using the TI-83 and TI BA II Plus Professional calculators and Microsoft® EXCEL. but will not attempt to teach the use of those tools. The technology sections will be clearly boxed off to separate them from the remainder of the text.   Students who do not have the technological background should be aware that this will in no way restrict their understanding of the theory. However, the technology discussions should be valuable to the many students who already use modern calculators or computer packages.

Chapter 2
Counting for Probability

2.1   What Is Probability?

People who have never studied the subject understand the intuitive ideas behind the mathematical concept of probability. Teachers (including the authors of this text) usually begin a probability course by asking the students if they know the probability of a coin toss coming up heads. The obvious answer is 50% or ½, and most people give the obvious answer with very little hesitation. The reasoning behind this answer is simple. There are two possible outcomes of the coin toss, heads or tails. If the coin comes up heads, only one of the two possible outcomes has occurred. There is one chance in two of tossing a head.

The simple reasoning here is based on an assumption — *the coin must be fair, so that heads and tails are **equally likely***. If your gambler friend Fast Eddie invites you into a coin tossing game, you might suspect that he has altered the coin so that he can get your money. However, if you are willing to assume that the coin is fair, you count possibilities and come up with ½.

Probabilities are evaluated by counting in a wide variety of situations. Gambling related problems involving dice and cards are typically solved using counting. For example, suppose you are rolling a single six-sided die whose sides bear the numbers 1, 2, 3, 4, 5 and 6. You wish to bet on the event that you will roll a number less than 5. The probability of this event is 4/6, since the outcomes 1, 2, 3 and 4 are less than 5 and there are six possible outcomes (assumed equally likely). The approach to probability used is summarized as follows:

Probability by Counting for Equally Likely Outcomes

$$Probability \ of \ an \ event = \frac{Number \ of \ outcomes \ in \ the \ event}{Total \ number \ of \ possible \ outcomes}$$

Part of the work of this chapter will be to introduce a more precise mathematical framework for this counting definition. However, this is not the only way to view probability. There are some cases in which outcomes may not be equally likely. A die or a coin may be altered so that all outcomes are not equally likely. Suppose that you are tossing a coin and suspect that it is not fair. Then the probability of tossing a head cannot be determined by counting, but there is a simple way to *estimate* that probability — simply toss the coin a large number of times and count the number of heads. If you toss the coin 1000 times and observe 650 heads, your best estimate of the probability of a head on one toss is $650/1000 = .65$. In this case you are using a **relative frequency estimate** of a probability.

Relative Frequency Estimate of the Probability of an Event

$$Probability \ of \ an \ event = \frac{Number \ of \ times \ the \ event \ occurs \ in \ n \ trials}{n}$$

We now have two ways of looking at probability, the counting approach for equally likely outcomes and the relative frequency approach. This raises an interesting question. If outcomes are equally likely, will both approaches lead to the same probability? For example, if you try to find the probability of tossing a head for a fair coin by tossing the coin a large number of times, should you expect to get a value of ½? The answer to this question is "not exactly, but for a very large number of tosses you are highly likely to get an answer close to ½." The more tosses, the more likely you are to be very close to ½. We had our computer simulate different numbers of coin tosses, and came up with the following results.

Number of Tosses	Number of Heads	Probability Estimate
4	1	.25
100	54	.54
1000	524	.524
10,000	4985	.4985

More will be said later in the text about the mathematical reasoning underlying the relative frequency approach. Many texts identify a third approach to probability. That is the **subjective** approach to probability. Using this approach, you ask a well-informed person for his or her personal estimate of the probability of an event. For example, one of your authors worked on a business valuation problem which required knowledge of the probability that an individual would fail to make a monthly mortgage payment to a company. He went to an executive of the company and asked what percent of individuals failed to make the monthly payment in a typical month. The executive, relying on his experience, gave an estimate of 3%, and the valuation problem was solved using a subjective probability of .03. The executive's subjective estimate of 3% was based on a personal recollection of relative frequencies he had seen in the past.

In the remainder of this chapter we will work on building a more precise mathematical framework for probability. The counting approach will play a big part in this framework, but the reader should keep in mind that many of the probability numbers actually used in calculation may come from relative frequencies or subjective estimates.

2.2 The Language of Probability; Sets, Sample Spaces and Events

If probabilities are to be evaluated by counting outcomes of a probability experiment, it is essential that all outcomes be specified. A person who is not familiar with dice does not know that the possible outcomes for a single die are 1, 2, 3, 4, 5 and 6. That person cannot find the probability of rolling a 1 with a single die because the basic outcomes are unknown. In every well-defined probability experiment, all possible outcomes must be specified in some way.

The language of set theory is very useful in the analysis of outcomes. Sets are covered in most modern mathematics courses, and the reader is assumed to be familiar with some set theory. For the sake of completeness, we will review some of the basic ideas of set theory. A **set** is a collection of objects such as the numbers $1, 2, 3, 4, 5$ and 6. These objects are called the **elements** or **members** of the set. If the set is finite and small enough that we can easily list all of its elements, we can describe the set by listing all of its elements in braces. For the set above, $S = \{1, 2, 3, 4, 5, 6\}$. For large or infinite sets, the set-builder notation is helpful. For example, the set of all positive real numbers may be written as

$$S = \{x \mid x \text{ is a real number and } x > 0\}.$$

Often it is assumed that the numbers in question are real numbers, and the set above is written as $S = \{x \mid x > 0\}$.

We will review more set theory as needed in this chapter. The important use of set theory here is to provide a precise language for dealing with the outcomes in a probability experiment. The definition below uses the set concept to refer to all possible outcomes of a probability experiment.

Definition 2.1 The **sample space** S for a probability experiment is the set of all possible outcomes of the experiment.

Example 2.1 A single die is rolled and the number facing up recorded. The sample space is $S = \{1, 2, 3, 4, 5, 6\}$. □

Example 2.2 A coin is tossed and the side facing up is recorded. The sample space is $S = \{H, T\}$. □

Many interesting applications involve a simple two-element sample space. The following examples are of this type.

Example 2.3 (Death of an insured) An insurance company is interested in the probability that an insured will die in the next year. The sample space is $S = \{death, survival\}$. □

Example 2.4 (Failure of a part in a machine) A manufacturer is interested in the probability that a crucial part in a machine will fail in the next week. The sample space is $S = \{failure, survival\}$. □

Example 2.5 (Default of a bond) Companies borrow money they need by issuing **bonds**. A bond is typically sold in $1000 units which have a fixed interest rate such as 8% per year for twenty years. When you buy a bond for $1000, you are actually loaning the company your $1000 in return for 8% interest per year. You are supposed to get your $1000 loan back in twenty years. If the company issuing the bonds has financial trouble, it may declare bankruptcy and *default* by failing to pay your money back. Investors who buy bonds wish to find the probability of default. The sample space is $S = \{default, no default\}$. □

Example 2.6 (Prepayment of a mortgage) Homeowners usually buy their homes by getting a **mortgage loan** which is repaid by monthly payments. The homeowner usually has the right to pay off the mortgage loan early if that is desirable — because the homeowner decides to move and sell the house, because interest rates have gone down, or because someone has won the lottery. Lenders may lose or gain money when a loan is prepaid early, so they are interested in the probability of prepayment. If the lender is interested in whether the loan will prepay in the next month, the sample space is $S = \{prepayment, no prepayment\}$. □

The simple sample spaces above are all of the same type. Something (a bond, a mortgage, a person, or a part) either continues or disappears. Despite this deceptive simplicity, the probabilities involved are of great importance. If a part in your airplane fails, you may become an insurance death — leading to the prepayment of your mortgage and a strain on your insurance company and its bonds. The probabilities are difficult and costly to estimate. Note also that the coin toss sample space $\{H, T\}$ was the only one in which the two outcomes were equally likely. Luckily for most of us, insured individuals are more likely to live than die and bonds are more likely to succeed than to default.

Not all sample spaces are so small or so simple.

Example 2.7 An insurance company has sold 100 individual life insurance policies. When an insured individual dies, the beneficiary named in the policy will file a claim for the amount of the policy. You wish to observe the number of claims filed in the next year. The sample space consists of all integers from 0 to 100, so $S = \{0, 1, 2, \ldots, 100\}$. □

Some of the previous examples may be looked at in slightly different ways that lead to different sample spaces. The sample space is determined by the question you are asking.

Example 2.8 An insurance company sells life insurance to a 30-year-old female. The company is interested in the age of the insured when she eventually dies. If the company assumes that the insured will not live to 110, the sample space is $S = \{30, 31, \ldots, 109\}$. ☐

Example 2.9 A mortgage lender makes a 30-year monthly payment loan. The lender is interested in studying the month in which the mortgage is paid off. Since there are 360 months in 30 years, the sample space is $S = \{1, 2, 3, \ldots, 359, 360\}$. ☐

The sample space can also be infinite.

Example 2.10 A stock is purchased for $100. You wish to observe the price it can be sold for in one year. Since stock prices are quoted in dollars and fractions of dollars, the stock could have any non-negative rational number as its future value. The sample space consists of all non-negative rational numbers, $S = \{x \mid x \geq 0 \text{ and } x \text{ rational}\}$. This does not imply that the price outcome of $1,000,000,000 is highly likely in one year — just that it is possible. Note that the price outcome of 0 is also possible. Stocks can become worthless. ☐

The above examples show that the sample space for an experiment can be a small finite set, a large finite set, or an infinite set.

In Section 2.1 we looked at the probability of events which were specified in words, such as "toss a head" or "roll a number less than 5." These events also need to be translated into clearly specified sets. For example, if a single die is rolled, the event "roll a number less than 5" consists of the outcomes in the set $E = \{1, 2, 3, 4\}$. Note that the set E is a subset of the sample space S, since every element of E is an element of S. This leads to the following set-theoretical definition of an event.

Definition 2.2 An **event** is a subset of the sample space S.

This set-theoretic definition of an event often causes some unnecessary confusion since people think of an event as something described in words like "roll a number less than 5 on a roll of a single die." There is no conflict here. The definition above reminds you that you must take the event described in words and determine precisely what outcomes are in the event. Below we give a few examples of events which are stated in words and then translated into subsets of the sample space.

Example 2.11 A coin is tossed. You wish to find the probability of the event "toss a head." The sample space is $S = \{H, T\}$. The event is the subset $E = \{H\}$.   □

Example 2.12 An insurance company has sold 100 individual life policies. The company is interested in the probability that at most 5 of the policies have death benefit claims in the next year. The sample space is $S = \{0, 1, 2, \ldots, 100\}$. The event E is the subset $\{0, 1, 2, 3, 4, 5\}$.   □

Example 2.13 You buy a stock for $100 and plan to sell it one year later. You are interested in the event E that you make a profit when the stock is sold. The sample space is $S = \{x \mid x \geq 0 \text{ and } x \text{ rational}\}$, the set of all possible future prices. The event E is the subset $E = \{x \mid x > 100 \text{ and } x \text{ rational}\}$, the set of all possible future prices which are greater than the $100 you paid.   □

Problems involving selections from a standard 52 card deck are common in beginning probability courses. Such problems reflect the origins of probability. To make listing simpler in card problems, we will adopt the following abbreviation system:

A: Ace	K: King	Q: Queen	J: Jack
S: Spade	H: Heart	D: Diamond	C: Club

We can then describe individual cards by combining letters and numbers. For example KH will stand for the king of hearts and $2D$ for the 2 of diamonds.

Example 2.14 A standard 52 card deck is shuffled and a card is picked at random. You are interested in the event that the card is a king. The sample space, $S = \{AS, KS, \ldots, 3C, 2C\}$, consists of all 52 cards. The event E consists of the four kings, $E = \{KS, KH, KD, KC\}$.   □

The examples of sample spaces and events given above are straightforward. In many practical problems things become much more complex. The following sections introduce more set theory and some counting techniques which will help in analyzing more difficult problems.

2.3 Compound Events; Set Notation

When we refer to events in ordinary language, we often negate them (the card drawn is *not* a king) or combine them using the words "and" or "or" (the card drawn is a king *or* an ace). Set theory has a convenient notation for use with such **compound events**.

2.3.1 Negation

The event *not E* is written as $\sim E$. (This may also be written as $\overline{E}$.)

Example 2.15 A single die is rolled, $S = \{1, 2, 3, 4, 5, 6\}$. The event E is the event of rolling a number less than 5, so $E = \{1, 2, 3, 4\}$. E does *not* occur when a 5 or 6 is rolled. Thus $\sim E = \{5, 6\}$. ☐

Note that the event $\sim E$ is the set of all outcomes in the sample space which are not in the original event set E. The result of removing all elements of E from the original sample space S is referred to as $S - E$. Thus $\sim E = S - E$. This set is called the **complement** of E.

Example 2.16 You buy a stock for \$100 and wish to evaluate the probability of selling it for a higher price x in one year. The sample space is $S = \{x | x \geq 0$ and x rational$\}$. The event of interest is $E = \{x \mid x > 100$ and x rational$\}$. The negation $\sim E$ is the event that no profit is made on the sale, so $\sim E$ can be written as

$$\sim E = \{x \mid 0 \leq x \leq 100 \text{ and } x \text{ rational}\} = S - E.$$

This can be portrayed graphically on a number line.

$\sim E$: no profit E: profit

☐

Graphical depiction of events is very helpful. The most common tool for this is the **Venn diagram**, in which the sample space is portrayed as a rectangular region and the event is portrayed as a circular region inside the rectangle. The Venn diagram showing E and $\sim E$ is given in the following figure.

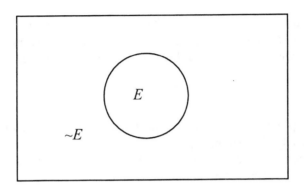

2.3.2   The Compound Events *A or B, A and B*

We will begin by returning to the familiar example of rolling a single die. Suppose that we have the opportunity to bet on two different events:

A: an even number is rolled B: a number less than 5 is rolled

$A = \{2, 4, 6\}$ $B = \{1, 2, 3, 4\}$

If we bet that *A or B* occurs, we will win if any element of the two sets above is rolled.

$$A \text{ or } B = \{1, 2, 3, 4, 6\}$$

In forming the set for *A or B* we have combined the sets A and B by listing all outcomes which appear in *either* A or B. The resulting set is called the **union** of A and B, and is written as $A \cup B$. It should be clear that for any two events A and B

$$A \text{ or } B = A \cup B.$$

For the single die roll above, we could also decide to bet on the event *A and B*. In that case, *both* the event *A* and the event *B* must occur on the single roll. This can happen only if an outcome occurs which is common to both events.

$$A \text{ and } B = \{2, 4\}$$

In forming the set for *A and B* we have listed all outcomes which are in both sets simultaneously. This set is referred to as the **intersection** of *A* and *B*, and is written as $A \cap B$. For any two events *A* and *B*

$$A \text{ and } B = A \cap B.$$

Example 2.17 Consider the insurance company which has written 100 individual life insurance policies and is interested in the number of claims which will occur in the next year. The sample space is $S = \{0, 1, 2, \ldots, 100\}$. The company is interested in the following two events:

A: there are at most 8 claims
B: the number of claims is between 5 and 12 (inclusive)

A and *B* are given by the sets

$$A = \{0, 1, 2, 3, 4, 5, 6, 7, 8\}$$
and
$$B = \{5, 6, 7, 8, 9, 10, 11, 12\}.$$

Then the events *A or B* and *A and B* are given by

$$A \text{ or } B = A \cup B = \{0, 1, 2, 3, 4, 5, 6, 7, 8, 9, 10, 11, 12\}$$

and

$$A \text{ and } B = A \cap B = \{5, 6, 7, 8\}. \qquad \square$$

The events *A or B* and *A and B* can also be represented using Venn diagrams, with overlapping circular regions representing *A* and *B*.

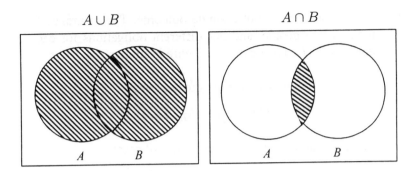

$A \cup B$ $A \cap B$

A B A B

2.3.3 New Sample Spaces from Old; Ordered Pair Outcomes

In some situations the basic outcomes of interest are actually pairs of simpler outcomes. The following examples illustrate this.

Example 2.18 (Insurance of a couple) Sometimes life insurance is written on a husband and wife. Suppose the insurer is interested in whether one or both members of the couple die in the next year. Then the insurance company must start by considering the following outcomes:

D_H: death of the husband $\qquad$ S_H: survival of the husband

D_W: death of the wife $\qquad$ S_W: survival of the wife

Since the insurance company has written a policy insuring both husband and wife, the sample space of interest consists of pairs which show the status of both husband and wife. For example, the pair (D_H, S_W) describes the outcome in which the husband dies but the wife survives. The sample space is

$$S = \{(D_H, S_W), (D_H, D_W), (S_H, S_W), (S_H, D_W)\}.$$

In this sample space, events may be more complicated than they sound. Consider the following event:

H: the husband dies in the next year

$$H = \{(D_H, S_W), (D_H, D_W)\}$$

The death of the husband is not a single outcome. The insurance company has insured two people, and has different obligations for each of the two outcomes in H. The death of the wife is similar.

W: the wife dies in the next year

$$W = \{(D_H, D_W), (S_H, D_W)\}$$

The events $H\ or\ W$ and $H\ and\ W$ are also sets of pairs.

$$H \cup W = \{(D_H, S_W), (D_H, D_W), (S_H, D_W)\}$$

$$H \cap W = \{(D_H, D_W)\} \qquad \square$$

Similar reasoning can be used in the study of the failure of two crucial parts in a machine or the prepayment of two mortgages.

2.4   Set Identities

2.4.1   The Distributive Laws for Sets

The distributive law for real numbers is the familiar

$$a(b + c) = ab + ac.$$

Two similar distributive laws for set operations are the following:

$$A \cap (B \cup C) = (A \cap B) \cup (A \cap C) \qquad (2.1)$$

$$A \cup (B \cap C) = (A \cup B) \cap (A \cup C) \qquad (2.2)$$

These laws are helpful in dealing with compound events involving the connectives *and* and *or*. They tell us that

$A\ and\ (B\ or\ C)$ is equivalent to $(A\ and\ B)\ or\ (A\ and\ C)$

and

$A\ or\ (B\ and\ C)$ is equivalent to $(A\ or\ B)\ and\ (A\ or\ C)$.

The validity of these laws can be seen using Venn diagrams. This is pursued in the exercises. These identities are illustrated in the following example.

Example 2.19 A financial services company is studying a large pool of individuals who are potential clients. The company offers to sell its clients stocks, bonds and life insurance. The events of interest are the following:

S: the individual owns stocks

B: the individual owns bonds

I: the individual has life insurance coverage

The distributive laws tell us that

$$I \cap (B \cup S) = (I \cap B) \cup (I \cap S)$$

and

$$I \cup (B \cap S) = (I \cup B) \cap (I \cup S).$$

The first identity states that

insured *and* (owning bonds *or* stocks)

is equivalent to

(insured *and* owning bonds) *or* (insured *and* owning stocks).

The second identity states that

insured *or* (owning bonds *and* stocks)

is equivalent to

(insured *or* owning bonds) *and* (insured *or* owning stocks).   □

2.4.2   De Morgan's Laws

Two other useful set identities are the following:

$$\sim(A \cup B) = \sim A \cap \sim B \qquad (2.3)$$
$$\sim(A \cap B) = \sim A \cup \sim B \qquad (2.4)$$

These laws state that

$$not(A \text{ or } B) \text{ is equivalent to } (not A) \text{ and } (not B)$$

and

$$not(A \text{ and } B) \text{ is equivalent to } (not A) \text{ or } (not B).$$

As before, verification using Venn diagrams is left for the exercises. The identity is seen more clearly through an example.

Example 2.20 We return to the events S (ownership of stock) and B (ownership of bonds) in the previous example. De Morgan's laws state that

$$\sim(S \cup B) = \sim S \cap \sim B$$

and

$$\sim(S \cap B) = \sim S \cup \sim B.$$

In words, the first identity states that if you don't own stocks *or* bonds then you don't own stocks *and* you don't own bonds (and vice versa). The second identity states that if you don't own both stocks *and* bonds, then you don't own stocks *or* you don't own bonds (and vice versa). □

De Morgan's laws and the distributive laws are worth remembering. They enable us to simplify events which are stated verbally or in set notation. They will be useful in the counting and probability problems which follow.

2.5   Counting

Since many (not all) probability problems will be solved by counting outcomes, this section will develop a number of counting principles which will prove useful in solving probability problems.

2.5.1   Basic Rules

We will first illustrate the basic counting rules by example and then state the general rules. In counting, we will use the convenient notation

$$n(A) = \text{the number of elements in the set (or event) } A.$$

Example 2.21 A neighborhood association has 100 families on its membership list. 78 of the families have a credit card[1] and 50 of the families are currently paying off a car loan. 41 of the families have both a credit card and a car loan. A financial planner intends to call on one of the 100 families today. The planner's sample space consists of the 100 families in the association. The events of interest to the planner are the following:

C: the family has a credit card L: the family has a car loan

We are given the following information:

$$n(C) = 78 \qquad n(L) = 50 \qquad n(L \cap C) = 41$$

The planner is also interested in the answers to some other questions. For example, she would first like to know how many families do not have credit cards. Since there are 100 families and 78 have credit cards, the number of families that do not have credit cards is $100 - 78 = 22$. This can be written using our counting notation as

$$n(\sim C) = n(S) - n(C). \qquad \square$$

This reasoning clearly works in all situations, giving the following general rule for any finite sample space S and event A.

$$n(\sim A) = n(S) - n(A) \qquad (2.5)$$

Example 2.22 The planner in the previous example would also like to know how many of the 100 families had a credit card or a car loan. If she adds $n(C) = 78$ and $n(L) = 50$, the result of 128 is clearly too high. This happened because in the 128 figure each of the 41 families with both a credit card and a car loan was counted twice. To reverse the double counting and get the correct answer, subtract 41 from 128 to get the correct count of 87. This is written below in our counting notation.

$$n(C \cup L) = n(C) + n(L) - n(C \cap L) = 78 + 50 - 41 = 87 \qquad \square$$

---

[1] In 2001, 72.7% of American families had credit cards. (*Statistical Abstract of the United States*, 2004-5, Table No. 1186.)

The reasoning in Example 2.22 also applies in general to any two events A and B in any finite sample space.

$$n(A \cup B) = n(A) + n(B) - n(A \cap B) \qquad (2.6)$$

Example 2.23 A single card is drawn at random from a well-shuffled deck. The events of interest are the following:

H: the card drawn is a heart $\qquad n(H) = 13$
K: the card is a king $\qquad\qquad n(K) = 4$
C: the card is a club $\qquad\qquad n(C) = 13$

The compound event $H \cap K$ occurs when the card drawn is both a heart and a king (i.e., the card is the king of hearts). Then $n(H \cap K) = 1$ and

$$n(H \cup K) = n(H) + n(K) - n(H \cap K) = 13 + 4 - 1 = 16.$$

The situation is somewhat simpler if we look at the events H and C. Since a single card is drawn, the event $H \cap C$ can only occur if the single card drawn is both a heart and a club, which is impossible. There are no outcomes in $H \cap C$, and $n(H \cap C) = 0$. Then

$$n(H \cup C) = n(H) + n(C) - n(H \cap C) = 13 + 13 - 0 = 26.$$

More simply,

$$n(H \cup C) = n(H) + n(C). \qquad \square$$

The two events H and C are called mutually exclusive because they cannot occur together. The occurrence of H excludes the possibility of C and vice versa. There is a convenient way to write this in set notation.

Definition 2.3 The **empty set** is the set which has no elements. It is denoted by the symbol $\emptyset$.

In the above example, we could write $H \cap C = \emptyset$ to show that H and C are mutually exclusive. The same principle applies in general.

Definition 2.4 Two events A and B are **mutually exclusive** if $A \cap B = \emptyset$.

> If A and B are mutually exclusive, then
>
> $$n(A \cup B) = n(A) + n(B). \qquad (2.7)$$

2.5.2   Using Venn Diagrams in Counting Problems

Venn diagrams are helpful in visualizing all of the components of a counting problem. This is illustrated in the following example.

Example 2.24   The following Venn diagram is labeled to completely describe all of the components of Example 2.22. In that example the sample space consisted of 100 families. Recall that the events of interest were C (the family has a credit card) and L (the family has a car loan). We were given that $n(C) = 78$, $n(L) = 50$ and $n(L \cap C) = 41$. We found that $n(L \cup C) = 87$. The Venn diagram below shows all this and more.

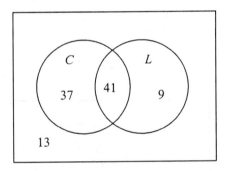

Since $n(C) = 78$ and $n(L \cap C) = 41$, there are 78 families with credit cards and 41 families with both a credit card and a car loan. This leaves $78 - 41 = 37$ families with a credit card and no car loan. We write the number 37 in the part of the region for C which does not intersect L. Since $n(L) = 50$, there are only 9 families with a car loan and no credit card, so we write 9 in the appropriate region. The total number of families with either a credit card or a car loan is clearly given by $37 + 41 + 9 = 87$. Finally, since $n(S) = 100$, there are $100 - 87 = 13$ families with neither a credit card nor a car loan. $\square$

The numbers on the previous page could all be derived using set identities and written in the following set theoretic terms:

$$n(L \cap C) = 41$$
$$n(\sim L \cap C) = 37$$
$$n(L \cap \sim C) = 9$$
$$n(\sim L \cap \sim C) = 13$$

However, the Venn diagram gives the relevant numbers much more quickly than symbolic manipulation. Some common counting problems are especially suited to the Venn diagram method, as the following example shows.

Example 2.25 A small college has 340 business majors. It is possible to have a double major in business and liberal arts. There are 125 such double majors, and 315 students majoring in liberal arts but not in business. How many students are in liberal arts or business?

Let B and L stand for majoring in business and liberal arts, respectively. The given information allows us to fill in the Venn diagram as follows.

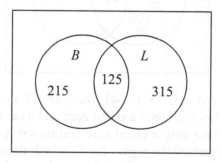

There are $215 + 125 + 315 = 655$ students in business or liberal arts. $\square$

The Venn diagram can also be used in counting problems involving three events, but requires the following slightly more complicated diagram.

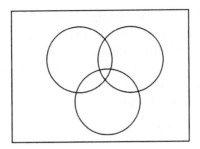

Some problems of this type are given in the exercises.

2.5.3 Trees

A **tree** gives a graphical display of all possible cases in a problem.

Example 2.26 A coin is tossed twice. The tree which gives all possible outcomes is shown below. We create one branch for each of the two outcomes on the first toss, and then attach a second set of branches to each of the first to show the outcomes on the second toss. The results of the two tosses along each set of branches are listed at the right of the diagram. □

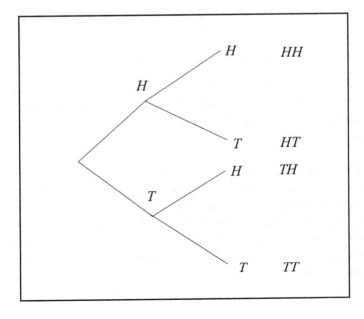

A tree provides a simple display of all possible pairs of outcomes in an experiment *if the number of outcomes is not unreasonably large*. It would not be reasonable to attempt a tree for an experiment in which two numbers between 1 and 100 were picked at random, but it is reasonable to give a tree to show the outcomes for three successive coin tosses. Such a tree is shown below.

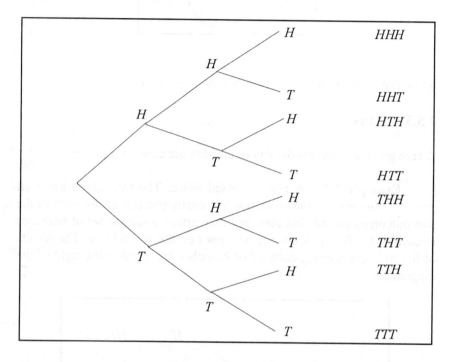

Trees will be used extensively in this text as visual aids in problem solving. Many problems in risk analysis can be better understood when all possibilities are displayed in this fashion. The next example gives a tree for disease testing.

Example 2.27 A test for the presence of a disease has two possible outcomes — positive or negative. A positive outcome indicates that the tested person *may* have the disease, and a negative outcome indicates that the tested person probably does not have the disease. Note that the test is not perfect. There may be some misleading results. The possibilities are shown in the tree below. We have the following outcomes of interest:

D: the person tested has the disease

$\sim D$: the person tested does not have the disease

Y: the test is positive

N: the test is negative

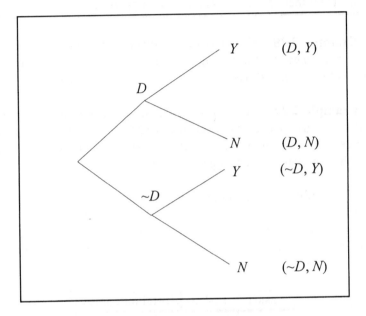

The outcome $(\sim D, Y)$ is referred to as a **false positive** result. The person tested does not have the disease, but nonetheless tests positive for it. The outcome (D, N) is a **false negative** result. □

2.5.4   The Multiplication Principle for Counting

The trees in the prior section illustrate a fundamental counting principle. In the case of two coin tosses, there were two choices for the outcome at the end of the first branch, and for each outcome on the first toss there were two more possibilities for the second branch. This led to a total of $2 \times 2 = 4$ outcomes. This reasoning is a particular instance of a very useful general law.

The Multiplication Principle for Counting

Suppose that the outcomes of an experiment consist of a combination of two separate tasks or actions. Suppose there are n possibilities for the first task, and that for each of these n possibilities there are k possible ways to perform the second task. Then there are nk possible outcomes for the experiment.

Example 2.28 A coin is tossed twice. The first toss has $n = 2$ possible outcomes and the second toss has $k = 2$ possible outcomes. The experiment (two tosses) has $nk = 2 \cdot 2 = 4$ possible outcomes.   □

Example 2.29 An employee of a southwestern state can choose one of three group life insurance plans and one of five group health insurance plans. The total number of ways she can choose her complete life and health insurance package is $3 \cdot 5 = 15$.   □

The validity of this counting principle can be seen by considering a tree for the combination of tasks. There are n possibilities for the first branch, and for each first branch there are k possibilities for the second branch. This will lead to a total of nk combined branches. Another way to present the rule schematically is the following:

Task 1	Task 2	Total outcomes
n ways	k ways	nk ways

The multiplication principle also applies to combined experiments consisting of more than two tasks. On page 26 we gave a tree to show all possible outcomes of tossing a coin three times. There were $2 \cdot 2 \cdot 2 = 8$ total outcomes for the combined experiment. This illustrates the general multiplication principle for counting.

Suppose that the outcomes of an experiment consist of a combination of k separate tasks or actions. If task i can be performed in n_i ways for each combined outcome of the remaining tasks for $i = 1, \ldots, k$, then the total number of outcomes for the experiment is $n_1 \times n_2 \times \ldots \times n_k$. Schematically, we have the following:

Task 1	Task 2	$\cdots$	Task k	Total outcomes
n_1	n_2	$\cdots$	n_k	$n_1 \times n_2 \times \cdots \times n_k$

Example 2.30 A certain mathematician owns 8 pairs of socks, 4 pairs of pants, and 10 shirts. The number of different ways he can get dressed is $8 \cdot 4 \cdot 10 = 320$. (It is important to note that this solution only applies if the mathematician will wear anything with anything else, which is a matter of concern to his wife.) □

The number of total possibilities in an everyday setting can be surprisingly large.

Example 2.31 A restaurant has 9 appetizers, 12 main courses, and 6 desserts. Each main course comes with a salad, and there are 6 choices for salad dressing. The number of different meals consisting of an appetizer, a salad with dressing, a main course, and a dessert is therefore $9 \cdot 6 \cdot 12 \cdot 6 = 3888$. □

2.5.5 Permutations

In many practical situations it is necessary to arrange objects in order. If you were considering buying one of four different cars, you would be interested in a $1, 2, 3, 4$ ranking which ordered them from best to worst. If you are scheduling a meeting in which there are 5 different speakers, you must create a program which gives the order in which they speak.

Definition 2.5 A **permutation** of n objects is an ordered arrangement of those objects.

The number of permutations of n objects can be found using the Multiplication Principal.

Example 2.32 The number of ways that four different cars can be ranked is shown schematically below.

Rank 1	Rank 2	Rank 3	Rank 4	Total ways to rank
4	3	2	1	$4 \cdot 3 \cdot 2 \cdot 1 = 24$

The successive tasks here are to choose Ranks 1, 2, 3 and 4. At the beginning there are 4 choices for Rank 1. After the first car is chosen, there are 3 cars left for Rank 2. After 2 cars have been chosen, there are only 2 cars left for Rank 3. Finally, there is only one car left for Rank 4. □

The same reasoning works for the problem of arranging 5 speakers in order. The total number of possibilities is $5 \cdot 4 \cdot 3 \cdot 2 \cdot 1 = 120$. To handle problems like this, it is convenient to use factorial notation.

$$n! = n(n-1)(n-2) \cdots 1$$

The notation $n!$ is read as "n factorial." The reasoning used in the previous examples leads to another counting principle.

First Counting Principle for Permutations

The number of permutations of n objects is $n!$.

Note: $0!$ is defined to be 1, the number of ways to arrange 0 objects.

Example 2.33 The manager of a youth baseball team has chosen nine players to start a game. The total number of batting orders that is possible is the number of ways to arrange nine players in order, namely $9! = 9 \cdot 8 \cdot 7 \cdot 6 \cdot 5 \cdot 4 \cdot 3 \cdot 2 \cdot 1 = 362,880$. (When the authors coached youth baseball, another coach stated that he had looked at all possible batting orders and had picked the best one. Sure.) □

The previous example shows that the number of permutations of n objects can be surprisingly large. Factorials grow rapidly as n increases, as shown in the following table.

n	$n!$
1	1
2	2
3	6
4	24
5	120
6	720
7	5,040
8	40,320
9	362,880
10	3,628,800
11	39,916,800

The number 52! has 68 digits and is too long to bother with presenting here. This may interest card players, since 52! is the number of ways that a standard card deck can be put in order (shuffled).

Some problems involve arranging only r of the n objects in order.

Example 2.34 Ten students are finalists in a scholarship competition. The top three students will receive scholarships for $1000, $500 and $200. The number of ways the scholarships can be awarded is found as follows:

Rank 1	Rank 2	Rank 3	Total ways to rank
10	9	8	$10 \cdot 9 \cdot 8 = 720$

This is similar to Example 2.32. Any one of the 10 students can win the $1000 scholarship. Once that is awarded, there are only 9 left for the $500. Finally, there are only 8 left for the $200. Note that we could also write

$$10 \cdot 9 \cdot 8 = \frac{10!}{7!} = \frac{10!}{(10 - 3)!}. \qquad \square$$

Example 2.34 is referred to as a problem of permuting 10 objects taken 3 at a time.

Definition 2.6 A permutation of n objects taken r at a time is an ordered arrangement of r of the original n objects, where $r \leq n$.

The reasoning used in the previous example can be used to derive a counting principle for permutations.

Second Counting Principle for Permutations

The number of permutations of n objects taken r at a time is denoted by $P(n, r)$.

$$P(n, r) = n(n - 1) \cdots (n - r + 1) = \frac{n!}{(n - r)!} \qquad (2.8)$$

Special Cases: $P(n, n) = n!$ $\qquad P(n, 0) = 1$

Technology Note

Calculation of $P(n, r)$ is simple using modern calculators. Inexpensive scientific calculators typically have a factorial function key. This makes the computation of $P(10, 3)$ above simple — find 10! and divide it by 7!.

More powerful calculators find quantities like $P(10, 3)$ directly. For example:

(a) On the TI-83 calculator, in the MATH menu under PRB, you will find the operator nPr. If you key in 10 nPr 3, you will get the answer 720 directly.

(b) On the TI BA II Plus Professional calculator, nPr is availble as a 2 ND function on the $\boxed{-}$ key.

Because modern calculators make these computations so easy, we will not avoid realistic problems in which answers involve large factorials.[2]

Many computer packages will compute factorials. The spreadsheet programs that are widely used on personal computers in business also have factorial functions. For example Microsoft® EXCEL has a function FACT(cell) which calculates the factorial of the number in the cell.

Example 2.35   Suppose a fourth scholarship for $100 is made available to the 10 students in Example 2.34. The number of ways the four scholarships can be awarded is

$$P(10, 4) = 10 \cdot 9 \cdot 8 \cdot 7 = \frac{10!}{6!} = 5040. \qquad \square$$

In some problems involving ordered arrangements the fact of ordering is not so obvious.

Example 2.36   The manager of a consulting firm office has 8 analysts available for job assignments. He must pick 3 analysts and assign one to a job in Bartlesville, Oklahoma, one to a job in Pensacola, Florida, and one to a job in Houston, Texas.[3] In how many ways can he do this?

---

[2] On most calculators factorials quickly become too large for the display mode, and factorials like 14! are given in scientific notation with some digits missing.

[3] This is real. Ben Wilson, a consultant and son-in-law of one of the authors, was recently sent to all three of those cities.

Solution This is a permutation problem, but it is not quite so obvious that order is involved. There is no implication that the highest ranked analyst will be sent to Bartlesville. However, order is implicit in making assignment lists like this one. The manager must fill out the following form:

City	Analyst
Bartlesville	?
Pensacola	?
Houston	?

There is no implication that the order of the cities ranks them in any way, but the list must be filled out with a first choice on the first line, a second choice on the second line and a final choice on the third line. This imposes an order on the problem. The total number of ways the job assignment can be done is

$$P(8, 3) = 8 \cdot 7 \cdot 6 = \tfrac{8!}{5!} = 336. \qquad \square$$

2.5.6 Combinations

In every permutation problem an ordering was stated or implied. In some problems, order is not an issue.

Example 2.37 A city council has 8 members. The council has decided to set up a committee of three members to study a zoning issue. In how many ways can the committee be selected?

Solution This problem does not involve order, since members of a committee are not identified by order of selection. The committee consisting of Smith, Jones and London is the same as the committee consisting of London, Smith and Jones. However, there is a way to look at the problem using what we already know about ordered arrangements. If we wanted to count all the ordered selections of 3 individuals from 8 council members, the answer would be

$$P(8, 3) = 336 = \text{number of ordered selections.}$$

In the 336 ordered selections, each group of 3 individuals is counted $3! = 6$ times. (Remember that 3 individuals can be ordered in 3! ways.)

Thus the number of unordered selections of 3 individuals is

$$\frac{336}{6} = \frac{P(8,3)}{3!} = 56.$$

In the language of sets, we would say that the number of possible three-element subsets of the set of 8 council members is 56, since a subset is a selection of elements in which order is irrelevant.   □

Definition 2.7 A **combination** of n objects taken r at a time is an r-element subset of the original n elements (or, equivalently, an unordered selection of r of the original n elements).

The number of combinations of n elements taken r at a time is denoted by $C(n,r)$ or $\binom{n}{r}$. The notation $\binom{n}{r}$ has traditionally been more widely used, but the $C(n,r)$ notation is more commonly used in mathematical calculators and computer programs — probably because it can be typed on a single line. We will use both notations in this text.

Example 2.37 above used the reasoning that since any 3-element subset can be ordered in 3! ways, then

$$C(8,3) = \binom{8}{3} = \frac{P(8,3)}{3!}.$$

Using Equation (2.8) for $P(8,3)$, we see that $P(8,3) = \frac{8!}{5!}$ and thus

$$C(8,3) = \frac{8!}{3!5!} = \frac{8 \cdot 7 \cdot 6}{3 \cdot 2 \cdot 1} = 56.$$

This reasoning applies to the r-element subsets of any n-element set, leading to the following general counting principle:

Counting Principle for Combinations

$$\binom{n}{r} = C(n,r) = \frac{P(n,r)}{r!} = \frac{n!}{r!(n-r)!} = \frac{n(n-1)\cdots(n-r+1)}{r!}$$

$$(2.9)$$

Special Cases: $C(n,n) = C(n,0) = 1$

Technology Note

Any calculator with a factorial function can be used to find $C(n, r)$. The TI-83 and TI-BA II Plus Professional calculators both have nCr functions which calculate $C(n, r)$ directly. Microsoft® EXCEL has a COMBIN function to evaluate $C(n, r)$.

Example 2.38 A company has ten management trainees. The company will test a new training method on four of the ten trainees. In how many ways can four trainees be selected for testing?
Solution

$$C(10, 4) = \frac{10!}{4!6!} = \frac{10 \cdot 9 \cdot 8 \cdot 7}{4!} = 210 \qquad \square$$

Example 2.39 It has become a tradition for authors of probability and statistics texts to include a discussion of their own state lottery. In the Arizona lottery, the player buys a ticket with six distinct numbers on it. The numbers are chosen from the numbers $1, 2, \ldots, 42$. What is the total number of possible combinations of 6 numbers chosen from 42 numbers?
Solution

$$C(42, 6) = \frac{42!}{6!36!} = \frac{42 \cdot 41 \cdot 40 \cdot 39 \cdot 38 \cdot 37}{6!} = 5,245,786 \qquad \square$$

2.5.7 Combined Problems

Many counting problems involve combined use of the multiplication principle, permutations, and combinations.

Example 2.40 A company has 20 male employees and 30 female employees. A grievance committee is to be established. The committee will have two male members and three female members. In how many ways can the committee be chosen?
Solution We will use the multiplication principle. We have the following two tasks:

Task 1: choose 2 males from 20
Task 2: choose 3 females from 30

The number of ways to choose the entire committee is

(Number of ways for Task 1) × (Number of ways for Task 2)

$$= \binom{20}{2}\binom{30}{3} = 190 \cdot 4060 = 771{,}400. \qquad \square$$

Example 2.41 A club has 40 members. Three of the members are running for office and will be elected president, vice-president and secretary-treasurer based on the total number of votes received. An advisory committee with 4 members will be selected from the 37 members who are not running for office. In how many ways can the club select its officers and advisory committee?

Solution In this problem, Task 1 is to rank the three candidates for office and Task 2 is select a committee of 4 from 37 members. The final answer is

$$3!\binom{37}{4} = 6 \cdot 66{,}045 = 396{,}270. \qquad \square$$

2.5.8 Partitions

Partitioning refers to the process of breaking a large group into separate smaller groups. The combination problems previously discussed are simple examples of partitioning problems.

Example 2.42 A company has 20 new employees to train. The company will select 6 employees to test a new computer-based training package. (The remaining 14 employees will get a classroom training course.) In how many ways can the company select the 6 employees for the new method?

Solution The company can select 6 employees from 20 in $C(20,6) = 38{,}760$ ways. Each possible selection of 6 employees results in a partition of the 20 employees into two groups — 6 employees for the computer-based training and 14 for the classroom. (We would get an identical answer if we solved the problem by selection of the 14 employees for classroom training.) The number of ways to partition the group of 20 into two groups of 6 and 14 is

$$\binom{20}{6} = \binom{20}{14} = \frac{20!}{6!14!} = 38{,}760. \qquad \square$$

A similar pattern develops when the partitioning involves more than two groups.

Example 2.43 The company in the last example has now decided to test televised classes in addition to computer-based training. In how many ways can the group of 20 employees be divided into 3 groups with 6 chosen for computer-based training, 4 for televised classes, and 10 for traditional classes?

Solution The partitioning requires the following two tasks:

Task 1: select 6 of 20 for computer-based training
Task 2: select 4 of the remaining 14 for the televised class

Once Task 2 is completed, only 10 employees will remain and they will take the traditional class. Thus the total number of ways to partition the employees is

$$\binom{20}{6}\binom{14}{4} = \frac{20!}{6!14!} \cdot \frac{14!}{4!10!} = \frac{20!}{6!4!10!} = 38{,}798{,}760. \qquad \square$$

The number of partitions of 20 objects into three groups of size 6, 4 and 10 is denoted by

$$\binom{20}{6,\,4,\,10}.$$

Example 2.43 showed that $\binom{20}{6,\,4,\,10} = \frac{20!}{6!4!10!}$, and, similarly, Example 2.42 showed that $\binom{20}{6,\,14} = \frac{20!}{6!14!}$.

The method of Example 2.43 can be used to show that this pattern always holds for the total number of partitions.

Counting Principle for Partitions

The number of partitions of n objects into k distinct groups of sizes $n_1, n_2, \ldots, n_k$ is given by

$$\binom{n}{n_1, n_2, \ldots, n_k} = \frac{n!}{n_1!n_2!\cdots n_k!}. \qquad (2.10)$$

Example 2.44 An insurance company has 15 new employees. The company needs to assign 4 to underwriting, 6 to marketing, 3 to accounting, and 2 to investments. In how many different ways can this be done? (Assume that any of the 15 can be assigned to any department.)

Solution

$$\binom{15}{4,\,6,\,3,\,2} = \frac{15!}{4!6!3!2!} = 6{,}306{,}300 \qquad \square$$

Many counting problems can be solved using partitions if they are looked at in the right way. Exercise 2-39, finding the number of ways to rearrange the letters in the word MISSISSIPPI, is a classical problem which can be done using partitions.

2.5.9 Some Useful Identities

In Example 2.42 we noted that

$$\binom{20}{6} = \binom{20}{14} = \frac{20!}{6!14!} = 38{,}760.$$

This is a special case of the general identity $C(n, k) = C(n, n-k)$, or

$$\binom{n}{k} = \binom{n}{n-k} = \frac{n!}{k!(n-k)!}.$$

In Exercise 2-46, the reader is asked to show that the total number of subsets of an n-element set is 2^n. Since $C(n, k)$ represents the number of k-element subsets of an n-element set, we can also find the total number of subsets of an n-element set by adding up all of the $C(n, k)$.

$$2^n = \binom{n}{0} + \binom{n}{1} + \cdots + \binom{n}{n-1} + \binom{n}{n}$$

For example,

$$2^3 = \binom{3}{0} + \binom{3}{1} + \binom{3}{2} + \binom{3}{3} = 1 + 3 + 3 + 1.$$

In Exercise 2-45, the reader is asked to use counting principles to derive the familiar Binomial Theorem

$$(x + y)^n = \binom{n}{0}x^n + \binom{n}{1}x^{n-1}y + \binom{n}{2}x^{n-2}y^2 + \cdots$$

$$+ \binom{n}{n-1}xy^{n-1} + \binom{n}{n}y^n.$$

This is useful for expansions such as

$$(x+y)^4 = \binom{4}{0}x^4 + \binom{4}{1}x^3y + \binom{4}{2}x^2y^2 + \binom{4}{3}xy^3 + \binom{4}{4}y^4$$

$$= x^4 + 4x^3y + 6x^2y^2 + 4xy^3 + y^4.$$

2.6   Exercises

2.2   The Language of Probability; Sets, Sample Spaces and Events

2-1.   From a standard deck of cards a single card is drawn. Let E be the event that the card is a red face card. List the outcomes in the event E.

2-2.   An insurance company insures buildings against loss due to fire.
(a)   What is the sample space of the amount of loss?
(b)   What is the event that the amount of loss is strictly between $1,000 and $1,000,000 (i.e., the amount x is in the open interval (1,000, 1,000,000))?

2-3.   An urn contains balls numbered from 1 to 25. A ball is selected and its number noted.
(a)   What is the sample space for this experiment?
(b)   If E is the event that the number is odd, what are the outcomes in E?

2-4.   An experiment consists of rolling a pair of fair dice, one red and one green. An outcome is an ordered pair (r, g), where r is the number on the red die and g is the number on the green die. List all outcomes of this experiment.

2-5.   Two dice are rolled. How many outcomes have a sum of (a) 7; (b) 8; (c) 11; (d) 7 *or* 11?

2-6.   Suppose a family has 3 children. List all possible outcomes for the sequence of births by sex in this family.

2.3   Compound Events; Set Notation

2-7.   Let S be the sample space for drawing a ball from an urn containing balls numbered from 1 to 25, and E be the event the number is odd. What are the outcomes in $\sim E$?

2-8.   In the sample space for drawing a card from a standard deck, let A be the event the card is a face card and B be the event the card is a club. List all the outcomes in $A \cap B$.

2-9.   Consider the insurance company that insures against loss due to fire. Let A be the event the loss is strictly between \$1,000 and \$100,000, and B be the event the loss is strictly between \$50,000 and \$500,000. What are the events in $A \cup B$ and $A \cap B$?

2-10.   An experiment consists of tossing a coin and then rolling a die. An outcome is an ordered pair, such as $(H, 3)$. Let A be the event the coin shows heads and B be the event the number on the die is greater than 2. What is $A \cap B$?

2-11.   In the experiment of tossing two dice, let E be the event the sum of the dice is 6 and F be the event both dice show the same number. List the outcomes in the events $E \cup F$ and $E \cap F$.

2-12.   In the sample space for the family with three children in Exercise 2-6, let E be the event that the oldest child is a girl and F the event that the middle child is a boy. List the outcomes in E, F, $E \cup F$ and $E \cap F$.

2.4   Set Identities

2-13.   Verify the two distributive laws by drawing the appropriate Venn diagrams.

2-14.   Verify De Morgan's laws by drawing the appropriate Venn diagrams.

2-15.　Let M be the set of students in a large university who are taking a mathematics class and E be the set taking an economics class.

　　(a)　Give a verbal statement of the identity
$$\sim(M \cup E) = \sim M \cap \sim E.$$

　　(b)　Give a verbal statement of the identity
$$\sim(M \cap E) = \sim M \cup \sim E.$$

2.5　Counting

2-16.　An insurance agent sells two types of insurance, life and health. Of his clients, 38 have life policies, 29 have health policies and 21 have both. How many clients does he have?

2-17.　A company has 134 employees. There are 84 who have been with the company more than 10 years and 65 of those are college graduates. There are 23 who do not have college degrees and have been with the company less than 10 years. How many employees are college graduates?

2-18.　A stockbroker has 94 clients who own either stocks or bonds. If 67 own stocks and 52 own bonds, how many own both stocks and bonds?

2-19.　In a survey of 185 university students, 91 were taking a history course, 75 were taking a biology course, and 37 were taking both. How many were taking a course in exactly one of these subjects?

2-20.　A broker deals in stocks, bonds and commodities. In reviewing his clients he finds that 29 own stocks, 27 own bonds, 19 own commodities, 11 own stocks and bonds, 9 own stocks and commodities, 8 own bonds and commodities, 3 own all three, and 11 have no current investments. How many clients does he have?

2-21.　An insurance agent sells life, health and auto insurance. During the year she met with 85 potential clients. Of these, 42 purchased life insurance, 40 health insurance, 24 auto insurance, 14 both life and health, 9 both life and auto, 11 both health and auto, and 2 purchased all three. How many of these potential clients purchased (a) no policies; (b) only health policies; (c) exactly one type of insurance; (d) life or health but not auto insurance?

2-22.   If an experiment consists of tossing a coin and then rolling a die, how many outcomes are possible?

2-23.   In purchasing a car, a woman has the choice of 4 body styles, 15 color combinations, and 6 accessory packages. In how many ways can she select her car?

2-24.   A student needs a course in each of history, mathematics, foreign languages and economics to graduate. In looking at the class schedule he sees he can choose from 7 history classes, 8 mathematics classes, 4 foreign language classes and 7 economics classes. In how many ways can he select the four classes he needs to graduate?

2-25.   An experiment has two stages. The first stage consists of drawing a card from a standard deck. If the card is red, the second stage consists of tossing a coin. If the card is black, the second stage consists of rolling a die. How many outcomes are possible?

2-26.   Let X be the n-element set $\{x_1, x_2, \ldots, x_n\}$. Show that the number of subsets of X, including X and $\emptyset$, is 2^n. (Hint: For each subset A of X, define the sequence $(a_1, a_2, \ldots, a_n)$ such that $a_i = 1$ if $x_i \in A$ and 0 otherwise. Then count the number of sequences).

2-27.   An arrangement of 4 letters from the set $\{A, B, C, D, E, F\}$ is called a (four-letter) word from that set. How many four-letter words are possible if repetitions are allowed? How many four-letter words are possible if repetitions are not allowed?

2-28.   Suppose any 7-digit number whose first digit is neither 0 nor 1 can be used as a telephone number. How many phone numbers are possible if repetitions are allowed? How many are possible if repetitions are not allowed?

2-29.   A row contains 12 chairs. In how many ways can 7 people be seated in these chairs?

2-30.   At the beginning of the basketball season a sportswriter is asked to rank the top 4 teams of the 10 teams in the PAC-10 conference. How many different rankings are possible?

2-31. A club with 30 members has three officers: president, secretary and treasurer. In how many ways can these offices be filled?

2-32. The speaker's table at a banquet has 10 chairs in a row. Of the ten people to be seated at the table, 4 are left-handed and 6 are right-handed. To avoid elbowing each other while eating, the left-handed people are seated in the 4 chairs on the left. In how many ways can these 10 people be seated?

2-33. Eight people are to be seated in a row of eight chairs. In how many ways can these people be seated if two of them insist on sitting next to each other?

2-34. A club with 30 members wants to have a 3-person governing board. In how many ways can this board be chosen? (Compare with Exercise 2-31.)

2-35. How many 5-card (poker) hands are possible from a deck of 52 cards?

2-36. How many of those poker hands consist of (a) all hearts; (b) all cards in the same suit; (c) 2 aces, 2 kings and 1 jack?

2-37. In a class of 15 boys and 13 girls, the teacher wants a cast of 4 boys and 5 girls for a play. In how many ways can she select the cast?

2-38. The Power Ball lottery uses two sets of balls, a set of white balls numbered 1 to 55 and a set of red balls numbered 1 to 42. To play, you select 5 of the white balls and 1 red ball. In how many ways can you make your selection?

2-39. How many different ways are there to arrange the letters in the word MISSISSIPPI?

2-40. An insurance company has offices in New York, Chicago and Los Angeles. It hires 12 new actuaries and sends 5 to New York, 3 to Chicago, and 4 to Los Angeles. In how many ways can this be done?

2-41.   A company has 9 analysts. It has a major project which has been divided into 3 subprojects, and it assigns 3 analysts to each task. In how ways can this be done?

2-42.   Suppose that, in Exercise 2-41, the company divides the 9 analysts into 3 teams of 3 each, and each team works on the whole project. In how many ways can this be done?

2-43.   Expand $(2s - t)^4$.

2-44.   In the expansion of $(2u - 3v)^8$, what is the coefficient of the term involving $u^5 v^3$?

2-45.   Prove the Binomial Theorem. (Hint: How many ways can you get the term $x^{n-k} y^k$ from the product of n factors, each of which is $(x + y)$?)

2-46.   Using the Binomial Theorem, give an alternate proof that the number of subsets of an n-element set is 2^n.

2.7   Sample Actuarial Examination Problem

2-47.   An auto insurance company has 10,000 policyholders. Each policyholder is classified as

   (i) young or old;
   (ii) male or female; and
   (iii) married or single.

   Of these policyholders, 3000 are young, 4600 are male, and 7000 are married. The policyholders can also be classified as 1320 young males, 3010 married males, and 1400young married persons. Finally, 600 of the policyholders are young married males.

   How many of the company's policyholders are young, female, and single?

Chapter 3
Elements of Probability

3.1   Probability by Counting for Equally Likely Outcomes

3.1.1   Definition of Probability for Equally Likely Outcomes

The lengthy Chapter 2 on counting may cause the reader to forget that our goal is to find probabilities. In Section 2.1 we stated an intuitively appealing definition of probability for situations in which outcomes were equally likely.

Probability by Counting for Equally Likely Outcomes

$$\textit{Probability of an event} = \frac{\textit{Number of outcomes in the event}}{\textit{Total number of possible outcomes}}$$

Chapter 2 gave us methods to count numbers of outcomes. The discussion of sets gave us a precise language for discussing collections of outcomes. Using the language and notation that have been developed, we can now give a more precise definition of probability.

Definition 3.1 Let E be an event from a sample space S in which all outcomes are equally likely. The probability of E, denoted $P(E)$, is defined by

$$P(E) = \frac{n(E)}{n(S)}.$$

Example 3.1 A company has 200 employees. 50 of these employees are smokers. One employee is selected at random. What is the probability that the selected employee is a smoker (Sm)?
  Solution

$$P(Sm) = \frac{n(Sm)}{n(S)} = \frac{50}{200} = .25 \qquad \square$$

Example 3.2 A standard 52 card deck is shuffled and one card is picked at random. What is the probability that the card is (a) a king (K); (b) a club (C); (c) a king and a club; (d) a heart and a club?
  Solution

(a) $P(K) = \dfrac{n(K)}{n(S)} = \dfrac{4}{52} = \dfrac{1}{13}$

(b) $P(C) = \dfrac{n(C)}{n(S)} = \dfrac{13}{52} = \dfrac{1}{4}$

(c)   The only card in the event $K \cap C$ is the king of clubs. Then
$$P(K \cap C) = \frac{n(K \cap C)}{n(S)} = \frac{1}{52}.$$

(d)   A single card cannot be both a heart and a club, so we have $n(H \cap C) = 0$. Then $P(H \cap C) = \dfrac{n(H \cap C)}{n(S)} = \dfrac{0}{52} = 0.$

$$\square$$

Part (d) of Example 3.2 illustrates an important point. It is impossible for a single card to be both a heart and a club. *If an event is impossible, n(E) will be 0 and P(E) will also be 0.*

3.1.2   Probability Rules for Compound Events

Some very useful probability rules can be derived from the counting rules in Section 2.5.1. The playing card experiment in Example 3.2 will provide simple illustrations of these rules. A standard deck is shuffled and a single card is chosen. We are interested in the following events:

H: the card drawn is a heart	$n(H) = 13$	$P(H) = 1/4$
K: the card is a king	$n(K) = 4$	$P(K) = 1/13$
C: the card is a club	$n(C) = 13$	$P(C) = 1/4$

Example 3.3 Find $P(\sim C)$.
Solution

$$P(\sim C) = \frac{n(\sim C)}{n(S)} = \frac{52-13}{52} = 1 - \frac{1}{4} = 1 - P(C) \qquad \square$$

The general rule for $P(\sim E)$ can be derived from Equation (2.5), $n(\sim E) = n(S) - n(E)$. Dividing by $n(S)$, we obtain

$$P(\sim E) = \frac{n(\sim E)}{n(S)} = \frac{n(S)}{n(S)} - \frac{n(E)}{n(S)} = 1 - P(E).$$

This gives a useful identity for $P(\sim E)$.

Negation Rule

$$P(\sim E) = 1 - P(E) \qquad\qquad (3.1)$$

Another useful rule comes from Equation (2.6), which states

$$n(A \cup B) = n(A) + n(B) - n(A \cap B).$$

Dividing by $n(S)$ here, we obtain

$$P(A \cup B) = \frac{n(A \cup B)}{n(S)} = \frac{n(A)}{n(S)} + \frac{n(B)}{n(S)} - \frac{n(A \cap B)}{n(S)}$$

$$= P(A) + P(B) - P(A \cap B).$$

This gives a useful identity for $P(A \cup B)$.

Disjunction Rule

$$P(A \cup B) = P(A) + P(B) - P(A \cap B) \qquad (3.2)$$

Example 3.4 A single card is drawn at random from a deck. Use Equation (3.2) to find (a) $P(K \cup C)$; (b) $P(H \cup C)$.
Solution

(a) $\qquad P(K \cup C) = P(K) + P(C) - P(K \cap C)$

$$= \frac{4}{52} + \frac{13}{52} - \frac{1}{52} = \frac{16}{52}$$

Note that this problem could also have been solved directly by counting $n(K \cup C)$ and dividing by 52. This should be obvious, since the rule used was based on counting. We will see later that Equation (3.2) still holds in situations where counting does not apply.

(b) $P(H \cup C) = P(H) + P(C) - P(H \cap C)$

$$= \frac{13}{52} + \frac{13}{52} - \frac{0}{52} = \frac{26}{52} \qquad \square$$

Part (b) of Example 3.4 illustrates a simple situation which occurs often. $P(H \cap C) = 0$, so that $P(H \cup C) = P(H) + P(C)$. Events like H and C are called mutually exclusive because the occurrence of one excludes the occurrence of the other. Mutually exclusive events were defined in Definition 2.4, which is repeated here for reinforcement.

Definition 2.4 Two events A and B are **mutually exclusive** if $A \cap B = \emptyset$.

For mutually exclusive events, $P(A \cap B) = 0$, and the following addition rule holds.

Addition Rule for Mutually Exclusive Events

If $A \cap B = \emptyset$, then $P(A \cup B) = P(A) + P(B)$.

Some care is needed in identifying mutually exclusive events. For example, if a single card is drawn from a deck, hearts and clubs are mutually exclusive. In some later problems we will look at the experiment of drawing two cards from a deck. In this case a first draw of a heart does not exclude a second draw of a club.

The rules developed here can be used in a wide range of applications.

Example 3.5 In Examples 2.21 and 2.22 we looked at a financial planner who intended to call on one family from a neighborhood association. In that association there were 100 families. 78 families had a credit card (C), 50 of the families were paying off a car loan (L), and 41 of the families had both a credit card and a car loan. The planner is going to pick one family at random. What is the probability that the family has a credit card or a car loan?

Solution

$$P(L \cup C) = P(L) + P(C) - P(L \cap C)$$

$$= \frac{50}{100} + \frac{78}{100} - \frac{41}{100} = .87 \qquad \square$$

The last problem could also have been solved directly by counting $n(L \cup C) = 87$. The identities used here will prove much more useful when we encounter problems which cannot be solved by counting.

3.1.3 More Counting Problems

It is a simple task to find the probability that a single card drawn from a deck is a king. Some probability calculations are a bit more complex. In this section we will give examples of individual probability calculations which are more interesting.

Example 3.6 In Example 2.40 we looked at a company with 20 male employees and 30 female employees. The company is going to choose 5 employees at random for drug testing. What is the probability that the five chosen employees consist of (a) 3 males and 2 females; (b) all males; (c) all females?

Solution The total number of ways to choose 5 employees from the entire company is $C(50,5)$. This will be the denominator of the solution in each part of this problem.

$$\binom{50}{5} = 2,118,760$$

(a) The total number of ways to choose a group of 3 males and 2 females is

$$\binom{20}{3}\binom{30}{2} = 1140 \cdot 435 = 495,900.$$

The probability of choosing a group of 3 males and 2 females is therefore

$$\frac{\binom{20}{3}\binom{30}{2}}{\binom{50}{5}} = \frac{495,900}{2,118,760} \approx .234.$$

(b)   An all-male group consists of 5 males and 0 females.
Reasoning as in part (a), we find that the probability of
choosing an all male group is

$$\frac{\binom{20}{5}\binom{30}{0}}{\binom{50}{5}} = \frac{\binom{20}{5}}{\binom{50}{5}} = \frac{15,504}{2,118,760} \approx .007.$$

(c)   Similarly, the probability of choosing an all-female group is

$$\frac{\binom{30}{5}}{\binom{50}{5}} = \frac{142,506}{2,118,760} \approx .067. \qquad \square$$

The above analysis is useful in many different applications. The
next example deals with testing defective parts; the mathematics is
identical.

Example 3.7 A manufacturer has received a shipment of 50 parts.
Unfortunately, 20 of the parts are defective. The manufacturer is going
to test a sample of 5 parts chosen at random from the shipment. What is
the probability that the sample contains (a) 3 defective parts and 2 good
parts; (b) all defective parts; (c) no defective parts?

Solution

(a) $\dfrac{\binom{20}{3}\binom{30}{2}}{\binom{50}{5}} = \dfrac{495,900}{2,118,760} \approx .234$

(b) $\dfrac{\binom{20}{5}\binom{30}{0}}{\binom{50}{5}} = \dfrac{\binom{20}{5}}{\binom{50}{5}} = \dfrac{15,504}{2,118,760} \approx .007$

(c) $\dfrac{\binom{30}{5}}{\binom{50}{5}} = \dfrac{142,506}{2,118,760} \approx .067$ $\qquad \square$

The range of different possible counting problems is very wide. The next example is not at all similar to the last two.

Example 3.8 Four people are subjected to an ESP experiment. Each one is asked to guess a number between 1 and 10. What is the probability that (a) no two of the four people guess the same number; (b) at least two of the four guess the same number?

Solution

(a) Each of the four people has the task of choosing from the numbers 1 to 10. The total number of ways this can be done is the number of ways to perform 4 tasks with 10 possibilities on each task, which is 10^4. The number of ways for the four people to choose 4 distinct numbers is $10 \cdot 9 \cdot 8 \cdot 7 = P(10, 4) = 5040$. (The first person has all 10 numbers to choose, leaving 9 for the second, 8 for the third, and 7 for the fourth.) Then the probability that none of the four guess the same number is

$$\frac{P(10, 4)}{10^4} = \frac{5,040}{10,000} = .504.$$

(b) At least two people guess the same number if it is *not* true that none of the 4 guess the same number.

P(at least two people guess the same)

$$= 1 - P(\text{no two people guess the same})$$

$$= 1 - \frac{P(10, 4)}{10^4} = .496 \qquad \square$$

In the previous example there were four people picking numbers from 1 to 10. A very similar problem occurs when you ask if any two of the four people have the same birthday. In this case, the birthday can be thought of as a number between 1 and 365, and we are asking whether any two of the people have the same number between 1 and 365. For a randomly chosen person, any day of the year has a probability of $\frac{1}{365}$ of being the birthday. The probability that at least two of the four have the same birthday is

$$1 - \frac{P(365, 4)}{365^4} \approx .016.$$

A surprising result appears when there are 40 people in a room. The probability that at least two have the same birthday is

$$1 - \frac{P(365, 40)}{365^{40}} \approx .891.$$

This result provides an interesting classroom demonstration for a teacher with 40 students and a little bit of nerve. (Remember that the probability of not finding 2 people with the same birthday is about .11.) The birthday problem is pursued further in the exercises.

Many more probability problems can be solved using counting. Most of the counting examples in this chapter can easily be used to solve related probability problems. A practical illustration of this is Example 2.39, which showed that the Arizona lottery has 5,245,786 possible combinations of 6 numbers between 1 and 42. This means that if you hold a lottery ticket and are waiting for the winning numbers to be drawn, the probability that your numbers will be drawn is 1/5,245,786.

3.2   Probability When Outcomes Are Not Equally Likely

The outcomes in an experiment are not always equally likely. We have already discussed the example of a biased coin which comes up heads 65% of the time and tails 35% of the time. Dice can be loaded so that the faces do not have equally likely probabilities. Outcomes in real data studies are rarely equally likely — e.g., the probability of a family having 5 children is much lower that the probability of having 2 children. In this section we will take a detailed look at a situation in which probabilities are not equally likely, and develop some of the key concepts which are used to analyze the probability in the general case.

Example 3.9 A large HMO is planning for future expenses. One component of their planning is a study of the percentage of births which involve more than one child — twins, triplets or more. The study leads to the following table:[1]

---

[1] These numbers are adapted from the 2006 edition of *Statistical Abstract of the United States*, Table 75.

Number of children	1	2	3
Percent of all births	96.70%	3.11%	0.19%

How will the company assign probabilities to multiple births for future planning?

Solution The table shows that the individual outcomes are not equally likely — a result which would not surprise anyone. The table also gives us numbers to use as the probabilities of individual outcomes.

$$P(1) = .9670 \qquad P(2) = .0311 \qquad P(3) = .0019$$

Once probabilities are defined for the individual outcomes, it is a simple matter to define the probability of any event. For example, consider the event E that a birth has more than one child. In set notation, $E = \{2, 3\}$. We can define

$$P(E) = P(2 \cup 3) = P(2) + P(3) = .0311 + .0019 = .0330.$$

What we have done here is to apply the addition rule to the mutually exclusive outcomes 2 and 3. We can define the probability for any event in the sample space $S = \{1, 2, 3\}$ in the same way — just add up the probabilities of the individual outcomes in the event. It is important to note that

$$P(S) = P(1) + P(2) + P(3) = .9670 + .0311 + .0019 = 1.$$

The sum of the probabilities of *all* the individual outcomes is 1.   ☐

3.2.1 Assigning Probabilities to a Finite Sample Space

Example 3.9 illustrated a natural method for assigning probabilities to events in any finite sample space with n individual outcomes denoted by $O_1, O_2, \ldots, O_n$.

(1) Assign a probability $P(O_i) \geq 0$ to each individual outcome O_i. The sum of all the individual outcome probabilities must be 1.

(2) Define the probability of any event E to be the sum of the probabilities of the individual outcomes in the event. (This is an application of the addition rule for mutually exclusive outcomes.) Then we have

$$P(E) = \sum_{O_i \in E} P(O_i).$$

Example 3.10 An automobile insurance company does a study to find the probability for the number of claims that a policyholder will file in a year. Their study gives the following probabilities for the individual outcomes $0, 1, 2, 3$.

Number of claims	0	1	2	3
Probability	.72	.22	.05	.01

The individual probabilities here are all non-negative and add to 1. We can now find the probability of any event by adding probabilities of individual outcomes.   □

3.2.2   The General Definition of Probability

Not all sample spaces are finite or as easy to handle as those above. To handle more difficult situations, mathematicians have developed an axiomatic approach that gives the general properties that an assignment of probabilities to events must have. If you define a way to assign a probability $P(E)$ to any event E, the following axioms should be satisfied:

(1) $P(E) \geq 0$ for any event E
(2) $P(S) = 1$
(3)   Suppose $E_1, E_2, \ldots, E_n, \ldots$ is a (possibly infinite) sequence of events in which each pair of events is mutually exclusive. Then

$$P\left(\bigcup_{i=1}^{\infty} E_i\right) = \sum_{i=1}^{\infty} P(E_i).$$

These axioms hold in Examples 3.9 and 3.10. Events have non-negative probabilities, individual probabilities add to one, and the addition rule works for mutually exclusive events.

In this text we will not take a strongly axiomatic approach. In situations where individual outcomes are not equally likely, we will define event probabilities in an intuitively natural way (as we did in the preceding examples) and then proceed directly to applied problems. The reader can assume that the above axioms hold, and in most cases it will be obvious that they do.

One advantage of the axiomatic approach is that the probability rules derived for equally likely outcomes can be shown to hold for any probability assignment that satisfies the axioms. In any probability problem we can use the following rules:

$$P(\sim E) = 1 - P(E)$$

$$P(A \cup B) = P(A) + P(B) - P(A \cap B)$$

$$P(A \cup B) = P(A) + P(B), \text{ if } A \text{ and } B \text{ are mutually exclusive}$$

The proof of the last rule from the axioms is simple — it is a special case of Axiom (3). Proofs of the first two properties from the axioms are outlined in the exercises. However, the emphasis here is not on proofs from the axioms. The important thing for the reader to know is that when probabilities have been properly defined, the above rules can be used.

3.3   Conditional Probability

In some probability problems a condition is given which restricts your attention to a subset of the sample space. When looking at the employees of a company, you might want to answer questions about males only or females only. When looking at people buying insurance, you might want to answer questions about smokers only or non-smokers only. The next section gives an example of how to find these conditional probabilities using counting.

3.3.1   Conditional Probability by Counting

Example 3.11 A health insurance pool includes 200 individuals. The insurer is interested in the number of smokers in the pool among both males and females. The following table (called a **contingency table**) shows the desired numbers.

	Males (M)	Females (F)	Total
Smokers (S)	28	22	50
Non-smokers ($\sim S$)	72	78	150
Total	100	100	200

Suppose one individual is to be chosen at random. Counting can be used to find the probability that the individual is a male, a female, a smoker, or both.

$$P(M) = \frac{100}{200} = .5 \qquad P(F) = \frac{100}{200} = .5 \qquad P(S) = \frac{50}{200} = .25$$

$$P(M \cap S) = \frac{28}{200} = .14 \qquad P(F \cap S) = \frac{22}{200} = .11$$

Suppose you were told that the selected individual was a male, and asked for the probability that the individual was a smoker, *given that the individual was a male*. (The notation for this probability is $P(S|M)$.) Since there are only 100 males and 28 of them are smokers, the desired probability can be found by dividing the number of male smokers by the total number of males.

$$P(S|M) = \frac{n(S \cap M)}{n(M)} = \frac{28}{100} = .28$$

This problem can also be solved using probabilities. If we divide the numerator and denominator of the last fractional expression by 200 (the total number of individuals), we see that

$$P(S|M) = \frac{28/200}{100/200} = \frac{.14}{.50} = \frac{P(S \cap M)}{P(M)} = .28.$$

The probability that the selected individual was a smoker, *given that the individual was a female*, can be found in the same two ways.

$$P(S|F) = \frac{n(S \cap F)}{n(F)} = \frac{22}{100} = .22$$

$$P(S|F) = \frac{P(S \cap F)}{P(F)} = \frac{.11}{.50} = .22$$

Note that the above conditional probabilities can be stated in words in another very natural way. In this group, 28% of the males smoke and 22% of the females smoke. □

3.3.2 Defining Conditional Probability

Example 3.11 showed two natural ways of finding a conditional probability. The first was based on counting.

Conditional Probability by Counting for Equally Likely Outcomes

$$P(A|B) = \frac{n(A \cap B)}{n(B)} \qquad (3.3)$$

When outcomes are not equally likely, this rule does not apply. Then we need a *definition* of conditional probability based on the probabilities that we can find. This definition is based on the second approach to conditional probability used in the example.

Definition 3.2 For any two events A and B, the **conditional probability** of A *given* B is defined as follows:

Definition of Conditional Probability

$$P(A|B) = \frac{P(A \cap B)}{P(B)} \qquad (3.4)$$

Example 3.12 In Example 3.9, probabilities were found for the number of children in a single birth.

$$P(1) = .9670 \qquad P(2) = .0311 \qquad P(3) = .0019$$

Suppose M is the event of a multiple birth, so that, $M = \{2, 3\}$. Find the probability of the birth of twins, *given that there is a multiple birth*.

Solution We need to find $P(2|M)$. We first note that

$$P(M) = .0311 + .0019 = .0330$$

and

$$P(M \cap 2) = P(2) = .0311.$$

Then by Definition 3.2,

$$P(2|M) = \frac{P(2 \cap M)}{P(M)} = \frac{.0311}{.0330} \approx .942.$$

The result tells us that approximately 96.7% of the multiple births are twins.   □

Example 3.13 In Example 3.10, probabilities were given for the possible numbers of insurance claims filed by individual policyholders.

Number of claims	0	1	2	3
Probability	.72	.22	.05	.01

Find the probability that a policyholder files exactly 2 claims, *given that the policyholder has filed at least one claim.*

Solution Let C be the event that at least one claim is filed. Then $C = \{1, 2, 3\}$ and $P(C) = .22 + .05 + .01 = .28$. We also need the value $P(2 \cap C) = P(2) = .05$. Then

$$P(2|C) = \frac{P(2 \cap C)}{P(C)} = \frac{.05}{.28} \approx .179.$$

This tells us that approximately 17.9% of the policyholders who file claims will file exactly 2 claims.   □

It is often simpler to find conditional probabilities by direct counting without using Equation (3.4).

Example 3.14 A card is drawn at random from a standard deck. The card is not replaced. Then a second card is drawn at random from the remaining cards. Find the probability that the second card is a king ($K2$), *given that the first card drawn was a king* ($K1$).

Solution If a king is drawn first and not replaced, then the deck will contain 51 cards and only 3 kings for the second draw.

$$P(K2|K1) = \frac{3}{51} \approx .0588$$

In this case the probability formula given by Equation (3.4) would require much more work to get this simple answer.   □

The definition of conditional probability, given by Equation (3.4), can be rewritten as a multiplication rule for probabilities.

> **Multiplication Rule for Probability**
>
> $$P(A \cap B) = P(A|B) \cdot P(B) \qquad (3.5)$$

Example 3.15 Two cards are drawn from a standard deck without replacement, as in Example 3.14. Find the probability that both are kings.

Solution
$$P(K1 \cap K2) = P(K1) \cdot P(K2|K1) = \frac{4}{52} \cdot \frac{3}{51} \approx .0045 \qquad \square$$

3.3.3   Using Trees in Probability Problems

Experiments such as drawing 2 cards without replacement and checking whether a king is drawn can be summarized completely using trees. The tree for Examples 3.14 and 3.15 is shown below.

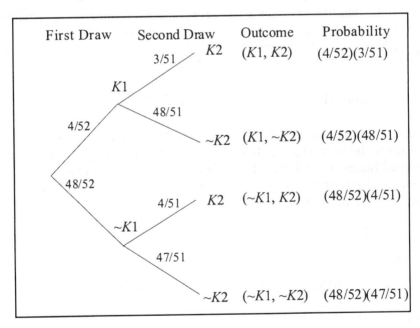

The first two branches on the left represent the possible first draws, and the next branches to the right represent the possible second draws. We write the probability of each first draw on its branch and the *conditional* probability of each second draw on its branch. At the end of each final branch we write the resulting 2-card outcome and the product of the two-branch probabilities. The multiplication rule tells us that the resulting product is the probability of the final 2-card outcome. For example, the product of the two fractions on the topmost branch is $P(K1 \cap K2)$, as calculated in the previous example.

The tree provides a rapid and efficient way to display all outcome pairs and their probabilities. This simplifies some harder problems, as the next example shows.

Example 3.16 Two cards are drawn at random from a standard deck without replacement. Find the probability that exactly one of the two cards is a king.

Solution The only pairs with exactly one king are $(K1, \sim K2)$ and $(\sim K1, K2)$. The desired probability is

$$P[(K1, \sim K2)] + P[(\sim K1, K2)] = \frac{4 \cdot 48}{52 \cdot 51} + \frac{48 \cdot 4}{52 \cdot 51} \approx .145. \quad \square$$

An intuitive description of our method for finding the probability of exactly one king would be to say that we have added up the final probabilities of all tree branches which contain exactly one king. This technique will be explored further in Section 3.5 on Bayes' Theorem.

3.3.4 Conditional Probabilities in Life Tables

Life tables give a probability of death for any given year of life. For example, Bowers, et al. [2] has a life table for the total population of the United States, 1979-1981. That table gives, for each integral age x, the estimated probability that an individual at integral age x will die in the next year. This probability is denoted by q_x.

$$q_x = P(\text{an individual aged } x \text{ will die before age } x + 1)$$

For example,

$$q_{25} = .00132 = P(\text{a 25-year-old will die before age 26})$$

and

$$q_{57} = .01059 = P(\text{a 57-year-old will die before age 58}).$$

Life tables are used in the pricing of insurance, the calculation of life expectancies, and a wide variety of other actuarial applications. They are mentioned here because the probabilities in them are really conditional. For example, q_{25} is the probability that a person dies before age 26, *given that the person has survived to age 25.*

3.4   Independence

3.4.1   An Example of Independent Events; The Definition of Independence

Example 3.17 A company specializes in coaching people to pass a major professional examination. The company had 200 students last year. Their pass rates, broken down by sex, are given in the following contingency table.

	Males	Females	Total
Pass	54	66	120
Fail	36	44	80
Total	90	110	200

This table can be used to calculate various probabilities for an individual selected at random from the 200 students.

$$P(Pass) = \frac{120}{200} = .60$$

$$P(Pass|Male) = \frac{54}{90} = .60 \qquad P(Pass|Female) = \frac{66}{110} = .60$$

These probabilities show that the overall pass rate was 60%, and that the pass rate for males and the pass rate for females were also 60%. When males and females have the same probability of passing, we say that passing is independent of gender.   □

The reasoning here leads to the following definition.

Definition 3.3 Two events A and B are **independent** if

$$P(A|B) = P(A).$$

In the above example, the events *Pass* and *Male* are independent because $P(Pass|Male) = P(Pass)$. When events are not independent they are called **dependent**.

In Example 3.11 we looked at an insurance pool in which there were males and females and smokers and non-smokers. For that pool, $P(S) = .25$ but $P(S|M) = .28$. The events S and M are dependent. (This was intuitively obvious in the original example. 28% of the males and only 22% of the females smoked. The probability of being a smoker depended on the sex of the individual.)

In many cases it appears obvious that two events are independent or dependent. For example, if a fair coin is tossed twice, most people agree that the second toss is independent of the first. This can be proven.

Example 3.18 The full sample space for two tosses of a fair coin is

$$\{HH, HT, TH, TT\}.$$

The four outcomes are equally likely. Let $H1$ be the event that the first toss is a head, and $H2$ the event that the second toss is a head. Show that the events $H1$ and $H2$ are independent.

Solution   We have $H2 = \{HH, TH\}$ and $P(H2) = .50$. Given that the first toss is a head, the sample space is reduced to the two outcomes $\{HH, HT\}$. Only one of these outcomes, HH, has a head as the second toss. Thus $P(H2|H1) = .50$. Then $P(H2|H1) = P(H2)$, and thus $H1$ and $H2$ are independent.   □

Coin-tossing problems are best approached by assuming that two successive tosses of a fair coin are independent. The counting argument above shows that is true.

There is another common problem in which independence and dependence are intuitively clear. If two cards are drawn from a standard deck *without* replacement of the first card, the probability for the second draw clearly depends on the outcome of the first. If a card is drawn and then replaced for the second random draw, the probability for the second draw is clearly independent of the first draw.

3.4.2 The Multiplication Rule for Independent Events

The general multiplication rule for any two events, given by Equation (3.5), is

$$P(A \cap B) = P(A|B) \cdot P(B).$$

If A and B are independent, then $P(A|B) = P(A)$ and the multiplication rule is simplified:

Multiplication Rule for Independent Events

$$P(A \cap B) = P(A) \cdot P(B) \qquad (3.6)$$

In some texts this identity is taken as the definition of independence and our definition is then derived. This multiplication rule makes some problems very easy if independence is immediately recognized.

Example 3.19 A fair coin is tossed twice. What is the probability of tossing two heads?

Solution The two tosses are independent. The multiplication rule yields

$$P(HH) = \tfrac{1}{2} \cdot \tfrac{1}{2} = \tfrac{1}{4}. \qquad \square$$

The multiplication rule extends to more than two independent events. If a fair coin is tossed three times, the three tosses are independent and

$$P(HHH) = \tfrac{1}{2} \cdot \tfrac{1}{2} \cdot \tfrac{1}{2} = \tfrac{1}{8}.$$

In fact, the definition of independence for $n > 2$ events states that the multiplication rule holds for any subset of the n events.

Definition 3.4 The events $A_1, A_2, \ldots, A_n$ are independent if

$$P(A_{i_1} \cap A_{i_2} \cap \cdots \cap A_{i_k}) = P(A_{i_1}) \times P(A_{i_2}) \times \cdots \times P(A_{i_k}),$$

for $1 \le i_1 < i_2 < \cdots < i_k \le n$.

The situation is more complicated than it appears. Exercise 3-30 will show that it is possible to have three events A, B and C such that each pair of events is independent but the three events together are not independent. Independence may be tricky to check for in some special problems. However, in this text there will be many problems where independence is intuitively obvious or simply given as an assumption of the problem. In those cases, the general multiplication rule should be applied immediately.

Example 3.20 A fair coin is tossed 30 times. What is the probability of tossing 30 heads in a row?
Solution

$$\left(\frac{1}{2}\right)^{30} = \frac{1}{1,073,741,824}$$

Don't bet on it!   ☐

Example 3.21 A student is taking a very difficult professional examination. Unlimited tries are allowed, and many people do not pass without first failing a number of times. The probability that this student will pass on any particular attempt is .60. *Assume that successive attempts at the exam are independent.* (If the exam is unreasonably tricky and changes every time, this may not be a bad assumption.) What is the probability that the student will not pass until his third attempt?
Solution

$$P(Fail \text{ and } Fail \text{ and } Pass) = (.40)(.40)(.60) = .096 \qquad ☐$$

Example 3.22 An insurance company has written two life insurance policies for a husband and wife. Policy 1 pays $10,000 to their children if both husband *and* wife die during this year. Policy 2 pays $100,000 to the surviving spouse if either husband *or* wife dies during this year. The probability that the husband will die this year (H_D) is .011. The probability that the wife will die this year (W_D) is .008. Find the probability that each policy will pay a benefit this year. You are to assume that the deaths of husband and wife are independent.
Solution
Policy 1: The probability of payment is

$$P(H_D \text{ and } W_D) = (.011)(.008) = .000088.$$

Policy 2: The probability of payment is

$$P(H_D \cup W_D) = P(H_D) + P(W_D) - P(H_D \cap W_D)$$

$$= .011 + .008 - .000088 = .018912. \qquad ☐$$

3.5 Bayes' Theorem

3.5.1 Testing a Test: An Example

In Example 2.27, we showed how to list the possible outcomes of a disease test using a tree. In the discussion, we mentioned that disease tests can have their problems. A test can indicate that you have the disease when you don't (a false positive) or indicate that you are free of the disease when you really have it (a false negative). Most of us are subjected to other tests that have similar problems — placement tests, college and graduate school admission tests, and job screening tests are a few examples. Bayes' Theorem and the related probability formulas presented in this section are quite useful in analyzing how well such tests are working, and we will begin discussion of Bayes' Theorem with a continuation of the disease-testing example. (This material has a wide variety of other applications.)

Example 3.23 The outcomes of interest in a disease test, from Example 2.27, are the following:

D: the person tested has the disease

$\sim D$: the person tested does not have the disease

Y: the test is positive

N: the test is negative

In this example, we will consider a hypothetical disease test which most people would think of as "95% accurate", defined as follows:

(a) $P(Y|D) = .95$; in words, if you have the disease there is a .95 probability that the test will be positive.

(b) $P(N|\sim D) = .95$; if you don't have the disease the probability is .95 that the test will be negative.

Only 1% of all people actually have the disease, so $P(D) = .01$. The tree for this test (with branch probabilities) is given on the following page.

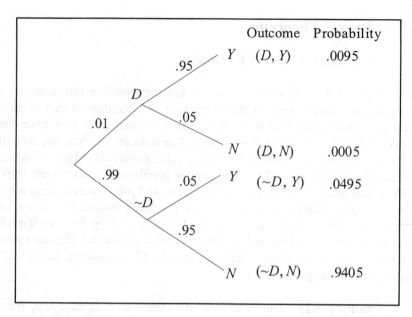

	Outcome	Probability
Y	(D, Y)	.0095
N	(D, N)	.0005
Y	(~D, Y)	.0495
N	(~D, N)	.9405

The tree illustrates that the test is misleading in some cases. 5% of individuals with the disease will test negative, and 5% of the individuals who do not have the disease will test positive. There are two important questions to ask about this test.

(a) What percentage of the population will test positive? This percentage is given by $P(Y)$.

(b) Suppose you know that someone has tested positive for the disease. What is the probability that the person does not actually have the disease? (This probability is $P(\sim D|Y)$.)

Solution

(a) $P(Y)$ is just the sum of the probabilities of all branches ending in Y.

$$P(Y) = P[(D, Y)] + P[(\sim D, Y)] = .0095 + .0495 = .059$$

(b) Note that the event $\sim D \cap Y$ corresponds to the branch $(\sim D, Y)$.

$$P(\sim D|Y) = \frac{P(\sim D \cap Y)}{P(Y)} = \frac{P(\sim D, Y)}{P(Y)} = \frac{.0495}{.0590} \approx .839$$

The practical information here is interesting. The "95% accurate" test will classify 5.9% of the population as positives — a classification which can be alarming and stressful. 83.9% of the individuals who tested positive will not actually have the disease.   □

In Example 3.23 we used Bayes' Theorem and the law of total probability without mentioning them by name. In the next section we will state these useful rules.

3.5.2   The Law of Total Probability; Bayes' Theorem

In Example 3.23 we found $P(Y)$ by breaking the event Y into two separate branch outcomes, so

$$Y = \{(D,Y),(\sim D,Y)\},$$

which enabled us to write

$$P(Y) = P[(D,Y)] + P[(\sim D,Y)].$$

Using set notation, we could rewrite the last two identities as

$$Y = (D \cap Y) \cup (\sim D \cap Y)$$

and

$$P(Y) = P(D \cap Y) + P(\sim D \cap Y).$$

Note that $D \cup \sim D = S$. The events D and $\sim D$ partition the sample space into two mutually exclusive pieces. Then the events $(D \cap Y)$ and $(\sim D \cap Y)$ break the event Y into two mutually exclusive pieces. This is illustrated in the following figure.

Sample Space

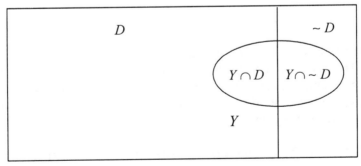

The events D and $\sim D$ are said to partition the sample space. This is a special case of a more general definition.

Definition 3.5 The events A_1, A_2, ..., A_n partition the sample space S if $A_1 \cup A_2 \cup \cdots \cup A_n = S$ and $A_i \cap A_j = \emptyset$ for $i \neq j$.

Sample Space

A_1	A_2	...	A_n

The **law of total probability** says that a partition of the sample space will lead to a partition of any event E into mutually exclusive pieces.

$$E = (A_1 \cap E) \cup (A_2 \cap E) \cup \cdots \cup (A_n \cap E)$$

Then we can write $P(E)$ as the sum of the probabilities of those pieces.

Law of Total Probability

Let E be an event. If A_1, A_2, ..., A_n partition the sample space, then

$$P(E) = P(A_1 \cap E) + P(A_2 \cap E) + \cdots + P(A_n \cap E). \quad (3.7)$$

This is the law we used intuitively when we wrote

$$Y = (D \cap Y) \cup (\sim D \cap Y) = \{(D, Y),(\sim D, Y)\}$$

and

$$P(Y) = P(D \cap Y) + P(\sim D \cap Y)$$

In that case $n = 2$, $A_1 = D$, and $A_2 = \sim D$.

The law of total probability can be rewritten in a useful way. In the disease testing example, the probabilities $P[(D, Y)]$ and $P[(\sim D, Y)]$ appeared to be read directly from the tree, but they were actually obtained by multiplying along branches.

$$P(D \cap Y) = P(D) \cdot P(Y|D) \qquad P(\sim D \cap Y) = P(\sim D) \cdot P(Y|\sim D)$$

Thus when we found $P(Y)$, we were really writing

$$P(Y) = P(D \cap Y) + P(\sim D \cap Y) = P(D) \cdot P(Y|D) + P(\sim D) \cdot P(Y|\sim D).$$

When we calculated $P(\sim D|Y)$, our reasoning could be summarized as

$$P(\sim D|Y) = \frac{P(\sim D \cap Y)}{P(Y)} = \frac{P(\sim D) \cdot P(Y|\sim D)}{P(D) \cdot P(Y|D) + P(\sim D) \cdot P(Y|\sim D)}.$$

The last expression on the right is referred to as **Bayes' Theorem**. It looks complicated, but can be stated simply in terms of trees.

$$P(\sim D|Y) = \frac{Probability\ for\ (\sim D \cap Y)\ branch}{Sum\ of\ probabilities\ for\ all\ branches\ ending\ in\ Y}$$

The general statement of Bayes' Theorem is simply an extension of the above reasoning for a partition of the sample space into n events.

Bayes' Theorem

Let E be an event. If $A_1, A_2, \ldots, A_n$ partition the sample space, then

$$P(A_i|E) = \frac{P(E \cap A_i)}{P(E)}$$
$$= \frac{P(A_i) \cdot P(E|A_i)}{P(A_1) \cdot P(E|A_1) + P(A_2) \cdot P(E|A_2) + \cdots + P(A_n) \cdot P(E|A_n)}.$$

$$(3.8)$$

We illustrate the use of Bayes' Theorem for a partition of the sample space into 3 events in the next example.

Example 3.24 An insurer has three types of auto insurance policyholders. 50% of the policyholders are low risk (L). The probability that a low-risk policyholder will file a claim in a given year is .10. Another 30% of the policyholders are moderate risk (M). The probability that a moderate-risk policyholder will file a claim in a given year is .20. Finally, 20% of the policyholders are high risk (H). The probability that a high-risk policyholder will file a claim in a given year is .50. A policyholder files a claim this year. Find the probability that he is a high-risk policyholder.

Solution The given probabilities lead to the following tree.

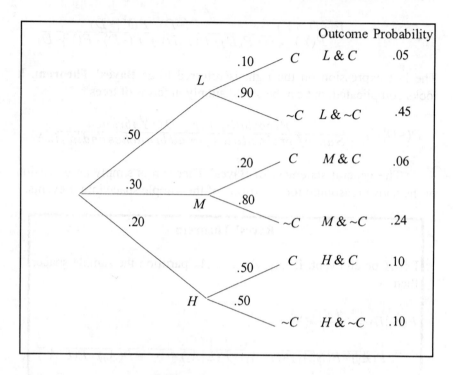

$$P(H|C) = \frac{P(H \cap C)}{P(C)} = \frac{.10}{.05 + .06 + .10} \approx .476$$

This shows that approximately 47.6% of the claims are filed by high-risk drivers.   □

Note that in a typical problem it is simpler to draw the tree and use branch probabilities than it is to memorize the formula and try to substitute numbers into it. For many people the tree provides the intuition to understand and memorize the formula.

3.6   Exercises

3.1   Probability by Counting for Equally Likely Outcomes

3-1.   You toss a fair coin 3 times. What is the probability that you get 2 heads and 1 tail? (Note: All possible outcomes for this experiment were given in a tree in Section 2.5.3.)

3-2.   If a fair coin is tossed 3 times what is the probability of getting at least 1 head?

3-3   An urn contains 3 red balls, 7 green balls and 6 blue balls. If a ball is selected at random from the urn, what is the probability that it is (a) red; (b) not green?

3-4.   A consulting company has 68 employees. Of these 21 have degrees in mathematics, 33 have degrees in economics and 7 have degrees in both. What is the probability that an employee chosen at random has a degree in either mathematics or economics?

3-5.   If a pair of dice is rolled, what is the probability that the sum of the two dice is (a) 7; (b) 11; (c) less than 5?

3-6.   An insurance agent has 78 clients. Of these 45 have life insurance, 32 have auto insurance, and 16 have both types. What is the probability that a client chosen at random has neither life nor auto insurance?

3-7.   An urn contains 4 red balls and 6 green balls. Three balls are selected at random. What is the probability (a) all 3 are red; (b) 1 is red and 2 are green; (c) all 3 are the same color?

3-8.   A computer company has a shipment of 40 computer components of which 5 are defective. If 4 components are chosen at random to be tested, what is the probability that (a) all are good; (b) 2 are good and 2 are defective?

3-9.   Ten people, 5 men and 5 women, are to be seated in a row of ten chairs. What is the probability that the men and women end up in alternate chairs?

3-10.   8 people were all born in January. What is the probability that at least 2 of them have the same birthday?

3-11.   What is the probability that at least 2 of a group of 4 people were born on the same day of the week?

3-12.   4 balls are picked at random from an urn containing 5 red balls and 6 blue balls. What is the probability that you get balls of both colors?

3-13.   A 5-card poker hand is dealt from a standard deck of cards. What is the probability that you get a full house (3 of one kind plus a different pair, such as KKK55) ?

3-14.   If a poker hand is dealt, what is the probability that you get 2 pairs (e.g., QQ993)?

3-15.   The odds for an event E are defined as the ratio $P(E)$ to $P(\sim E)$. Odds are generally written as the ratio of two integers, such as 5:4, which is read "5 to 4". The odds against E are given by the reverse ratio (i.e., 4:5). If a pair of dice are rolled, what are   (a) the odds for a 7; (b) the odds against an 11?

3-16.   If the odds for E are known, say $r{:}s$, then $P(E) = r/(r + s)$. If the odds against F are $a{:}b$, what is the $P(F)$?

3.2   Probability When Outcomes Are Not Equally Likely

3-17.   Prove $P(\sim E) = 1 - P(E)$.

3-18.   Prove $P(A \cup B) = P(A) + P(B) - P(A \cap B)$ using the axioms in Section 3.2.2. Hint: First show that

$$(A \cup B) = (A \cap \sim B) \cup (A \cap B) \cup (\sim A \cap B).$$

3-19. A four-year college has the following enrollment by class: 27.8% freshman, 26.3% sophomore, 24.4% junior and 21.5% senior. What is the probability that a student chosen at random is a junior or senior.

3-20. An auto insurance company finds that in the past 10 years 22% of its policyholders have filed liability claims, 37% have filed comprehensive claims, and 13% have filed both types of claims. What is the probability that a policyholder chosen at random has not filed a claim of either kind?

3-21. A teacher's grade distribution for the year is as follows: A, 13.1%; B, 27.8%; C, 31.2%; D, 8.9%; E, 9.4%; and W, 9.6%. What is the probability that a student of this teacher got (a) a grade C or better; (b) a grade of D or E?

3-22. In a survey of college students it was discovered that 37% had received flu shots, 58% had a skin test for tuberculosis, and 21% had received neither. What is the probability that a student received both?

3.3   Conditional Probability

3-23. In Exercise 3-21 what is the probability that a randomly selected student got an A, given that she got a grade of C or better?

3-24. In the first quarter of a year, a company's records showed that 63.5% of its employees missed no work, 23.7% missed one day of work, 8.1% missed two days, and 4.7% missed three days. What is the probability that an employee who missed work missed only one day?

3-25. An insurance company classifies its claims as low if they are under $10,000, and high otherwise. During the year 79.2% of its policyholders filed no claims, 16.9% filed low claims, and 3.9% filed high claims. If a policyholder filed a claim, what is the probability that it was a low claim?

3-26. Two cards are drawn from a standard deck without replacement. What is the probability that (a) both are hearts; (b) neither is a heart; (c) exactly one is a heart?

3-27.   For the experiment of tossing a single fair coin 3 times, what is the probability of getting exactly 2 heads, given that you get at least one head?

3-28.   For the experiment in Exercise 3-27 what is the probability of getting exactly 2 heads, given that the first toss is a head?

3-29.   Three cards are drawn from a standard deck. What is the probability that all three are hearts, given that at least two of them are hearts?

3.4   Independence

3-30.   Let X be the experiment of drawing a single card from a deck. Let A be the event the card is a spade or a heart, B be the event it is a spade or a diamond, and C be the event it is a spade or a club. Show that each of the pairs (A, B), (A, C) and (B, C) is independent. Show that $P(A \cap B \cap C) \neq P(A) \cdot P(B) \cdot P(C)$.

3-31.   Two cards are drawn from a standard deck with replacement. Let A1 be the event the first card is an ace and A2 be the event the second card is an ace. Show that A1 and A2 are independent.

3-32.   Let S be the sample space for rolling a single die. Let $A = \{1, 2, 3, 4\}$, $B = \{2, 3, 4\}$, and $C = \{3, 4, 5\}$. Which of the pairs (A, B), (A, C) and (B, C) is independent?

3-33.   A company needs some of its employees for a task that requires that they not be color blind. In testing them it finds that 7 of the 130 men are color blind and 2 of the 170 women are color blind. Are the events male and color blind independent or dependent?

3-34.   A student is taking a history course and an English course. He decides that the probability of passing the history course is .75 and the probability of passing the English course is .84. If these events are independent, what is the probability that (a) he passes both courses; (b) he passes exactly one of them?

3-35. A company has three identical machines operating independently of each other. The probability of any one machine breaking down during the next year is .05. What is the probability that during the next year there will be no breakdowns?

3-36. A machine has two parts that could fail and have to be replaced. The probabilities of failure of parts A and B are .17 and .12, respectively. If failures of these parts are independent of each other, what is the probability that at least one of them will fail?

3-37. For the experiment of tossing a single fair coin 3 times, let E be the event the first toss is a head and F be the event 2 heads and 1 tail are tossed. Are E and F independent?

3.5   Bayes' Theorem

3-38. A manufacturing company has a fabrication plant and an assembly line. The fabrication plant has 60% of the employees and the assembly line 40%. During the past year 35% of the workers in the fabrication plant sustained injuries and 20% of the assembly line workers had injuries.
   (a)   What percentage of all workers had injuries in this period?
   (b)   If an employee had an injury, what is the probability that he worked on the assembly line?

3-39. Two jars contain coins. Jar I contains 5 pennies, 4 nickels and 6 dimes. Jar II contains 6 pennies, 4 nickels and 2 dimes. A jar is selected at random and a coin is selected from that jar. If the coin is a nickel, what is the probability that it came from Jar II?

3-40. An insurance company divides its policyholders into low-risk and high-risk classes. For the year, of those in the low-risk class, 80% had no claims, 15% had one claim, and 5% had 2 claims. Of those in the high-risk class, 50% had no claims, 30% had one claim, and 20% had two claims. Of the policyholders, 60% were in the low-risk class and 40% in the high-risk class.
   (a)   If a policyholder had no claims in the year, what is the probability that he is in the low-risk class?
   (b)   If a policyholder had two claims in the year, what is the probability that he is in the high-risk class?

3-41. A manufacturer has three machines producing light bulbs. Machine A produces 40% of the light bulbs with 1% of them defective. Machine B produces 35% of them with 2% being defective. Machine C produces 25% with 4% being defective. If a light bulb is tested and found to be defective, what is the probability that it was produced by machine A?

3-42. A skin test for a disease is less expensive but less accurate than an X-ray. In a country 20% of the adult population has this disease. For a person with the disease, the skin test is positive 95% of the time. If a person does not have the disease, it will be positive 30% of the time.
       (a)   What is the probability that a person who tests positive does not have the disease?
       (b)   What is the probability that a person who tests negative has the disease?

3-43. A card is drawn from a deck, not replaced, and a second card is drawn. What is the probability that the second card is a heart?

3-44. A company classifies injuries to its workers as minor if the worker does not have to take time off and severe if the worker has to take time off. The company has two plants, A and B. In plant A 60% of the workers had no injuries, 30% had minor injuries, and 10% had severe injuries. In plant B 50% had no injuries, 35% minor injuries, and 15% severe injuries. 70% of all workers work in plant A and 30% in plant B. What is the probability that a worker with a severe injury worked in plant A?

3-45. In Exercise 3-44, what is the probability that a worker who had an injury worked in plant B and had a minor injury?

3.7   Sample Actuarial Examination Problems

3-46. The probability that a visit to a primary care physicians (PCP) office results in neither lab work nor referral to a specialist is 35%. Of those coming to a PCP's office, 30% are referred to specialists and 40% require lab work.

       Determine the probability that a visit to a PCP's office results in both lab work and referral to a specialist.

3-47.   You are given $P(A \cup B) = 0.7$ and $P(A \cup B') = 0.9$.
Determine $P[A]$.

3-48.   An insurance company examines its pool of auto insurance customers and gathers the following information:

(i)   All customers insure at least one car.
(ii)   64% of the customers insure more than one car.
(iii)   20% of the customers insure a sports car.
(iv)   Of those customers who insure more than one car, 15% insure a sports car.

What is the probability that a randomly selected customer insures exactly one car, and that car is not a sports car?

3-49.   Among a large group of patients recovering from shoulder injuries, it is found that 22% visit both a physical therapist and a chiropractor, whereas 12% visit neither of these. The probability that a patient visits a chiropractor exceeds by 0.14 the probability that a patient visits a physical therapist.

Determine the probability that a randomly chosen member of this group visits a physical therapist.

3-50.   A survey of a group's viewing habits over the last year revealed the following information:

(i)   28% watched gymnastics
(ii)   29% watched baseball
(iii)   19% watched soccer
(iv)   14% watched gymnastics and baseball
(v)   12% watched baseball and soccer
(vi)   10% watched gymnastics and soccer
(vii)   8% watched all three sports.

Calculate the percentage of the group that watched none of the three sports during the last year.

3-51. An actuary studying the insurance preferences of automobile owners makes the following conclusions:

    (i)   An automobile owner is twice as likely to purchase collision coverage as disability coverage.

    (ii)   The event that an automobile owner purchases collision coverage is independent of the event that he or she purchases disability coverage.

    (iii) The probability that an automobile owner purchases both collision and disability coverages is 0.15.

What is the probability that an automobile owner purchases neither collision nor disability coverage?

3-52. An insurance company pays hospital claims. The number of claims that include emergency room or operating room charges is 85% of the total number of claims. The number of claims that do not include emergency room charges is 25% of the total number of claims. The occurrence of emergency room charges is independent of the occurrence of operating room charges on hospital claims.

Calculate the probability that a claim submitted to the insurance company includes operating room charges.

3-53. The number of injury claims per month is modeled by a random variable N with $P[N=n] = \frac{1}{(n+1)(n+2)}$, where $n \geq 0$.

Determine the probability of at least one claim during a particular month, given that there have been at most four claims during that month.

3-54. A public health researcher examines the medical records of a group of 937 men who died in 1999 and discovers that 210 of the men died from causes related to heart disease.

Moreover, 312 of the 937 men had at least one parent who suffered from heart disease, and, of these 312 men, 102 died from causes related to heart disease.

Determine the probability that a man randomly selected from this group died of causes related to heart disease, given that neither of his parents suffered from heart disease.

3-55.   An urn contains 10 balls: 4 red and 6 blue. A second urn contains 16 red balls and an unknown number of blue balls. A single ball is drawn from each urn. The probability that both balls are the same color is 0.44.

Calculate the number of blue balls in the second urn.

3-56.   An actuary is studying the prevalence of three health risk factors, denoted by A, B, and C, within a population of women. For each of the three factors, the probability is 0.1 that a woman in the population has only this risk factor (and no others). For any two of the three factors, the probability is 0.12 that she has exactly these two risk factors (but not the other). The probability that a woman has all three risk factors, given that she has A and B, is 1/3.

What is the probability that a woman has none of the three risk factors, given that she does not have risk factor A?

3-57.   An insurer offers a health plan to the employees of a large company. As part of this plan, the individual employees may choose exactly two of the supplementary coverages A, B, and C, or they may choose no supplementary coverage. The proportions of the company's employees that choose coverages A, B, and C are 1/4, 1/3, and 5/12, respectively.

Determine the probability that a randomly chosen employee will choose no supplementary coverage.

3-58.   An insurance company estimates that 40% of policyholders who have only an auto policy will renew next year and 60% of policyholders who have only a homeowners policy will renew next year. The company estimates that 80% of policyholders who have both an auto and a homeowners policy will renew at least one of those policies next year. Company records show that 65% of policyholders have an auto policy, 50% of policyholders have a homeowners policy, and 15% of policyholders have both an auto and a homeowners policy.

Using the company's estimates, calculate the percentage of policyholders that will renew at least one policy next year.

3-59.   A blood test indicates the presence of a particular disease 95% of
         the time when the disease is actually present. The same test
         indicates the presence of the disease 0.5% of the time when the
         disease is not present. One percent of the population actually has
         the disease.

         Calculate the probability that a person has the disease given that
         the test indicates the presence of the disease.

3-60.   An insurance company issues life insurance policies in three
         separate categories: standard, preferred, and ultra-preferred. Of the
         company's policyholders, 50% are standard, 40% are preferred,
         and 10% are ultra-preferred. Each standard policyholder has prob-
         ability 0.010 of dying in the next year, each preferred policyholder
         has probability 0.005 of dying in the next year, and each ultra-
         preferred policyholder has probability 0.001 of dying in the next
         year. A policyholder dies in the next year.

         What is the probability that the deceased policyholder was ultra-
         preferred?

3-61.   Upon arrival at a hospital's emergency room, patients are catego-
         rized according to their condition as critical, serious, or stable. In
         the past year:

         (i)   10% of the emergency room patients were critical;
         (ii)   30% of the emergency room patients were serious;
         (iii)   the rest of the emergency room patients were stable;
         (iv)   40% of the critical patients died;
         (vi)   10% of the serious patients died; and
         (vii)   1% of the stable patients died.

         Given that a patient survived, what is the probability that the
         patient was categorized as serious upon arrival?

3-62. An actuary studied the likelihood that different types of drivers would be involved in at least one collision during any one-year period. The results of the study are presented below.

Type of Driver	Percentage of all drivers	Probability of at least one collision
Teen	8%	0.15
Young Adult	16%	0.08
Midlife	45%	0.04
Senior	31%	0.05
Total	100%	

Given that a driver has been involved in at least one collision in the past year, what is the probability that the driver is a young adult driver?

3-63. The probability that a randomly chosen male has a circulation problem is 0.25. Males who have a circulation problem are twice as likely to be smokers as those who do not have a circulation problem.

What is the conditional probability that a male has a circulation problem, given that he a smoker?

3-64. A health study tracked a group of persons for five years. At the beginning of the study, 20% were classified as heavy smokers, 30% as light smokers, and 50% as nonsmokers. Results of the study showed that light smokers were twice as likely as nonsmokers to die during the five-year study, but only half as likely as heavy smokers. A randomly selected participant from the study died over the five-year period.

Calculate the probability that the participant was a heavy smoker.

Chapter 4
Discrete Random Variables

4.1   Random Variables

4.1.1   Defining a Random Variable

Random variables surround us. The (unknown) number of years that you are going to live is a random variable, as is the number of auto insurance claims you will file in your lifetime and the number of TV sets owned by a randomly selected American family. Next year's return on your stock portfolio is a random variable, and so is your weight after Thanksgiving. The number you roll when you toss dice at a table in Las Vegas is also a random variable — gambling is always with us in probability. The key feature in each of these random variables is that the outcome of interest is a number (a count of insurance claims or a weight measurement) and it depends on chance. Most of us try not to have accidents or gain weight, but somehow those things are forced on us by chance. This leads to an intuitive definition of a random variable.

Definition 4.1 A **random variable** is a numerical quantity whose value depends on chance.[1]

---

[1]   This nice intuitive description of a random variable is taken from Weiss [18], who adapted it from the words of the mathematician B.V. Gnedenko.

Example 4.1 You are tossing a coin twice and will bet on the number of heads. The outcome is a number (0, 1 or 2) which depends on chance. The number of heads is a random variable.   □

Example 4.2 You are tossing a coin twice and will bet on specific outcomes such as "first a head then a tail" or HT. The outcome depends on chance, but is not a number. This is *not* a random variable.   □

Example 4.3 A resident of Winsted, Connecticut, is selected at random and his height is measured. The height is a number which depends on the chance event of random selection. The height is a random variable.   □

Example 4.4 You go to Las Vegas and begin to put quarters in a slot machine. Let X be the number of quarters you play before your first win of any amount. X is a number and depends on chance. X is a random variable.   □

There is an important difference between the height random variable in Example 4.3 and the other random variables. Height can be measured with such precision that any number between two given heights is still a theoretically possible height — if you are given the two heights (in inches) 66 and 66.01, any number between 66 and 66.01 is still a theoretically possibly height. For this reason, height is said to be measured on a continuous scale, and the height random variable is called a **continuous** random variable. In contrast, the outcomes 0, 1 and 2 for the numbers in Example 4.1 are distinct, and the values between them are not possible. This kind of random variable is called a **discrete** random variable. In Example 4.4, the possible numbers of attempts before the first win at a slot machine are $\{0, 1, 2, 3, \ldots\}$. This sample space is discrete and infinite — as any visitor to a casino will attest.

In this chapter we will study only discrete random variables. Continuous random variables require a different approach, which requires the use of calculus. They will be studied in Chapter 7.

Intelligent people often get into ridiculous arguments over whether a certain random variable is truly discrete or continuous. For example, one of our students became quite excited over the argument that he would measure heights to at most 3 decimal places, which meant that heights were discrete for him. That is an unproductive argument. The real point is that calculus-based continuous mathematics is the most efficient way to analyze heights. When we say that heights are continuous, we are really just identifying the kind of mathematical model we will use.

4.1.2   Redefining a Random Variable

Our approach in this text is intuitive and applied. More advanced books in probability give more rigorous definitions which are a bit harder to understand at first sight. A widely used definition of a random variable is the following.

Definition 4.1a   A random variable is a function mapping the sample space to the real numbers.

The idea behind this definition can be visualized by looking at the example of the number of heads when two coins are tossed. When we look at the results of the tosses, we assign numerical results to the physical outcomes we see.

Original Outcome		Number of Heads
HH	$\longrightarrow$	2
HT	$\longrightarrow$	1
TH	$\longrightarrow$	1
TT	$\longrightarrow$	0

This assignment of numerical values is a function from the sample space to the real numbers — as the last definition states. We will not use the more rigorous definition any further in this text.

4.1.3   Notation; The Distinction Between X and x

Random variables are usually denoted by capital letters. If we were to look at the random variable for the number of heads in two coin tosses, we might use X to represent the entire random variable which can take on any of the values 0, 1 or 2. However, specific outcomes are usually referred to using small letters. Thus the reader will see statements like "let x be the number of heads in the first two coin tosses." This refers to a single realized outcome, *not* to the entire random variable. This confuses students, and the confusion is increased by the convention that if x heads are tossed the notation is mixed — we write "$X = x$." The reader should be aware that we are not arbitrarily mixing capital and small letters in our notation. The notation has a purpose, and the statement "$X = x$" is not nonsense. It means that the random variable X was realized with a specific value x.

4.2   The Probability Function of a Discrete Random Variable

4.2.1   Defining the Probability Function

If we decide to bet on the number of heads which will occur when a fair coin is tossed twice, we can better manage our risk if we have a table of all possible outcomes and their probabilities. The following table gives this useful information.

Number of heads (x)	0	1	2
$p(x)$	.25	.50	.25

This table assigns a probability to each individual outcome. Once we have such a function, we can use it to find the probability of any event by adding the probabilities of the individual outcomes in the event.

   Definition 4.2 Let X be a discrete random variable. A **probability function** for X is a function $p(x)$ which assigns a probability to each value of the random variable, such that

(a) $p(x) \geq 0$ for all x, and

(b) $\sum p(x) = 1$. (The sum of all individual outcome probabilities is 1).

The probability function is also referred to as the **probability mass function** or the **discrete density function** for X.

   For discrete random variables with a finite number of individual outcomes, the probability function can be given by a table. This was done for the two coin toss problem at the beginning of this section.

Example 4.5 In Example 3.9, a large HMO studied the number of children in a given birth. The probability function was as follows:

Number of children (x)	1	2	3
$p(x)$	.9670	.0311	.0019

□

Example 4.6 In Example 3.10, an automobile insurer studied the number of claims filed by a policyholder in a given year. The probability function was as follows:

Number of claims (x)	0	1	2	3
$p(x)$	.72	.22	.05	.01

□

If a discrete random variable has a very large or infinite number of possible outcomes, a simple table is not possible, and $p(x)$ must be specified in some other way — usually by a formula.

Example 4.7 On a certain slot machine, the probability of winning on an individual play is .05. Let X be the number of unsuccessful attempts before the first win. If we assume that successive plays are independent, the probability of k unsuccessful plays before the first win is given by the multiplication rule for independent events.

$$p(k) = P(X = k) = .95^k(.05), k = 0, 1, 2, \ldots$$ □

4.2.2 The Cumulative Distribution Function

Example 4.8 A clinical researcher is studying a fatal disease. The random variable of interest to her is X, the number ($x = 1, 2, \ldots$) of the year following diagnosis in which a patient dies. Her studies lead to the probability table given below.

Year of death (x)	1	2	3	4	5
$p(x)$	.53	.25	.12	.07	.03

This probability function gives the probability that someone who is diagnosed will die in a specific year following diagnosis. For example, the empirical probability that a person diagnosed today will die sometime during the third year from today is .12. However, the table does not directly give the probability that a person will die during the first two years or the first three years. These probabilities are given by

$$P(X \leq 2) = p(1) + p(2) = .53 + .25 = .78$$
and

$$P(X \leq 3) = p(1) + p(2) + p(3) = .53 + .25 + .12 = .90. \qquad \square$$

These useful probabilities are obtained by cumulatively adding successive probabilities in the table above. If we do this throughout the table, we obtain the cumulative distribution function $F(x)$.

Definition 4.3 Let X be a random variable. The **cumulative distribution function** $F(x)$ for X is defined by

$$F(x) = P(X \leq x).$$

For a discrete random variable, we can find $F(x)$ by adding all values of $p(y)$ for $y \leq x$.

Example 4.9 The cumulative distribution function for the probability function of Example 4.8 is given by the following table:

Year of death (x)	1	2	3	4	5
$F(x)$	.53	.78	.90	.97	1.00

This tells us, for example, that for those diagnosed with the disease, the probability of death within 3 years of diagnosis is 90%. $\qquad \square$

Note that the last entry in the table for $F(x)$ is 1.00. This will always hold for a finite discrete random variable.

Example 4.10 In Example 4.6 we looked at the distribution of the number of claims filed in a year by a policyholder in a large insurance company. The cumulative distribution function is given by the following table:

Number of claims (x)	0	1	2	3
$F(x)$	.72	.94	.99	1.00

This tells us that 94% of policyholders file one claim or less in a year —
leaving 6% who file more than one claim.   □

In Example 4.10 we gave values of $F(x)$ only for $x = 0, 1, 2, 3$,
since those x-values represent the numbers of claims that actually
occurred. Although it is not possible to have 0.5 claims, we can define
$F(.5)$.

$$F(.5) = P(X \leq .5) = P(X \leq 0) = P(X = 0) = .72$$

Since it is not possible to have an actual claim number in the open
interval $(0, 1)$, we can see that

$$F(x) = P(X \leq x) = P(X \leq 0) = .72, 0 \leq x < 1.$$

Continuing this reasoning, we can write a definition $F(x)$ for any real
number.

$$F(x) = \begin{cases} 0 & x < 0 \\ .72 & 0 \leq x < 1 \\ .94 & 1 \leq x < 2 \\ .99 & 2 \leq x < 3 \\ 1.00 & 3 \leq x \end{cases}$$

The graph of $F(x)$ is as follows:

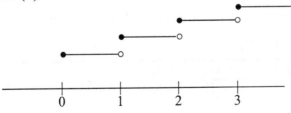

The cumulative distribution function for an infinite discrete
random variable requires a bit more work. For example, the cumulative
distribution function for the random variable in Example 4.7 requires use
of the formula for the sum of a geometric series. This is reviewed next.

Geometric Series Review

A geometric series is a series of the form a, ar, ar^2, ar^3, $\ldots$, ar^n. The sum of the series for $r \neq 1$ is given by

$$a + ar + ar^2 + \cdots + ar^n = a\left(\frac{1 - r^{n+1}}{1 - r}\right). \qquad (4.1)$$

The number r is called the **ratio** or **common ratio**. If $|r| < 1$, we can sum the infinite geometric series.

$$a + ar + ar^2 + \cdots + ar^n + \cdots = a\left(\frac{1}{1 - r}\right) \qquad (4.2a)$$

Example 4.11 You play a slot machine repeatedly. (How else?) The probability of winning on a single play is .05, and successive plays are independent. The random variable of interest is X, the number of unsuccessful attempts before the first win. Find an expression for $F(x)$.

   Solution In Example 4.7, we showed that

$$p(k) = P(X = k) = .95^k(.05).$$

The cumulative distribution function is given by

$$
\begin{aligned}
F(x) &= p(0) + p(1) + \cdots + p(x) \\
&= .05 + .95(.05) + .95^2(.05) + \cdots + .95^x(.05) \\
&= .05\left(\frac{1 - .95^{x+1}}{1 - .95}\right) = 1 - .95^{x+1}. \qquad \square
\end{aligned}
$$

The first five values of $p(x)$ and $F(x)$ are given in the table below.

x	0	1	2	3	4
$p(x)$	.05	.0475	.045125	.04286875	.0407253125
$F(x)$	.05	.0975	.142625	.18549375	.2262190625

It is interesting to interpret these values of $F(x)$. For example, the value $F(4) = P(X \leq 4) \approx .226$ is the probability that at most 4 unsuccessful plays will occur before the first win. Then $1 - F(4) = P(X > 4) \approx .774$ is the probability that at least 5 unsuccessful plays will occur before the first win. You have a 77.4% probability of losing at least 5 times before the first win. This means that if you play the slot machine five times in a row, the probability of losing all 5 times is approximately .774 and the probability of winning at least once in the 5 plays is $F(4) = .226$.

This interpretation of the cumulative distribution in the slot machine problem holds for any x. $F(x)$ is the probability that you win at least once in $x + 1$ successive plays. This is used in the next example.

Example 4.12 How many times would you need to play the slot machine in Example 4.11 in order to be sure that your probability of winning at least once is greater than or equal to .99?

Solution $F(k - 1) = 1 - .95^k$ is the probability that you win at least once in k successive plays. We need this probability to be at least .99. Set

$$1 - .95^k = .99.$$

Then

$$.95^k = .01$$

$$ln(.95^k) = k[ln(.95)] = ln(.01)$$

$$k = \frac{ln(.01)}{ln(.95)} \approx 89.78.$$

You need $k = 89.78$ (round up to 90) plays for the probability to be 99% that you win at least once. Note that since k was between 89 and 90, the probability of winning at least once in 89 plays is less than .99 and the probability of winning at least once in 90 plays is more than .99. Rounding up to 90 guarantees that the probability is at least .99. In problems like this one, the value of k is always rounded up. If k had been 89.12, we still would have rounded up. $\square$

4.3   Measuring Central Tendency; Expected Value

4.3.1   Central Tendency; The Mean

When we try to interpret numerical information that has a wide range of values, we like to reduce our confusion by looking at a single number which summarizes the information. For example, when tests are returned to a class, students are usually interested in the test average as well as the distribution of grades. In the next example, we will introduce a basic concept by looking at a distribution of grades.

Example 4.13 A large lecture class with 100 students was given a 10-point quiz. The lowest score actually recorded was a 5. The distribution of scores (from 5 to 10) is given in the following table.

Grade	5	6	7	8	9	10
Count	5	10	45	20	10	10

Students are interested in two things: the percentage of students at each grade level and the class average. The percentage of students at each grade level is given next.

Grade	5	6	7	8	9	10
Percent	5%	10%	45%	20%	10%	10%

Note that we could reinterpret this table as a probability function of a random variable X. Suppose a student score X is chosen at random from the class. What is the probability $p(x)$ that the student score is x? The next table repeats the previous one in probability function format.

Grade (x)	5	6	7	8	9	10
$p(x)$	.05	.10	.45	.20	.10	.10

The previous tables show the grade distribution, but people still want to know what the "average" is. The word "average" is in quotes here because there are different kinds of averages that can be calculated. More will be said about this later. The "average" that is most familiar to students is the **mean**, which is calculated by adding up all 100 student scores and dividing by 100. We do not really have to add 100 separate scores, since we can add 5 scores of 5 by multiplying 5×5, add 10 scores of 6 by multiplying 6×10, and so on. The mean is given by

$$\text{Class Mean} = \frac{5 \cdot 5 + 6 \cdot 10 + 7 \cdot 45 + 8 \cdot 20 + 9 \cdot 10 + 10 \cdot 10}{100} = 7.5.$$

This mean can be rewritten in terms of the probabilities for the grade random variable by a little rearrangement of numbers.

$$\text{Class Mean} = 5 \cdot \frac{5}{100} + 6 \cdot \frac{10}{100} + 7 \cdot \frac{45}{100} + 8 \cdot \frac{20}{100} + 9 \cdot \frac{10}{100} + 10 \cdot \frac{10}{100}$$

$$= 5(.05) + 6(.10) + 7(.45) + 8(.20) + 9(.10) + 10\,(.10)$$

$$= \sum x \cdot p(x) \qquad\qquad \square$$

This example shows that if we are given numerical results in the form of a probability function, we can calculate the familiar mean (or average) using the above result.

$$Mean = \sum x \cdot p(x)$$

When we are given a discrete random variable X, we are usually given only the probability function $p(x)$. The mean of the random variable X can be obtained from $p(x)$ by using the simple equation above.

The mean of the random variable is also called the expected value of the random variable.

Definition 4.4 Let X be a discrete random variable. The **expected value** of X is defined by

$$E(X) = \sum x \cdot p(x).$$

The expected value of the random variable X is often denoted by the Greek letter μ (pronounced "mew").

$$E(X) = \mu$$

Example 4.14 The probability function for the random variable in Example 4.5 (number of children in a birth) was as follows:

Number of children (x)	1	2	3
$p(x)$	.9670	.0311	.0019

Then the mean is

$$\mu = E(X) = 1(.9670) + 2(.0311) + 3(.0019) = 1.0349. \qquad \square$$

The calculations become more interesting if the discrete random variable is infinite. It is necessary to look at another infinite series formula before the next example.

Series Formula

The infinite geometric series given by Equation (4.2a) tells us that for $|x| < 1$,

$$\sum_{k=0}^{\infty} x^k = 1 + x + x^2 + x^3 + \cdots = \frac{1}{1-x}. \qquad (4.2b)$$

If we differentiate this infinite series term by term, and differentiate the expression on the right in the usual manner, we see that for $|x| < 1$,

$$\sum_{k=1}^{\infty} k \cdot x^{k-1} = 1 + 2x + 3x^2 + 4x^3 + \cdots = \frac{1}{(1-x)^2}. \qquad (4.3)$$

Example 4.15 Let X be the random variable for the number of unsuccessful plays before the first win on the slot machine in Examples 4.7 and 4.11. The probability function is $p(k) = P(X = k) = .95^k(.05)$. Then

$$\mu = E(X) = \sum_{k=0}^{\infty} k \cdot p(k) = \sum_{k=0}^{\infty} k(.95^k)(.05)$$

$$= 0(.05) + 1(.05)(.95) + 2(.05)(.95^2) + \cdots$$

$$= (.05)(.95)[1 + 2(.95) + 3(.95)^2 + \cdots]$$

$$= (.05)(.95)\left(\frac{1}{(1-.95)^2}\right) = \frac{.95}{.05} = 19. \quad \square$$

One common way of interpreting this result is to say that the average (mean) number of unsuccessful plays before the first win is 19. We could also say that the expected number of unsuccessful plays before the first win is 19. These verbal interpretations can be misleading. They do *not* say that you should expect to have exactly 19 unsuccessful plays and then the first win. Some players win on the first play and some on the fortieth. The expected value is not what you "expect" to happen. It is an average.

4.3.2   The Expected Value of $Y = aX$

Example 4.16   In Example 4.6 we looked at the probability function for the random variable X, the number of claims filed by a policyholder in a large insurance company in a year.

Number of claims (x)	0	1	2	3
$p(x)$	.72	.22	.05	.01

The expected number of claims is

$$E(X) = 0(.72) + 1(.22) + 2(.05) + 3(.01) = .35.$$

Suppose this table is for a type of policy which guarantees a fixed payment of $1000 for each claim. Then the amount paid to a policyholder in a year is just $1000 multiplied by the number of claims filed. The total claim amount is a new random variable $Y = 1000X$. We now have two random variables, X and Y, and each random variable has its own probability function. To avoid confusion, we will subscript the probability function. The probability function for X is $p_X(x)$ and the probability function for Y is $p_Y(y)$. The probability function for Y has the same second row as the probability function for X, since $p_Y(1000x) = p_X(x)$.

Total claim amount (y)	0	1000	2000	3000
$p_Y(y)$	.72	.22	.05	.01

The expected claim amount is

$$E(Y) = 0(.72) + 1000(.22) + 2000(.05) + 3000(.01) = \$350. \quad \square$$

Since $E(X) = .35$, then $E(1000X) = E(Y) = 1000E(X)$. This simple multiplication rule always works.

For any constant a and random variable X,
$$E(aX) = a \cdot E(X). \tag{4.4a}$$

The derivation of Equation (4.4a) should be clear from Example 4.16. If $Y = aX$, $p_Y(y) = p_Y(ax) = p_X(x)$. Then

$$E(Y) = E(aX) = \sum ax \cdot p_Y(ax) = a \sum x \cdot p_X(x) = a \cdot E(X).$$

The expected claim amount for the year is often called the **pure premium** for the insurance policy. If the company charges the mean amount of \$350 per year for each policy sold, and its experience actually follows the assumed probability function, then there will be just enough money to pay all claims. This is pursued in Exercises 4-7 and 4-8.

The useful rule for $Y = aX$ can be extended to a rule for $aX + b$.

For any constants a and b and random variable X,

$$E(aX + b) = a \cdot E(X) + b. \qquad (4.4b)$$

The derivation of Equation (4.4b) is left as Exercise 4-9.

Example 4.17   The company in Example 4.16 has a yearly fixed cost of \$100 per policyholder for administering the insurance policy. Thus its total cost in a year for a policy is the sum of the claim payments and the administrative cost.

$$\text{Total cost per policy} = 1000X + 100$$

The expected cost per policy per year is

$$E(1000X + 100) = 1000E(X) + 100 = \$450. \qquad \square$$

4.3.3   The Mode

The mean of a random variable is the most widely used single measure of central tendency. There are other measures which are also informative. One of these, the median or fiftieth percentile, will be covered in Chapter 7. The other, the mode, is discussed below.

Definition 4.5   The **mode** of a probability function is the value of x which has the highest probability $p(x)$.

Example 4.18   The mode of the probability function for the number of claims is $x = 0$, as the table clearly shows.

Number of claims (x)	0	1	2	3
$p(x)$	.72	.22	.05	.01

The mode will be used infrequently in this text. The more widely used tools in probability theory rely more on the mean. $\square$

4.4   Variance and Standard Deviation

4.4.1   Measuring Variation

The mean of a random variable gives a nice single summary number to measure central tendency. However, two different random variables can have the same mean and still be quite different. The next example illustrates this.

Example 4.19   Below we give probability functions representing quiz scores for two different classes.

First class: random variable X

Score (x)	7	8	9
$p(x)$	.20	.60	.20

Second class: random variable Y

Score (y)	6	8	10
$p(y)$	.20	.60	.20

Each random variable function has a mean of 8.

$$E(X) = 7(.20) + 8(.60) + 9(.20) = 8$$
$$E(Y) = 6(.20) + 8(.60) + 10(.20) = 8$$

However, the two random variables are clearly quite different. There is much more variation or dispersion in Y than in X. The question is how to measure that variation. One possible suggestion is to measure dispersion by looking at the distance of each individual value x or y from the mean of its distribution. This is shown in the tables below.

First class: random variable for distance from mean, $X - 8$

$x - 8$	$7 - 8 = -1$	$8 - 8 = 0$	$9 - 8 = 1$
$p(x)$	.20	.60	.20

Second class: random variable $Y - 8$

$y - 8$	$6 - 8 = -2$	$8 - 8 = 0$	$10 - 8 = 2$
$p(y)$	.20	.60	.20

The expected value of each of the random variables $X - 8$ and $Y - 8$ gives an average distance from the original mean. Unfortunately, this average is of no use in measuring dispersion. Positive and negative values cancel each other out, and we find $E(X - 8) = E(Y - 8) = 0$. ($E(X - \mu) = 0$ for any distribution with $\mu = E(X)$.) However, if we look at the *square* of the distance from the mean, this problem does not occur.

First class: random variable $(X - 8)^2$

$(x - 8)^2$	$(7 - 8)^2 = 1$	$(8 - 8)^2 = 0$	$(9 - 8)^2 = 1$
$p(x)$	.20	.60	.20

Second class: random variable $(Y - 8)^2$

$(y - 8)^2$	$(6 - 8)^2 = 4$	$(8 - 8)^2 = 0$	$(10 - 8)^2 = 4$
$p(y)$	.20	.60	.20

The expected value of each of these new random variables gives an *average squared distance from the mean.*

$$E[(X - 8)^2] = 1(.20) + 0(.60) + 1(.20) = 0.4$$
$$E[(Y - 8)^2] = 4(.20) + 0(.60) + 4(.20) = 1.6$$

This is the single measure of variation that is most widely used in probability theory.   □

Definition 4.6 The **variance** of a random variable X is defined to be

$$V(X) = E[(X - \mu)^2] = \sum (x - \mu)^2 \cdot p(x).$$

The **standard deviation** of a random variable is the square root of its variance. It is denoted by the greek letter σ.

$$\sigma = \sqrt{V(X)}$$

The variance is also written as $V(X) = \sigma^2$.

If more than one random variable is being studied, subscripts are used to associate mean and standard deviation with the proper random variable.

Example 4.20 For the random variables X and Y in Example 4.19, we write the following:

$$\mu_X = \mu_Y = 8$$

$$V(X) = \sigma_X^2 = .40 \qquad V(Y) = \sigma_Y^2 = 1.6$$

$$\sigma_X = \sqrt{\sigma_X^2} = \sqrt{.40} = .632 \qquad \sigma_Y = \sqrt{\sigma_Y^2} = \sqrt{1.6} = 1.265$$

Note that the random variable Y, which is more dispersed, has a greater variance and standard deviation. □

4.4.2 The Variance and Standard Deviation of $Y = aX$

If $Y = aX$, we already know that $\mu_Y = E(Y) = a \cdot E(X) = a \cdot \mu_X$. Recall that if $Y = aX$, then $p_Y(y) = p_Y(ax) = p_X(x)$. Then

$$V(Y) = \sum (y - \mu_Y)^2 \cdot p_Y(y) = \sum (ax - a \cdot \mu_X)^2 \cdot p_X(x)$$

$$= a^2 \sum (x - \mu_X)^2 \cdot p_X(x) = a^2 \cdot V(X).$$

This gives us a simple way to find $V(Y) = V(aX)$.

$$V(aX) = a^2 \cdot V(X) \qquad (4.5a)$$

The standard deviation of aX can now be obtained by taking the square root.

$$\sigma_{aX} = |a| \cdot \sigma_X \qquad (4.6)$$

Example 4.21 We return to the distributions of claim number and claim amount given in Example 4.16. The probability function for claim number random variable X was as follows:

Number of claims (x)	0	1	2	3
$p(x)$	.72	.22	.05	.01

We found that $E(X) = .35$. Using Definition 4.6, $V(X)$ is given by

$$\sigma^2 = E[(X - \mu_X)^2]$$

$$= .72(0-.35)^2 + .22(1-.35)^2 + .05(2-.35)^2 + .01(3-.35)^2$$

$$= .3875.$$

$$\sigma = \sqrt{.3875} \approx .622495$$

The probability function for the claim amount random variable Y was

Total claim amount (y)	0	1000	2000	3000
$p(y)$	.72	.22	.05	.01

We previously found $E(Y) = 1000(.35) = 350$. $V(Y)$ does not have to be calculated directly. Instead we write

$$V(Y) = V(1000X) = 1000^2 \cdot V(X) = 1,000,000(.3875) = 387,500.$$

The reader can check this result by direct calculation.   □

The useful rule (4.5a) can be extended to handle $Y = aX + b$.

$$V(aX + b) = a^2 \cdot V(X) \qquad\qquad (4.5b)$$

A derivation of Equation (4.5b) is outlined in Exercise 4-14. The intuitive idea is that if all values are shifted by exactly b units, the mean changes but the dispersion around the new mean is exactly as before.

Example 4.22 In Example 4.17 we looked at the total cost random variable $Y = 1000X + 100$, where X is the claim number random variable. In Example 4.20 we showed $V(X) = .3875$. Then

$$V(1000X + 100) = 1000^2(.3875) = 387,500. \qquad\qquad □$$

4.4.3 Comparing Two Stocks

Suppose you are considering an investment in one of two stocks, imaginatively named A and B. You have a forecast of the value of the stocks in the future.

Forecast: The value of each stock will increase by 5% if the national economy stays as it is. If the economic outlook improves, Stock A will increase in value by 10% and Stock B will increase in value by 15%. If the economic outlook deteriorates, Stock A will decrease in value by 10% and Stock B will decrease in value by 15%. You believe that probabilities for the future states of the economy are given by the following table:

State of the economy	Deteriorate	Unchanged	Improve
Probability	.20	.60	.20

This information enables you to create probability function tables for the return on each of the two stocks.

% Change in value of Stock A: a	$-.10$	.05	$+.10$
Probability: $p(a)$	.20	.60	.20

% Change in value of Stock B: b	$-.15$	.05	$+.15$
Probability: $p(b)$	.20	.60	.20

We cannot use expected value to choose between these stocks, since they have the same expected value.

$$E(A) = (-.10)(.20) + .05(.60) + .10(.20) = .03$$
$$E(B) = (-.15)(.20) + .05(.60) + .15(.20) = .03$$

However, there is a real difference between the two stocks. There is much more variation in the return of Stock B than the return of Stock A. Modern financial theory says that Stock B is riskier than Stock A because of that increased variation. You can make a greater profit with B, but you risk a greater loss.

One number that can be used to measure the risk in a stock is the standard deviation of returns. For the stocks above, we can easily compute the variances and standard deviations of the random variables representing change in value.

$$V(A) = (-.10-.03)^2(.20) + (.05-.03)^2(.60) + (.10-.03)^2(.20) = .0046$$
$$V(B) = (-.15-.03)^2(.20) + (.05-.03)^2(.60) + (.15-.03)^2(.20) = .0096$$

Then $\sigma_A \approx .068$ and $\sigma_B \approx .098$. The standard deviation of the riskier stock is higher.

Modern finance texts use the standard deviation of an investment as one possible measure of risk.[2] Many books of investment information give the mean and standard deviation of recent historical returns for stocks and mutual funds.[3]

4.4.4 *z*-scores; Chebychev's Theorem

Example 4.23 In Example 4.13, we studied the probability distribution of grades for a class.

Grade (x)	5	6	7	8	9	10
$p(x)$	.05	.10	.45	.20	.10	.10

The expected value is 7.5. The variance and standard deviation are

$$V(X) = .05(-2.5)^2 + .10(-1.5)^2 + .45(-0.5)^2$$
$$+ .20(0.5)^2 + .10(1.5)^2 + .10(2.5)^2 = 1.550$$

and

$$\sigma_X = \sqrt{1.55} \approx 1.245.$$

Suppose a student scored 10 on this quiz. The student is 2.5 points above the mean of 7.5. However, if we think of variability as measured in standard deviation units, those 2.5 points are

$$\frac{10 - 7.5}{1.245} = \frac{2.5}{1.245} \approx 2.008$$

standard deviation units above the mean. We have just computed a *z*-score. □

---

[2] See, for example, page 143 of Bodie et al. [1].
[3] On page 146 of [1] you will find this information for the entire Standard and Poor's Composite index of common stocks, 1926-2002. The mean is 12.04% and the standard deviation is 20.55%.

Definition 4.7 For any possible value x of a random variable, the **z-score** is

$$z = \frac{x - \mu}{\sigma}.$$

The z-score measures the distance of x from $\mu = E(X)$ in standard deviation units.

Example 4.24 For the test example above, a student with a score of 6 has a z-score of

$$z = \frac{6 - 7.5}{1.245} \approx -1.205.$$

That student's score is approximately 1.205 standard deviations below the mean. We could say that the student's score of 6 is within 1.21 standard deviations of the mean, since the score is below the mean by less than 1.21 standard deviations. □

Definition 4.8 We say that a value x of the random variable X is *within k standard deviations of the mean* if $|z| \leq k$.

Example 4.25 In the grade example, the highest z-score is approximately 2.008. The lowest z-score is found for $x = 5$; it is -2.008. Thus we could say that *all* of the x-values are within 2.01 standard deviations of the mean. This means that the probability is 1 that a score will be within 2.01 standard deviations of the mean. Below we give all the values of x with their approximate z-scores and probabilities.

Grade (x)	5	6	7	8	9	10
z	-2.008	-1.205	$-.402$	$.402$	1.205	2.008
$p(x) = p(z)$	.05	.10	.45	.20	.10	.10

The values 6, 7, 8, and 9 are within 1.21 standard deviations of the mean. Then

$P(X$ is within 1.21 standard deviations of the mean)

$$= P(6 \leq X \leq 9) = .10 + .45 + .20 + .10 = .85.$$

For the original data, we could simply say that 85% of the scores are within 1.21 standard deviations of the mean. □

It is common to discuss the percentage of values of a random variable that lie within a certain number of standard deviations of the mean. The results can vary widely from one random variable to another.

Example 4.26 The claim amount distribution in Example 4.22 had $\mu = 350$ and $\sigma = \sqrt{387,500} \approx 622.495$. The probability function table with approximate z-scores is as follows:

Total claim amount (y)	0	1000	2000	3000
z	$-.562$	1.044	2.651	4.257
$p(y)$	.72	.22	.05	.01

For this distribution, the probability that X is within 2.01 standard deviations of the mean is .94, not 1.00 as in the previous example. □

Usually discussions of this type depend on what specific probability function is being studied. However, there is a general result which holds for all probability functions.

Chebychev's Theorem For any random variable X, the probability that X is within k standard deviations of the mean is at least $1 - \frac{1}{k^2}$.

$$P(\mu - k\sigma \leq X \leq \mu + k\sigma) \geq 1 - \frac{1}{k^2}$$

Example 4.27 For the grade random variable, the mean was 7.5 and the standard deviation was approximately 1.245. Chebychev's Theorem says that the probability that a grade is within 3 standard deviations of the mean is at least $1 - \frac{1}{3^2}$, or approximately .889.

$$P(7.5 - 3(1.245) \leq X \leq 7.5 + 3(1.245))$$
$$= P(3.765 \leq X \leq 11.235) \geq 1 - \frac{1}{3^2} \approx .889$$

This last result is certainly true. All values of X are between 3.765 and 11.235, so the exact probability that X is in this range is 1.00. The true probability of 1.00 is certainly greater than or equal to .889. □

Chebychev's Theorem was quite conservative here: it estimated a lower bound of .889 for a probability that was actually 1.00. For the distributions studied in this text, we will calculate exact probabilities for problems like this. Chebychev's Theorem will see very little use.

4.5 Population and Sample Statistics

4.5.1 Population and Sample Mean

Most people are familiar with the calculation of an average or mean for a set of numbers, such as the test scores for a class. Modern calculator technology makes this calculation easy. However, it takes a little work to relate our standard deviation calculations to calculator technology. This is required because most calculators have two different standard deviation keys — one for a population and one for a sample. The difference between a population and a sample can be illustrated by returning to our probability function for the number of claims X filed by a policyholder with a large insurance company.

Number of claims (x)	0	1	2	3
$p(x)$	.72	.22	.05	.01

This is the probability function for all policyholders of the company — the entire **population** of policyholders. The mean and standard deviation were calculated in Examples 4.16 and 4.21 by using the probabilities above and the formulas

$$\mu = \sum x \cdot p(x) = .35$$

and

$$\sigma = \sqrt{\sum (x - \mu)^2 \cdot p(x)} = .622495.$$

Suppose the company had $n = 100,000$ policyholders and had compiled the above table by looking at all records to obtain the following table:

Number of claims (x)	0	1	2	3
Number of policyholders with x claims (f)	72,000	22,000	5,000	1,000

If we rewrite each $p(x)$ as f/n, the formulas for population mean and standard deviation can be rewritten as follows:

Population Mean and Standard Deviation

$$\mu = \frac{1}{n}\sum f \cdot x \qquad\qquad (4.7a)$$

$$\sigma = \sqrt{\frac{1}{n}\sum f \cdot (x - \mu)^2} \qquad\qquad (4.7b)$$

These formulas essentially add up all 100,000 individual values instead of using the probability table. They are equivalent, and give the correct answers for the entire population.

In many cases, it is not possible to gather complete data on an entire population. Then people who need information might take a **sample** of records to get an estimate of the mean and standard deviation of the population. Suppose an analyst does not know the true values of μ and σ for the entire company population. She picks a sample of $n = 10$ policyholder records at random from the company files, and finds the following numbers of claims on the 10 records.

$$0, 0, 1, 0, 2, 0, 0, 0, 1, 0$$

This sample leads to the following frequency table.

Number of claims (x)	0	1	2
Number of policyholders with x claims (f)	7	2	1

There are now two means and two standard deviations to consider: a) the original population mean and standard deviation, which are unknown to the analyst, and b) the sample mean and standard deviation. We picture this as follows:

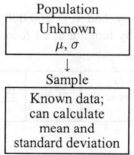

To *estimate* the true mean and standard deviation, the analyst would compute the sample mean and sample standard deviation from the sample values using a slightly different set of formulas. The difference is that the sum of squares in the standard deviation formula is divided by $n - 1$ instead of n when the calculation is done for sample data. This is done to make the estimates come out better on the average[4], but the details are the subject of another course. The real issue here is that calculations using sample data require a new and different formula.

Sample Mean and Standard Deviation

$$\bar{x} = \frac{1}{n}\sum f \cdot x \tag{4.8a}$$

$$s = \sqrt{\frac{1}{n-1}\sum f \cdot (x - \bar{x})^2} \tag{4.8b}$$

For the sample data above,

$$\bar{x} = \frac{1}{10}(7 \cdot 0 + 2 \cdot 1 + 1 \cdot 2) = .40$$

and

$$s = \sqrt{\frac{1}{9}[7(0-.40)^2 + 2(1-.40)^2 + 1(2-.40)^2]} \approx .699206.$$

These numbers are *estimates* of μ and σ; the analyst did not know those values (and still does not). A major difference between statistics and probability is that the subject of statistics deals primarily with estimating unknown values like μ and σ from sample data, whereas probability deals with solving problems for populations with known (or assumed) distributions. More will be said about this in later sections. This text covers probability and deals very little with estimation from sample data. However, it is important for the student to realize that the concepts of mean and standard deviation are widely used in two different ways with two different sets of formulas. This occasionally leads to confusion in calculator use.

---

4   The technical term is that the estimators are *unbiased*.

4.5.2   Using Calculators for the Mean and Standard Deviation

Modern calculators typically give both the sample and population standard deviations. Thus the student must be familiar with both and be able to determine which one is required for any given problem.

The TI-83 calculator calculates both sample and population standard deviation. On this calculator, the values of x and the frequencies f are entered in separate lists, say, L_1 and L_2. Then the command

$$1 - Var\, Stats\, L_1, L_2$$

will lead to a screen which shows the mean as $\overline{x}$, sample standard deviation as s_x, and population standard deviation as σ_x.

The TI BA II Plus calculator has a STAT menu. Under the 1-V option the calculator will show the mean as $\overline{x}$, sample standard deviation as s_x, and population standard deviation as σ_x just as the TI-83 does.

In Microsoft EXCEL® the function AVERAGE gives the mean, the function STDEV gives the sample standard deviation and the function STDEVP gives the population standard deviation.

4.6   Exercises

4.2   The Probability Function of a Discrete Random Variable

4-1.   Let X be the random variable for the number of heads obtained when three fair coins are tossed. What is the probability function for X?

4-2.   Ten cards are face down in a row on a table. Exactly one of them is an ace. You turn the cards over one at a time, moving from left to right. Let X be the random variable for the number of cards turned *before* the ace is turned over. What is the probability function for X?

4-3.   A fair die is rolled repeatedly. Let X be the random variable for the number of times the die is rolled *before* a six appears. What are the probability function and the cumulative distribution function for X?

4-4.   Let X be the random variable for the sum obtained by rolling two fair dice. What are the $p(x)$ and $F(x)$ functions for X?

4.3   Measuring Central Tendency; Expected Value

4-5.   For the X defined in Exercise 4-4, what is $E(X)$?

4-6.   The GPA (grade point average) random variable X assigns to the letter grades A, B, C, D and E the numerical values 4, 3, 2, 1 and 0. Find the expected value of X for a student selected at random from a class in which there were 15 A grades, 33 B grades, 51 C grades, 6 D grades, and 3 E grades. (This expected value can be thought of as the class average GPA for the course.)

4-7.   A construction company whose workers are used on high-risk projects insures its workers against injury or death on the job. One unit of insurance for an employee pays $1,000 for an injury and $10,000 for death. Studies have shown that in a year 7.3% of the workers suffer an injury and 0.41% are killed. What is the expected unit claim amount (pure premium) for this insurance? If the company has 10,000 employees and exactly 7.3% are injured and exactly 0.41% are killed, what is the average cost per unit of the insurance claims?

4-8.   Suppose that in the above problem the administrative costs are $50 per person insured. The company purchases 10 units of insurance for each worker. Let X be the total of expected claim amount and administrative costs for each worker. Find $E(X)$.

4-9.   Verify Equation (4.4b).

4-10.   Let X be the random variable for the number of times a fair die is tossed before a six appears (Exercise 4-3). Find $E(X)$.

4-11.   The mode of a probability function does not have to be unique. Find the mode of the probability function in Exercise 4-1, for the random variable for the number of heads obtained when three fair coins are tossed.

4.4   Variance and Standard Deviation

4-12.   If X is the random variable for the sum obtained by rolling two
        fair dice (Exercise 4-4), what is $V(X)$?

4-13.   For the insurance policy that pays $1,000 for an injury and
        $10,000 for death (Exercise 4-7), what is the standard deviation
        for the claim amount on 5 units of insurance? (Note: Some
        employees receive $0 of claim payment. This value of the
        random variable must be included in your calculation.)

4-14.   Verify Equation (4.5b). (Hint: It is sufficient to show that
        $V(X + b) = V(X)$. If $Y = X + b$ and $E(X) = \mu_X$, what is
        $Y - \mu_Y$?)

4-15.   Let X be the random variable for the sum obtained by rolling
        two fair dice (Exercise 4-4).
        (a)   Using Chebychev's Theorem, what is a lower bound for
               the probability that the value of X is within 2 standard
               deviations of the mean of X?
        (b)   What is the exact probability that this sum is within this
               range?

4.5   Population and Sample Statistics

4-16.   An auto insurance company has 15,000 policyholders with
        comprehensive automobile coverage. In the past year 11,425
        filed no claims, 3,100 filed one claim, 385 filed two claims, and
        90 filed three claims. What are the mean and the standard
        deviation for the number of claims filed by a policyholder?

4-17.   A marketing company polled 50 people at a mall about the
        number of movies they had seen in the previous month. The
        results of this poll are as follows:

Number of movies	0	1	2	3	4	5	6	7	8
Number of viewers	3	5	6	9	11	7	5	3	1

        What are the sample mean and sample standard deviation for the
        number of movies seen by an individual in a month?

4.7   Sample Actuarial Examination Problems

4-18. A probability distribution of the claim sizes for an auto insurance
policy is given in the table below:

Claim Size	Probability
20	0.15
30	0.10
40	0.05
50	0.20
60	0.10
70	0.10
80	0.30

What percentage of the claims are within one standard deviation of
the mean claim size?

4-19. A recent study indicates that the annual cost of maintaining and
repairing a car in a town in Ontario averages 200 with a variance
of 260.

If a tax of 20% is introduced on all items associated with the
maintenance and repair of cars (i.e., everything is made 20% more
expensive), what will be the variance of the annual cost of
maintaining and repairing a car?

4-20. A tour operator has a bus that can accommodate 20 tourists. The
operator knows that tourists may not show up, so he sells 21
tickets. The probability that an individual tourist will not show up
is 0.02, independent of all other tourists.

Each ticket costs 50, and is non-refundable if a tourist fails to
show up. If a tourist shows up and a seat is not available, the tour
operator has to pay 100 (ticket cost + 50 penalty) to the tourist.

What is the expected revenue of the tour operator?

Chapter 5
Commonly Used Discrete Distributions

In Chapter 4 we saw a number of examples of discrete probability distributions. In this chapter we will study some special distributions that are extremely useful and widely applied. Examples of some of these distributions have already appeared in Chapter 4.

5.1 The Binomial Distribution

We have already seen an example of a binomial distribution problem: tossing a coin three times and finding the probability of observing exactly two heads. The binomial distribution is useful for modeling problems in which you need to find probabilities for the number of successes in a series of independent trials; how many times will you toss a head, hit a target, or guess a right answer on a test. We will introduce the binomial distribution by looking at the coin-tossing example.

5.1.1 Binomial Random Variables

Suppose you are going to toss a fair coin three times and record the number of heads X. The process of tossing the coin three times and observing whether or not each toss is a head is called a binomial experiment because it satisfies all the conditions given in the following definition.

Definition 5.1 An experiment is called a **binomial experiment** if all of the following hold:

(a)   The experiment consists of n identical trials.

(b)   Each trial has exactly two outcomes, which are usually referred to as success (S) or failure (F).

(c)   The probability of success on each individual trial is always the same number $P(S) = p$. (The probability of failure is then always $P(F) = 1 - p$. It is traditional to use the notation $P(F) = q = 1 - p$.)

(d)   The trials are independent.

Definition 5.2 If X is the number of successes in a binomial experiment, X is called a **binomial random variable**.

Example 5.1 A fair coin is tossed three times and the number of heads X is recorded. The experiment is a binomial experiment since all of the following hold:

(a)   There are $n = 3$ identical trials (coin tosses).

(b)   Each trial has two outcomes: heads (a success, S) or tails (a failure, F).

(c)   The probability of success is the same on each trial; in this case, $P(S) = P(H) = .50$ for each toss.

(d)   Successive tosses of a fair coin are independent.

Thus X is a binomial random variable.   □

Example 5.2 A student takes a multiple choice examination with $n = 10$ questions. He has not attended class or studied for three weeks and plans to guess on each question by having his calculator display a random integer from 1 to 5. (There are 5 choices for each question.) Let X be the number of questions out of 10 for which the student guesses correctly. Then X is a binomial random variable, since all of the following hold:

(a)   There are $n = 10$ identical trials.

(b)   Each trial has two outcomes: right (a success, S) or wrong.

(c) $P(S) = p = 1/5 = .20$ on each trial.

(d)   Successive guesses are independent.   □

5.1.2 Binomial Probabilities

In Section 3.4.2 we used the multiplication rule for independent events to show that the probability of tossing 3 heads in a row with a fair coin was 1/8. That was an example of a binomial probability problem — we found the probability $P(X = 3)$ for the binomial random variable X in Example 5.1. There is a formula which will enable us to find $P(X = k)$ for any binomial random variable X and any k. We will show how this formula works by looking at the example of tossing a fair coin 3 times.

Example 5.3 Below is the tree for three tosses of a fair coin. Probabilities for each branch are included.

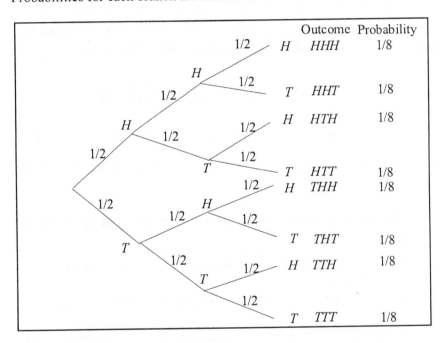

Let X be the number of heads observed. There is only one branch (HHH) with $X = 3$. Since the probability of each branch is 1/8,

$$P(X = 3) = \text{(number of branches with 3 heads)}\tfrac{1}{8} = 1\left(\tfrac{1}{8}\right) = \tfrac{1}{8}.$$

This reasoning works for any possible value of X. For example

$$P(X = 2) = \text{(number of branches with 2 heads)}\tfrac{1}{8} = 3\left(\tfrac{1}{8}\right) = \tfrac{3}{8}. \ \square$$

The above results above could also have been obtained from the general formula for $P(X = k)$.

Binomial Distribution

If X is a binomial random variable with n trials and $P(S) = p$,

$$P(X = k) = \binom{n}{k}p^k(1 - p)^{n-k} = \binom{n}{k}p^k(q)^{n-k}, \qquad (5.1)$$

for $k = 0, 1, \ldots, n$.

Example 5.4 Let X be the number of heads in 3 tosses of a fair coin. Then $n = 3$ and $p = \frac{1}{2}$. Using Equation (5.1) for $k = 2$, we can replicate the value of $P(X = 2)$ obtained in the last example.

$$P(X = 2) = \binom{3}{2}\left(\frac{1}{2}\right)^2\left(\frac{1}{2}\right)^1 = 3\left(\frac{1}{8}\right) = \frac{3}{8}$$

Note that the term $\binom{3}{2}$ gives the number of branches with exactly 2 heads, and the term $\left(\frac{1}{2}\right)^2\left(\frac{1}{2}\right)^1$ gives the probability of a single branch with 2 heads. □

The example should make clear the meaning of the terms in Equation (5.1).

(1) $p^k q^{n-k}$ gives the probability of a single branch with exactly k successes.

(2) $\binom{n}{k}$ gives the number of branches with exactly k successes.

Example 5.5 We return to the student who is guessing on a ten-question multiple choice quiz, with $n = 10$ and $p = .20$. The probability that the student gets exactly 2 questions right is

$$\binom{10}{2}(.20)^2(.80)^8 \approx .30199.$$

The probability that the student who guessed on all 10 questions got only 2 right answers is approximately .302. There is some justice in this. □

5.1.3 Mean and Variance of the Binomial Distribution

The mean and variance of a binomial distribution depend on the underlying values of n and p. It is not too hard to find the mean and variance for a binomial distribution when there is only one trial — i.e., with $n = 1$. The probability distribution for a binomial random variable with $n = 1$ and $P(S) = p$ is given below.

Number of successes (x)	0	1
$p(x)$	$q = 1 - p$	p

$$E(X) = q \cdot 0 + p \cdot 1 = p$$

$$V(X) = E[(X - p)^2] = q(0-p)^2 + p(1-p)^2$$
$$= q(p)^2 + p(q)^2 = pq(p + q) = pq$$

Exercise 5-10 asks the reader to show that for a binomial random variable X with $n = 2$ and $P(S) = p$,

$$E(X) = 2p$$

and

$$V(X) = 2pq.$$

The general formulas for the mean and variance of any binomial distribution X follow the pattern established above. Methods for proving these rules in general will be developed later in the text.

Binomial Distribution Mean and Variance

If X is a binomial random variable with n trials and $P(S) = p$,

$$E(X) = np \qquad (5.2a)$$

and

$$V(X) = np(1 - p) = npq. \qquad (5.2b)$$

Example 5.6 Let X be the number of heads in 3 tosses of a fair coin. Since X is binomial with $n = 3$ and $p = .50$,

$$E(X) = 3(.50) = 1.5 \quad \text{and} \quad V(X) = 3(.50)(1 - .50) = .75. \qquad \square$$

Example 5.7 Let X be the number of correct answers for a student guessing on a 10 question ($n = 10$) multiple choice test with 5 choices on each question ($p = .20$).

$$E(X) = 10(.20) = 2 \qquad V(X) = 10(.20)(.80) = 1.6 \qquad \square$$

Technology Note

We have already noted that calculators like the TI-83 or TI-BA II Plus will calculate the coefficient $\binom{n}{k}$ needed for the binomial probability formula. Thus it is fairly easy to calculate binomial probabilities on these calculators. Since the binomial distribution is widely used, many calculators and computer packages have special functions for finding binomial probabilities. On the TI-83, entering

binompdf(10, .20, 2)

gives the probability of .30199 found in Example 5.5. (The function binompdf( ) can be found in the DISTR menu.)

Microsoft® EXCEL has a function BINOMDIST which finds binomial probabilities. The statistical package MINITAB will quickly give the entire probability distribution for a binomial random variable X. Below is the entire probability distribution for the binomial random variable X with $n = 10$ and $p = .20$, as calculated by MINITAB.

Binomial (10, .20)

K	$P(X = K)$
0.00	0.1074
1.00	0.2684
2.00	0.3020
3.00	0.2013
4.00	0.0881
5.00	0.0264
6.00	0.0055
7.00	0.0008
8.00	0.0001
9.00	0.0000
10.00	0.0000

The last two probabilities in the MINITAB printout are not 0; they round to 0 when four decimal places are used. The computer-generated table can be used to rapidly answer questions about the binomial experiment

Example 5.8   Consider the guessing student with $n = 10$ and $p = .20$. What is the probability that he has 6 or more correct answers?

$$P(X \geq 6) = .0055 + .0008 + .0001 + .0000 + .0000 = .0064$$

The guessing student will score 60% or more on this quiz less than 1% of the time.   □

5.1.4   Applications

Example 5.9   (Insurance) The 1979-81 United States Life Table given in Bowers et al. [2] gives the probability of death within one year for a 57-year-old person as .01059. (In actuarial notation, $q_{57} = .01059$.) Suppose that you are an insurance agent with 10 clients who have just reached age 57. You are willing to assume that deaths of the clients are independent events.

  (a)   What is the probability that all 10 survive the next year?
  (b)   What is the probability that 9 will survive and exactly one will die during the next year?

Solution   If client deaths are independent, the number of survivors X will be a binomial random variable with parameters $n = 10$ and $p = 1 - .01059 = .98941$.

  (a) $P(X = 10) = \binom{10}{10}(.98941)^{10} \approx .89901$

  (b) $P(X = 9) = \binom{10}{9}(.98941)^{9}(.01059)^{1} \approx .09622$ □

Example 5.10   (Polling) Suppose you live in a large city which has 1,000,000 registered voters. The voters will vote on a bond issue in the next month, and you want to estimate the percent of the voters who favor the issue. You cannot ask each of 1,000,000 people for his or her opinion, so you decide to randomly select a sample of 100 voters and ask each of them if they favor the issue. What are your chances of getting reasonably close to the true percentage in favor of the issue?

Solution To answer this question concretely, we will make an assumption. Suppose the true percent of the voters who favor the bond issue is 65%. You don't know this number; you are trying to estimate it. In polling voters, you are really doing a binomial experiment. A success S is finding a voter in favor of the bond issue, and $P(S) = p = .65$. You are polling 100 voters, so $n = 100$. Your random selection is designed to make the successive voter opinions independent. Below is a table of probabilities $p(x)$ and cumulative probabilities $F(x)$ for values of x from 59 to 70.

x	$p(x)$	$F(x)$
59		0.1250
60	0.0474	0.1724
61	0.0577	0.2301
62	0.0674	0.2976
63	0.0755	0.3731
64	0.0811	0.4542
65	0.0834	0.5376
66	0.0821	0.6197
67	0.0774	0.6971
68	0.0698	0.7669
69	0.0601	0.8270
70	0.0494	0.8764

The probability that 65 out of the 100 voters sampled favor the bond issue is .0834, so that you will estimate the true percentage of 65% exactly with a probability of .0834. The probability that your estimate is in the range 60%–70% is the sum of all the $p(x)$ values above, since it equals

$$P(60 \leq X \leq 70) = p(60) + p(61) + \cdots + p(70).$$

The cumulative distribution function $F(x)$ helps to simplify this calculation, since

$$P(60 \leq X \leq 70) = P(X \leq 70) - P(X \leq 59) = .8764 - .1250 = .7514$$

to four places.[1]   Even though you do not know the true value of $p = .65$, your estimate will be in the range .60 to .70 with probability .7514. ☐

---

[1]   The $p(x)$ values add to .7513 due to rounding.

Polling problems are really statistical estimation problems. A statistics course would demonstrate how to increase sample size to give an even higher probability of getting an estimate very close to the true value of p. However, the statistical methods taught in other classes are based on the kind of reasoning used in the last example.

5.1.5 Checking Assumptions for Binomial Problems

There are some applied problems in textbooks in which independence of trials is questionable. A standard example is the following problem:

A baseball player has a batting average of .350.[2] What is the probability that he gets exactly 4 hits in his next 10 at bats?

This problem usually appears at the end of the section on binomial probabilities. The obvious intent is to treat the next 10 at bats as $n = 10$ independent trials with $p = .350$ on each trial. Many students question this problem, either because they do not believe that successive at bats are independent or they do not believe that $p = .350$ on each trial. (The authors also question these assumptions.) The best way to simplify this situation for the student is simply to add a clause to the problem:

Assume that successive at bats are independent and the same value of p applies in each at bat.

The polling problem in Example 5.10 also raises issues about the validity of assumptions. The usual method of sampling voters is called **sampling without replacement**. Once you have polled a specific voter, you will not sample him or her again. This means that when the first voter is selected for polling, the next selection will not be from all 1,000,000 voters, but from the remaining 999,999. This changes the probability of favoring the bond issue very slightly for the second trial. The usual response to this problem is to say that with 1,000,000 voters and a sample of only 100, the removal of a few voters changes things very little on each trial, and it is still reasonable to use the binomial probability model. This practical argument depends heavily on the underlying population being very large and the sample very small in comparison. In the next section we will introduce the hypergeometric distribution, which will handle sampling without replacement exactly for any population size.

---

[2] This often gives textbook authors a chance to put in their favorite hitters, so that the problem becomes the Ted Williams problem or the Tony Gwynn problem.

5.2 The Hypergeometric Distribution

5.2.1 An Example

We have already solved counting problems that were truly sampling without replacement problems in Chapter 3. The first of these problems was in Example 3.6, which is reviewed below.

Example 5.11 In Example 3.6, we looked at a company with 20 male employees and 30 female employees. The company is going to choose 5 employees at random for drug testing. We found, for example, that the probability of choosing a group of 3 males and 2 females is

$$\frac{\binom{20}{3}\binom{30}{2}}{\binom{50}{5}} = \frac{495,900}{2,118,760} \approx .234.$$

The numerator in the above expression is the product of (a) the number of ways to choose 3 males from 20, and (b) the number of ways to choose 2 females from 30. The denominator represents the number of ways to choose a random sample of 5 from 50 people.

It is easy to follow the reasoning in this calculation and find the probability that the group selected for testing contains any number of females between 0 and 5. If X is the number of females selected, then

$$P(X = k) = \frac{\binom{20}{5-k}\binom{30}{k}}{\binom{50}{5}}, \ k = 0, 1, 2, 3, 4, 5.$$

The probability function for X is given in the following table:

Number of females x	$p(x)$
0	0.0073
1	0.0686
2	0.2341
3	0.3641
4	0.2587
5	0.0673

The problem of selecting five employees for testing is a sampling without replacement problem. Once a person is selected for a drug test, that person is no longer in the pool for future selection. This makes successive selections dependent on what has gone before. Originally the pool of employees is 40% male and 60% female. If a male is selected on the first pick, the remaining pool consists of 49 people. The proportion of males changes to $19/49 \approx .388$ and the proportion of females changes to $30/49 \approx .612$.   □

5.2.2   The Hypergeometric Distribution

The probability function given for the number of females selected in Example 5.11 is hypergeometric. A useful intuitive interpretation of the **hypergeometric distribution** can be obtained from Example 5.11.

(1)   A sample of size n is being taken from a finite population of size N. In Example 5.11, $N = 50$ (the number of employees in the entire company) and $n = 5$ (the size of the group selected for testing).

(2)   The population has a subgroup of size $r \geq n$ that is of interest. In our problem, there were $r = 30$ females in the population of 50. We were interested in the number of females in the group selected for testing.

(3)   The random variable of interest is X, the number of members of the subgroup in the sample taken. In Example 5.11, X is the number of females in the group selected for testing.

(4)   The probability function for X is given below.

Hypergeometric Distribution

$$P(X = k) = \frac{\binom{N-r}{n-k}\binom{r}{k}}{\binom{N}{n}}, \quad k = 0, \dots, n \text{ and } r \geq n$$

(5.3)[3]

---

[3] All applications here will satisfy $r \geq n$ and this is the most common situation. If we do not require $r \geq n$, the formula will still be applicable, with k ranging from $max(0, n + r - N)$ to $min(r, n)$.

124

Chapter 5

A common textbook example of the hypergeometric distribution involves testing for defective parts. This was covered in Example 3.7, and is reviewed here.

Example 5.12 A manufacturer receives a shipment of 50 parts. 20 of the parts are defective. The manufacturer does not know this number, and is going to test a sample of 5 parts chosen at random from the shipment.

Solution In this problem there is a population of $N = 50$ parts. A sample of size $n = 5$ will be taken. The manufacturer would like to study the subgroup of defective parts, and this subgroup has $r = 20$ members. The random variable of interest is X, the number of defective parts in the sample of size 5. The probability function for X is

$$P(X = k) = \frac{\binom{20}{k}\binom{30}{5-k}}{\binom{50}{5}}, \quad k = 0, 1, 2, 3, 4, 5. \qquad \square$$

5.2.3 The Mean and Variance of the Hypergeometric Distribution

The mean and variance of the hypergeometric distribution are given without proof by the following:

Hypergeometric Distribution Mean and Variance

$$E(X) = n\left(\frac{r}{N}\right) \qquad (5.4a)$$

$$V(X) = n\left(\frac{r}{N}\right)\left(1 - \frac{r}{N}\right)\left(\frac{N-n}{N-1}\right) \qquad (5.4b)$$

An example will enable us to relate this to the binomial distribution mean and variance.

Example 5.13 We return to the parts testing of Example 5.12. A sample of size $n = 5$ was taken from a population of size $N = 50$ which contained $r = 20$ defectives. If X is the number of defectives, the mean number of defectives in a sample is

$$E(X) = 5\left(\frac{20}{50}\right) = 5(.40) = 2.$$

In this problem, we are conducting $n = 5$ trials in which a success S occurs if and when we find a defective part. On the first trial, $P(S) = 20/50 = .40 = p$. Since parts are not replaced, $P(S) = p$ changes on later trials, but the mean is still $np = 5(.40)$ as in the binomial case.

A similar relationship appears when we find the variance of the number of defective parts in the sample.

$$V(X) = 5\left(\frac{20}{50}\right)\left(1 - \frac{20}{50}\right)\left(\frac{50-5}{50-1}\right) = 5(.40)(.60)\frac{45}{49} \approx 1.102.$$

A binomial distribution with $n = 5$ would have a variance of $npq = 5(.40)(.60) = 1.20$. The hypergeometric variance is adjusted by multiplying 1.20 by 45/49. The final term in the hypergeometric variance is often called the **finite population correction factor**.

5.2.4 Relating the Binomial and Hypergeometric Distributions

Both the binomial and hypergeometric distributions can be thought of as involving n success-failure trials. In binomial problems, successive trials are independent and have the same success probability. In hypergeometric problems, successive trials are influenced by what has happened before and the success probability changes. When the population is large and the sample is small, the hypergeometric distribution looks much like the binomial. Meyer [10] states that "In general, the approximation of the hypergeometric distribution by the binomial is very good if $n/N \le .10$."[4] In our Example 5.13, we found

Binomial		Hypergeometric	
n	5	Sample size (r)	5
p	0.6	Population size (N)	50
		Subgroup size (n)	30
x	$p(x)$	Successes in sample (x)	$p(x)$
0	0.0102	0	0.0073
1	0.0768	1	0.0686
2	0.2304	2	0.2341
3	0.3456	3	0.3641
4	0.2592	4	0.2587
5	0.0778	5	0.0673

---

[4] See page 176.

$n/N = 5/50 = .10$. For the reader's comparison, the probability tables for the hypergeometric distribution with $N = 50$, $n = 5$ and $r = 30$, and for the binomial with $n = 5$ and $p = .60$, are shown at the bottom of page 117.

Technology Note

The formulas for hypergeometric probabilities use the combinatorial coefficients $\binom{n}{k} = C(n, k)$ and can easily be calculated on modern calculators. Microsoft® EXCEL has a spreadsheet function HYPGEOMDIST which calculates hypergeometric probabilities directly. The comparison table on the previous page is an EXCEL spreadsheet.

5.3   The Poisson Distribution

In the last two sections, we have used the binomial distribution and the hypergeometric distribution to find the probability of a given number of successes in a series of trials — e.g., the number of heads in 3 coin tosses or the number of females selected for drug testing. In this section, we will study the Poisson distribution, which is also used to find the probability of a number of occurrences — e.g., the number of accidents at an intersection in a week or the number of claims an insured files with a company in a year. We will first look at the example of the number of accidents at an intersection to get an idea of the kind of problems that are modeled by the Poisson distribution.

5.3.1   The Poisson Distribution

Example 5.14   A busy intersection is the scene of many traffic accidents. An analyst studies data on the accidents and concludes that accidents occur there at "an average rate of $\lambda = 2$ per month". This does not mean that there are exactly 2 accidents in each month. In any given month there may be any number of accidents, $k = 0, 1, 2, 3, \ldots$. The number of accidents X in a month is a random variable. The **Poisson distribution** can be used to find the probabilities $P(X = k)$ in terms of k and λ, the average rate.

Poisson Distribution

The random variable X follows the Poisson distribution with parameter (or average rate) λ if

$$P(X = k) = \frac{e^{-\lambda}\lambda^k}{k!}, \quad k = 0, 1, 2, 3, \ldots . \qquad (5.5a)$$

For this distribution,

$$E(X) = \lambda \qquad (5.5b)^5$$

and

$$V(X) = \lambda. \qquad (5.5c)^5$$

The number of accidents in a month at this intersection can be modeled using the Poisson distribution with an average rate of $\lambda = 2$ if we make a few reasonable assumptions about how accidents occur. We will discuss why the Poisson distribution works well for this problem later in this section and again in Chapter 8. Once we accept that the Poisson distribution is the right one to use here, it is a simple matter to calculate probabilities, mean and variance. If X is the number of accidents in a month, then

$$P(X = 0) = \frac{e^{-2}2^0}{0!} \approx .1353353,$$

$$P(X = 1) = \frac{e^{-2}2^1}{1!} \approx .2706706,$$

$$P(X = 2) = \frac{e^{-2}2^2}{2!} \approx .2706706,$$

$$E(X) = 2 \quad \text{and} \quad V(X) = 2.$$

It should not be too surprising that the mean of X is 2, since 2 was given as the average rate of accidents per month. $\qquad\qquad\square$

The Poisson distribution is used to model a wide variety of situations in which some event (such as an accident) is said to occur at an average rate λ per time period.

---

[5] A derivation of $E(X) = \lambda$ will be provided in Section 5.3.4. The proof that $V(X) = \lambda$ is outlined in Exercise 5-22.

Example 5.15 The holders of an insurance policy file claims at an average rate of 0.45 per year. Use the Poisson model to answer the following questions.

(a)   Find the probability that a policyholder files at least one claim in a year.

(b)   Find the mean number of claims per policyholder per year.

(c)   Suppose each claim pays exactly $1000. Find the mean claim amount for a policyholder in a year. (This is the pure premium for the policy.)

Solution

(a)   Let X be the number of claims.

$$P(\text{at least one claim}) = 1 - P(\text{no claims})$$
$$= 1 - P(X = 0)$$
$$= 1 - \frac{e^{-.45} .45^0}{0!} \approx .3624$$

(b) $E(X) = \lambda = .45$ claims per client per year.

(c)   The annual claim amount random variable is $Y = 1000X$. Equation (4.4a) states that $E(aX) = a \cdot E(X)$. Thus the pure premium is

$$E(Y) = E(1000X) = 1000E(X) = 1000(.45) = 450. \qquad \square$$

5.3.2   The Poisson Approximation to the Binomial for Large n and Small p

With two reasonable assumptions we can demonstrate why the Poisson distribution gives realistic answers for the probabilities in Example 5.14:

Assumption 1   *The probability of exactly one accident in a small time interval of length t is approximately* λt. For example, if a month consists of 30 days, the month will have $30(24) = 720$ hours so that an hour is a time interval of length $t = 1/720$ of a month. If the rate of accidents is $\lambda = 2$ per month, the probability of an accident in a single hour is $\lambda t = 2/720$ (or 2 accidents per 720 hours).

Assumption 2 *Accidents occur independently in time intervals which do not intersect.*

With these two assumptions, we can find the probability of any given number of accidents in a month using the binomial distribution. Divide the month into 720 distinct hours which do not intersect. In each hour, the probability of an accident is $p = 2/720$. Since accidents occur independently in these 720 hours, we can think of observing accidents over a month as a binomial experiment with $n = 720$ trials and $p = 2/720$. Let X be the number of accidents in a month. Using the binomial distribution

$$P(X = 1) = \binom{720}{1} \left(\frac{2}{720}\right)^1 \left(1 - \frac{2}{720}\right)^{719} \approx .2706702.$$

In Example 5.14 we found $P(X = 1)$ to be .2706706 using the Poisson formula. The binomial calculation gives the same answer as the Poisson, to 5 places, for $P(X = 1)$.

This relationship between Poisson and binomial probabilities is no accident. The binomial distribution with $n = 720$ and $p = 2/720$ is very closely approximated by the Poisson distribution with $\lambda = 2$. In the following table we give probability values for (a) the binomial distribution with $n = 720$ and $p = 2/720$, and (b) the Poisson distribution with $\lambda = 2$ for $x = 0, 1, \dots, 10$. The values are very close.

Poisson $\lambda = 2$		Binomial $n = 720$ $p = 2/720$	
x	$p(x)$	x	$p(x)$
0	0.1353	0	0.1350
1	0.2707	1	0.2707
2	0.2707	2	0.2710
3	0.1804	3	0.1807
4	0.0902	4	0.0902
5	0.0361	5	0.0360
6	0.0120	6	0.0119
7	0.0034	7	0.0034
8	0.0009	8	0.0008
9	0.0002	9	0.0002
10	0.0000	10	0.0000

Thus we can think of the Poisson probabilities for an average rate of 2 accidents per month as approximately binomial probabilities for $n = 720$ hourly trials per month, with a probability of $p = 2/720$ for one accident in an hour. In general, the Poisson probabilities for any rate λ approximate binomial probabilities for large n and small $p = \lambda/n$.

Poisson Approximation to the Binomial

If n is large and $p = \frac{\lambda}{n}$ is small, then $P(X = k)$ can be calculated using the Poisson or the binomial with approximately the same answer.

$$\frac{e^{-\lambda}\lambda^k}{k!} \approx \binom{n}{k}\left(\frac{\lambda}{n}\right)^k\left(1 - \frac{\lambda}{n}\right)^{n-k} \qquad (5.6)$$

We will give some idea of why this is true in the next section.

Example 5.16 In Example 5.15 we looked at an insurance company whose clients file claims at an average rate of $\lambda = .45$ per year. The company has 500 clients. What is the probability that a client files exactly one claim?

Solution   Let X be the number of claims filed. If we use the Poisson distribution,

$$P(X = 1) = \frac{e^{-.45}.45^1}{1!} \approx .2869.$$

If we are willing to assume that the 500 clients are independent, we can look at X as the number of successes in 500 trials with $n = 500$ and $p = .45/500$. Then

$$P(X = 1) = \binom{500}{1}\left(\frac{.45}{500}\right)^1\left(1 - \frac{.45}{500}\right)^{499} \approx .2871. \qquad \square$$

5.3.3   Why Poisson Probabilities Approximate Binomial Probabilities

To understand the Poisson approximation to the binomial, we need to review the definition of the number e and the implied value of $e^{-\lambda}$.

$$e = \lim_{n\to\infty}\left(1 + \frac{1}{n}\right)^n \qquad e^{-\lambda} = \lim_{n\to\infty}\left(1 - \frac{\lambda}{n}\right)^n$$

This means that for large n,

$$e^{-\lambda} \approx \left(1 - \frac{\lambda}{n}\right)^n.$$

To see how this identity can be used to establish the approximation, we will look at the simplest cases — i.e., $P(X = 0)$ and $P(X = 1)$. For $X = 0$, the Poisson gives

$$P(X = 0) = e^{-\lambda}.$$

The binomial with large n and $p = \lambda/n$ gives

$$P(X = 0) = \binom{n}{0}\left(\frac{\lambda}{n}\right)^0\left(1 - \frac{\lambda}{n}\right)^n = \left(1 - \frac{\lambda}{n}\right)^n \approx e^{-\lambda}.$$

For $X = 1$, the Poisson gives

$$P(X = 1) = e^{-\lambda}\lambda.$$

The binomial with large n and $p = \lambda/n$ gives

$$P(X = 1) = \binom{n}{1}\left(\frac{\lambda}{n}\right)^1\left(1 - \frac{\lambda}{n}\right)^{n-1}$$

$$= \lambda\left(1 - \frac{\lambda}{n}\right)^{n-1}$$

$$= \frac{\lambda}{\left(1 - \frac{\lambda}{n}\right)}\left(1 - \frac{\lambda}{n}\right)^n \approx \lambda e^{-\lambda},$$

since $\left(1 - \frac{\lambda}{n}\right) \approx 1$.

The general proof of the approximation is based on the same principles, but requires much more rearranging of terms.

5.3.4 Derivation of the Expected Value of a Poisson Random Variable

In order to prove that $E(X) = \lambda$ for a Poisson distribution with rate λ, we need to review the series expansion for e^x:

$$e^x = 1 + x + \frac{x^2}{2!} + \frac{x^3}{3!} + \cdots + \frac{x^n}{n!} + \cdots$$

The expected value of X is also an infinite series.

$$E(X) = \sum k \cdot P(X = k)$$

$$= 0 \frac{e^{-\lambda} \lambda^0}{0!} + 1 \frac{e^{-\lambda} \lambda^1}{1!} + 2 \frac{e^{-\lambda} \lambda^2}{2!} + 3 \frac{e^{-\lambda} \lambda^3}{3!} + \cdots$$

$$= \lambda e^{-\lambda} \left(1 + \lambda + \frac{\lambda^2}{2!} + \frac{\lambda^3}{3!} + \cdots \right) = \lambda e^{-\lambda} e^{\lambda} = \lambda$$

Technology Note

The Poisson formulas are simple to evaluate on any modern calculator. However, the distribution is used so often that the TI-83 calculator has a time-saving function (poissonpdf) which calculates Poisson probabilities. For example, if $\lambda = 2$, entering

poissonpdf(2, 1)

from the DISTR menu gives $.27067 = P(X = 1)$.

Microsoft® EXCEL has a POISSON function to calculate Poisson probabilities, and MINITAB will generate tables of Poisson probabilities. The table which compared Poisson and binomial probabilities in Section 5.3.2 was calculated in both EXCEL and in MINITAB.

5.4 The Geometric Distribution

5.4.1 Waiting Time Problems

The **geometric distribution** is used to study how many failures will occur before the first success in a series of independent trials. We have already looked at a geometric distribution problem in Example 4.7. This example dealt with a slot machine for which the probability of winning on an individual play was .05 and successive plays were independent. The random variable of interest was X, the number of unsuccessful plays before the first win. This is a **waiting time** random variable — it represents the number of losses we must wait through before our first win.

The general setting for a geometric distribution problem has many features in common with a binomial distribution problem:

(1) The experiment consists of repeating identical success-or-failure trials until the first success occurs.
(2) The trials are independent.
(3) On each trial $P(S) = p$ and $P(F) = 1 - p = q$.
(4) The random variable of interest is X, the number of failures before the first success.

The probability of k failures before the first success can be found by the multiplication rule for independent events:

Geometric Distribution

$$P(X = k) = q^k p, \quad k = 0, 1, 2, 3, \ldots \qquad (5.7)$$

Example 5.17 Let X be the number of unsuccessful plays before the first win on the slot machine in Example 4.7. X follows the geometric distribution with $p = .05$ and $q = .95$. Then

$$P(X = k) = .95^k(.05), \quad k = 0, 1, 2, 3, \ldots.$$

This was derived in Example 4.7 using the multiplication rule. $\square$

Example 5.18 A telemarketer makes repeated calls to persons on a computer generated list. The probability of making a sale on any individual call is $p = .10$. Successive calls are independent. Let X be the number of unsuccessful calls before the first sale. Then X has a geometric distribution with

$$P(X = k) = .90^k(.10), \quad k = 0, 1, 2, 3, \ldots. \qquad \square$$

Example 5.19[6] An unemployed worker goes out to look for a job every day. The probability of finding a job on any single day is λ. Let X be the number of days of job search before the worker finds a job. If we assume that successive days are independent, then

$$P(X = k) = (1 - \lambda)^k \lambda, \quad k = 0, 1, 2, 3, \ldots. \qquad \square$$

---

[6] This example is taken from London [9].

5.4.2   The Mean and Variance of the Geometric Distribution

The mean and variance of the geometric distribution are given below.

Geometric Distribution Mean and Variance

$$E(X) = \frac{q}{p} \qquad (5.8a)$$

and

$$V(X) = \frac{q}{p^2} \qquad (5.8b)$$

Example 5.20 Let X be the number of unsuccessful plays on the slot machine in Example 5.17.

(a) $E(X) = \frac{q}{p} = \frac{.95}{.05} = 19$

(b) $V(X) = \frac{q}{p^2} = \frac{.95}{.05^2} = 380$ □

The expected value of 19 in the last example was previously derived in Example 4.15 using Equation (4.3). We can follow the steps of Example 4.15 to derive the general expression for the mean of a geometric random variable X with $P(S) = p$.

$$E(X) = 0q + 1pq + 2pq^2 + 3pq^3 + \cdots + kpq^k + \cdots$$
$$= pq(1 + 2q + 3q^2 + 4q^3 + \cdots + kq^{k-1} + \cdots)$$
$$= pq\left(\frac{1}{(1-q)^2}\right) = \frac{q}{p} \qquad □$$

We will show how to derive the expression for $V(X)$ in a later section.

5.4.3   An Alternate Formulation of the Geometric Distribution

We defined the geometric random variable X to be the number of failures before the first success. Other texts define the geometric random variable to be Y, the total number of trials needed to obtain the first success — *including the trial on which the success occurs*. This implies that $Y = X + 1$, and changes things slightly.

<u>Our text</u> $P(X = k) = q^k p$ $k = 0, 1, 2, 3, \ldots$

<u>Alternative</u> $P(Y = k) = P(X + 1 = k)$

$$= P(X = k - 1)$$

$$= q^{k-1} p \qquad k = 1, 2, 3, \ldots$$

When the alternative form is used, the expression for the mean changes slightly and the expression for the variance remains the same. We can show this using the relationships $E(aX + b) = a \cdot E(X) + b$ and $V(aX + b) = a^2 \cdot V(X)$.

$$E(Y) = E(X + 1) = E(X) + 1 = \frac{q}{p} + 1 = \frac{p + q}{p} = \frac{1}{p}$$

$$V(Y) = V(X + 1) = V(X) = \frac{q}{p^2}$$

Our use of X as the geometric random variable is consistent with Bowers et al. [2]. The reader needs to exercise care in problems to be sure that X is not mistaken for Y or vice versa.

Example 5.21 The telemarketer in Example 5.18 makes successive independent calls with success probability $p = .10$. The calls cost $0.50 each. What is the expected cost of obtaining the first success (sale)?

Solution The total number of calls needed to obtain the first sale includes the call on which the sale is made. Thus $Y = X + 1$ is the number of calls to make the first sale, and $.50Y$ is the cost of the first sale.

$$E(.50Y) = .50E(Y) = .50 \ E(X + 1)$$

$$= .50[E(X) + 1]$$

$$= .50\left(\frac{.90}{.10} + 1\right)$$

$$= \$5.00 \qquad \qquad \Box$$

Technology Note

The TI-83 calculator has a function

$$\text{geometpdf}(p, x)$$

for which p is the probability of success and x is the number of trials needed for the first success. Thus the TI-83 calculates probabilities for the random variable $Y = X + 1$. Entering

$$\text{geometpdf}(.10, 2)$$

from the DISTR menu will return the answer .09.

Microsoft® EXCEL will calculate geometric probabilities as a special case of the negative binomial distribution. This will be covered in the next section.

5.5   The Negative Binomial Distribution

5.5.1   Relation to the Geometric Distribution

The geometric random variable X represents the number of failures before the first success. In some cases, it may be useful to study the number of failures before the second success, or the third or the fourth. The **negative binomial distribution** gives probabilities for X, the number of failures before the nth success. We will solve a problem of this type directly before giving the general probability formulas.

Example 5.22 You are playing the slot machine on which the probability of a win on any individual trial is .05. You will play until you win twice. What is the probability that you will lose exactly 4 times before the second win?

Solution There are a number of different sequences of wins and losses which will give exactly four losses before the second win. For example, if S stands for a success (win) and F stands for a failure (loss), two such sequences are $SFFFFS$ and $FSFFFS$. Note that the probability of each of the above sequences can be obtained using the multiplication rule for independent events.

$$P(SFFFFS) = P(FSFFFS) = (.95)^4(.05)^2$$

The probability of *any* sequence with exactly four losses before the second win will be the same value $(.95)^4(.05)^2$. However, there are clearly more such sequences than the two above. The number of such sequences can be counted using a simple idea. The last letter in the sequence must be an S. We really only need to count the number of ways to put a five letter sequence consisting of 1 S and four Fs in front of the last S.

$$\{5 \text{ letter sequence with one } S\} \longrightarrow \{\text{final } S\}$$

We can create a 5 letter sequence with one S by simply choosing the one place in the sequence where the single S appears. The number of ways this can be done is $\binom{5}{1} = 5$. Thus there are 5 sequences with exactly 4 losses before the second win. Each sequence has a probability of $(.95)^4(.05)^2$. The probability of exactly 4 losses before the second win is

$$P(X = 4) = 5(.95)^4(.05)^2 \approx .01018. \qquad \square$$

In the general negative binomial problem, the number of desired successes is denoted by r. (In the last example, $r = 2$ and a win was a success.) The random variable of interest is X, the number of failures before success r in a series of independent trials. As before X will assume the value k if there is a sequence of r successes (S) and k failures (F) with last letter S. (In the last example we looked at $k = 4$.) The probability of any such sequence will be $q^k p^r$. Each such sequence will have $r + k$ entries, with S as a final entry. The form of a sequence is

$$\{r + k - 1 \text{ letters with exactly } r - 1 \text{ copies of } S\} \longrightarrow \{\text{final } S\}.$$

The number of ways to choose the location of the $r - 1$ copies of S in the first $r + k - 1$ letters is $\binom{r + k - 1}{r - 1}$. (In the last example, $r + k - 1 = 5$ and $r - 1 = 1$.) The probability that $X = k$ will be given by the product

$$(Number\ of\ sequences)(Probabality\ of\ an\ individual\ sequence).$$

Negative Binomial Distribution

A series of independent trials has $P(S) = p$ on each trial.
Let X be the number of failures before success r.

$$P(X = k) = \binom{r + k - 1}{r - 1} q^k p^r, \; k = 0, 1, 2, 3, \ldots \quad (5.9)$$

Example 5.23 The telemarketer in Example 5.18 makes success-ful calls with probability $p = .10$. What is the probability of making exactly 5 unsuccessful calls before the third sale is made?

Solution In this problem, $r = 3$ and $k = 5$.

$$P(X = 5) = \binom{3 + 5 - 1}{3 - 1}(.90)^5(.10)^3 = \binom{7}{2}.00059049$$

$$= 21(.00059049) \approx .0124$$

Rote memorization of the distribution formula is not recommended. An intuitive approach is more effective. In this problem, one should think of sequences of 8 letters (calls) ending in S with exactly 2 copies of S in the first 7 letters. Each sequence has probability $(.90)^5(.10)^3$ and there are $\binom{7}{2} = 21$ such sequences.   □

It is important to note one special case. When $r = 1$, X is the number of failures before the first success — a geometric random variable. This is intuitively obvious, and can also be verified in the distribution formula. For $r = 1$

$$P(X = k) = \binom{1 + k - 1}{1 - 1} q^k p^1 = \binom{k}{0} q^k p = q^k p.$$

5.5.2 The Mean and Variance of the Negative Binomial Distribution

The expressions given below will not be derived until a later chapter. However, we will give examples which should make these formulas intuitively reasonable.

> ## Negative Binomial Distribution Mean and Variance
>
> $$E(X) = \frac{rq}{p} \qquad (5.10a)$$
>
> and
>
> $$V(X) = \frac{rq}{p^2} \qquad (5.10b)$$

Example 5.24 We return to Example 5.22 and the slot machine player who wishes to win twice. For this player, $r = 2$ and $p = .05$. Thus

$$E(X) = \frac{2(.95)}{.05} = 2 \cdot 19 = 38 \text{ and } V(X) = \frac{2(.95)}{.05^2} = 2 \cdot 380 = 760.$$

These answers can be related to the geometric distribution. Recall that we have already calculated the mean and variance for the geometric distribution case ($r = 1$) in Example 5.17. The mean number of losses before the first win was 19. Now we see that the mean number of losses before the second win is 2×19. The player waits through 19 losses on the average for the first win. After the first win occurs, the player starts over and must wait through an average of 19 losses for the second time. Similarly, the variance of the number of losses for the first win was 380. For the second win it is 2×380. □

This example illustrates that we can look at X, the number of failures before the second success, as a sum of independent random variables. Let X_1 be the number of failures before the first success and X_2 the number of subsequent failures before the second success. Then X_1 and X_2 are independent random variables, and $X = X_1 + X_2$. If we are waiting for the second success, we wait through X_1 failures for the first success and then repeat the process as we go through X_2 subsequent failures before the second success, for a total of $X = X_1 + X_2$ failures. Note that although the separate waits X_1 and X_2 follow the same kind of geometric distribution, X_1 and X_2 can have different values. Thus $X_1 + X_2$ is not the same as $2X_1$. (A common student mistake is to confuse $X_1 + X_2$ and $2X_1$.) Sums of random variables will be studied further in Chapter 11.

Technology Note

Microsoft® EXCEL has a NEGBINOMDIST function which calculates probabilities for this distribution. The table below was done in EXCEL. It shows the negative binomial probabilities for $p = .10$ and $r = 1, 2$ and 3. $p(k) = P(X = k)$ is given for $k = 0, 1, \ldots, 10$. We have also included the cumulative probability $F(k) = P(X \leq k)$.

Negative Binomial Distribution

k	$r = 1$ $p = 0.1$		$r = 2$ $p = 0.1$		$r = 3$ $p = 0.1$	
	$p(k)$	$F(k)$	$p(k)$	$F(k)$	$p(k)$	$F(k)$
0	0.10000	0.10000	0.01000	0.01000	0.00100	0.00100
1	0.09000	0.19000	0.01800	0.02800	0.00270	0.00370
2	0.08100	0.27100	0.02430	0.05230	0.00486	0.00856
3	0.07290	0.34390	0.02916	0.08146	0.00729	0.01585
4	0.06561	0.40951	0.03281	0.11427	0.00984	0.02569
5	0.05905	0.46856	0.03543	0.14969	0.01240	0.03809
6	0.05314	0.52170	0.03720	0.18690	0.01488	0.05297
7	0.04783	0.56953	0.03826	0.22516	0.01722	0.07019
8	0.04305	0.61258	0.03874	0.26390	0.01937	0.08956
9	0.03874	0.65132	0.03874	0.32064	0.02131	0.11087
10	0.03487	0.68619	0.03835	0.34100	0.02301	0.13388

The value of $p = .10$ was used in our analysis of the telemarketer. The above table tells the telemarketer (or his manager) quite a bit about the risks of his job. There is a reasonable probability (.68619) that the first sale will be made with 10 or fewer unsuccessful calls. There is a low probability (.13388) that three sales will be made with 10 or fewer unsuccessful calls.

This table was stopped at $k = 10$ only for reasons of space. The reader who constructs it for herself will find that it takes only a few additional seconds to extend the table to $k = 78$. This gives a fairly complete picture of the probabilities involved.

5.6 The Discrete Uniform Distribution

One of our first probability examples dealt with the experiment of rolling a single fair die and observing the number X that came up. The sample space was $S = \{1, 2, 3, 4, 5, 6\}$ and each of the outcomes was equally likely with probability 1/6. The random variable X is said to have a **discrete uniform distribution** on 1, ..., 6. This is a special case of the discrete uniform distribution on 1, ..., n.

Discrete Uniform Distribution on 1, ..., n

$$p(x) = \tfrac{1}{n}, \, x = 1, \ldots, n \qquad (5.11a)$$

$$E(X) = \tfrac{n+1}{2} \qquad (5.11b)$$

$$V(X) = \tfrac{n^2-1}{12} \qquad (5.11c)$$

Example 5.25 Let X be the number that appears when a single fair die is rolled. Then

$$E(X) = \tfrac{6+1}{2} = 3.5$$

and

$$V(X) = \tfrac{6^2-1}{12} = \tfrac{35}{12} = 2.91\dot{6}. \qquad \square$$

In Exercise 5-33 you will be asked to verify the results of Example 5.25 by direct calculation using the definitions of $E(X)$ and $V(X)$. The derivations of $E(X)$ and $V(X)$ using summation formulas are outlined in Exercise 5-35.

5.7   Exercises

5.1   The Binomial Distribution

5-1. A student takes a 10 question true-false test. He has not attended class nor studied the material, and so he guesses on every question. What is the probability that he gets (a) exactly 5 questions correct; (b) he gets 8 or more correct?

5-2. A single fair die is rolled 10 times. What is the probability of getting (a) exactly 2 sixes; (b) at least 2 sixes?

5-3. An insurance agent has 12 policyholders who are considered high risk. The probability that one of these clients will file a major claim in the next year is .023. What is the probability that exactly 3 of them will file major claims in the next year?

5-4. A company produces light bulbs of which 2% are defective.
  (a) If 50 bulbs are selected for testing, what is the probability that exactly 2 are defective?
  (b) If a distributor gets a shipment of 1,000 bulbs, what are the mean and the variance of the number of defective bulbs?

5-5. In the game of craps (dice table) the simplest bet is the pass line. The probability of winning such a bet is .493 and the payoff is even money, i.e., if you win you receive $1 more for each dollar that you bet. A gambler makes a series of 100 $10 bets on the pass line. What is his expected gain or loss at the end of this sequence of bets?

5-6. In a large population 10% of the people have type B+ blood. At a blood donation center 20 people donate blood. What is the probability that (a) exactly 4 of these have B+ blood; (b) at most 3 have B+ blood?

5-7. In the population of Exercise 5-6, 50,000 pints of blood are donated. What is the expected number of pints of B+ blood? What is the variance of the number of pints of B+ blood?

5-8. An experiment consists of picking a card at random from a standard deck and replacing it. If this experiment is performed 12 times, what is the probability that you get (a) exactly 2 aces; (b) exactly 3 hearts; (c) more than 1 heart?

5-9. Suppose that 5% of the individuals in a large population have a certain disease. If 15 individuals are selected at random, what is the probability that no more than 3 have the disease?

5-10. For a binomial random variable X with $n = 2$ and $P(S) = p$, show that (a) $E(X) = 2p$; (b) $V(X) = 2p(1 - p)$.

5.2   The Hypergeometric Distribution

5-11. There are 10 cards lying face down on a table, and 2 of them are aces. If 5 of these cards are selected at random, what is the probability that 2 of them are aces?

5-12. In a hospital ward there are 16 patients, 4 of whom have AIDS. A doctor is assigned to 6 of these patients at random. What is the probability that he gets 2 of the AIDS patients?

5-13. A baseball team has 16 non-pitchers on its roster. Of these, 6 bat left-handed and 10 right-handed. The manager, having already selected the pitcher for the game, randomly selects 8 players for the remaining positions.
  (a)   What is the probability that he selects 4 left-handed batters and 4 right-handed batters?
  (b)   What is the expected number of left-handed batters chosen?

5-14. The United States Senate has 100 members. Suppose there are 54 Republicans and 46 Democrats.
  (a)   If a committee of 15 is selected at random, what is the expected number of Republicans on this committee?
  (b)   What is the variance of the number of Republicans?

5-15.   A bridge hand consists of 13 cards. If X is the random variable
        for the number of spades in a bridge hand, what are $E(X)$ and
        $V(X)$?

5.3   The Poisson Distribution

5-16.   An auto insurance company has determined that the average
        number of claims against the comprehensive coverage of a
        policy is 0.6 per year. What is the probability that a policyholder
        will file (a) 1 claim in a year; (b) more than 1 claim in a year?

5-17.   A city has an intersection where accidents have occurred at an
        average rate of 1.5 per year. What is the probability that in a
        year there will be (a) 0; (b) 1; (c) 2 accidents in a year?

5-18.   Policyholders of an insurance company file claims at an average
        rate of 0.38 per year. If the company pays $5,000 for each claim,
        what is the mean claim amount for a policyholder in a year?

5-19.   An insurance company has 5,000 policyholders who have had
        policies for at least 10 years. Over this period there have been a
        total of 12,200 claims on these policies. Assuming a Poisson
        distribution for these claims, answer each of the following.
        (a)   What is λ, the average number of claims per policy per
              year?
        (b)   What is the probability that a policyholder will file less
              than 2 claims in a year?
        (c)   If all claims are for $1,000, what is the mean claim amount
              for a policyholder in a year?

5-20.   Claims filed in a year by a policyholder of an insurance company
        have a Poisson distribution with $\lambda = .40$. The number of claims
        filed by two different policyholders are independent events.
        (a)   If two policyholders are selected at random, what is the
              probability that each of them will file one claim during the
              year?
        (b)   What is the probability that at least one of them will file no
              claims?

5-21. Show that a Poisson distribution with parameter $\lambda = k$ (an integer) has two modes, $k - 1$ and k.

5-22. Show that $V(X) = \lambda$ for a Poisson random variable X with parameter λ. Hint: Show $V(X) = E(X^2) + E(-2\lambda X + \lambda^2)$ and $E(X^2) = \lambda^2 + \lambda$.

5.4 The Geometric Distribution

5-23. If you roll a pair of fair dice, the probability of getting an 11 is 1/18. (See Exercise 4-4.) If you roll the dice repeatedly, what is the probability that the first 11 occurs on the eighth roll?

5-24. An experiment consists of drawing a card at random from a standard deck and replacing it. If this experiment is done repeatedly, what is the probability that (a) the first heart appears on the fifth draw; (b) the first ace appears on the tenth draw?

5-25. For the experiment in Exercise 5-24, let X be the random variable for the number of unsuccessful draws before the first ace is drawn. Find $E(X)$ and $V(X)$.

5-26. At a medical clinic, patients are given X-rays to test for tuberculosis.
 (a) If 15% of these patients have the disease, what is the probability that on a given day the first patient to have the disease will be the fifth one tested?
 (b) What is the probability that the first with the disease will be the tenth one tested?

5.5 The Negative Binomial Distribution

5-27. Consider the experiment of drawing from a deck of cards with replacement (Exercise 5-24).
 (a) What is the probability that the third heart appears on the tenth draw?
 (b) What is the mean number of non-hearts drawn before the fifth heart is drawn?

5-28.   A single fair die is rolled repeatedly.
        (a)   What is the probability that the fourth six appears on the twentieth roll?
        (b)   What is the mean number of total rolls needed to get 4 sixes?

5-29.   For the experiment in Exercise 5-28, let X be the random variable for the number of non-sixes rolled before the fifth six is rolled. What are $E(X)$ and $V(X)$?

5-30.   A telemarketer makes successful calls with probability .20. What is the probability that her fifth sale will be on her sixteenth call?

5-31.   If each sale made by the person in Exercise 5-30 is for $250, what is the mean number of total calls she will have to make to reach $2,000 in total sales?

5-32.   Consider the clinic in Exercise 5-26, where 15% of the patients have tuberculosis.
        (a)   What is the probability that the fifteenth patient tested will be the third with tuberculosis?
        (b)   What is the mean number of patients without tuberculosis tested before the sixth patient with tuberculosis is tested?

5.6   The Discrete Uniform Distribution

5-33.   Verify the results of Example 5.25 by direct calculation using the definitions of $E(X)$ and $V(X)$.

5-34.   A contestant on a game show selects a ball from an urn containing 25 balls numbered from 1 to 25. His prize is $1,000 times the number of the ball selected. If X is the random variable for the amount he wins, find the mean and standard deviation of X.

5-35.   Derive the formulas for $E(X)$ and $V(X)$ for the discrete uniform distribution. (Recall that $1 + 2 + 3 + \cdots + n = \dfrac{n(n+1)}{2}$ and $1^2 + 2^2 + 3^2 + \cdots + n^2 = \dfrac{n(n+1)(2n+1)}{6}$.)

5.8   Sample Actuarial Examination Problems

5-36.   A company prices its hurricane insurance using the following assumptions:
   (i) In any calendar year, there can be at most one hurricane.
   (ii) In any calendar year, the probability of a hurricane is 0.05.
   (iii) The number of hurricanes in any calendar year is independent of the number of hurricanes in any other calendar year.

   Using the company's assumptions, calculate the probability that there are fewer than 3 hurricanes in a 20-year period.

5-37.   A study is being conducted in which the health of two independent groups of ten policyholders is being monitored over a one-year period of time. Individual participants in the study drop out before the end of the study with probability 0.2 (independently of the other participants).

   What is the probability that at least 9 participants complete the study in one of the two groups, but not in both groups?

5-38.   A hospital receives 1/5 of its flu vaccine shipments from Company X and the remainder of its shipments from other companies. Each shipment contains a very large number of vaccine vials.

   For Company X's shipments, 10% of the vials are ineffective. For every other company, 2% of the vials are ineffective. The hospital tests 30 randomly selected vials from a shipment and finds that one vial is ineffective.

   What is the probability that this shipment came from Company X?

5-39.   An actuary has discovered that policyholders are three times as likely to file two claims as to file four claims. If the number of claims filed has a Poisson distribution, what is the variance of the number of claims filed?

5-40.   A company buys a policy to insure its revenue in the event of major snowstorms that shut down business. The policy pays nothing for the first such snowstorm of the year and 10,000 for each one thereafter, until the end of the year. The number of major snowstorms per year that shut down business is assumed to have a Poisson distribution with mean 1.5.

What is the expected amount paid to the company under this policy during a one-year period?

5-41.   In modeling the number of claims filed by an individual under an automobile policy during a three-year period, an actuary makes the simplifying assumption that for all integers $n \geq 0$, $p_{n+1} = \frac{1}{5}p_n$, where p_n represents the probability that the policyholder files n claims during the period.

Under this assumption, what is the probability that a policyholder files more than one claim during the period?

Chapter 6
Applications for Discrete
Random Variables

6.1 Functions of Random Variables and Their Expectations

6.1.1 The Function $Y = aX + b$

We have already looked at functions of random variables. In Sections 4.3 and 4.4, we looked at the function $f(X) = aX + b$ and used the identities

$$E[f(X)] = E(aX + b) = a \cdot E(X) + b$$

and

$$V[f(X)] = V(aX + b) = a^2 \cdot V(X).$$

For example, we looked at a random variable X for the number of claims filed by an insurance policyholder in Example 4.6.

Number of claims (x)	0	1	2	3
$p(x)$	.72	.22	.05	.01

The expected value $E(X)$ was .35 and the variance $V(X)$ was .3875. In Examples 4.17 and 4.22, we looked at the total cost random variable $f(X) = 1000X + 100$. We then found

$$E[f(X)] = E(1000X + 100) = 1000E(X) + 100 = 450$$

and

$$V[f(X)] = V(1000X + 100) = 1000^2 V(X) = 387,500.$$

Simple derivations of these results were sketched previously, but a closer look at the reasoning is needed. The reasoning used previously relied on the observation that $Y = f(X)$ had a distribution table with the same underlying probabilities as X.

Cost: $f(x) = 1000x + 100$	100	1100	2100	3100
$p(x)$	.72	.22	.05	.01

For example, since the probability of 0 claims is .72, the probability of a total cost of $f(0) = 1000(0) + 100$ will also be .72. We could check the expected value above using this distribution table.

$$E[f(X)] = .72(100) + .22(1100) + .05(2100) + .01(3100)$$
$$= 450 = \sum f(x) \cdot p(x)$$

6.1.2   Analyzing $Y = f(X)$ in General

The identity

$$E[f(X)] = \sum_x f(x) \cdot p(x) \qquad (6.1)$$

holds for any discrete random variable X and function $f(x)$. However, there is a subtle point here. This point is illustrated in the next example.

Example 6.1 Let the random variable X have the distribution below.

x	-1	0	1
$p(x)$	.20	.60	.20

If $f(x) = x^2$, the naive table extension technique just used in Section 6.1.1 gives us a similar distribution.

$f(x) = x^2$	$-1^2 = 1$	$0^2 = 0$	$1^2 = 1$
$p(x)$	.20	.60	.20

Calculating the mean for X^2 gives

$$E(X^2) = \sum x^2 \cdot p(x) = .20(1) + .60(0) + .20(1) = .40.$$

The subtle point is that the previous table is not exactly the probability distribution table for X^2, since the value of 1 is repeated twice in the top row. The true distribution table for $Y = X^2$ is the following:

$y = f(x) = x^2$	0	1
$p(y)$	.60	.40

Using this table, we still get the same result.

$$E(Y) = \sum y \cdot p(y) = .60(0) + .40(1) = .40. \qquad \square$$

This example illustrates two major points:

(1) The distribution table for X can be converted into a preliminary table for $f(X)$ with entries for $f(x)$ and $p(x)$, but some grouping and combination may be necessary to get the actual distribution table for $Y = f(X)$.

(2) Even though the tables are not the same, they lead to the same result for the expected value of $Y = f(x)$.

$$E(Y) = \sum y \cdot p(y) = E[f(X)] = \sum f(x) \cdot p(x)$$

The final summation above is the expression in Equation (6.1). It is usually the simplest one to use to find $E[f(X)]$. The general proof of Equation (6.1) follows the reasoning of the previous example, but will not be given here.

6.1.3. Applications

In this section we will give an elementary example from economics: **the expected utility of wealth**.

Example 6.2 For most (but not all of us), the satisfaction obtained from an extra dollar depends on how much wealth we have already. A single dollar may be much less important to someone who has $500,000 in the bank than it is to someone who has nothing saved. Economists describe this by using **utility functions** that measure the importance of various levels of wealth to an individual. One utility function which fits the attitude described above is $u(w) = \sqrt{w}$, for wealth $w > 0$. The graph of $u(w)$ is given in the following figure.

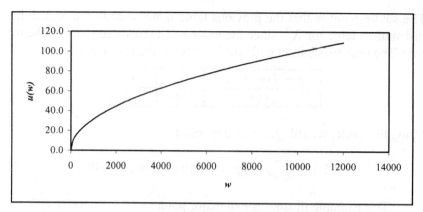

We can see from this graph that utility increases more rapidly at first and then more slowly at higher levels of wealth, w. We will now look at how a person with the utility function $u(w) = \sqrt{w}$ might make financial decisions. (The reader should be aware that this is only one possible utility function. Other individuals may have very different utility functions which lead to very different financial decisions.)

Suppose a person with the utility function $u(w) = \sqrt{w}$ can choose between two different methods for managing his wealth. Using Method 1, he has a 10% chance of ending up with $w = 0$ and a 90% chance of ending up with $w = 10,000$. Using Method 2, he has a 2% chance of ending up with $w = 0$ and a 98% chance of ending up with $w = 9,025$. (Which would you choose?) These two methods of managing wealth are really two random variables, W_1 and W_2.

Random variable W_1 for Method 1

Wealth (w)	0	10,000
$p(w)$	.10	.90

Random variable W_2 for Method 2

Wealth (w)	0	9,025
$p(w)$	.02	.98

One way to evaluate these two alternatives would be to compare their expected values.

$$E(W_1) = .10(0) + .90(10,000) = 9,000$$

$$E(W_2) = .02(0) + .98(9,025) = 8,844.50$$

This comparison implies that Method 1 should be chosen, since it has the higher expected value. However, this method does not take into account the utility that is attached to various levels of wealth. The **expected utility method** compares the two methods by calculating $u(w)$ for each outcome and comparing the two expected utilities $E[u(W_1)]$ and $E[u(W_2)]$. We can expand the two tables for wealth outcomes to include $u(w) = \sqrt{w}$ for this calculation.

Method 1

Wealth (w)	0	10,000
$u(w) = \sqrt{w}$	0	$\sqrt{10{,}000}$
$p(w)$	.10	.90

Method 2

Wealth (w)	0	9,025
$u(w) = \sqrt{w}$	0	$\sqrt{9{,}025}$
$p(w)$	.02	.98

We can now compute expected utility.

$$E[u(W_1)] = .10(0) + .90\sqrt{10{,}000} = 90$$
$$E[u(W_2)] = .02(0) + .98\sqrt{9{,}025} = 93.10$$

Using expected utility, the person with $u(w) = \sqrt{w}$ would choose Method 2 instead of Method 1. □

Expected utility is analyzed much more deeply in other texts. The important point here is that this economic decision-making method makes use of the identity

$$E[u(W)] = \sum u(w) \cdot p(w),$$

which was discussed in this section.

6.1.4 Another Way to Calculate the Variance of a Random Variable

In Section 4.4.1 we defined the variance of a random variable X by

$$V(X) = E[(X - \mu)^2] = \sum (x - \mu)^2 \cdot p(x).$$

In that definition, we were implicitly using Equation (6.1) with $f(x) = \sum(x - \mu)^2$. There is another way to write the variance. If we expand the expression $(x - \mu)^2$, we obtain

$$V(X) = \sum(x^2 - 2\mu x + \mu^2) \cdot p(x)$$

$$= \sum x^2 \cdot p(x) - 2\mu \sum x \cdot p(x) + \mu^2 \sum p(x)$$

$$= E(X^2) - 2\mu \cdot E(X) + \mu^2 \cdot 1$$

$$= E(X^2) - 2\mu \cdot \mu + \mu^2 \cdot 1$$

$$= E(X^2) - \mu^2.$$

Thus we can write

$$V(X) = E(X^2) - \mu^2 = E(X^2) - (E(X))^2. \qquad (6.2)$$

Example 6.3 We will verify the variance calculated for the claim number distribution from Example 4.6.

Number of claims (x)	0	1	2	3
$p(x)$	.72	.22	.05	.01

We know that $E(X) = .35$. Using Equation (6.1),

$$E(X^2) = .72(0^2) + .22(1^2) + .05(2^2) + .01(3^2) = .51.$$

Then Equation (6.2) gives

$$V(X) = E(X^2) - (E(X))^2 = .51 - .35^2 = .3875.$$

This verifies our previous calculation obtained directly from the definition. $\square$

It is important to know Equation (6.2). It is widely used in probability and statistics texts. These texts often note that the *calculation* of $V(X)$ can be done more easily using Equation (6.2) than from the definition. This is true for computations done by hand, but computations are rarely done by hand in our computer age. In fact, examples have been developed to show that Equation (6.2) has a disadvantage for computer work when large values of X are present; there are problems with overflow due to the magnitude of X^2. This is pursued in Exercise 6-4.

6.2 Moments and the Moment Generating Function

6.2.1 Moments of a Random Variable

We saw in Section 6.1.4 that $E(X^2)$ could be used in the calculation of $V(X)$. $E(X^2)$ is called the **second moment** of the random variable X. There are useful applications of expected values of higher powers of X as well.

Definition 6.1 The nth **moment** of X is $E(X^n)$.

Note that the first moment is simply $E(X)$.

Example 6.4 The third moment of the claim number random variable in Example 6.3 is

$$E(X^3) = .72(0^3) + .22(1^3) + .05(2^3) + .01(3^3) = .89. \qquad \square$$

6.2.2 The Moment Generating Function

The definition of the moment generating function does not have an immediate intuitive interpretation. In this section, we will define the moment generating function and show how it is applied. In Section 6.2.9 we will give an infinite series interpretation which may help the reader to understand the motivation behind the definition.

Definition 6.2 Let X be a discrete random variable. The **moment generating function**, denoted $M_X(t)$, is defined by

$$M_X(t) = E(e^{tX}) = \sum e^{tx} \cdot p(x).$$

Example 6.5 Below is the probability function table for the claim number random variable X. We have added a row for e^{tX} so that $M_X(t)$ can be calculated .

Number of claims (x)	0	1	2	3
e^{tx}	$e^{0t} = 1$	e^{1t}	e^{2t}	e^{3t}
$p(x)$	.72	.22	.05	.01

Then

$$M_X(t) = .72(1) + .22(e^t) + .05(e^{2t}) + .01(e^{3t}).$$

$M_X(t)$ is called the moment generating function because its derivatives can be used to find the moments of X. For the function above the derivative is

$$M_X'(t) = 0 + .22(e^t) + .05(2)(e^{2t}) + .01(3)(e^{3t}).$$

If we evaluate the derivative at $t = 0$, we obtain

$$M_X'(0) = 0 + .22(1) + .05(2) + .01(3) = .35 = E(X).$$

This is the first moment of X. The higher derivatives can be used in the same way.

$$M_X''(t) = 0 + .22(e^t) + .05(2^2)(e^{2t}) + .01(3^2)(e^{3t})$$

$$M_X''(0) = 0 + .22(1^2) + .05(2^2) + .01(3^2) = .51 = E(X^2) \qquad \square$$

This result holds in general.

$$M_X(t) = \sum e^{tx} \cdot p(x)$$

$$M_X'(t) = \sum x \cdot e^{tx} \cdot p(x) \text{ and } M_X'(0) = \sum x \cdot p(x) = E(X)$$

$$M_X''(t) = \sum x^2 \cdot e^{tx} \cdot p(x) \text{ and } M_X''(0) = \sum x^2 \cdot p(x) = E(X^2)$$

The general form is the following:

$$M_X^{(n)}(0) = \sum x^n \cdot p(x) = E(X^n) \qquad\qquad (6.3)$$

Many standard probability distributions have moment generating functions which can be found fairly easily. In the next sections, we will give the moment generating functions for all of the random variables in this chapter except the hypergeometric. This will give us a way of deriving the mean and variance formulas stated in the previous chapter.

6.2.3 Moment Generating Function for the Binomial Random Variable

We begin with the binomial random variable with $n = 1$ and $P(S) = p$. The distribution table needed for the moment generating function is the following:

x	0	1
e^{tx}	1	e^t
$p(x)$	$q = 1 - p$	p

Then

$$M_X(t) = E(e^{tX}) = q + pe^t.$$

For $n = 2$, the table and moment generating function are as follows:

x	0	1	2
e^{tx}	1	e^t	e^{2t}
$p(x)$	q^2	$2pq$	p^2

$$M_X(t) = q^2 + 2pqe^t + p^2 e^{2t} = q^2 + 2q(pe^t) + (pe^t)^2 = (q + pe^t)^2$$

The pattern should be clear.

Binomial Distribution Moment Generating Function
(n trials, $P(S) = p$)

$$M_X(t) = (q + pe^t)^n \qquad (6.4)$$

The general proof is similar to the proof for $n = 2$, and is outlined in Exercise 6-5. Once the moment generating function is derived, the mean and variance of the binomial distribution can be easily found.

$$M_X'(t) = n(q + pe^t)^{n-1}pe^t$$

$$M_X'(0) = n(p + q)^{n-1}p = np = E(X)$$

$$M_X''(t) = n[(q+pe^t)^{n-1}pe^t + (n-1)(q+pe^t)^{n-2}(pe^t)^2]$$

$$M_X''(0) = n[p + (n-1)p^2] = np + (np)^2 - np^2 = E(X^2)$$

$$V(X) = E(X^2) - (E(X))^2 = (np+(np)^2-np^2) - (np)^2$$

$$= np(1 - p)$$

6.2.4 Moment Generating Function f for the Poisson Random Variable

Poisson Distribution Moment Generating Function
(Rate λ)

$$M_X(t) = e^{\lambda(e^t-1)} \tag{6.5}$$

The derivation of this result makes use of the series for e^x.

$$E(e^{tX}) = \sum_{k=0}^{\infty} p(k) \cdot e^{tk} = \sum_{k=0}^{\infty} \left(\frac{e^{-\lambda}\lambda^k}{k!} \right) e^{tk}$$

$$= e^{-\lambda} \sum_{k=0}^{\infty} \left(\frac{(\lambda e^t)^k}{k!} \right)$$

$$= e^{-\lambda}e^{\lambda e^t} = e^{\lambda(e^t-1)}$$

We have already shown that $E(X) = \lambda$. Exercise 6-6 asks the reader to use the moment generating function to verify that $E(X) = V(X) = \lambda$.

6.2.5 Moment Generating Function for the Geometric Random Variable

Geometric Distribution Moment Generating Function
($P(S) = p$)

$$M_X(t) = \frac{p}{1 - qe^t} \tag{6.6}$$

The derivation of this result relies on the sum of an infinite geometric series.

$$E(e^{tX}) = \sum_{k=0}^{\infty} p(k) \cdot e^{tk} = \sum_{k=0}^{\infty} (pq^k)e^{tk} = p\sum_{k=0}^{\infty}(qe^t)^k = p \cdot \frac{1}{1 - qe^t}$$

We have already shown that $E(X) = q/p$. Exercise 6-7 asks the reader to use the moment generating function to find the mean and variance for X.

6.2.6 Moment Generating Function for the Negative Binomial Random Variable

---

Negative Binomial Distribution Moment Generating Function
$(P(S) = p; \ X =$ number of failures before success $r)$

$$M_X(t) = \left(\frac{p}{1 - qe^t}\right)^r \qquad (6.7)$$

Note that the moment generating function for the geometric random variable, given by Equation (6.6), is just Equation (6.7) with $r = 1$. We will not give a derivation of this result at this time. In Chapter 11 we will develop machinery which will make it easier to establish this result by looking at the negative binomial random variable as a sum of independent geometric random variables.

6.2.7 Other Uses of the Moment Generating Function

Moment generating functions are unique. This means that if a random variable X has the moment generating function of a known random variable, it must be that kind of random variable.

Example 6.6 You are working with a random variable X, and find that its moment generating function is

$$M_X(t) = (.2 + .8e^t)^7.$$

This is the moment generating function for a binomial random variable with $p = .80$ and $n = 7$. Thus X is a binomial random variable with $p = .80$ and $n = 7$. $\square$

The technique of recognizing a random variable by its moment generating function is common. Thus it will be very useful to be able to recognize the moment generating functions given in this section.

6.2.8   A Useful Identity

If $Y = aX + b$, the moment generating function of Y is as follows:

$$M_{aX+b}(t) = e^{tb} \cdot M_X(at) \qquad (6.8)$$

Example 6.7   Suppose X is Poisson with $\lambda = 2$. Let $Y = 3X + 5$. Then

$$M_X(t) = e^{2(e^t-1)}$$

and

$$M_Y(t) = e^{5t} \cdot M_X(3t) = e^{5t}e^{2(e^{3t}-1)}.$$

A proof of this identity is outlined in Exercise 6-11.   □

6.2.9   Infinite Series and the Moment Generating Function

We can understand why $M_X^{(n)}(0) = E(X^n)$ if we look at an infinite series representation of e^{tx}.

The series expansion for e^x about $x = 0$ is

$$e^x = 1 + x + \frac{x^2}{2!} + \frac{x^3}{3!} + \cdots.$$

If we substitute the random variable tX for x in this series, we obtain

$$e^{tX} = 1 + tX + \frac{t^2 X^2}{2!} + \frac{t^3 X^3}{3!} + \cdots.$$

If we take the expected value of each side of the last equation (assuming that the expected value of the infinite sum is the sum of the expected values of the terms on the right-hand side), we obtain

$$M_X(t) = E(e^{tX}) = 1 + t \cdot E(X) + \frac{t^2}{2!} \cdot E(X^2) + \frac{t^3}{3!} \cdot E(X^3) + \cdots.$$

Now we can look at the derivatives of $M_X(t)$ by differentiating the series for $M_X(t)$. For example,

$$M_X'(t) = \frac{d}{dt}[M_X(t)]$$

$$= E(X) + t \cdot E(X^2) + \frac{t^2}{2!} \cdot E(X^3) + \cdots.$$

It is clear from this series representation that $M_X'(0) = E(X)$. Similarly,

$$M_X''(t) = \frac{d}{dt}[M_X'(t)]$$

$$= E(X^2) + tE(X^3) + \frac{t^2}{2!}E(X^4) + \cdots,$$

and we see that $M_X''(0) = E(X^2)$.

6.3   Distribution Shapes

We can visualize the probability pattern in a distribution by plotting the probability values in a bar graph or histogram. For example, the geometric distribution with $p = .60$ has the following probability values (rounded to three places):

x	$p(x)$
0	0.600
1	0.240
2	0.096
3	0.038
4	0.015
5	0.006
6	0.002
7	0.001

The histogram is shown in the following figure.

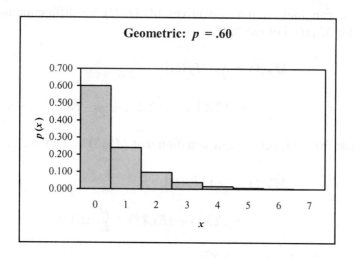

The binomial distribution with $n = 20$ and $p = .15$ has the histogram below. (Values of $x > 11$ are omitted because $p(x)$ is very small.)

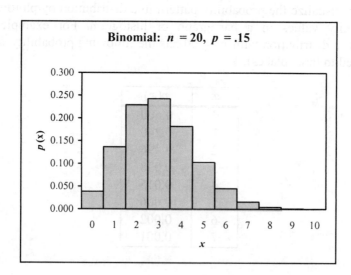

The Poisson distribution with $\lambda = 3$ has a very similar histogram.

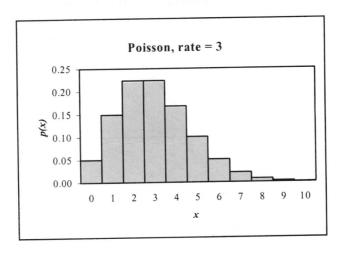

In many applied problems, researchers look at histograms of the data in their application to try to detect the underlying distribution. These histograms also provide a useful hint as to the method for analyzing continuous distributions. Suppose we look at the binomial distribution for $n = 10$ and $p = .60$.

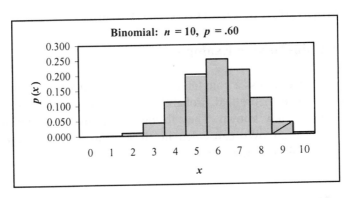

The area of the marked bar in this histogram represents the probability that $X = 9$. The pattern of this distribution might be represented by a continuous curve fitted through the tops of these rectangles.

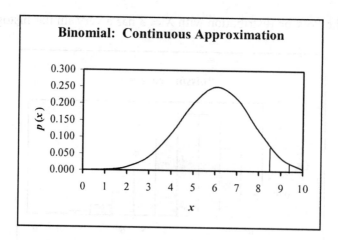

This curve describes the pattern very well, and the area under the curve between 8.5 and 9.5 is a good approximation of the area of the marked bar in the histogram area which represents $P(X = 9)$. This approximation is helpful in understanding the probability methods for continuous distributions in the next chapter. These methods are based on calculating probability as an area under a curve between two points.

6.4   Simulation of Discrete Distributions

6.4.1   A Coin-Tossing Example

Suppose you plan to toss a coin ten times and bet that it will show a head on each toss. The theoretical probabilities of each possible number of heads are completely known. They follow a binomial distribution with $n = 10$ and $p = .50$. We can calculate these probabilities easily. They are given in the following table:

x	$p(x)$
0	.000977
1	.009766
2	.043945
3	.117188
4	.205078
5	.246094
6	.205078
7	.117188
8	.043945
9	.009766
10	.000977

However, knowing these probabilities does not enable you to experience what happens when you actually toss the coin ten times. You could do this simple experiment by actually tossing a coin ten times, but you could do it more rapidly and simply using a **computer simulation**. To simulate a single toss, have the computer generate a random number from the interval $[0, 1)$. If the number is less than .50, call the toss a head. If the number is greater than or equal to .50, call the toss a tail. To simulate ten tosses, have the computer generate ten random numbers for the same procedure. We did this in EXCEL. The results of one series of ten "tosses" are given below.

Random Number	Outcome	Random Number	Outcome
0.32957	H	0.86690	T
0.96496	T	0.03550	H
0.10965	H	0.84940	T
0.10876	H	0.20878	H
0.38750	H	0.64528	T

Since the number used is chosen at random from $[0, 1)$, the probability that the number is in the interval $[0, .50)$ for heads is .50 and the probability that the number is in the interval $[.50, 1)$ for tails is .50. Thus $P(H) = .50$ and $P(T) = .50$, as is desired for a fair coin.

The simulation in this example merely allows us to play a game whose probabilities we already understand. Simulation is also used to study complicated probability problems which cannot be solved easily in closed form. We will not look at problems of that level of difficulty until

Chapter 12. In this section we will discuss how to simulate the discrete random variables studied in this chapter.

6.4.2   Generating Random Numbers from $[0, 1)$

The intuitive procedure used in the last section relied on the ability to pick a number at random from the interval $[0, 1)$. This random pick must give all numbers in the interval an equal probability of being chosen, so that the probability of a number in the interval $[0, .50)$ is .50. In practice, most people simply use the random number generator on their computers or calculators to find random numbers. In this section we will illustrate the kind of method that might be used to build a random number generator for a computer program. In later sections of this text, we will use computers to generate random numbers without showing the background calculations.

A basic method for generating a sequence of random numbers is the **linear congruential method**. When using this method, you must start by selecting four non-negative integers, a, b, m and x_1. The number x_1 must be less than m, and is your first number in the random sequence. It is called the **seed**. To generate the second number in the sequence x_2, calculate $y = ax_1 + b$, divide it by m, and find the remainder. This process can be repeated to find more numbers in the sequence. In practice, the values used for a, b and m are quite large, but we will illustrate the procedure for the simpler case where $a = 5, b = 7, m = 16$ and $x_1 = 5$.

Step 1: $y = ax_1 + b = 5(5) + 7 = 32$

Remainder when 32 is divided by 16: $x_2 = 0$

Step 2: $y = ax_2 + b = 5(0) + 7 = 7$

Remainder when 7 is divided by 16: $x_3 = 7$

The successive numbers in the sequence are all between 0 and 15. We can generate numbers in $[0, 1)$ by dividing by 16.

$$\frac{5}{16} = .3125 \qquad \frac{0}{16} = 0 \qquad \frac{7}{16} = .4375$$

The results of repeating this procedure 16 times are given in the next table.

k	x_k	$5x_k + 7$	$x_k/16$
1	5	32	.3125
2	0	7	.0000
3	7	42	.4375
4	10	57	.6250
5	9	52	.5625
6	4	27	.2500
7	11	62	.6875
8	14	77	.8750
9	13	72	.8125
10	8	47	.5000
11	15	82	.9375
12	2	17	.1250
13	1	12	.0625
14	12	67	.7500
15	3	22	.1875
16	6	37	.3750

In the preceding example the numbers x_k were remainders after dividing by 16, so there are only 16 possible values for x_k. In fact, if we use the last number in the table ($x_{16} = 6$) to find x_{17}, we will find that $x_{17} = 5$ which was our starting point. The sequence will repeat itself after $m = 16$ entries.

The random number generators used in computers are based on much larger values of a, b, and m. For example, Klugman et al. [8] discuss using $a = 742{,}938{,}285$, $b = 0$ and $m = 2^{31} - 1$. These numbers provide reasonable random number generators for practical use, and researchers have discovered other values of a, b and m which also appear to work well. However, the example above with $m = 16$ illustrates an important point. Any linear congruential generator will eventually enter a deterministic repeating pattern. Thus it is not truly random. For this reason, these useful generators are called **pseudo-random**.

In the remainder of this text, we will not require linear congruen-tial generator calculations for random numbers. Computers can do these calculations for us. We will simply use computer generated random numbers in the interval $[0, 1)$.

Technology Note

The TI-83 will generate a random number from $[0, 1)$ using the command "RAND" in the MATH menu under PRB. EXCEL has a RAND() function which will give a random number in $[0, 1)$. MINITAB will generate numbers from $[0, 1)$ using the menu choices Calc, Random Data, and Uniform.

6.4.3   Simulating Any Finite Discrete Distribution

We can use random numbers from $[0, 1)$ to simulate any finite discrete distribution by using an extension of the coin toss simulation reasoning. This is best shown by an example. Suppose we are looking at the random variable with the following probability function.

x	0	1	2
$p(x)$	.25	.50	.25

Given a random number x from $[0, 1)$, we assign the outcome 0, 1 or 2 using the rule

$$outcome = \begin{cases} 0 & \text{if } 0 \leq x < .25 \\ 1 & \text{if } .25 \leq x < .75. \\ 2 & \text{if } .75 \leq x < 1 \end{cases}$$

We did this in an EXCEL spreadsheet. The results of 10 trials are shown in the next table.

Trial	Random Number	Outcome
1	.109371	0
2	.449958	1
3	.253222	1
4	.108458	0
5	.377789	1
6	.481501	1
7	.027924	0
8	.452472	1
9	.936474	2
10	.318389	1

The frequencies of the individual outcomes in the preceding table are shown in the next table.

Outcome	Frequency	Percent
0	3	30%
1	6	60%
2	1	10%

Note that with only ten trials, you should not expect to see the outcomes occur with exactly the same percentages as given in the original distribution. Even with 100 trials, the percentages of the outcomes do not always match the original distribution very well. The next table gives the results of a simulation of 100 trials for this distribution.

Outcome	Frequency	Percent
0	34	34%
1	42	42%
2	24	24%

A simulation of 1000 trials gives results closer to the original distribution. The results of a single simulation of 1000 trials are given in the next table.

Outcome	Frequency	Percent
0	245	24.5%
1	514	51.4%
2	241	24.1%

6.4.4   Simulating a Binomial Distribution

The reader may have noticed that the finite discrete distribution simulated in the last section was a binomial distribution with $n = 2$ and $p = .50$. The method was easy to implement for that binomial due to the small number of outcomes, but programming may become tedious if n is large. There is another way to simulate any binomial by having the computer simulate n trials and total the number of successes. For example, if you wish to simulate the binomial with $n = 10$ and $p = .30$, generate 10 random numbers x. If $x < .30$ on a trial, a success has occurred. Otherwise, the trial was a failure. The computer can be used to add up the number of successes to obtain the binomial outcome. In the next table we show the result of one simulation for $n = 10$ and $p = .30$.

Trial	Random Number	Outcome	Trial	Random Number	Outcome
1	.53917995	F	6	.414125	F
2	.49763993	F	7	.335325	F
3	.53307458	F	8	.438872	F
4	.5367283	F	9	.377748	F
5	.41993715	F	10	.076637	S

This ten-trial experiment led to nine failures and one success.

6.4.5   Simulating a Geometric Distribution

The geometric random variable X represents the number of failures before the first success in a series of binomial experiment trials. To simulate it, have the computer generate random numbers for a success-failure experiment until the first success is obtained and then count the number of prior failures. The table in Section 6.4.4 demonstrates how this might be done for $p = .30$. In that table, the first success was obtained on trial 10, so that the geometric random variable X assumes the value 9.

6.4.6 Simulating a Negative Binomial Distribution

The negative binomial random variable measures the number of failures before the rth success. This can be simulated in the same manner as the geometric distribution.

6.4.7 Simulating Other Distributions

Simulations are widely used, and a number of ingenious methods have been developed for them. Many of those methods are beyond the scope of this course, but the designers of computer programs have implemented them so that they are available to the ordinary user. In this section we have tried to give a basic idea of how simulations may be done, not to show the reader how to implement every possible kind of simulation. In practice, most people simply use computer routines which simulate the most widely-used distributions directly (without the intermediate step of starting with random numbers from $[0, 1)$). The spreadsheet Microsoft® EXCEL and the statistical program MINITAB both will simulate the binomial and Poisson distributions directly. In addition, each program will allow the user to input any finite discrete distribution for simulation.

6.5 Exercises

6.1 Functions of Random Variables and Their Expectations

6-1. In a year, a policyholder with an insurance company has no claims with probability .69, 1 claim with probability .23, 2 claims with probability .07, and 3 claims with probability .01. If X is the random variable for the number of claims, find (a) $E(500X + 50)$; (b) $E(X^2)$; (c) $E(X^3)$.

6-2. Let X be the random variable for the sum obtained by rolling a pair of fair dice (see Exercise 4-4). Find $V(X)$ by using the alternate formula $V(X) = E(X^2) - E(X)^2$.

6-3. Rework Example 6.2 using the logarithmic utility function $u(w) = ln(w + 1)$. What are $E[u(W_1)]$ and $E[u(W_2)]$ for this utility function?

6-4.   Overflow problems occur when you exceed the precision of the
        computer or calculator you are using. Consider the distribution
        whose values of x are 1,000,000,000.1, 1,000,000,000 and
        999,999,999.9, each with probability 1/3. The variance for this
        distribution is .00666. If you try to compute the variance using
        Equation (6.2), the value you get will depend on the precision of
        your computer or calculator and may not be correct. Use your
        calculator to find $E(X^2)$ and $E(X)$. Then use Equation (6.2) and
        determine whether or not you found the correct value of $V(X)$.

6.2   Moments and the Moment Generating Function

6-5.   Show that the moment generating function for the binomial
        distribution is $(q + pe^t)^n$. Hint: Expand $(q + p)^n$ using the bino-
        mial theorem and use it to get the moment generating function.

6-6.   Use the moment generating function for the Poisson distribution
        to verify that $E(X) = V(X) = \lambda$.

6-7.   Use the moment generating function for the geometric distribu-
        tion to obtain its mean and variance.

6-8.   Use the moment generating function for the negative binomial
        distribution to obtain its mean and variance.

6-9.   Let X be a discrete random variable with $p(x) = \frac{1}{n}$ for
        $x = 1, \ldots, n$. (X is a discrete uniform random variable.)
        (a)   Show that the moment generating function for X is
        $$M_X(t) = \frac{1}{n}\sum_{x=1}^{n} e^{xt}.$$
        (b)   Find $E(X)$ and $V(X)$.

6-10.   Let X be a random variable whose probability function is given
        below.

x	0	1	2	3
$p(x)$	.42	.30	.17	.11

        Find $M_X(t)$ and use its derivatives to find $E(X)$ and $E(X^2)$.

6-11.   Prove $M_{aX+b}(t) = e^{tb} \cdot M_X(at)$.

6-12.   If X is a binomial random variable with $p = .60$ and $n = 8$, and
        if $Y = 3X + 4$, what is $M_Y(t)$?

6-13.   If $M_X(t) = [.70/(1 - .3e^t)]^5$, what is the distribution of X.

6.4   Simulation of Discrete Distributions

6-14.   Using the linear congruence $y = 9x + 11 \pmod{16}$, with seed
        $x_1 = 6$, find $x_2, x_3, \ldots, x_{16}$.

        For Exercises 6-15 and 6-16, use the following sequence of
        random numbers from $[0, 1)$.

1. .5619	6. .9983	11. .7855	16. .3729
2. .4500	7. .0225	12. .9955	17. .1326
3. .3566	8. .8026	13. .6558	18. .9246
4. .5844	9. .3516	14. .1280	19. .6867
5. .8638	10. .4584	15. .3908	20. .9638

6-15.   Random numbers from $[0, 1)$ are used to simulate a binomial
        distribution with $n = 20$ and $p = .40$. If the random number x is
        less than .40 on a trial, then a success has occurred. Count the
        number of successes in the 20 trials.

6-16.   Random numbers from $[0, 1)$ are used to simulate repeated trials
        of the experiment of tossing 5 fair coins. The first five numbers
        represent the first trial, the second five numbers the second, and
        so on. If the random number x is less than .50, the coin is a head.
        How many heads appear on each of the first four repetitions of
        this experiment?

6.6   Sample Actuarial Examination Problems

6-17.   A baseball team has scheduled its opening game for April 1. If it rains on April 1, the game is postponed and will be played on the next day that it does not rain. The team purchases insurance against rain. The policy will pay 1000 for each day, up to 2 days, that the opening game is postponed.

The insurance company determines that the number of consecutive days of rain beginning on April 1 is a Poisson random variable with mean 0.6.

What is the standard deviation of the amount the insurance company will have to pay?

6-18.   Let X_1, X_2, X_3 be a random sample from a discrete distribution with probability function

$$p(x) = \begin{cases} \frac{1}{3} & \text{for } x = 0 \\ \frac{2}{3} & \text{for } x = 1 \\ 0 & \text{otherwise} \end{cases}$$

Determine the moment generating function, $M(t)$, of $Y = X_1 X_2 X_3$.

Chapter 7
Continuous Random Variables

7.1   Defining a Continuous Random Variable

7.1.1   A Basic Example

Suppose you are asked to pick a number at random from the interval $[0, 1]$ with all numbers in the interval being equally likely.[1] The number X that you pick is a random variable, since it is a numerical quantity whose value depends on chance. However, X is not discrete. The interval $[0, 1]$ is continuous, and you can pick any number from it. X is therefore continuous.

Probabilities for continuous random variables will be calculated in a new way. The discrete methods used in the previous chapters will not apply. The continuous probability method is nicely illustrated by looking at the random variable X above. For example, suppose that you wished to calculate the probability $P(.50 \leq X \leq .75)$. Intuitively, it is natural to guess that this probability is .25, since 25% of the numbers in the interval $[0, 1]$ are between .50 and .75. The probability calculation method for continuous random variables should give this natural answer.

The method that is used involves the standard calculus problem of finding areas under curves. In Section 6.3 we noted that probabilities (represented by histogram areas) for a discrete random variable could be approximated by areas under a suitable curve. For this random variable,

---

[1] The random number generator introduced in Chapter 6 would pick a rational number from $[0, 1)$, so that 1 was not a possible value. In this example, we pick a real number from $[0, 1]$, and 1 is possible.

we will find probabilities exactly by looking at areas under the curve $y = f(x)$ defined by

$$f(x) = \begin{cases} 1 & 0 \le x \le 1 \\ 0 & \text{otherwise} \end{cases}.$$

This function $f(x)$ is called the density function for X. We will calculate the probability $P(.50 \le X \le .75)$ by finding the area bounded by $f(x)$ and the x-axis between $x = .50$ and $x = .75$. This is pictured in the next figure.

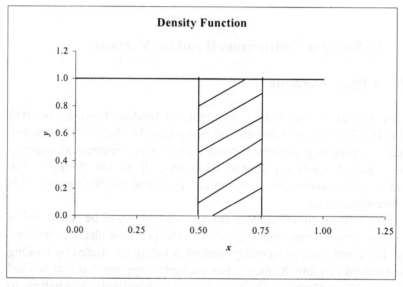

The desired area is .25, which is the intuitively natural answer for $P(.50 \le X \le .75)$.

To find the general probability $P(a \le X \le b)$, we find the area bounded by the graph of $f(x)$ and the x-axis between $x = a$ and $x = b$. This is the area of a rectangle, but we could calculate it by integration.

$$P(a \le X \le b) = \int_a^b f(x)\, dx$$

For example,

$$P(.10 \le X \le .32) = \int_{.10}^{.32} 1\, dx = .22.$$

This also is the intuitively natural answer, since 22% of the interval is between .10 and .32.

It is important to note that the total area bounded by $f(x)$ and the x-axis is 1.00. This tells us that $P(0 \leq X \leq 1) = 1$, which is certainly true if we are picking a number in the interval $[0, 1]$.

7.1.2 The Density Function and Probabilities for Continuous Random Variables

Probabilities for any continuous random variable are computed in a similar fashion, using a density function and areas under the density function curve. The density function used will depend on the random variable. The following definition of a density function is based on properties which were illustrated in the example in Section 7.1.1.

Definition 7.1 The **probability density function** of a random variable X is a real-valued function satisfying the following properties:

(a) $f(x) \geq 0$ for all x.
(b) The total area bounded by the graph of $y = f(x)$ and the x-axis is 1.00.

$$\int_{-\infty}^{\infty} f(x)\,dx = 1 \qquad (7.1)$$

(c) $P(a \leq X \leq b)$ is given by the area under $y = f(x)$ between $x = a$ and $x = b$.

$$P(a \leq X \leq b) = \int_{a}^{b} f(x)\,dx \qquad (7.2)$$

Example 7.1 A risky investment has widely varying possible return percentages for the next year. The best that can happen for this particular investment is a return of 100%. (The investor doubles her money by getting back the amount invested plus 100% of the amount invested.) The worst that can happen is a return of -100%. (The investor loses 100% of the amount she invests.) The percentage return is a random variable X which could be anything from -1 (-100%) to 1 (100%), depending on the state of the economy in one year. The probability density function is

$$f(x) = \begin{cases} .75(1 - x^2) & -1 \leq x \leq 1 \\ 0 & \text{otherwise} \end{cases}.$$

Find the probability that the return is greater than 10%.

Solution Since we are told that $f(x)$ is a density function, we know that $f(x) \geq 0$ and the total area under the curve is 1.00. It is still a good idea for the reader to check these key properties. The graph of $f(x)$ is given in the next figure.

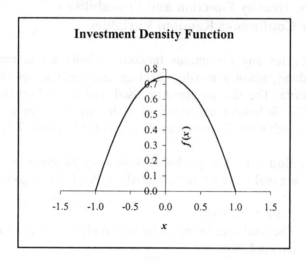

The graph shows that $f(x)$ is non-negative. The total area under the curve is

$$\int_{-1}^{1} f(x)\,dx = .75 \left(x - \frac{x^3}{3} \right) \Bigg|_{-1}^{1} = 1.$$

The probability that X is greater that 10% is

$$\int_{.10}^{1} f(x)\,dx = .75 \left(x - \frac{x^3}{3} \right) \Bigg|_{.10}^{1} = .42525. \qquad \square$$

The probability density function in this example makes intuitive sense for a risky investment. The investor can make a lot or lose a lot. In fact, the probability that X is less than -10% is also .42525. The shape of the curve shows that the greatest gains and losses have somewhat lower probabilities.

7.1.3 Building a Straight-Line Density Function for an Insurance Loss

In this section we will look at an example in which we derive the density function for a random variable based on simple assumptions about its behavior.

Example 7.2 You are going to offer a warranty insurance policy which pays for repairs on a new appliance in the next year. Your experience indicates that repair costs X on a single policy will be in the interval $[0, 1000]$. Probability will be highest for the lowest costs (those near 0), and will fall off in a straight line fashion until x reaches 1000. Find an appropriate density function, and calculate $P(X > 600)$.

Solution The density function will be a straight line segment of negative slope, starting at $x = 0$ and ending at $x = 1000$. It is pictured in the graph below.

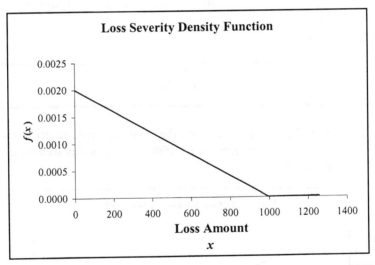

The straight line and the two axes bound a triangle with base 1000. To make the total area under the curve equal 1.00, we need a height of .002. Thus $f(0) = .002$ and $f(1000) = 0$. Once these values are specified, we can find the equation of the straight line.

$$f(x) = \begin{cases} .002 - .000002x & 0 \le x \le 1000 \\ 0 & \text{otherwise} \end{cases}$$

The probability $P(X > 600)$ is the area of the triangle to the right of $x = 600$ and below the line segment. Thus

$$P(X > 600) = \frac{400 \cdot f(600)}{2} = 200(.0008) = .16.$$

For straight-line densities, it is usually easier to find probabilities as areas of trapezoids or triangles. The reader can check that integration would give the same answer.

$$\int_{600}^{1000} (.002 - .000002x)\, dx = .16 \qquad\qquad \square$$

7.1.4   The Cumulative Distribution Function $F(x)$

In Chapter 4 we defined the cumulative distribution function $F(x)$ by

$$F(x) = P(X \le x).$$

The definition of $F(x)$ is the same for discrete and continuous random variables, but the calculations for continuous random variables use integration rather than discrete summation.

$$F(x) = \int_{-\infty}^{x} f(u)\, du \qquad\qquad (7.3)$$

Example 7.3   We return to the loss severity distribution in Example 7.2. For x in the interval $(0, 1000]$, $F(x)$ is the area under the density curve from 0 to x.

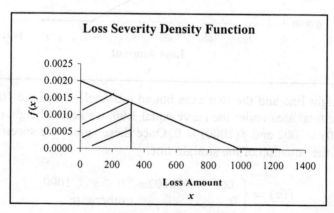

We can calculate this area as the area of a trapezoid or by integration.

$$F(x) = \int_0^x (.002 - .000002u)\,du = .002x - .000001x^2, 0 \leq x \leq 1000$$

Note that $F(x) = 0$ for $x \leq 0$ and $F(x) = 1$ for $x \geq 1000$. The graph of $F(x)$ is shown below.

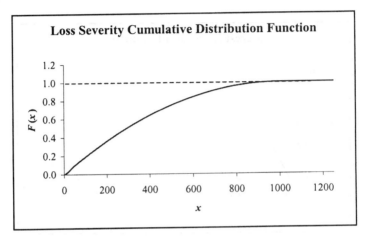

Since $F(x)$ is defined by integrating $f(x)$, it is clear that the derivative of $F(x)$ is $f(x)$. This simple relationship is very important when the derivative $F'(x)$ exists.

$$F'(x) = f(x) \qquad\qquad (7.4)$$

7.1.5 A Piecewise Density Function

The density function for a continuous random variable can be defined piecewise and fail to be continuous at some points, as the following example shows.

Example 7.4 A company has made a loan which has a variable interest rate. One month from now interest will be due, but the rate is not known now. It will be set then, based on the value of a short-term borrowing rate which changes daily. The company believes that the density function given below is a reasonable one for this future interest rate.

$$f(x) = \begin{cases} 0 & x < 0 \\ 560x & 0 \le x \le .05 \\ -15x + 3.75 & .05 < x \le .25 \\ 0 & x > .25 \end{cases}$$

The graph of $f(x)$ for $0 \le x \le .25$ is shown below. Note that $f(x)$ is not continuous at $x = .05$.

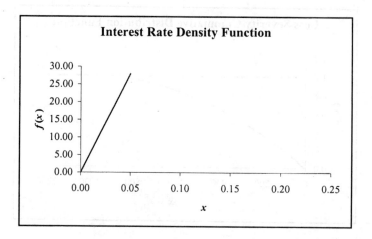

The company is projecting higher probabilities for rates below 5%, but is allowing the possibility of rates above 5%. The total area under this density function breaks into two triangular pieces whose areas can be easily calculated.

$$P(0 \le X \le .05) = \int_0^{.05} 560x \, dx = .70$$

$$P(.05 \le X \le .25) = \int_{.05}^{.25} (-15x + 3.75) \, dx = .30$$

The total area is 1.00. Other probabilities may also involve two calculations similar to the above. For example,

$$P(.03 \le X \le .07) = \int_{.03}^{.05} 560x \, dx + \int_{.05}^{.07} (-15x + 3.75) \, dx$$

$$= .448 + .057 = .505.$$

It is important to note that the values of $f(x)$ are not themselves probabilities; they define areas which give probabilities. *The values of $f(x)$ must be positive, but they can be greater than one as in this example.* For example, $f(.04) = 560(.04) = 22.40$. This value of 22.40 cannot be a probability, but

$$P(.039 \leq x \leq .041) = \int_{.039}^{.041} 560x \, dx = .0448.$$

The cumulative distribution function $F(x)$ must be calculated in pieces.

$$F(x) = P(0 \leq X \leq x) = \int_0^x 560u \, du = 280x^2, \ 0 \leq x \leq .05$$

$$F(.05) = .70$$

$$F(x) = P(0 \leq X \leq x) = .70 + \int_{.05}^x (-15u + 3.75)du$$

$$= -7.5x^2 + 3.75x + .53125, \ .05 < x \leq .25$$

The graph of $F(x)$ for $0 \leq x \leq .25$ is pictured below.

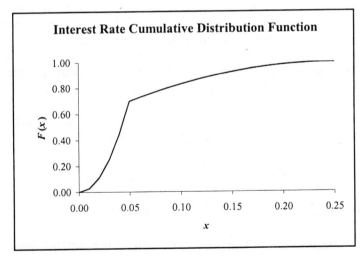

Note that even though $f(x)$ is not continuous, $F(x)$ is continuous. However, $F(x)$ is not differentiable everywhere, since $F'(x)$ is not defined at .05. *Values of $F(x)$ are probabilities and must be in the interval [0, 1].* □

Technology Note

The density functions used in this section were simple enough that no special help was needed to integrate them. In later sections we will deal with more complex density functions which must be integrated numerically. The TI-83, TI 89 or TI-92 calculators will do those integrals for us.

The piecewise function in this section was not demanding, but it required a tedious calculation. Piecewise functions can be defined on the TI 89 or TI-92 using the "when" operator. Once this is done, calculations can be done more rapidly. For example, the author found $F(x)$ for the piecewise function in Example 7.4 with a single integration statement on the TI-89.

7.2   The Mode, the Median, and Percentiles

In Chapter 4, we looked at two measures of central tendency for discrete random variables: the mean and the mode. We will look at the mean of a continuous random variable in Section 7.3. In this section, we will look at the mode of a continuous random variable and introduce another commonly used measure of central tendency, the median.

For a discrete random variable, the mode was defined to be the value of x for which the probability $p(x)$ was highest. For a continuous random variable, we look at the density function $f(x)$.

Definition 7.2 The **mode** of a continuous random variable is the value of x for which the density function $f(x)$ is a maximum.

Example 7.5 In Example 7.1, we looked at X, the percentage return on an investment. The density function was

$$f(x) = \begin{cases} .75(1 - x^2) & -1 \le x \le 1 \\ 0 & \text{otherwise} \end{cases}.$$

$f(x)$ is maximized when $x = 0$, so the mode is 0.   □

Example 7.6 In Example 7.4, we looked at a variable interest rate whose density function $f(x)$ was defined piecewise. The maximum value of $f(x)$ occurred at $x = .05$. The mode is .05.   □

Example 7.7 Let X be the random variable for the value of a number picked at random from $[0, 1]$. Then

$$f(x) = \begin{cases} 1 & 0 \le x \le 1 \\ 0 & \text{otherwise} \end{cases}.$$

$f(x)$ is constant on $[0, 1]$ and does not have a unique maximum. Any x in the interval $[0, 1]$ is a mode. □

Definition 7.3 The **median** m of a continuous random variable X is the solution of the equation

$$F(m) = P(X \le m) = .50. \tag{7.5}$$

Example 7.8 The loss severity distribution in Example 7.2 had the following density and cumulative distribution functions.

$$f(x) = \begin{cases} .002 - .000002x & 0 \le x \le 1000 \\ 0 & \text{otherwise} \end{cases}$$

$$F(x) = \int_0^x (.002 - .000002x)du = .002x - .000001x^2,$$
$$0 \le x \le 1000$$

The median m can be found by solving $F(m) = .50$ for m.

$$.002m - .000001m^2 = .50$$

The solution to this quadratic equation, in the interval $[0, 1000]$, is $m \approx 292.89$. This has a nice intuitive interpretation. Half of all losses will be less than 292.89; the other half will be greater. Note that the mode of this distribution is 0. The median and the mode are not necessarily equal. □

If the density function is symmetric, the median can be found without calculation. For example, if X is a random number chosen from $[0, 1]$, the median is clearly $m = .50$. If X is the random variable of investment returns in Example 7.1, the density function graph is symmetric about 0.

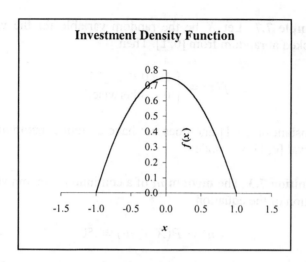

It should be clear from the graph that $m = 0$.

For the loss severity example, the median could be interpreted as separating the top 50% of losses from the bottom 50%. For this reason, the median is called the 50th percentile. Other percentiles can be defined using similar reasoning. For example, the 90th percentile separates the top 10% from the bottom 90%. Percentiles are defined in general in the next definition.

Definition 7.4   Let X be a continuous random variable and $0 \leq p \leq 1$. The $\mathbf{100}p^{th}$ **percentile** of X is the number x_p defined by

$$F(x_p) = p.$$

Example 7.9 The 90th percentile of the loss severity distribution is found by solving

$$.002x_{.90} - .000001x_{.90}^2 = .90.$$

The solution in the interval $[0, 1000]$ is $x_{.90} \approx 683.77$.   ☐

The median and percentiles are more difficult to find for piecewise densities, since one must first find which piece contains the median or the desired percentile. This will be necessary in Exercise 7-7.

7.3 The Mean and Variance of a Continuous Random Variable

7.3.1 The Expected Value of a Continuous Random Variable

In Chapter 4, the expected value of a discrete random variable X was defined as

$$E(X) = \sum x \cdot p(x).$$

Using the integral as a continuous sum, we can similarly define the expected value of a continuous random variable X.

Definition 7.5 Let X be a continuous random variable with density function $f(x)$. The **expected value** of X is

$$E(X) = \int_{-\infty}^{\infty} x \cdot f(x)\, dx. \qquad (7.6)$$

$E(X)$ is also denoted by μ, and referred to as the **mean** of X.

Example 7.10 Let X be the loss severity random variable from Example 7.2.

$$f(x) = \begin{cases} .002 - .000002x & 0 \le x \le 1000 \\ 0 & \text{otherwise} \end{cases}$$

$$E(X) = \int_0^{1000} (.002x - .000002x^2)\, dx = \frac{1000}{3} = 333.3\dot{3} \qquad \square$$

Note that the mean is not equal to the median for the loss severity distribution. (The median is approximately 292.89.) *This illustrates that the mean and median are not necessarily equal.* The next example illustrates a case where the two are equal.

Example 7.11 Let X be a number chosen at random from $[0, 1]$.

$$E(X) = \int_0^1 x \cdot 1\, dx = .50 \qquad \square$$

The mean equals the median for the random number X. The reader will be asked to show in Exercise 7-10 that for the random variable of investment values in Example 7.1, the mean equals the median of 0. *The mean will equal the median when the graph of the density function is symmetric.*

Finding the mean when the density function is defined piecewise requires a bit more calculation.

Example 7.12 The interest rate random variable in Example 7.4 had density function

$$f(x) = \begin{cases} 560x & 0 \le x \le .05 \\ -15x + 3.75 & .05 < x \le .25. \\ 0 & \text{otherwise} \end{cases}$$

$$E(X) = \int_0^{.05} 560x^2 \, dx + \int_{.05}^{.25} (-15x^2 + 3.75x) \, dx$$

$$= .0233 + .035 = .05833 \qquad \qquad \square$$

7.3.2   The Expected Value of a Function of a Random Variable

Suppose X is a random variable, but we are actually interested in the random variable $g(X)$. In Section 6.1 we discussed how to find $E[g(X)]$ if X is discrete with probability function $p(x)$,

$$E[g(X)] = \sum g(x) \cdot p(x).$$

The result for continuous random variables is similar, with summation replaced by integration.

Expected Value of a Function of a Continuous Random Variable
X continuous with density function $f(x)$

$$E[g(X)] = \int_{-\infty}^{\infty} g(x) \cdot f(x) \, dx \qquad (7.7)$$

Dealing with functions of random variables can be tricky. We will not give a proof of Equation (7.7) here, but we will discuss finding the density function for $g(X)$ in a later section. At this point, we will concentrate on applying Equation (7.7). One common application occurs when $g(x) = ax + b$.

$$E[g(X)] = \int_{-\infty}^{\infty} (ax + b) \cdot f(x)\, dx = a\int_{-\infty}^{\infty} x \cdot f(x)\, dx + b\int_{-\infty}^{\infty} f(x)\, dx$$

$$= a \cdot E(X) + b \cdot 1$$

Thus for any discrete or continuous random variable X,

$$E(aX + b) \;=\; a \cdot E(X) + b. \qquad (7.8)$$

Example 7.13 Let X be the loss severity random variable of Example 7.2. In Example 7.10 we showed that $E(X) = 333.3\overline{3}$. The random variable is the amount of loss on one policy in the next year. Suppose that next year is 1999, but you also wish to project costs Y for the year 2000. You believe that costs will inflate by 5% for the year 2000. Then the inflated cost for the year 2000 is $Y = 1.05X$, and

$$E(Y) = E(1.05X) = 1.05 \cdot E(X) \;=\; 350. \qquad \square$$

We will use Equation (7.7) in many applications throughout this chapter. In the next section, we will use it in the definition of the variance of a continuous random variable.

7.3.3 The Variance of a Continuous Random Variable

In Chapter 4 we defined the variance of a discrete random variable to be $E[(X - \mu)^2]$. This expectation also defines the variance of a continuous random variable, but the expectation is calculated using integration instead of summation.

Definition 7.6 Let X be a continuous random variable with density function $f(x)$ and mean μ. Then the **variance** of x is defined by

$$V(X) = E[(X - \mu)^2] = \int_{-\infty}^{\infty} (x - \mu)^2 \cdot f(x)\, dx. \qquad (7.9)$$

The square root of the variance is called the **standard deviation** and denoted by the Greek letter sigma.

$$\sigma = \sqrt{V(X)}$$

$$\sigma^2 = V(X)$$

Example 7.14 Let X be a number chosen at random from $[0, 1]$. In Example 7.11, we showed that $E(X) = .50$. Then

$$V(X) = E[(X - .50)^2] = \int_0^1 \left(x - \frac{1}{2}\right)^2 \cdot 1\, dx = \frac{1}{12}. \qquad \square$$

In Chapter 6 we showed that for a discrete random variable X

$$\boxed{V(X) \;=\; E(X^2) - [E(X)]^2 \;=\; E(X^2) - \mu^2. \qquad (7.10)}$$

This result can also be derived for continuous random variables.

$$E[(X - \mu)^2] = \int_{-\infty}^{\infty} (x^2 - 2\mu x + \mu^2) \cdot f(x)\, dx$$

$$= \int_{-\infty}^{\infty} x^2 \cdot f(x)\, dx - 2\mu \int_{-\infty}^{\infty} x \cdot f(x)\, dx + \mu^2 \int_{-\infty}^{\infty} f(x)\, dx$$

$$E(X^2) - 2\mu \cdot \mu + \mu^2 \cdot 1 = E(X^2) - \mu^2$$

We noted in Chapter 6 that Equation (7.10) is often preferred for calculations that must be done by hand. The definition of variance in Equation (7.9) gives a calculation method which avoids certain round-off error problems, and is preferred for computer solutions. In the next example we illustrate how Equation (7.10) might be used to shorten computation time for a traditional hand calculation.

Example 7.15 Let X be the loss severity random variable of Example 7.2. We showed in Example 7.10 that

$$E(X) = \frac{1000}{3} = 333.3\dot{3}.$$

In order to use Equation (7.10), we need only calculate $E(X^2)$.

$$E(X^2) = \int_0^{1000} x^2(.002 - .000002x)\, dx = 166{,}666.6\dot{6}.$$

$$V(X) = 166{,}666.6\dot{6} - 333.3\dot{3}^2 = \frac{500{,}000}{9} = 55{,}555.5\dot{5}$$

Calculation of $V(X)$ from the defining Equation (7.9) would require evaluation of the integral

$$\int_0^{1000} \left(x - \frac{1000}{3}\right)^2 (.002 - .000002x)\, dx.$$

This calculation is straightforward, but much more time-consuming if done by hand. If the calculation is done on a computer or powerful calculator, calculation time is not an issue. □

We have already used Equation (7.7) to derive the expected value of a linear function of a continuous random variable X, which was $E(aX + b) = a \cdot E(X) + b = a\mu + b$. We can also derive a formula for $V(aX + b)$. If $Y = aX + b$, then

$$Y - E(Y) = aX + b - (a\mu + b) = a(X - \mu).$$

Then

$$V(Y) = E[(Y - E(Y))^2] = E[a^2(X - \mu)^2] = a^2 \cdot E[(X - \mu)^2]$$
$$= a^2 \cdot V(X).$$

$$\boxed{V(aX + b) = a^2 \cdot V(X) \qquad (7.11)}$$

The expressions for $E(aX + b)$ and $V(aX + b)$ derived here for continuous random variables are identical with those derived earlier for discrete random variables.

Example 7.16 In Example 7.13, we looked at the effect of 5% inflation on the loss severity random variable X. The random variable for loss severity after inflation was $Y = 1.05X$. In Example 7.15 we showed that $V(X) = 55{,}555.5\dot{5}$. Then

$$V(Y) = V(1.05X) = 1.05^2(55{,}555.5\dot{5}) = 61{,}250. \qquad □$$

7.4   Exercises

7.1   Defining a Continuous Random Variable

7-1.   Let $f(x) = 1.5x + .25$, for $0 \leq x \leq 1$, and $f(x) = 0$ elsewhere.
     (a)   Show that $f(x)$ is a probability density function.
     (b)   What is the cumulative distribution function?
     (c)   Find $P(0 \leq X \leq \frac{1}{2})$ and $P(\frac{1}{4} \leq X \leq \frac{3}{4})$.

7-2.   Let $f(x) = a(e^{-2x} - e^{-3x})$, for $x \geq 0$, and $f(x) = 0$ elsewhere.
     (a)   Find a so that $f(x)$ is a probability density function.
     (b)   What is $P(X \leq 1)$?

7-3   Let
$$f(x) = \begin{cases} 25x & 0 \leq x \leq .20 \\ 1.5625(1 - x) & .20 < x \leq 1. \\ 0 & \text{elsewhere} \end{cases}$$

     Find $P(.10 \leq X \leq .60)$.

7-4.   Let $f(x) = a/(1 + x^2)$, for $x \geq 0$, and $f(x) = 0$ elsewhere.
     (a)   Find a so that $f(x)$ is a probability density function.
     (b)   What is $P(X \leq 1)$?

7.2   The Mode, the Median, and Percentiles

7-5.   For the density function in Exercise 7-1, find $x_{.25}$, $x_{.50}$ and $x_{.75}$.

7-6.   Let $f(x) = e^x$, for $0 \leq x \leq ln2$, and $f(x) = 0$ elsewhere.
     (a)   Find $x_{.50}$ and $x_{.90}$.
     (b)   What is the mode of this distribution?

7-7.   For the density function in Exercise 7-3, find the median and
     $x_{.80}$.

7.3 The Mean and Variance of a Continuous Random Variable

7-8. If X is the random variable whose density function is defined in Exercise 7-1, what are $E(X)$ and $V(X)$?

7-9. If X is the random variable whose density function is defined in Exercise 7-3, what is $E(X)$?

7-10. For the random variable in Example 7.1 whose density function is $f(x) = .75(1-x^2)$, for $-1 \le x \le 1$, and $f(x) = 0$ elsewhere, show that both the mean and the median are equal to 0.

7-11. Let X be a random variable whose density function is $\dfrac{2}{\pi(1+x^2)}$, for $x \ge 0$, and 0 elsewhere (Exercise 7-4). Show that $E(X)$ does not exist.

7.5 Sample Actuarial Examination Problems

7-12. The lifetime of a machine part has a continuous distribution on the interval $(0,40)$ with probability density function f, where $f(x)$ is proportional to $(10+x)^{-2}$.

Calculate the probability that the lifetime of the machine part is less than 6.

7-13. An insurer's annual weather-related loss, X, is a random variable with density function

$$f(x) = \begin{cases} \dfrac{2.5(200)^{2.5}}{x^{3.5}} & \text{for } x > 200 \\ 0 & \text{otherwise} \end{cases}$$

Calculate the difference between the 30th and 70th percentiles of X.

7-14.   An insurance company's monthly claims are modeled by a
continuous, positive random variable X, whose probability
density function is proportional to $(1+x)^{-4}$ where $0 < x < \infty$.

Determine the company's expected monthly claims.

7-15.   Let X be a continuous random variable with density function

$$f(x) = \begin{cases} \dfrac{|x|}{10} & \text{for} \quad -2 \le x \le 4 \\ 0 & \text{otherwise} \end{cases}$$

Calculate the expected value of X.

7-16.   The loss due to a fire in a commercial building is modeled by a
random variable X with density function

$$f(x) = \begin{cases} .005(20-x) & \text{for} \quad 0 < x < 20 \\ 0 & \text{otherwise} \end{cases}$$

Given that a fire loss exceeds 8, what is the probability that it
exceeds 16?

7-17.   An insurance company insures a large number of homes. The
insured value, X, of a randomly selected home is assumed to
follow a distribution with density function

$$f(x) = \begin{cases} 3x^{-4} & \text{for} \quad x > 1 \\ 0 & \text{otherwise} \end{cases}$$

Given that a randomly selected home is insured for at least 1.5,
what is the probability that it is insured for less than 2?

Chapter 8
Commonly Used Continuous Distributions

8.1 The Uniform Distribution

8.1.1 The Uniform Density Function

The **uniform distribution** is the first of a series of useful continuous probability distributions which will be studied in this chapter. It is covered first because it is the simplest. We have already seen an example of a random variable X which has a uniform distribution. In Section 7.1.1, we looked at X, the value of a number picked at random from the interval $[0, 1]$. The density function was constant (at 1) on the interval $[0, 1]$, and 0 otherwise.

$$f(x) = \begin{cases} 1 & 0 \leq x \leq 1 \\ 0 & \text{otherwise} \end{cases}$$

The general uniform density function is constant on an interval $[a, b]$, and 0 otherwise. To assure that the area bounded by the density function and the x-axis is 1, the constant value must be $\frac{1}{b - a}$.

Uniform Density Function
X uniform on $[a, b]$

$$f(x) = \begin{cases} \dfrac{1}{b - a} & a \leq x \leq b \\ 0 & \text{otherwise} \end{cases} \qquad (8.1)$$

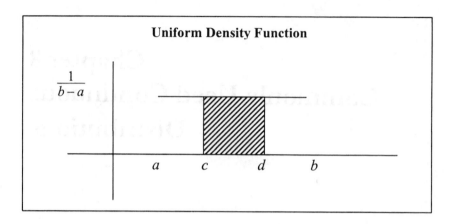

The graph of the uniform density function is pictured above. The graph shows that

$$P(c \le X \le d) = \frac{d - c}{b - a}, \quad \text{for} \quad a \le c \le d \le b. \quad (8.2)$$

Example 8.1 A company is expecting to receive payment of a large bill sometime today. The time X until the payment is received is uniformly distributed over the interval $[1, 9]$, sometime between 1 and 9 hours from now, with all times in the interval being equally likely. The density function for X is

$$f(x) = \begin{cases} \frac{1}{8} & 1 \le x \le 9 \\ 0 & \text{otherwise} \end{cases}.$$

The probability that the time of receipt is between 2 and 5 hours from now is

$$P(2 \le X \le 5) = \frac{5 - 2}{9 - 1} = \frac{3}{8}. \qquad \qquad \square$$

8.1.2 The Cumulative Distribution Function for a Uniform   Random Variable

Equation (8.2) can be used to find $P(X \le x)$ for values of x in the interval $[a, b]$.

$$P(X \leq x) = P(a \leq X \leq x) = \frac{x-a}{b-a}, \quad \text{for } a \leq x \leq b$$

Then the cumulative distribution function $F(x)$ for a uniform random variable X on $[a, b]$ can be defined.

Uniform Cumulative Distribution Function
X uniform on $[a, b]$

$$F(x) = \begin{cases} 0 & x < a \\ \frac{x-a}{b-a} & a \leq x \leq b \\ 1 & x > b \end{cases} \qquad (8.3)$$

Example 8.2 Let X be the random variable for time of payment receipt in Example 8.1. X is uniform on $[1, 9]$. The cumulative distribution is given by

$$F(x) = \begin{cases} 0 & x < 1 \\ \frac{x-1}{8} & 1 \leq x \leq 9 \\ 1 & x > 9 \end{cases}.$$

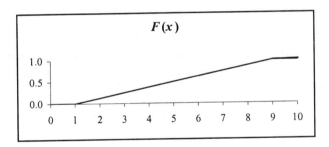

As the graph shows, the cumulative distribution function is a straight line between $a = 1$ and $b = 9$. □

8.1.3 Uniform Random Variables for Lifetimes; Survival Functions

In many applied probability problems, the random variable of interest is a time variable T. This time variable could be the time until death of a person, which is a standard insurance application. However, the same mathematics can be used to analyze the time until a machine part fails, the time until a disease ends, or the time it takes to serve a customer in a store. The uniform distribution does not give a very realistic model for human lifetimes, but it is often used as an illustration of a lifetime model because of its simplicity.

Example 8.3 Let T be the time from birth until death of a randomly selected member of a population. Assume that T has a uniform distribution on $[0, 100]$[1]. Then

$$f(t) = \begin{cases} \frac{1}{100} & 0 \le t \le 100 \\ 0 & \text{otherwise} \end{cases}$$

and

$$F(t) = \begin{cases} 0 & t < 0 \\ \frac{t}{100} & 0 \le t \le 100 \\ 1 & t > 100 \end{cases}.$$

The function $F(t)$ gives us the probability that the person dies by age t. For example, the probability of death by age 57 is

$$P(T \le 57) = F(57) = \frac{57}{100} = .57.$$

Most of us are interested in the probability that we will survive past a certain age. In this example, we might wish to find the probability that we survive beyond age 57. This is simply the probability that we do *not* die by age 57.

$$P(T > 57) = 1 - F(57) = 1 - \frac{57}{100} = .43 \qquad \square$$

The probability of surviving from birth past a given age t is called a **survival probability** and denoted by $S(t)$.

Definition 8.1 The **survival function** is

$$S(t) = P(T > t) = 1 - F(t). \qquad (8.4)$$

In the last example, we could have written $S(57) = .43$.

---

[1] Actuarial texts refer to this as a de Moivre distribution.

8.1.4 The Mean and Variance of the Uniform Distribution

The mean and variance of the uniform distribution are given below.

Uniform Distribution Mean and Variance
X uniform on $[a, b]$

$$E(X) = \frac{a+b}{2} \tag{8.5a}$$

$$V(X) = \frac{(b-a)^2}{12} \tag{8.5b}$$

We will discuss the derivation of these formulas at the end of the section. First we will look at some examples.

Example 8.4 Let X be the payment time in Example 8.1, where X is uniform on $[1, 9]$. Then

$$E(X) = \frac{1+9}{2} = 5$$

and

$$V(X) = \frac{(9-1)^2}{12} = \frac{64}{12} = 5.3\dot{3}.$$

Note that the expected value of the uniform X is the midpoint of the interval $[a, b]$. □

Example 8.5 Let T be the time until death in Example 8.3, where T is uniform on $[0, 100]$. Then

$$E(T) = \frac{0+100}{2} = 50$$

and

$$V(T) = \frac{(100-0)^2}{12} = \frac{10{,}000}{12} = 833.3\dot{3}. \qquad \square$$

The formulas for the mean and the variance can be derived by integrating polynomials. The mean is derived below.

$$E(X) = \int_a^b x \cdot \frac{1}{b-a}\, dx = \frac{1}{b-a} \cdot \frac{x^2}{2}\Big|_a^b = \frac{1}{b-a} \cdot \frac{b^2 - a^2}{2} = \frac{a+b}{2}$$

To derive the variance, find $E[X^2]$ and use Equation (7.10). This is left for the reader in Exercise 8-1.

8.1.5   A Conditional Probability Problem Involving the Uniform Distribution

In some problems we are given information about an individual and end up solving conditional probability problems based on that information. In Example 8.3 we looked at a random variable T which represented the lifetime of a member of a population. If you are a twenty-year-old in that population, you are interested in lifetime probabilities for twenty-year-old individuals. This requires conditional probability calculations in which you are given that an individual is at least twenty years old.

Example 8.6   Let T be the lifetime random variable in Example 8.3, where T is uniform on $[0, 100]$. Find (a) $P(T \geq 50 \mid T \geq 20)$ and (b) $P(T \geq x \mid T \geq 20)$, for x in $[20, 100]$.

Solution

(a) $$P(T \geq 50 \mid T \geq 20) = \frac{P(T \geq 50 \text{ and } T \geq 20)}{P(T \geq 20)}$$

$$= \frac{P(T \geq 50)}{P(T \geq 20)} = \frac{.50}{.80} = .625$$

(b)   If x is any real number in the interval $[20, 100]$, then

$$P(T \geq x \mid T \geq 20) = \frac{P(T \geq x \text{ and } T \geq 20)}{P(T \geq 20)}$$

$$= \frac{P(T \geq x)}{P(T \geq 20)}$$

$$= \frac{1 - \frac{x}{100}}{.80} = \frac{100 - x}{80}.$$

The final expression in part (b) is the survival function $S(x)$ for a random variable which is uniformly distributed on $[20, 100]$. This has a nice intuitive interpretation. If the lifetime of a newborn is uniformly distributed on $[0, 100]$, the lifetime of a twenty-year-old is uniformly distributed on the remaining interval $[20, 100]$.   □

8.2   The Exponential Distribution

8.2.1   Mathematical Preliminaries

The exponential distribution formula uses the exponential function $f(x) = e^{-ax}$. It is helpful to review some material from calculus. The following limit will be useful in evaluating definite integrals.

$$\lim_{x \to \infty} x^n \cdot e^{-ax} = \lim_{x \to \infty} \frac{x^n}{e^{ax}} = 0, \quad \text{for} \quad a > 0 \qquad (8.6)$$

Many applications will require integration of expressions of the form $x^n e^{-ax}$, from 0 to ∞, for positive a. The simplest case occurs when $n = 0$. In this case

$$\int_0^\infty e^{-ax}\, dx = \left. \frac{e^{-ax}}{-a} \right|_0^\infty = 0 - \frac{1}{-a} = \frac{1}{a}.$$

The 0 term in the evaluation results from Equation (8.6).

If $n = 1$, we can use integration by parts with $u = x$ and $dv = e^{-ax}\, dx$ to show that

$$\int x \cdot e^{-ax}\, dx = \frac{-x \cdot e^{-ax}}{a} - \frac{e^{-ax}}{a^2} + C.$$

This antiderivative enables us to show that, for $a > 0$,

$$\int_0^\infty x \cdot e^{-ax}\, dx = \left. \left(\frac{-x \cdot e^{-ax}}{a} - \frac{e^{-ax}}{a^2} \right) \right|_0^\infty = (0-0) - \left(0 - \frac{1}{a^2} \right) = \frac{1}{a^2}.$$

Repeated integration by parts can be used to show that

$$\int_0^\infty x^n \cdot e^{-ax}\, dx = \frac{n!}{a^{n+1}}, \quad \text{for } a > 0 \text{ and } n \text{ a positive integer.} \qquad (8.7)$$

Equation (8.7) will be used frequently. It is worth remembering.

An interesting question is what happens to the integral in Equation (8.7) if n is not a positive integer. The answer to this question involves a special function $\Gamma(x)$ called the **gamma function**. (Gamma (Γ) is a capital "G" in the classical Greek alphabet.) The gamma function is defined for $n > 0$ by

$$\Gamma(n) = \int_0^\infty x^{n-1} \cdot e^{-x}\, dx. \qquad (8.8)$$

Equation (8.7) can be used to show that for any positive integer n,

$$\Gamma(n) = (n-1)!. \qquad (8.9)$$

The gamma function is defined by an integral, and gives a value for any n. If n is a positive integer, the value is $(n-1)!$, but we can also evaluate it for other values of n. For example, it can be shown that

$$\Gamma\left(\tfrac{3}{2}\right) = \tfrac{1}{2}\pi^{\frac{1}{2}} \approx .88623.$$

If we look at the relation between the gamma function and the factorial function in Equation (8.9), we might think of the above value as the factorial of $\tfrac{1}{2}$.

$$\tfrac{1}{2}! = \Gamma\left(\tfrac{3}{2}\right) = \tfrac{1}{2}\pi^{\frac{1}{2}} \approx .88623$$

The gamma function will be used in Section 8.3 when we study the gamma distribution. It can be used here to give a version of Equation (8.7) that works for any $n > -1$.

$$\int_0^\infty x^n \cdot e^{-ax}\, dx = \frac{\Gamma(n+1)}{a^{n+1}}, \quad \text{for } a > 0 \text{ and } n > -1 \qquad (8.10)$$

8.2.2   The Exponential Density: An Example

In Section 5.3 we introduced the Poisson distribution, which gave the probability of a specified number of random events in an interval. The **exponential distribution** gives the probability for the waiting time between those Poisson events. We will introduce this by returning to the accident analysis in Example 5.14. The mathematical reasoning which shows that the waiting time in this example has an exponential distribution will be covered in Section 8.2.9.

Example 8.7 Accidents at a busy intersection occur at an average rate of $\lambda = 2$ per month. An analyst has observed that the number of accidents in a month has a Poisson distribution. (This was studied in Section 5.3.2.). The analyst has also observed that the time T between accidents is a random variable with density function

$$f(t) = 2e^{-2t}, \text{ for } t \geq 0.$$

The time T is measured in months. The shape of the density function is given in the next graph.

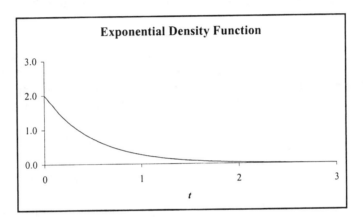

Exponential Density Function

The graph decreases steadily, and appears to indicate that the time between accidents is almost always less than 2 months. We can use the density function to calculate the probability that the waiting time for the next accident is less than 2 months.

$$P(0 \leq T < 2) = \int_0^2 2e^{-2x}\,dx = -e^{-2x}\Big|_0^2 = -e^{-4} + 1 \approx .98168 \quad \square$$

8.2.3 The Exponential Density Function

The density function in the preceding section was an example of an exponential density function.

Exponential Density Function
Random variable T, parameter λ

$$f(t) = \lambda e^{-\lambda t}, \text{ for } t \geq 0 \qquad\qquad (8.11)$$

This definition of $f(t)$ satisfies the definition of a density function, since $f(t) \geq 0$ and the total area bounded by the curve and the x-axis is 1.00.

$$\int_0^\infty \lambda e^{-\lambda t} dt = -e^{-\lambda t}\Big|_0^\infty = 0 - (-1) = 1$$

In many applications the parameter λ represents the rate at which events occur in a Poisson process, and the random variable T represents the waiting time between events.[2] A common application of the exponential distribution is the analysis of the time until failure of a machine part.

Example 8.8 A company is studying the reliability of a part in a machine. The time T (in hours) from installation to failure of the part is a random variable. The study shows that T follows an exponential distribution with $\lambda = .001$. The probability that a part fails within 100 hours is

$$P(0 \leq T \leq 100) = \int_0^{100} .001 e^{-.001x} dx = -e^{-.001x}\Big|_0^{100}$$
$$= -e^{-.1} + 1 \approx .095. \qquad \square$$

If we replace the failure of a part by the death of a human, we can apply the exponential distribution to human lifetimes. We will show in Section 8.2.10 that the exponential distribution is not a good model for the length of a normal human life, but it has been used to study the remaining lifetime of humans with a disease.

Example 8.9 Panjer [13] studied the progression of individuals who had been infected with the AIDS virus. Modern treatments have greatly improved the treatment of AIDS, and Panjer's numbers are no longer valid for modern patients. However, for the data available in 1988, Panjer found that the time in each stage of the disease until progression to the next stage could be modeled by an exponential distribution. For example, the time T (in years) from reaching the actual Acquired Immune Deficiency Syndrome (AIDS) stage until death could be modeled by an exponential distribution with $\lambda \approx 1/.91$. $\qquad \square$

---

[2] λ might also be described as the average number of events occuring per unit of time.

8.2.4 The Cumulative Distribution Function and Survival Function of the Exponential Random Variable

In Example 8.8 we found the probability $P(T \leq 100)$. This is $F(100)$, where $F(t)$ is the cumulative distribution function. The cumulative distribution for any exponential random variable is derived below.

$$P(T \leq t) = \int_0^t \lambda e^{-\lambda x} dx = -e^{-\lambda x}\Big|_0^t = 1 - e^{-\lambda t}, \text{ for } t \geq 0$$

Exponential Cumulative Distribution and Survival Functions
Random variable T, parameter λ

$$F(t) = 1 - e^{-\lambda t} \tag{8.12a}$$

$$S(t) = 1 - F(t) = e^{-\lambda t} \tag{8.12b}$$

for $t \geq 0$

These simple formulas make the exponential distribution an easy one with which to deal.

Example 8.10 Let T be the time until failure of the part in Example 8.8. T has an exponential distribution with $\lambda = .001$. Find (a) the probability that the part fails within 200 hours; (b) the probability that the part lasts for more than 500 hours.
Solution
(a) $F(200) = 1 - e^{-.20} \approx .181$
(b) $S(500) = e^{-.50} \approx .607$ □

8.2.5 The Mean and Variance of the Exponential Distribution

The mean and variance of the exponential distribution with parameter λ can be derived using Equation (8.7).

$$E(T) = \int_0^\infty t \cdot \lambda e^{-\lambda t} dt = \lambda \int_0^\infty t \cdot e^{-\lambda t} dt = \lambda \frac{1}{\lambda^2} = \frac{1}{\lambda}$$

$$E(T^2) = \int_0^\infty t^2 \cdot \lambda e^{-\lambda t} dt = \lambda \int_0^\infty t^2 \cdot e^{-\lambda t} dt = \lambda \frac{2}{\lambda^3} = \frac{2}{\lambda^2}$$

$$V(T) = E(T^2) - [E(T)]^2 = \frac{2}{\lambda^2} - \left(\frac{1}{\lambda}\right)^2 = \frac{1}{\lambda^2}$$

Exponential Distribution Mean and Variance
Random variable T, parameter λ

$$E(T) = \frac{1}{\lambda} \qquad\qquad (8.13a)$$

$$V(T) = \frac{1}{\lambda^2} \qquad\qquad (8.13b)$$

Example 8.11 Let T be the random variable for the time from reaching the AIDS stage to death in Example 8.9. T is exponential with $\lambda = 1/.91$. Then

$$E(T) = \frac{1}{\lambda} = .91$$

and

$$V(T) = \frac{1}{\lambda^2} = .91^2 = .8281. \qquad\qquad \square$$

Example 8.12 Let T be the time to failure of the machine part in Example 8.8. T is exponential with $\lambda = .001$. Then

$$E(T) = \frac{1}{\lambda} = 1000$$

and

$$V(T) = \frac{1}{\lambda^2} = 1{,}000{,}000. \qquad\qquad \square$$

Although the part in Example 8.12 has an expected life of 1000 hours, you might not want to use it for 1000 hours if your life depended on it. The probability that the part fails within 1000 hours is

$$P(T \le 1000) = F(1000) = 1 - e^{-1} \approx .632.$$

It is true for any exponential distribution that $F[E(T)] = 1 - e^{-1} \approx .632$. The reader is asked to verify this in Exercise 8-14.

8.2.6 Another Look at the Meaning of the Density Function

We have mentioned before that density function values are not probabilities, but rather they define areas which give probabilities. We can illustrate this in a new way by looking at the previous exponential graph from Example 8.8. At the time value t we have inserted a rectangle of height $f(t)$ with a small base dt. The rectangle area is $f(t)\,dt$, and it approximates the area under the curve between t and $t+dt$. Thus

$$P(t < T < t+dt) \approx f(t)\,dt.$$

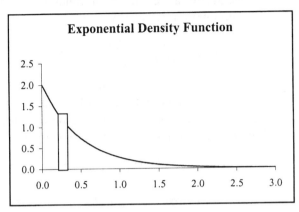

Exponential Density Function

When $f(t)$ is the density function, $f(t)\,dt$ represents the probability that the random variable T falls in the small interval from t to $t+dt$.

8.2.7 The Failure (Hazard) Rate

We will introduce the failure rate (also called the hazard rate) by returning to the machine part failure time random variable T. Since $\lambda = .001$, the survival function is

$$S(t) = e^{-.001t}.$$

This formula is identical with the familiar formula for exponential decay at a rate of .001. Thus it is intuitively natural to think of the machine part as one member of a population which is failing at a rate of .001 per hour, and to refer to .001 as the **failure rate** of the part.

The above reasoning is intuitive, but probability theory has a more careful definition of the failure rate.

Definition 8.2 Let T be a random variable with density function $f(t)$ and cumulative distribution function $F(t)$. The **failure rate function** $\lambda(t)$ is defined by

$$\lambda(t) = \frac{f(t)}{1 - F(t)} = \frac{f(t)}{S(t)}. \tag{8.14}$$

The failure rate can be defined for any random variable, but is simplest to understand for an exponential random variable. For the exponential distribution with parameter λ,

$$\lambda(x) = \frac{f(x)}{S(x)} = \frac{\lambda e^{-\lambda x}}{e^{-\lambda x}} = \lambda.$$

Thus our intuitive idea of $\lambda = .001$ as the failure rate of the machine part agrees with the probabilistic definition of the failure rate. To get a better understanding of the reasoning behind the definition of the failure rate, multiply through the defining equation for $\lambda(t)$ by dt.

$$\lambda(t)\, dt = \frac{f(t)\, dt}{1 - F(t)} = \frac{f(t)\, dt}{S(t)}$$

The numerator $f(t)\, dt$ is approximately $P(t < T < t+dt)$. The denominator is $P(T > t)$. The quotient of the two can be thought of as a conditional probability.

$$\lambda(t)\, dt \approx \frac{P(t < T < t+dt)}{P(T > t)} = P(t < T < t+dt \mid t < T)$$

In words, $\lambda(t)\, dt$ is the conditional probability of failure in the next dt time units for a part that has survived to time t.

The situation for now is simple. For an exponential distribution, the failure rate is constant; it is always equal to λ. The same general definition of failure rate can lead to much more complicated functions for other random variables. The reader is asked to derive the failure rate function for the uniform distribution in Exercise 8-12.

When we look at a human being subject to death, instead of a part exposed to failure, we think of death as a hazard. In this case, we might refer to the failure (death) rate as the **hazard rate**. In Example 8.9, the parameter $\lambda = 1/.91$ for the exponential distribution of time to death would be referred to as a hazard rate.

8.2.8   Use of the Cumulative Distribution Function

Once the cumulative distribution $F(x)$ is known for a random variable X, it can be used to find the probability that X lies in any interval, since

$$\boxed{P(a < X \leq b) = P(X \leq b) - P(X \leq a) = F(b) - F(a).\ (8.15)^3}$$

---

[3] For continuous distributions, $P(a < X \leq b) = P(a \leq X \leq b)$. For discrete and mixed distributions, this will not be the case.

Equation (8.15) is true for any random variable X. For the exponential random variable, it leads to the simple formula

$$P(a < X \le b) = e^{-\lambda a} - e^{-\lambda b}.$$

We have not emphasized the use of technology in Sections 8.1 and 8.2 because there is little need for it in dealing with the uniform and exponential distributions. The probability integrals for uniform probabilities are rectangle areas, and the cumulative distribution for the exponential distribution is a simple exponential expression which can be evaluated on any scientific calculator. This situation will change in the following sections, where we will see much more complicated density functions and integrals which cannot be done in closed form. It is worth noting that the exponential distribution is important enough that a function for it is included in Microsoft® EXCEL. The function EXPONDIST() will calculate values of the cumulative distribution function of an exponential random variable.

8.2.9 Why the Waiting Time is Exponential for Events Whose Number Follows a Poisson Distribution

In Section 8.2.2 we stated that the exponential distribution gave the waiting time between events when the number of events followed a Poisson distribution. To see why this is true, we need to make one more assumption about the events in question: *If the number of events in a time period of length 1 is a Poisson random variable with parameter λ, then the number of events in a time period of length t is a Poisson random variable with parameter λt.*

This is a reasonable assumption. For example, if the number of accidents in a month at an intersection is a Poisson random variable with rate parameter $\lambda = 2$, then the assumption says that accidents in a two-month period will be Poisson with a rate parameter of $2\lambda = 4$.

Using this assumption, the probability of no accidents in an interval of length t is

$$P(X = 0) = \frac{e^{-\lambda t}(\lambda t)^0}{0!} = e^{-\lambda t}.$$

However, there are no accidents in an interval of length t if and only if the waiting time T for the next accident is greater than t. Thus

$$P(X = 0) = P(T > t) = S(t) = e^{-\lambda t}.$$

This is the survival function for an exponential distribution, so the waiting time T is exponential with parameter λ.

8.2.10 A Conditional Probability Problem Involving the Exponential Distribution

In Section 8.1.5 we looked at a conditional probability problem involving the uniform distribution. We can use the same kind of reasoning for conditional problems in which the underlying random variable is exponential.

Example 8.13 Let T be the time to failure of the machine part in Example 8.8, where T is exponential with $\lambda = .001$. Find each of (a) $P(T \geq 150|\ T \geq 100)$ and (b) $P(T \geq x+100|T \geq 100)$, for x in $[0, \infty)$.

Solution

(a) $P(T \geq 150|\ T \geq 100) = \dfrac{P(T \geq 150 \text{ and } T \geq 100)}{P(T \geq 100)}$

$$= \frac{P(T \geq 150)}{P(T \geq 100)}$$

$$= \frac{e^{-.001(150)}}{e^{-.001(100)}} = e^{-.05} \approx .951$$

(b)   If x is any real number in the interval $[0, \infty)$, then

$$P(T \geq x + 100|\ T \geq 100) = \frac{P(T \geq x + 100 \text{ and } T \geq 100)}{P(T \geq 100)}$$

$$= \frac{P(T \geq x + 100)}{P(T \geq 100)}$$

$$= \frac{e^{-.001(x+100)}}{e^{-.001(100)}} = e^{-.001x}.$$

The final expression in part (b) is the survival function $S(x)$ for a random variable which is exponentially distributed on $[0, \infty)$ with $\lambda = .001$. This has a nice intuitive interpretation, since we can think of x as representing hours survived past the 100th hour. If the lifetime of a new part is exponentially distributed on $[0, \infty)$ with $\lambda = .001$, the *remaining* lifetime of a 100-hour-old part is also exponentially distributed on $[0, \infty)$ with $\lambda = .001$. The lifetime random variable of the part is called **memoryless**, because the future lifetime of an aged part has the same distribution as the lifetime of a new part. All exponential distributions are memoryless. (Exercise 8-18 asks for a proof of this fact.) The memoryless property makes the exponential distribution a poor model for a normal human life.   □

8.3   The Gamma Distribution

In the following sections we will discuss a number of distributions which are quite useful in applications. The mathematics for these distributions is complex, and derivations of most key properties will be left for more advanced courses. We will focus on the application of these distributions in applied problems. The first of these distributions is the **gamma distribution**.

8.3.1   Applications of the Gamma Distribution

In Section 5.4, we showed that the geometric probability function $p(x)$ gave the probability of x failures before the first success in a series of independent success-failure trials. In Section 5.5 we showed that the negative binomial probability function $p(x)$ gave the probability of x failures before the rth success in a series of independent success-failure trials. The gamma distribution is related to the exponential distribution in a similar way. The exponential random variable T can be used to model the waiting time for the first occurrence of an event of interest, such as the waiting time for the next accident at an intersection. The gamma random variable X can be used to model the waiting time for the nth occurrence of the event if successive occurrences are independent. In this section, we will use the gamma random variable as a model for the waiting time for a total of two accidents at an intersection. The gamma distribution can also be used in other problems where the exponential distribution is useful; examples include the analysis of failure time of a machine part or survival time for a disease.

There are a number of insurance applications of the gamma distribution. The distribution has mathematical properties which make it a convenient model for the average rate of claims filed by different policyholders of an insurance company. (See, for example, page 152 of Herzog [4] or page 98 of Hossack et al. [6].) Bowers et al. [2] use a translated gamma distribution as a model for the aggregate claims of an insurance company.

8.3.2 The Gamma Density Function

The density function for the gamma distribution has two parameters, α and β. It requires use of the gamma function, $\Gamma(x)$, which was defined in Equation (8.8) in Section 8.2.1. The key property of the gamma function which will be needed in this section was given by Equation (8.9). For any positive integer n, $\Gamma(n) = (n-1)!$.

Gamma Density Function
Parameters $\alpha, \beta > 0$

$$f(x) = \frac{\beta^\alpha}{\Gamma(\alpha)} x^{\alpha-1} e^{-\beta x}, \quad for \quad x \geq 0 \qquad (8.16)$$

Note that for $\alpha = 1$,

$$f(x) = \frac{\beta^1}{\Gamma(1)} x^0 e^{-\beta x} = \beta e^{-\beta x}.$$

This is the exponential density function, so the exponential distribution is a special case of the gamma distribution.

The next figure shows the shape of the gamma density functions for, $\beta = 2$ and $\alpha = 1$, 2 and 4.

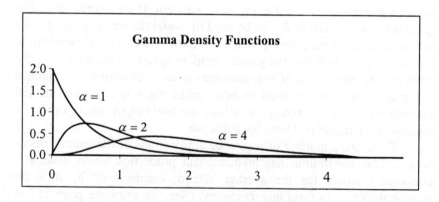

The familiar negative exponential curve for $\alpha = 1$ is clearly visible. For the higher values of α, the curve increases to a maximum and then decreases.

8.3.3 Sums of Independent Exponential Random Variables

We will state without proof an important theorem which will aid us in understanding the application of the gamma distribution. This theorem will be proved using moment generating functions in Chapter 11.

Theorem Let $X_1, X_2, \ldots, X_n$ be independent random variables, all of which have the same exponential distribution with $f(x) = \beta e^{-\beta x}$. Then the sum $X_1 + X_2 + \cdots + X_n$ has a gamma distribution with parameters $\alpha = n$ and β.

Example 8.14 In Example 8.7 we studied T, the time in months between accidents at a busy intersection. T was modeled as an exponential random variable with parameter $\beta = 2$. T represents the waiting time for the first accident after observation begins. If we assume that accidents occur independently, it is natural to assume that once the first accident occurs we will again have an exponential waiting time with $\beta = 2$ for the second accident. The total waiting time from the start of observation will be the sum of the waiting time for the first accident and the waiting time from the first accident until the second. In the notation of the preceding theorem,

X_1 is the waiting time for the first accident,

X_2 is the waiting time between the first and second accidents,

and, in general,

X_i is the waiting time between accidents $i - 1$ and i.

Then

$$\sum_{i=1}^{n} X_i = X,$$

the total waiting time for accident n. For example, $X = X_1 + X_2$ is the random variable for the waiting time from the start of observation until the second accident. According to the theorem, X has a gamma distribution with parameters $\alpha = 2$ and $\beta = 2$. The density function is

$$f(x) = \frac{2^2}{\Gamma(2)} x^{2-1} e^{-2x} = 4x \cdot e^{-2x}.$$

Its graph was given in the previous figure. We can now use this density function to find probabilities. For example, the probability that the total waiting time for the second accident is between one and two months is

$$P(1 \leq X \leq 2) = \int_1^2 4x \cdot e^{-2x} dx.$$

Using integration by parts, we can evaluate this as

$$-2x \cdot e^{-2x} - e^{-2x} \Big|_1^2 = 3e^{-2} - 5e^{-4} \approx .314. \qquad \square$$

8.3.4   The Mean and Variance of the Gamma Distribution

The mean and variance of the gamma distribution can be derived using Equation (8.10). This is left for the exercises.

Gamma Distribution Mean and Variance
Parameters $\alpha, \beta > 0$

$$E(X) = \frac{\alpha}{\beta} \qquad\qquad\qquad (8.17a)$$

$$V(X) = \frac{\alpha}{\beta^2} \qquad\qquad\qquad (8.17b)$$

Example 8.15 Let $X = X_1 + X_2$ be the random variable for the waiting time from the start of observation until the second accident in Example 8.14. X has a gamma distribution with $\alpha = 2$ and $\beta = 2$. Then

$$E(X) = \frac{2}{2} = 1$$

and

$$V(X) = \frac{2}{2^2} = \frac{1}{2}. \qquad \square$$

Example 8.16   Let $Y = X_1 + X_2 + X_3 + X_4$ be the random variable for the waiting time from the start of observation until the fourth accident in Example 8.14. Y has a gamma distribution with $\alpha = 4$ and $\beta = 2$. Then

$$E(X) = \frac{4}{2} = 2$$

and

$$V(X) = \frac{4}{2^2} = 1. \qquad \square$$

8.3.5   Notational Differences Between Texts

Probability textbooks are divided on notational issues. Many textbooks follow our presentation for the gamma distribution. Others replace β by $1/\beta$, giving the alternate formulation

$$f(x) = \frac{1}{\beta^\alpha \Gamma(\alpha)} x^{\alpha-1} e^{-x/\beta}$$

for the density function. This version leads to $E(X) = \alpha\beta$ and $V(X) = \alpha\beta^2$. This alternate formulation may also be used for the exponential distribution. The reader needs to be aware of this difference because different versions may be used in different applied studies.

Technology Note

Technology is very helpful when working with the gamma distribution, since integrating the gamma density function can be quite tedious for most values of α and β. Consider, for example, the gamma random variable $Y = X_1 + X_2 + X_3 + X_4$ with parameters $\alpha = 4$ and $\beta = 2$ from Example 8.16. The density function is

$$f(x) = \frac{2^4}{\Gamma(4)} x^{4-1} e^{-2x} = \tfrac{8}{3} x^3 e^{-2x}.$$

To find the probability $P(1 \leq Y \leq 2)$, we must evaluate the integral

$$P(1 \leq Y \leq 2) = \int_1^2 \tfrac{8}{3} x^3 e^{-2x} dx.$$

This can be done by repeated integration by parts, but that is time consuming. The TI-83 calculator can approximate this integral in a few seconds using the function **fnInt**. It gives the answer .42365334. The TI 89 or TI-92 will rapidly do the integration by parts exactly. Each calculator gives the answer

$$\frac{(19e^2 - 71)e^{-4}}{3}.$$

This exact value approximated to eight places leads to the same answer given by the TI-83.

Microsoft® EXCEL has a function GAMMADIST which will calculate values of the gamma cumulative distribution function. (Parameters must be entered in the alternative format of Section 8.3.5.) For the random variable Y, EXCEL gave the values

$$F(2) = .56652988 \text{ and } F(1) = .14287654.$$

This gives the same answer to our problem.

$$P(1 \leq Y \leq 2) = F(2) - F(1) = .42365334$$

The reader may have noted that in this section the values of α and β were integers in all examples. This was done only for computational simplicity. The parameters α and β may assume any non-negative real values. Technology will enable us to find probabilities for any gamma random variable. This is important. For example, the Chi-square random variable used in statistical work is a gamma random variable with $\beta = \frac{1}{2}$ and $\alpha = \frac{n}{2}$, for some non-negative integer n.

8.4   The Normal Distribution

8.4.1   Applications of the Normal Distribution

The **normal distribution** is the most widely-used of all the distributions found in this text. It can be used to model the distributions of heights, weights, test scores, measurement errors, stock portfolio returns, insurance portfolio losses, and a wide range of other variables. A classic example of the application of the normal distribution was a study of the chest sizes of 5732 Scottish militiamen in 1817. (This study is nicely summarized in Weiss [18].) An army contractor who provided uniforms to the military collected the data for planning purposes. The histogram of chest sizes is shown in the next figure.

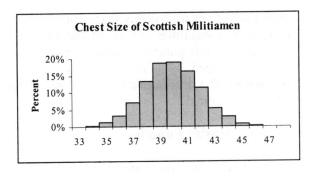

We can see a pattern to the histogram. The pattern is the shape of the normal density curve. The next figure shows the histogram with a normal density curve fitted to it.

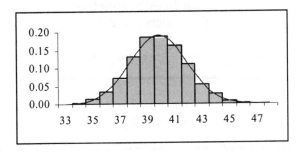

A wide range of natural phenomena follow the symmetric pattern observed here.[4] People often refer to the normal density curve as a "bell-shaped curve." The normal curve for the chest sizes is shown below without the histogram so that its bell shape can be seen more clearly.

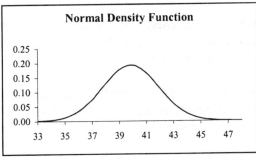

---

[4] We will see why the normal curve is so widely applicable when we discuss the Central Limit Theorem in Section 8.4.4.

Every normal density curve has this shape, and the normal density model is used to find probabilities for all of the natural phenomena whose histograms display this pattern. Random variables whose histograms are well-approximated by a normal density curve are called **approximately normal**. The distribution of chest sizes of Scottish militiamen is approximately normal.

8.4.2   The Normal Density Function

The normal density function has two parameters, μ and σ. The function is difficult to integrate, and we will not find normal probabilities by integration in closed form.

Normal Density Function
Parameters μ and σ

$$f(x) = \frac{1}{\sqrt{2\pi}\sigma}e^{-\frac{(x-\mu)^2}{2\sigma^2}}, \quad \text{for } -\infty < x < \infty \qquad (8.18)$$

It can be shown that $\mu = E(X)$ and $\sigma^2 = V(X)$. (Derivations of $E(X)$ and $V(X)$ will be given in Section 9.2.3.)

Normal Distribution Mean and Variance
Parameters μ and σ

$$E(X) = \mu \qquad (8.19a)$$
$$V(X) = \sigma^2 \qquad (8.19b)$$

Example 8.17   The chest sizes of Scottish militiamen in 1817 were approximately normal with $\mu = 39.85$ and $\sigma = 2.07$. The density function is graphed in the preceding figure.   □

Example 8.18   The SAT aptitude examinations in English and Mathematics were originally designed so that scores would be approximately normal with $\mu = 500$ and $\sigma = 100$.   □

Note that in each of the previous examples we gave the value of the standard deviation σ rather than the variance σ^2. This is the usual practice when dealing with the normal distribution.

8.4.3 Calculation of Normal Probabilities; The Standard Normal

Suppose we are looking at a national examination whose scores X are approximately normal with $\mu = 500$ and $\sigma = 100$. If we wish to find the probability that a score falls between 600 and 750, we must evaluate a difficult integral.

$$P(600 \leq X \leq 750) = \int_{600}^{750} \frac{1}{\sqrt{2\pi} \cdot 100} e^{-\frac{(x-500)^2}{20,000}} \, dx$$

This cannot be done in closed form using the standard techniques of calculus, but it can be approximated using numerical methods. We did this using the **fnInt** operation on the TI-83 calculator, and found that the answer was approximately .152446.

We will discuss use of technology in more detail at the end of this section. Until recently, numerical integration was not readily available to most people, so another way of finding normal probabilities involving tables of areas for a standard normal distribution was developed. It is still the most common way of finding normal probabilities. In the rest of this section we will cover this method, and the basic properties of normal distributions which are behind it, in a series of steps. We begin with an important property of normal distributions which is stated without a complete proof.

Step 1: Linear transformation of normal random variables. Let X be a normal random variable with mean μ and standard deviation σ. Then the transformed random variable $Y = aX + b$ is also normal, with mean $a\mu + b$ and standard deviation $|a|\sigma$.

The crucial statement which is *not* proved here is the assertion that Y is also normal. This will be proved using moment generating functions in Section 9.2.3. We can easily derive the mean and variance of Y.

$$E(aX + b) = a \cdot E(X) + b = a\mu + b$$

$$V(aX + b) = a^2 \cdot V(X) = a^2\sigma^2$$

$$\sigma_Y = \sqrt{a^2\sigma^2} = |a|\sigma$$

Step 2: Transformation to a standard normal. Using the linear transformation property of normal random variables, we can transform any normal random variable X with mean μ and standard deviation σ into a **standard normal** random variable Z with mean 0 and standard deviation 1. The linear transformation that is used to do this is

$$Z = \frac{X - \mu}{\sigma} = \frac{1}{\sigma}X - \frac{\mu}{\sigma}. \qquad (8.20)$$

Note that this is the transformation used to define the z-score in Section 4.4.4. The linear transformation property tells us that Z is normal, with

$$E(Z) = \frac{1}{\sigma}E(X) - \frac{\mu}{\sigma} = 0$$

and

$$\sigma_Z = \frac{1}{\sigma}\sigma = 1.$$

The standard normal random variable Z has a density function which is somewhat simpler in appearance. This density function still requires numerical integration, but it will be the only density function we need to integrate to find normal probabilities.

Standard Normal Density Function

Parameters $\mu = 0$ and $\sigma^2 = \sigma = 1$

$$f(z) = \frac{1}{\sqrt{2\pi}}e^{-\frac{z^2}{2}}, \text{ for } -\infty < z < \infty \qquad (8.21)$$

The density function for the distribution of Z is shown in the next figure.

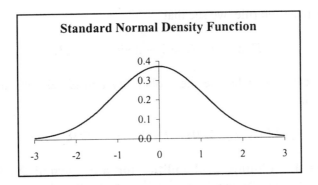

Step 3: Using z-tables. Tables of areas under the density curve for the distribution of Z have been constructed for use in probability calculations. In Appendix A, we have provided a table of values of the cumulative distribution function for Z, $F_Z(z) = P(Z \leq z)$. The left hand column of the table gives the value of z to one decimal place and the upper row gives the second decimal place for z. The areas $F_Z(z)$ are found in the body of the table. Below we have reproduced a small part of the table and highlighted the key points for finding the value $F_Z(1.28) = .8997$.

z	Second Decimal Place in z									
	0.00	0.01	0.02	0.03	0.04	0.05	0.06	0.07	0.08	0.09
0.0	0.5000	0.5040	0.5080	0.5120	0.5160	0.5199	0.5239	0.5279	0.5319	0.5359
0.1	0.5398	0.5438	0.5478	0.5517	0.5557	0.5596	0.5636	0.5675	0.5714	0.5753
0.2	0.5793	0.5832	0.5871	0.5910	0.5948	0.5987	0.6026	0.6064	0.6103	0.6141
0.3	0.6179	0.6217	06255	0.6293	0.6331	0.6368	0.6406	0.6443	0.6480	0.6517
0.4	0.6554	0.6591	0.6628	0.6664	0.6700	0.6736	0.6772	0.6808	0.6844	0.6879
0.5	0.6915	0.6950	0.6985	0.7019	0.7054	0.7088	0.7123	0.7157	0.7190	0.7224
0.6	0.7257	0.7291	0.7324	0.7357	0.7389	0.7422	0.7454	0.7486	0.7517	0.7549
0.7	0.7580	0.7611	0.7642	0.7673	0.7704	0.7734	0.7764	0.7794	0.7823	0.7852
0.8	0.7881	0.7910	0.7939	0.7967	0.7995	0.8023	0.8051	0.8078	0.8106	0.8133
0.9	0.8159	0.8186	0.8212	0.8238	0.8264	0.8289	0.8315	0.8340	0.8365	0.8389
1.0	0.8413	0.8438	0.8461	0.8485	0.8508	0.8531	0.8554	0.8577	0.8599	0.8621
1.1	0.8643	0.8665	0.8686	0.8708	0.8729	0.8749	0.8770	0.8790	0.8810	0.8830
1.2	0.8849	0.8869	0.8888	0.8907	0.8925	0.8944	0.8962	0.8980	0.8997	0.9015
1.3	0.9032	0.9049	0.9066	0.9082	0.9099	0.9115	0.9131	0.9147	0.9162	0.9177
1.4	0.9192	0.9207	0.9222	0.9236	0.9251	0.9265	0.9279	0.9292	0.9306	0.9319

The table tells us that

$$P(Z \leq 1.28) = F_Z(1.28) = .8997.$$

Using the negation rule, we see that

$$P(Z > 1.28) = 1 - .8997 = .1003.$$

We can also calculate the probability that Z falls in an interval. For example,

$$P(1 \leq Z \leq 2.5) = F_Z(2.50) - F_Z(1.00) = .9938 - .8413 = .1525.$$

Step 4: Finding probabilities for any normal X. Once we know how to find probabilities for Z, we can use the transformation given by Equation (8.20) to find probabilities for any normal random variable X with mean μ and standard deviation σ, using the identity

$$P(x_1 \leq X \leq x_2) = P\left(\frac{x_1 - \mu}{\sigma} \leq \frac{X - \mu}{\sigma} \leq \frac{x_2 - \mu}{\sigma}\right) = P(z_1 \leq Z \leq z_2),$$

where $z_1 = \frac{x_1 - \mu}{\sigma}$ and $z_2 = \frac{x_2 - \mu}{\sigma}$.

Example 8.19 The national examination scores X in Example 8.18 were normally distributed with $\mu = 500$ and $\sigma = 100$. Then the probability of a score in the interval $[600, 750]$ is

$$P(600 \leq X \leq 750) = P\left(\frac{600 - 500}{100} \leq \frac{X - 500}{100} \leq \frac{750 - 500}{100}\right)$$

$$= P(1 \leq Z \leq 2.5)$$

$$= F_Z(2.50) - F_Z(1.00)$$

$$= .9938 - .8413 = .1525.$$

We might also calculate

$$P(X \leq 600) = F_Z(1.00) = .8413,$$

$$P(X \leq 400) = F_Z(-1.00) = .1587,$$

and

$$P(X \geq 750) = 1 - F_Z(2.50) = 1 - .9938 = .0062. \qquad \square$$

The observant reader will note that we previously calculated the probability $P(600 \le X \le 750)$ by numerical integration of the density function and got an answer of .1524, *not* the .1525 found above. Each z-value is rounded to two places and each entry in the table is rounded to four places. This rounding can produce small inaccuracies in the last decimal place of answers found using the tables.

Example 8.20 The chest sizes of Scottish militiamen in 1817 were approximately normally distributed with $\mu = 39.85$ and $\sigma = 2.07$. Find the probability that a randomly selected militiaman had a chest size in the interval $[38, 42]$.

Solution

$$P(38 \le X \le 42) = P\left(\frac{38-39.85}{2.07} \le \frac{X-39.85}{2.07} \le \frac{42-39.85}{2.07}\right)$$

$$= P(-0.89 \le Z \le 1.04)$$

$$= F_Z(1.04) - F_Z(-0.89)$$

$$= .8508 - .1867 = .6641 \qquad \qquad \square$$

Technology Note

Calculation of normal probabilities using Z-tables is not as quick or convenient as direct calculator use. The probability $P(38 \le X \le 42)$ from Example 8.20 can be done in seconds on the TI-83, which has a special function for normal probabilities. The function, **normalcdf**, is found in the DISTR menu. Entering

normalcdf(38, 42, 39.85, 2.07)

will give the answer .6648 to 4 places. Note that this answer is not identical with the less-accurate answer obtained from table use. If we wish an independent check on this answer, we could use the TI-92 to do the integral

$$P(38 \le X \le 42) = \int_{38}^{42} \frac{1}{\sqrt{2\pi} \cdot 2.07} e^{-\frac{(x-39.85)^2}{2(2.07^2)}} \, dx.$$

The answer is .6648 to four places. The calculator is using numerical methods to approximate the probability to a higher degree of accuracy than is possible using the tables.

Microsoft® EXCEL has a NORMDIST() function which will calculate values of either the density function $f(x)$ or the cumulative distribution function $F(x)$. Using EXCEL,

$$P(38 \leq X \leq 42) = F(42) - F(38) = .8505 - .1857 = .6648.$$

Although modern technology is quicker and more accurate than use of z-tables, we will continue to find normal probabilities using the table method in this text. The old method is so widely used that it must be learned for use in standardized examinations which do not allow powerful calculators, and for use in other probability and statistics courses.

---

z-scores are useful for purposes other than table calculation. In Chapter 4 we observed that a z-value gives a distance from the mean in standard deviation units. Thus for the national examination with $\mu = 500$ and $\sigma = 100$, a student with an exam score of $x = 750$ and a transformed value of $z = 2.5$ can be described as being "2.5 standard deviations above the mean." This is a useful type of description.

8.4.4   Sums of Independent, Identically Distributed, Random Variables

Sums of random variables will be fully covered in Chapter 11. A brief discussion here may help the reader to have a greater appreciation of the usefulness of the normal distribution. We will use the loss severity random variable X of Examples 7.2, 7.10 and 7.15 to illustrate the need for adding random variables. The random variable X represented the loss *on a single insurance policy*. It was not normally distributed. We found that

$$E(X) = \frac{1000}{3} \text{ and } V(X) = \frac{500,000}{9}.$$

We also found probabilities for X. However, this information applies only to a single policy. The company selling insurance has more than one policy, and must look at its total business. Suppose that the company has 1000 policies. The company is willing to assume that all of the policies are independent, and that each is governed by the same (non-normal) distribution given in Example 7.2. Then the company is really responsible for 1000 random variables, X_1, X_2, ..., X_{1000}. The total claim loss S for the company is the sum of the losses on all the individual policies.

$$S = X_1 + X_2 + \cdots + X_{1000}$$

There is a key theorem, called the **Central Limit Theorem**, which shows that this important sum is approximately normal, even though the individual policies X_i are not.

Central Limit Theorem Let X_1, X_2, ..., X_n be independent random variables, all of which have the same probability distribution and thus the same mean μ and variance σ^2. If n is large[5], the sum

$$S = X_1 + X_2 + \cdots + X_n$$

will be approximately normal with mean $n\mu$ and variance $n\sigma^2$.

This theorem shows that the total loss $S = X_1 + X_2 + \cdots + X_{1000}$ will be approximately normal with mean and variance equal to 1000 times the original mean and variance.

$$E(S) = 1000 \cdot \frac{1000}{3} \qquad V(S) = 1000 \cdot \frac{500,000}{9}$$

This means that even though the original single claim distribution is *not* normal, the normal distribution probability methods can be used to find probabilities for the total claim loss of the company. Suppose the company wishes to find the probability that total claims S were less that $350,000. We know that S is approximately normal, and the calculations for $E(S)$ and $V(S)$ show that

$$\mu_S = 333,333.33 \text{ and } \sigma_S = 7453.56.$$

---

[5] How large n must be depends on how close the original distribution is to the normal. Some elementary statistics books define $n \geq 30$ as "large", but this will not always be the case.

Then we can use Z-tables to find

$$P(S \leq 350,000 = P\left(\frac{S - 333,333.33}{7453.56}\right) \leq \frac{350,000 - 333,333.33}{7453.56}$$
$$= P(Z \leq 2.24) = F_Z(2.24) = .9875.$$

This shows the company that it is not likely to need more than $350,000 to pay claims, which is helpful in planning. In general, the normal distribution is quite valuable because it applies in so many situations where independent and identical components are being added.

The Central Limit Theorem enables us to understand why so many random variables are approximately normally distributed. This occurs because many useful random variables are themselves sums of other independent random variables.

8.4.5   Percentiles of the Normal Distribution

The percentiles of the standard normal can be determined from the tables. For example,

$$P(Z \leq 1.96) = .975$$

Thus the 97.5 percentile of the Z distribution is 1.96.

The 90th, 95th and 99th percentiles are often asked for in problems. They are listed for the standard normal distribution below.

Z	0.842	1.036	1.282	1.645	1.960	2.326	2.576
$P(Z < z)$	0.800	0.850	0.900	0.950	0.975	0.990	0.995

If X is a normal random variable with mean μ and standard deviation σ, then we can easily find x_p, the $100p^{th}$ percentile of X, using the $100p^{th}$ percentile of Z and the basic relationship of X and Z.

$$z_p = \frac{x_p - \mu}{\sigma} \quad \rightarrow \quad x_p = \mu + z_p \sigma.$$

For example, if X is a standard test score random variable with mean $\mu = 500$ and standard deviation $\sigma = 100$, then the 99th percentile of X is

$$x_{.99} = \mu + z_{.99}\sigma = 500 + 2.326(100) = 732.6.$$

8.4.6 The Continuity Correction

When the normal model is used to approximate a discrete distribution (such as integer test scores), you might be asked to apply the **continuity correction**. This is covered in detail in basic statistics courses.[2]

If you are finding $P(a \leq X \leq b)$ for a normal random variable X, the continuity correction merely decreases the lower limit by 0.5 and raises the upper limit by 0.5. Suppose, for example, that for the test score random variable in example 8.20 you wanted to find the probability that a score was in the range from 600 to 700. Without the continuity correction you would calculate:

$$P(500 \leq X \leq 700) = P\left(\frac{500-500}{100} \leq Z \leq \frac{700-500}{100}\right)$$
$$= P(0 \leq Z \leq 2) = .9772 - .5 = .4772$$

With the continuity correction you would calculate

$$P(499.5 \leq X \leq 700.5) = P\left(\frac{499.5-500}{100} \leq Z \leq \frac{700.5-500}{100}\right)$$
$$= P(-.005 \leq Z \leq 2.005)$$

Your tables for Z do not go to three places. If you rounded to two places you would get

$$P(-.01 \leq Z \leq 2.01) = .9778 - .4960 = .4818$$

In this example the use of the continuity correction would make no difference in your final answer if exam choices are rounded to two places –each method would give you .48. You should use the continuity correction if you are instructed to in an exam question or if σ is small enough that the change of $.5/\sigma$ would change the second place in your z-score.

---

[2] You can review the continuity correction in introductory texts such as *Introductory Statistics*, (Seventh edition) by Neil Weiss, Pearson Addison-Wesley 2005.

8.5   The Lognormal Distribution

8.5.1   Applications of the Lognormal Distribution

Although the normal distribution is very useful, it does not fit every situation. The normal distribution curve is symmetric, and this is not appropriate for some real phenomena such as insurance claim severity or investment returns. The **lognormal distribution** curve has a shape that is not symmetric and fits the last two phenomena fairly well. The next figure shows the lognormal curve for a claim severity problem which will be examined in Example 8.21.

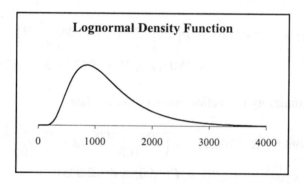

This curve gives the highest probability to claims in a range around $x = 1000$, but does give a non-zero probability to much higher claim amounts.

The use of the lognormal distribution as a model for claim severity in insurance is discussed by Hossack et al. [6]. The reader interested in using the lognormal to model investment returns should see page 187 of Bodie et al. [1], or page 281 of Hull [7].

8.5.2   Defining the Lognormal Distribution

A random variable is called lognormal if its natural logarithm is normally distributed. This is said in a slightly different way in the usual definition of the lognormal.

Definition 8.3   A random variable Y is lognormal if $Y = e^X$ for some normal random variable X with mean μ and standard deviation σ.

Example 8.21 Let X be a normal random variable with $\mu = 7$ and $\sigma = 0.5$. $Y = e^X$ is the lognormal random variable whose density curve is shown in the last figure. The shape of the curve makes it a reasonable model for some insurance claim analyses. □

The density function of a lognormal distribution is given below.

Density Function for Lognormal $Y = e^X$
X normal with mean μ and standard deviation σ

$$f(y) = \frac{1}{\sigma y \sqrt{2\pi}} e^{-\frac{1}{2}\left(\frac{\ln y - \mu}{\sigma}\right)^2}, \text{ for } y \geq 0 \qquad (8.22)$$

This function is difficult to work with, but we will not need it. We will show how to find lognormal probabilities using normal probabilities in Section 8.5.3.

Note that the parameters μ and σ represent the mean and standard deviation of the normal random variable X which appears in the exponent. The mean and variance of the actual lognormal distribution Y are given below.

Mean and Variance for Lognormal $Y = e^X$
X normal with mean μ and standard deviation σ

$$E(Y) = e^{\mu + \frac{\sigma^2}{2}} \qquad (8.23a)$$

$$V(Y) = e^{2\mu + \sigma^2}(e^{\sigma^2} - 1) \qquad (8.23b)$$

Example 8.22 Let X be a normal random variable with $\mu = 7$ and $\sigma = 0.5$, and let $Y = e^X$ as in the Example 8.21.

$$E(Y) = e^{7 + \frac{0.5^2}{2}} \approx 1242.65$$

$$V(Y) = e^{2(7) + 0.5^2}(e^{0.5^2} - 1) \approx 438{,}584.80$$

If we think of Y as a model for insurance claim amounts, the mean claim amount is \$1,242.65. □

8.5.3 Calculating Probabilities for a Lognormal Random Variable

We do not need to integrate the density function for the lognormal random variable Y. The cumulative distribution function can be found directly from the cumulative distribution for the normally distributed exponent X.

$$F_Y(c) = P(Y \le c) = P(e^X \le c) = P(X \le \ln c) = F_X(\ln c)$$

Example 8.23 Suppose the random variable Y of Examples 8.21 and 8.22 is used as a model for claim amounts. We wish to find the probability of the occurrence of a claim greater than $1300. Since X is normal with $\mu = 7$ and $\sigma = 0.5$, we can use Z-tables. The probability of a claim less than or equal to 1300 is

$$P(Y \le 1300) = P(e^X \le 1300)$$

$$= P(X \le \ln 1300)$$

$$= P\left(Z \le \frac{\ln 1300 - 7}{.50}\right) = F_Z(.34) = .6331.$$

The probability of a claim greater than 1300 is

$$1 - P(Y \le 1300) = 1 - .6331 = .3669. \qquad \square$$

Technology Note

Microsoft® EXCEL has a function LOGNORMDIST() which calculates values of the cumulative distribution function for a given lognormal. For the preceding example, EXCEL gives the answers

$$P(Y \le 1300) = .6331617 \text{ and } P(Y > 1300) = .3668383.$$

Note the difference from the Z-table answer in the fourth decimal place. Recall that EXCEL will give more accurate normal probabilities than the Z-table method. (The TI-83 gives the same answer as EXCEL when used to calculate the $P(X \le \ln 1300)$ for the normal X with $\mu = 7$ and $\sigma = 0.5$.)

8.5.4 The Lognormal Distribution for a Stock Price

The value of a single stock at some future point in time is a random variable. The lognormal distribution gives a reasonable probability model for this random variable. This is due to the fact that the exponential function is used to model continuous growth.

Continuous Growth Model

Value of asset at time t if growth is continuous at rate r

$$A(t) = A(0) \cdot e^{rt} \qquad (8.24)$$

Example 8.24 A stock was purchased for $A(0) = 100$. Its value grows at a continuous rate of 10% per year. What is its value in (a) 6 months; (b) one year?

Solution

(a) $A(.5) = 100e^{.10(.5)} \approx 105.13$

(b) $A(1) = 100e^{.10(1)} \approx 110.52$ □

In the last example, the stock is known to have grown at a given rate of 10% over a time period in the past. When we look to the future, the rate of growth X is a random variable. If we assume that X is normally distributed, then the future value $Y = 100 \cdot e^X$ is a multiple of a lognormal random variable.

Example 8.25 A stock was purchased for $A(0) = 100$. Its value will grow at a continuous rate X which is normal with mean $\mu = .10$ and standard deviation $\sigma = .03$. Then the value of the stock in one year is the random variable $Y = 100e^X$, where e^X is lognormal. □

The use of the lognormal distribution for a stock price is discussed in more detail by Hull [7][6].

---

[6] See page 281.

8.6   The Pareto Distribution

8.6.1   Application of the Pareto Distribution

In Section 8.5 the lognormal distribution was used to model the amounts of insurance claims. The **Pareto distribution** can also be used to model certain insurance loss amounts. The next figure shows the graph of a Pareto density function for loss amounts measured in hundreds of dollars (i.e., a claim of $300 is represented by $x = 3$).

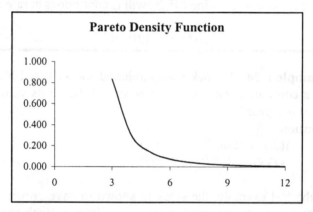

Note that the distribution starts at $x = 3$. This insurance policy has a **deductible** of $300. The insurance company pays the loss amount minus $300. Thus claims for $300 or less are not filed and the only losses of interest are those for more than $300.

8.6.2   The Density Function of the Pareto Random Variable

The Pareto distribution has a number of different equivalent formulations. The one we have chosen involves two constants, α and β.

Pareto Density Function
Constants α and β

$$f(x) = \frac{\alpha}{\beta}\left(\frac{\beta}{x}\right)^{\alpha+1}, \quad \alpha > 2, \ x \geq \beta > 0 \qquad (8.25)^7$$

---

[7] The Pareto density function can be defined for $\alpha > 0$, but the restriction that $\alpha > 2$ guarantees the existence of the mean and variance.

Example 8.26 The Pareto density in the previous figure has $\alpha = 2.5$ and $\beta = 3$. The density curve is

$$f(x) = \tfrac{2.5}{3}\left(\tfrac{3}{x}\right)^{3.5}, \quad \text{for } x \geq 3.$$ □

Note that the value of β must be set in advance to define the domain of the density function. Once β is set, the value of α can vary. The Pareto distribution shown here is often referred to as a single parameter Pareto distribution with parameter α. There is a different Pareto distribution called the two parameter Pareto distribution. We will not cover the two parameter distribution in this text, but it is useful to know that the term "Pareto distribution" can refer to different things.

8.6.3 The Cumulative Distribution Function; Evaluating Probabilities

In dealing with the normal and lognormal distributions we had density functions which were difficult to integrate in closed form, and numerical integration was used for evaluation of $F(x)$. Since the Pareto distribution has a density which is a power function, $F(x)$ can be easily found. The details are left for the reader in Exercise 8-42.

Pareto Cumulative Distribution Function
Parameters α and β

$$F(x) = 1 - \left(\tfrac{\beta}{x}\right)^{\alpha}, \quad \alpha > 2, x \geq \beta > 0 \qquad (8.26)$$

Once $F(x)$ is known, it can be used to find probabilities for a Pareto random variable. There is no need for further integration.

Example 8.27 The Pareto random variable in Example 8.26 had $\alpha = 2.5$ and $\beta = 3$. The cumulative distribution function is

$$F(x) = 1 - \left(\tfrac{3}{x}\right)^{2.5}, \quad \text{for } x \geq 3.$$

If the random variable X represents a loss amount, find the probability that a loss is (a) between 400 and 600; (b) greater than 1000.

Solution

(a) $P(4 \leq X \leq 6) = F(6) - F(4) = \left(\tfrac{3}{4}\right)^{2.5} - \left(\tfrac{3}{6}\right)^{2.5} \approx .3104$

(b) $P(X > 10) = S(10) = 1 - F(10) = \left(\tfrac{3}{10}\right)^{2.5} \approx .0493$ □

8.6.4   The Mean and Variance of the Pareto Distribution

The mean and variance of the Pareto distribution can be obtained by straightforward integration of power functions. This is left for the exercises.

Pareto Distribution Mean and Variance
Parameters α and β

$$E(X) = \frac{\alpha\beta}{\alpha - 1} \qquad (8.27a)$$

$$V(X) = \frac{\alpha\beta^2}{\alpha-2} - \left(\frac{\alpha\beta}{\alpha-1}\right)^2 \qquad (8.27b)$$

Example 8.28 The Pareto random variable in Example 8.26 had $\alpha = 2.5$ and $\beta = 3$. The mean and variance are

$$E(X) = \frac{2.5(3)}{2.5-1} = 5$$

and

$$V(X) = \frac{2.5(3)^2}{2.5-2} - \left(\frac{2.5(3)}{2.5-1}\right)^2 = 20. \qquad \square$$

Note that if we look at X as a loss amount in hundreds of dollars, Example 8.28 says that the expected loss is \$500. However, we have interpreted the insurance modeled as insurance for the loss less a deductible of \$300. The random variable for the amount paid on a single claim is $X - 3$. Thus the expected amount of a single claim is

$$E(X - 3) = E(X) - 3 = 2.$$

8.6.5   The Failure Rate of a Pareto Random Variable

In Equation (8.14) we defined the failure (hazard) rate of a random variable to be

$$\lambda(t) = \frac{f(t)}{1 - F(t)}.$$

The reader may wonder why we did not calculate the failure rates of the gamma, normal and lognormal distributions. The answer is that those calculations do not provide a simple answer in closed form. The Pareto distribution, however, does have a failure rate that is easy to find.

$$\lambda(x) = \frac{\frac{\alpha}{\beta}\left(\frac{\beta}{x}\right)^{\alpha+1}}{\left(\frac{\beta}{x}\right)^{\alpha}} = \frac{\alpha}{x}$$

This failure rate does not make sense if x represents the age of a machine part or a human being, since it decreases with age. Unfortunately, humans and their cars tend to fail at higher rates as the age x increases.

Although the Pareto model may not be appropriate for failure time applications, it is used to model other phenomena such as claim amounts. The decreasing failure rate causes the Pareto density curve to give higher probabilities for large values of x than you might expect. For example, despite the fact that the density graph for the claim distribution in this section appears to be approaching zero when $x = 12$, the probability $P(X \geq 12)$ is .031. The section of the density graph to the right of $x = 12$ is called the **tail** of the distribution. The Pareto distribution is referred to as **heavy-tailed**[8].

8.7 The Weibull Distribution

8.7.1 Application of the Weibull Distribution

Researchers who study units that fail or die often like to think in terms of the failure rate. They might decide to use an exponential distribution model if they believe the failure rate is constant. If they believe that the failure rate increases with time or age, then the **Weibull distribution** can provide a useful model. We will show that the failure rate of a Weibull distribution is of the form $\lambda(x) = \alpha\beta x^{\alpha-1}$. When $\alpha > 1$ and $\beta > 0$, this failure rate increases with x and older units really do have a higher rate of failure.

8.7.2 The Density Function of the Weibull Distribution

This density function has two parameters, α and β. It looks complicated, but it is easy to integrate and has a simple failure rate.

---

[8] See [8] Klugman et al., Second Edition, page 48 for a discussion of this.

Weibull Density Function
Parameters $\alpha > 0$ and $\beta > 0$

$$f(x) = \alpha\beta x^{\alpha-1}e^{-\beta x^{\alpha}}, \text{ for } x \geq 0 \qquad (8.28)$$

Example 8.29 When $\alpha = 2$ and $\beta = 2.5$, the density function is

$$f(x) = 5x \cdot e^{-2.5x^2}, \text{ for } x \geq 0.$$

It is graphed in the next figure.

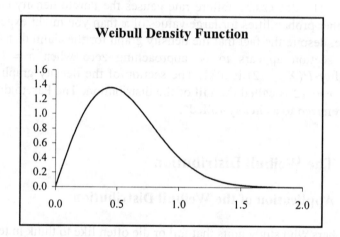

The reader should note that if $\alpha = 1$, the density function becomes the exponential density $\beta e^{-\beta x}$. Thus the exponential distribution is a special case of the Weibull distribution.   □

8.7.3   The Cumulative Distribution Function and Probability Calculations

The Weibull density function can be integrated by substitution since $\alpha x^{\alpha-1}$ is the derivative of x^{α}. Thus the cumulative distribution function can be found in closed form. (The reader can check the $F(x)$ given below without integration by showing that $F'(x) = f(x)$.)

> **Weibull Cumulative Distribution Function**
> Parameters $\alpha > 0$ and $\beta > 0$
>
> $$F(x) = 1 - e^{-\beta x^{\alpha}}, \text{ for } x \geq 0 \qquad (8.29)$$

For the density function in Example 8.29,

$$F(x) = 1 - e^{-2.5x^2}, \text{ for } x \geq 0.$$

Once we have $F(x)$, we can use it to find probabilities as we did with the Pareto distribution.

Example 8.30 Suppose the Weibull random variable X with $\alpha = 2$ and $\beta = 2.5$ represents the lifetime in years of a machine part. Find the probability that (a) the part fails during the first 6 months; (b) the part lasts longer than one year.

Solution

(a) Convert 6 months to 0.5 years.
$$P(X \leq .5) = F(.5) = 1 - e^{-2.5(.5^2)} \approx .465$$

(b) $P(X > 1) = S(1) = 1 - F(1) = e^{-2.5(1^2)} \approx .082$ □

8.7.4 The Mean and Variance of the Weibull Distribution

The mean and variance of the Weibull distribution are calculated using values of the gamma function $\Gamma(x)$, which was defined in Equation (8.8) of Section 8.2.1. We will not give derivations here. The reader will be asked to derive $E(X)$ using Equation (8.10) in Exercise 8-49.

> **Weibull Distribution Mean and Variance**
> Parameters $\alpha > 0$ and $\beta > 0$
>
> $$E(X) = \frac{\Gamma(1 + \frac{1}{\alpha})}{\beta^{\frac{1}{\alpha}}} \qquad (8.30a)$$
>
> $$V(X) = \frac{1}{\beta^{\frac{2}{\alpha}}}\left[\Gamma\left(1+\frac{2}{\alpha}\right) - \Gamma\left(1+\frac{1}{\alpha}\right)^2\right] \qquad (8.30b)$$

The reader may recall that when n is a non-negative integer, then $\Gamma(n) = (n-1)!$. In cases where the above gamma functions are applied to non-integral arguments, calculation of the mean and variance may require some work. However, the calculations can be done using numerical integration on modern calculators. In the following example we will be able to avoid this by using the known gamma function value

$$\Gamma\left(\tfrac{3}{2}\right) = \frac{\sqrt{\pi}}{2}.$$

Example 8.31 We return to the Weibull random variable X with $\alpha = 2$ and $\beta = 2.5$. The mean and variance of X are

$$E(X) = \frac{\Gamma\left(1+\tfrac{1}{2}\right)}{2.5^{\frac{1}{2}}} = \frac{\left(\frac{\sqrt{\pi}}{2}\right)}{2.5^{\frac{1}{2}}} \approx .560499$$

and

$$V(X) = \frac{1}{2.5^{\frac{2}{2}}}\left[\Gamma\left(1+\tfrac{2}{2}\right) - \Gamma\left(1+\tfrac{1}{2}\right)^2\right]$$

$$= \frac{1}{2.5}\left[1 - \left(\frac{\sqrt{\pi}}{2}\right)^2\right] \approx .085841. \qquad \square$$

8.7.5   The Failure Rate of a Weibull Random Variable

The Weibull distribution is of special interest due to its failure rate.

$$\lambda(x) = \frac{f(x)}{1 - F(x)} = \frac{\alpha\beta(x^{\alpha-1}e^{-\beta x^\alpha})}{e^{-\beta x^\alpha}} = \alpha\beta(x^{\alpha-1}) \quad (8.31)$$

As previously mentioned, the Weibull failure rate is proportional to a positive power of x. Thus the Weibull random variable can be used to model phenomena for which the failure rate increases with age.

Example 8.32 For the Weibull random variable X with $\alpha = 2$ and $\beta = 2.5$, the failure rate is $\lambda(x) = 5x$. $\qquad \square$

Technology Note

Probability calculations for the Weibull distribution do not require sophisticated technology, since $F(x)$ has an exponential form that can be easily evaluated. Microsoft® EXCEL does have a WEIBULL() function to calculate values of $f(x)$ and $F(x)$. The reader needs to use this with some care, since a different (equivalent) form of the Weibull is used there, and parameters must be converted from our form to EXCEL form.

Technology can be used to evaluate the mean and variance when the gamma function has arguments that are not integers. We can either evaluate the defining integral for the gamma function to complete the calculation of Equations (8.30a) and (8.30b), or directly evaluate the integrals which define $E(X)$ and $E(X^2)$. The latter approach was used by the authors to check the values found in Example 8.31 using the TI-92 calculator.

8.8 The Beta Distribution

8.8.1 Applications of the Beta Distribution

The **beta distribution** is defined on the interval $[0, 1]$. Thus the beta distribution can be used to model random variables whose outcomes are percents ranging from 0% to 100% and written in decimal form. It can be applied to study the percent of defective units in a manufacturing process, the percent of errors made in data entry, the percent of clients satisfied with their service, and similar variables. Herzog [4] used properties of the beta distribution to study errors in the recording of FHA mortgages.[9]

8.8.2 The Density Function of the Beta Distribution

The beta distribution has two parameters, α and β. The gamma function $\Gamma(x)$ is used in this density function.

Beta Density Function
Parameters $\alpha > 0$ and $\beta > 0$

$$f(x) = \frac{\Gamma(\alpha + \beta)}{\Gamma(\alpha) \cdot \Gamma(\beta)} x^{\alpha-1}(1 - x)^{\beta-1}, \text{ for } 0 < x < 1 \quad (8.32)$$

[9] See Chapter 11.

The density function $f(x)$ may be difficult to integrate if α or β is not an integer, but it will be a polynomial for integral values of α and β.

Example 8.33 A management firm handles investment accounts for a large number of clients. The percent of clients who telephone the firm for information or services in a given month is a beta random variable with $\alpha = 4$ and $\beta = 3$. The density function is given by

$$f(x) = \frac{6!}{2!3!}x^{4-1}(1-x)^{3-1} = 60x^3(1-x)^2$$

$$= 60(x^3 - 2x^4 + x^5), \text{ for } 0 < x < 1.$$

The graph is shown in the next figure.

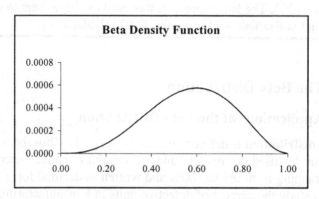

Beta Density Function

8.8.3 The Cumulative Distribution Function and Probability Calculations

When $\alpha - 1$ and $\beta - 1$ are non-negative integers, the cumulative distribution function can be found by integrating a polynomial.

Example 8.34 For the random variable X in Example 8.33, $F(x)$ is found by integration. For $0 < x < 1$,

$$F(x) = \int_0^x f(u)du = \int_0^x 60(u^3 - 2u^4 + u^5)du = 60\left(\frac{x^4}{4} - 2\frac{x^5}{5} + \frac{x^6}{6}\right).$$

The probability that the percent of clients phoning for service in a month is less than 40% is

$$F(.40) = .17920.$$

The probability that the percent of clients phoning for service in a month is greater than 60% is

$$1 - F(.60) = 1 - .54432 = .45568.$$

Calculations are more difficult when α and β are not integers, but technology will help us obtain the desired results. □

8.8.4 A Useful Identity

The area between the density function graph and the x-axis must be 1, so the integral of the density function from 0 to 1 must be 1.

$$\int_0^1 f(x)dx = \int_0^1 \frac{\Gamma(\alpha + \beta)}{\Gamma(\alpha) \cdot \Gamma(\beta)} x^{\alpha-1}(1 - x)^{\beta-1}dx = 1$$

We have stated this result without proof. A proof would be required to show that $f(x)$ is truly a density function. Once we accept the result, we can derive a useful identity.

$$\int_0^1 x^{\alpha-1}(1 - x)^{\beta-1}dx = \frac{\Gamma(\alpha) \cdot \Gamma(\beta)}{\Gamma(\alpha + \beta)} \qquad (8.33)$$

Example 8.35 Let $\alpha = 4$ and $\beta = 3$. Then

$$\int_0^1 x^3(1 - x)^2 dx = \frac{3!2!}{6!} = \frac{1}{60}. \qquad □$$

8.8.5 The Mean and Variance of a Beta Random Variable

The identity in Equation (8.33) can be used to find the mean and variance of a beta random variable X. The reader is asked to find $E(X)$ in Exercise 8-55. The mean and variance are given below.

Beta Distribution Mean and Variance	
Parameters $\alpha > 0$ and $\beta > 0$	
$E(X) = \dfrac{\alpha}{\alpha + \beta}$	(8.34a)
$V(X) = \dfrac{\alpha\beta}{(\alpha + \beta)^2(\alpha + \beta + 1)}$	(8.34b)

Example 8.36 The mean and variance of the percent of clients calling in for service in the preceding examples are

$$E(X) = \frac{4}{4+3} = \frac{4}{7} \approx .5714$$

and

$$V(X) = \frac{4 \cdot 3}{(4+3)^2(4+3+1)} \approx .0306. \qquad \square$$

Technology Note

When either α or β is not an integer, technology can be used to find probabilities for a beta random variable. Microsoft® EXCEL has a function BETADIST() which gives values of $F(x)$ for the beta distribution. Alternatively, the TI-83 or TI-89 can be used to integrate the density function. For example, when $\alpha = 4$ and $\beta = 1.5$, Microsoft EXCEL gives the value $F(.40) = .05189$. The reader will be asked to show in Exercise 8-50 that the density function for $\alpha = 4$ and $\beta = 1.5$ is

$$f(x) = \frac{5 \cdot 7 \cdot 9}{2^5} x^3 \sqrt{1-x}.$$

The TI-83 gives the numerical result

$$\int_0^{.40} f(x)\, dx \approx .05189.$$

8.9   Fitting Theoretical Distributions to Real Problems

The reader may be wondering how a researcher first decides that a particular distribution fits a specific applied problem. Why are claim amounts modeled by Pareto or lognormal distributions? Why do heights follow normal distributions? This kind of model selection is difficult, and it may involve many methods which are not developed in this text. However, there is one simple approach which is commonly used. If a researcher is familiar with the shapes of various distributions, he or she can collect real data on claims and try to match the shapes of the real data histograms with the patterns of known distributions. There are statistical methods for testing **goodness of fit** which the researcher can then use to see if the chosen theoretical distribution fits the data fairly well.

The choice of distribution to apply to a problem is really the subject of another text. In a probability text, we discuss how to use the distribution that applies to a particular problem, not how to find the distribution. The distribution appears somewhat like a rabbit pulled out of a hat. The reader should be aware that a good deal of work may have gone into the selection of the particular rabbit that suddenly appeared.

8.10 Exercises

8.1 The Uniform Distribution

8-1.   Derive Equation (8.5b).

8-2.   If T is the random variable in Example 8.3 whose distribution is uniform on $[0, 100]$, find $E(T)$ and $V(T)$.

8-3.   In a hospital the time of birth of a baby within an hour interval (e.g. between 5:00 and 6:00 in the morning) is uniformly distributed over that hour. What is the probability that a baby is born between 5:15 and 5:25, given that it was born between 5:00 and 6:00?

8-4.   On a large construction site the lengths of pieces of lumber are rounded off to the nearest centimeter. Let X be the rounding error random variable (the actual length of a piece of lumber minus the rounded-off value). Suppose that X is uniformly distributed over $[-.50, .50]$. Find (a) $P(-.10 \le X \le .20)$; (b) $V(X)$.

8-5.   A professor gives a test to a large class. The time limit for the test is 50 minutes, and the first student to finish is done in 35 minutes. The professor assumes that the random variable T for the time it takes a student to finish the test is uniformly distributed over $[35, 50]$.
(a)   Find $E(T)$ and $V(T)$.
(b)   At what time T will 60 percent of the students be finished?

8-6.   Let T be a random variable whose distribution is uniform on $[a,b]$ and $a \leq c \leq d \leq b$. Suppose you are given that the value of T falls in the interval $[c,d]$. Let Y be the conditional random variable for those values of T that are in $[c,d]$. Show that the distribution of Y is uniform over $[c,d]$.

8-7.   Suppose you consider the subset of the population in Example 8.3 who survive to age 40. If T is the random variable for the age at time of death of these survivors, T has a uniform distribution over $[40, 100]$.
  (a)   Find $E(T)$ and $V(T)$.
  (b)   What is $P(T > 57)$ for this group? (Compare this with the result in Example 8.3.)

8-8.   For the population in Example 8.3 where the time until death random variable T is uniform over $[0, 100]$, consider a couple whose ages are 45 and 50. Assume that their deaths are independent events.
  (a)   What is the probability that they both live at least 20 more years?
  (b)   What is the probability that both die in the next 20 years?

8.2   The Exponential Distribution

8-9.   Tests on a certain machine part have determined that the mean time until failure of this part is 500 hours. Assume that the time T until failure of this part is exponentially distributed.
  (a)   What is the probability that one of these parts will fail within 300 hours?
  (b)   What is the probability that one of these parts will still be working after 900 hours?

8-10.   If T has an exponential distribution with parameter λ, what is the median of T?

8-11.   For a certain population the time until death random variable T has an exponential distribution with mean 60 years.
  (a)   What is the probability that a member of this population will die by age 50?
  (b)   What is the probability that a member of this population will live to be 100?

8-12. If T is uniformly distributed over $[a, b]$, what is its failure rate?

8-13. Researchers at a medical facility have discovered a virus whose mean incubation period (time from being infected until symptoms appear) is 38 days. Assume the incubation period has an exponential distribution
   (a) What is the probability that a patient who has just been infected will show symptoms in 25 days?
   (b) What is the probability that a patient who has just been infected will not show symptoms for at least 30 days?

8-14. If T has an exponential distribution, show that $P[T \le E(T)]$ is $F[E(T)] = 1 - e^{-1} \approx .632$.

8-15. A city engineer has studied the frequency of accidents at two busy intersections. He has determined that the time T in months between accidents at each intersection has an exponential distribution. The parameters for these two distributions are 2 and 2.5. Assume that the occurrence of accidents at these intersections is independent.
   (a) What is the probability that there are no accidents at either intersection in the next month?
   (b) What is the probability that there will be no accidents for at least one of these intersections in the next month?

8-16. If T has an exponential distribution with parameter .15, what are the 25th and 75th percentiles for T?

8-17. Using Equation (8.8) and integration by parts, derive the identity $\Gamma(n) = (n - 1) \cdot \Gamma(n - 1)$.

8-18. Let T be a random variable whose distribution is exponential with parameter λ. Show that $P(T \ge a + b | T \ge a) = P(T \ge b)$.

8-19. Consider the population in Exercise 8-11.
   (a) What is the probability that a member of this population who lives to age 40 will die by age 50?
   (b) What is the probability that a person who lives to age 40 will then live to age 100?

8.3   The Gamma Distribution

8-20.   Using Equation (8.10) and the result in Exercise 8.17, show that the mean of the gamma distribution with parameters α and β is α/β.

8-21.   Use Equation (8.10) and Exercise 8.17 to show if X has a gamma distribution with parameters α and β, then $E(X^2) = \alpha(\alpha + 1)/\beta^2$ and hence $V(X) = \alpha/\beta^2$.

8-22.   At a dangerous intersection accidents occur at a rate of 2.5 per month, and the time between accidents is exponentially distributed. Let T be the random variable for the waiting time from the beginning of observation until the third accident. Find $E(T)$ and $V(T)$.

8-23.   Suppose a company hires new people at a rate of 8 per year and the time between new hires is exponentially distributed. What are the mean and variance of the time until the company hires its 12th new employee?

8-24.   A gamma distribution has a mean of 18 and a variance of 27. What are α and β for this distribution?

8-25.   A gamma distribution has parameters $\alpha = 2$ and $\beta = 3$. Find (a) $F(x)$; (b) $P(0 \le X \le 3)$; (c) $P(1 \le X \le 2)$.

8-26.   The length of stay X in a hospital for a certain disease has a gamma distribution with parameters $\alpha = 2$ and $\beta = 1/3$. The cost of treatment in the hospital is $C = 500X + 5X^2$. What is the expected cost of a hospital treatment for this disease?

8.4   The Normal Distribution

8-27.   Using the z-table in Appendix A, find the following probabilities:

    (a) $P(-1.15 \le Z \le 1.56)$ (b) $P(0.15 \le Z \le 2.13)$
    (c) $P(|Z| \le 1.0)$ (d) $P(|Z| \ge 1.65)$.

8-28. Using the z-tables in Appendix A, find the value of z that satisfies the following probabilities:

(a) $P(Z \leq z) = .8238$ (b) $P(Z \leq z) = .0287$
(c) $P(Z \geq z) = .9115$ (d) $P(Z \geq z) = .1660$
(e) $P(|Z| \geq z) = .10$ (f) $P(|Z| \leq z) = .95$

8-29. Let z be the standard normal random variable. If $z > 0$ and
$F_Z(z) = \alpha$, what are $F_Z(-z)$ and $P(-z \leq Z \leq z)$?

8-30. If X is a normal random variable with a mean of 17.1 and a
standard deviation of 3.2, what is $P(14 \leq X \leq 25)$?

8-31. An insurance company has 5000 policies and assumes these
policies are all independent. Each policy is governed by the
same distribution with a mean of \$495 and a variance of
\$30,000. What is the probability that the total claims for the year
will be less than \$2,500,000?

8-32. A company manufactures engines. Specifications require that the
length of a certain rod in this engine be between 7.48 cm. and
7.52 cm. The lengths of the rods produced by their supplier have
a normal distribution with a mean of 7.505 cm. and a standard
deviation of .01 cm.

(a) What is the probability that one of these rods meets these
specifications?
(b) If a worker selects 4 of these rods at random, what is the
probability that at least 3 of them meet these specifications?

8-33. The lifetimes of light bulbs produced by a company are normally
distributed with mean 1500 hours and standard deviation 125
hours.

(a) What is the probability that a bulb will last at least 1400
hours?
(b) If 3 new bulbs are installed at the same time, what is the
probability that they will all still be burning after 1400
hours?

8-34.   If a number is selected at random from the interval $[0, 1]$, its value has a uniform distribution over that interval. Let S be the random variable for the sum of 50 numbers selected at random from $[0, 1]$. What is $P(24 \leq S \leq 27)$?

8-35.   Let X have a normal distribution with mean 25 and unknown standard deviation. If $P(X \leq 29.9) = .9192$, what is σ?

8.5   The Lognormal Distribution

8-36.   If $Y = e^X$, where X is a normal random variable with $\mu = 5$ and $\sigma = .40$, what are $E(Y)$ and $V(Y)$?

8-37.   If Y is lognormal and X, the normally distributed exponent, has parameters $\mu = 5.2$ and $\sigma = .80$, what is $P(100 \leq Y \leq 500)$?

8-38.   The claim severity random variable for an insurance company is lognormal, and the normally distributed exponent has mean 6.8 and standard deviation 0.6. What is the probability that a claim is greater than \$1750?

8-39.   If Y is a lognormal random variable, and the normally distributed exponent has parameters μ and σ, what is the median of Y?

8-40.   For the stock in Example 8.24, whose value in one year is $Y = 100e^X$ where X is normal with parameters $\mu = .10$ and $\sigma = .03$, what is the probability that the value of the stock in one year will be (a) greater than 112.50; (b) less than 107.50.

8-41.   If $Y = e^X$ is a lognormal random variable with $E(Y) = 2,500$ and $V(Y) = 1,000,000$, what are the parameters μ and σ for X?

8.6   The Pareto Distribution

8-42.   Let X be the Pareto random variable with parameters α and β, $\alpha > 2$ and $x \geq \beta > 0$.

(a)   Verify that $F(x) = 1 - (\beta/x)^{\alpha}$.
(b)   Verify that $E(X) = \alpha\beta/(\alpha - 1)$.
(c)   Verify that $E(X^2) = \alpha\beta^2/(\alpha - 2)$, and use this result to obtain $V(X)$.

8-43.   For the Pareto random variable with $\alpha = 3.5$ and $\beta = 4$, find (a) $E(X)$; (b) $V(X)$; (c) the median of X; (d) $P(6 \leq X \leq 12)$.

8-44.   A comprehensive insurance policy on commercial trucks has a deductible of \$500. The random variable for the loss amount (before deductible) on claims filed has a Pareto distribution with a failure rate of $3.5/x$ (x measured in hundreds of dollars). Find (a) the mean loss amount; (b) the expected value of the amount paid on a single claim; and (c) the variance of the amount of a single loss.

8.7   The Weibull Distribution

8-45.   It can be shown (although beyond the scope of this text) that $\Gamma(1/2) = \pi^{1/2}$. Using this and the result of Exercise 8-17, find (a) $\Gamma(3/2)$; (b) $\Gamma(5/2)$; (c) $\Gamma(7/2)$. (Can you see a pattern?)

8-46.   Let X be the Weibull random variable with $\alpha = 3$ and $\beta = 3.5$. Find (a) $P(X \leq 0.4)$; (b) $P(X > 0.8)$.

8-47.   What is the failure rate for the random variable in Exercise 8-46?

8-48.   For the Weibull random variable X with $\alpha = 2$ and $\beta = 3.5$, find (a) $E(X)$; (b) $V(X)$; (c) $P(.25 \leq X \leq .75)$.

8-49.   Using Equation (8.10), verify that the mean of a Weibull distribution is $\Gamma(1 + 1/\alpha)/\beta^{1/\alpha}$. (Hint: Transform the integral using the substitution $u = x^{\alpha}$.)

8.8   The Beta Distribution

8-50.   Find the density function for the beta distribution with $\alpha = 4$ and $\beta = 1.5$. (Hint: Use the results of Exercise 8.17.)

8-51.   Find the value of k so that $f(x) = kx^4(1-x)^2$ for $0 \le x \le 1$ is a beta density function.

8-52.   A meter measuring the volume of a liquid put into a bottle has an accuracy of $\pm$ 1 cm^3. The absolute value of the error has a beta distribution with $\alpha = 3$ and $\beta = 2$. What are the mean and variance for this error?

8-53.   In Exercise 8-52, what is the probability that the error is no more than 0.5cm^3?

8-54.   A company markets a new product and surveys customers on their satisfaction with this product. The fraction of customers who are dissatisfied has a beta distribution with $\alpha = 2$ and $\beta = 4$. What is the probability that no more than 30 percent of the customers are dissatisfied?

8.11   Sample Actuarial Examination Problems

8-55.   Using Equation (8.33), verify that the mean of the beta distribution is $\alpha/(\alpha+\beta)$.

8-56.   The time to failure of a component in an electronic device has an exponential distribution with a median of four hours.

Calculate the probability that the component will work without failing for at least five hours.

8-57.   The waiting time for the first claim from a good driver and the waiting time for the first claim from a bad driver are independent and follow exponential distributions with 6 years and 3 years, respectively.

What is the probability that the first claim from a good driver will be filed within 3 years and the first claim from a bad driver will be filed within 2 years?

8-58.   The lifetime of a printer costing 200 is exponentially distributed with mean 2 years. The manufacturer agrees to pay a full refund to a buyer if the printer fails during the first year following its purchase, and a one-half refund if it fails during the second year.

If the manufacturer sells 100 printers, how much should it expect to pay in refunds?

8-59.   The number of days that elapse between the beginning of a calendar year and the moment a high-risk driver is involved in an accident is exponentially distributed. An insurance company expects that 30% of high-risk drivers will be involved in an accident during the first 50 days of a calendar year.

What portion of high-risk drivers are expected to be involved in an accident during the first 80 days of a calendar year?

8-60.   An insurance policy reimburses dental expense, X, up to a maximum benefit of 250. The probability density function for X is:

$$f(x) = \begin{cases} ce^{-0.004x} & \text{for } x \geq 0 \\ 0 & \text{otherwise} \end{cases}$$

where c is a constant.

Calculate the median benefit for this policy.

8-61.   You are given the following information about N, the annual number of claims for a randomly selected insured:

$$P(N=0) = \frac{1}{2} \qquad P(N=1) = \frac{1}{3} \qquad P(N>1) = \frac{1}{6}$$

Let S denote the total annual claim amount for an insured. When $N = 1$, S is exponentially distributed with mean 5. When $N > 1$, S is exponentially distributed with mean 8.

Determine $P(4 < S < 8)$.

8-62.   An insurance company issues 1250 vision care insurance policies. The number of claims filed by a policyholder under a vision care insurance policy during one year is a Poisson random variable with mean 2. Assume the numbers of claims filed by distinct policyholders are independent of one another.

What is the approximate probability that there is a total of between 2450 and 2600 claims during a one-year period?

8-63.   The total claim amount for a health insurance policy follows a distribution with density function

$$f(x) = \frac{1}{1000} e^{-\frac{x}{1000}} \quad \text{for} \quad x \geq 0.$$

The premium for the policy is set at 100 over the expected total claim amount.

If 100 policies are sold, what is the approximate probability that the insurance company will have claims exceeding the premiums collected?

8-64.   A city has just added 100 new female recruits to its police force. The city will provide a pension to each new hire who remains with the force until retirement. In addition, if the new hire is married at the time of her retirement, a second pension will be provided for her husband. A consulting actuary makes the following assumptions:

(i)   Each new recruit has a 0.4 probability of remaining with the police force until retirement.

(ii) Given that a new recruit reaches retirement with the police force, the probability that she is not married at the time of retirement is 0.25.

(iii) The number of pensions that the city will provide on behalf of each new hire is independent of the number of pensions it will provide on behalf of any other new hire.

Determine the probability that the city will provide at most 90 pensions to the 100 new hires and their husbands.

8-65.   In an analysis of healthcare data, ages have been rounded to the nearest multiple of 5 years. The difference between the true age and the rounded age is assumed to be uniformly distributed on the interval from –2.5 years to 2.5 years. The healthcare data are based on a random sample of 48 people.

What is the approximate probability that the mean of the rounded ages is within 0.25 years of the mean of the true ages?

8-66.   A charity receives 2025 contributions. Contributions are assumed to be independent and identically distributed with mean 3125 and standard deviation 250.

Calculate the approximate 90th percentile for the distribution of the total contributions received.

Chapter 9
Applications for Continuous Random Variables

9.1   Expected Value of a Function of a Random Variable

9.1.1   Calculating $E[g(X)]$

In Section 7.3.2 we gave the integral which is used for the expected value of $g(X)$, where X is a continuous random variable with density function $f(x)$.

$$E[g(X)] = \int_{-\infty}^{\infty} g(x) \cdot f(x)\, dx$$

In this section we will give a number of applications which require calculations of this type.

9.1.2   Expected Value of a Loss or Claim

Example 9.1   The amount of a single loss X for an insurance policy is exponential, with density function

$$f(x) = .002e^{-.002x},$$

for $x \geq 0$. The expected value of a single loss is

$$E(X) = \frac{1}{.002} = 500. \qquad \square$$

Example 9.2 (Insurance with a deductible) Suppose the insurance in Example 9.1 has a deductible of $100 for each loss. Find the expected value of a single claim.

Solution The amount paid for a loss x is given by the function $g(x)$ below.

$$g(x) = \begin{cases} 0 & 0 < x < 100 \\ (x - 100) & 100 \le x \end{cases}$$

The expected amount of a single claim is

$$E[g(X)] = \int_0^\infty g(x) \cdot (.002e^{-.002x}) \, dx$$

$$= \int_{100}^\infty (x - 100)(.002e^{-.002x}) \, dx$$

$$= -e^{-.002x}(x+400)\Big|_{100}^\infty = 500e^{-.20} \approx 409.37. \qquad \square$$

Example 9.3 (Insurance with a deductible and a cap) Suppose the insurance in Example 9.1 has a deductible of $100 per claim and a restriction that the largest amount paid on any claim will be $700. (Payments are **capped** at $700, so that any loss of $800 or larger will receive a payment of $800 − $100 = $700.) Find the expected value of a single claim for this insurance.

Solution The amount paid for a loss x is given by the function $h(x)$ below.

$$h(x) = \begin{cases} 0 & 0 < x < 100 \\ (x - 100) & 100 \le x \le 800 \\ 700 & x > 800 \end{cases}$$

The expected claim amount $E[h(X)]$ is

$$E[h(X)] = \int_0^\infty h(x) \cdot (.002e^{-.002x}) \, dx$$

$$= \int_{100}^{800} (x - 100)(.002e^{-.002x}) \, dx + \int_{800}^\infty 700(.002e^{-.002x}) \, dx$$

$$= -e^{-.002x}(x+400)\Big|_{100}^{800} + 700(-e^{-.002x})\Big|_{800}^\infty$$

$$\approx 167.09 + 141.33 = 308.42. \qquad \square$$

Calculations of the expected value of the amount paid for insurance with a deductible or for an insurance with a cap are very important in actuarial mathematics. Because of this, there is a special notation for each of them.

The expected value of the amount paid on an insurance with loss random variable X and deductible x is written as $E\big[(X-x)_+\big]$. In Example 9.2 we found $E\big[(X-100)_+\big]$.

The expected value of the amount paid on the insurance with loss random variable X and cap x is written as $E\big[(X \wedge x)\big]$.

In the advanced actuarial text *Loss Models: From Data to Decisions*[1] there are formula tables that give simple algebraic formulas for these amount paid expected values for many random variables (including the exponential), thus enabling you to skip the integrations and proceed rapidly to the answer. It is not necessary to master this advanced material at this point, but it is good to know that a very useful simplification is available in many cases.

9.1.3 Expected Utility

In Section 6.1.3 we looked at economic decisions based on expected utility. The next example illustrates the use of expected utility analysis for continuous random variables.

Example 9.4 A person has the utility function $u(w) = \sqrt{w}$, which measures the utility attached to a given level of wealth w. She can choose between two methods of managing her wealth. Under each method, the wealth W is a random variable in units of 1000.

Method 1: W_1 is uniformly distributed on $[9, 11]$. Then the expected value is $E(W_1) = 10$ and the density function is

$$f_1(w) = \tfrac{1}{2}, \text{ for } 9 \le w \le 11.$$

Method 2: W_2 is uniformly distributed on $[5, 15]$. Then the expected value is $E(W_2) = 10$ and the density function is

$$f_2(w) = \tfrac{1}{10}, \text{ for } 5 \le w \le 15.$$

---

[1] See [8]

The two methods have identical expected values, but the investor bases decisions on expected utility. The expected utilities under the two methods are as follows:

Method 1: $E[u(W_1)] = \displaystyle\int_9^{11} \sqrt{w} \cdot \tfrac{1}{2} dw$

$$= \frac{w^{1.5}}{3}\Big|_9^{11} \approx 3.16$$

Method 2: $E[u(W_2)] = \displaystyle\int_5^{15} \sqrt{w} \cdot \tfrac{1}{10} dw$

$$= \frac{w^{1.5}}{15}\Big|_5^{15} \approx 3.13$$

The person here will choose Method 1 because it has higher expected utility. Economists would say that a person with a square root utility function is **risk averse** and will choose W_1 because W_2 is riskier.   □

9.2   Moment Generating Functions for Continuous Random Variables

9.2.1   A Review

The moment generating function and its properties were presented in Section 6.2. The moment generating function of a random variable X was defined by

$$M_X(t) = E(e^{tX}).$$

The moment generating function has a number of useful properties.

(1)   The derivatives of $M_X(t)$ can be used to find the moments of the random variable X.

$$M_X'(0) = E(X), \quad M_X''(0) = E(X^2), \quad \ldots, \quad M_X^{(n)}(0) = E(X^n)$$

(2)   The moment generating function of $aX + b$ can be found easily if the moment generating function of X is known.

$$M_{aX+b}(t) = e^{tb} \cdot M_X(at)$$

(3)   If a random variable X has the moment generating function of a known distribution, then X has that distribution.

All of the above properties were developed for discrete random variables in Chapter 6. All of them also hold for continuous random variables. The only difference for continuous random variables is that the expectation in the definition is now calculated using an integral.

Moment Generating Function

X continuous with density function $f(x)$

$$M_X(t) = E(e^{tX}) = \int_{-\infty}^{\infty} e^{tx} \cdot f(x)\,dx \qquad (9.1)$$

Some continuous random variables have useful moment generating functions which can be written in closed form and easily applied, and others do not. In the following sections, we will give the moment generating functions for the gamma and normal random variables because these can be found and will have useful applications for us. The moment generating function of the uniform distribution will be left as an exercise. The beta and lognormal distributions do not have useful moment generating functions, and the Pareto moment generating function does not exist.

9.2.2   The Gamma Moment Generating Function

The gamma distribution provides a nice example of a distribution which looks complex, but has a simple moment generating function which can be derived in a few lines. To derive it, we will need to use the integral given in Equation (8.10).

$$\int_{0}^{\infty} x^n e^{-ax}\,dx = \frac{\Gamma(n+1)}{a^{n+1}}, \text{ for } a > 0 \text{ and } n > -1$$

This identity is valid if n is not an integer. If n is an integer, then $\Gamma(n+1) = n!$. Using the identity we can find $M_X(t)$ for a gamma random variable X with parameters α and β. We will need to assume that we are only working with values of t for $t < \beta$, so that $\beta - t > 0$.

$$M_X(t) = \int_0^\infty e^{tx} \cdot f(x) \, dx$$

$$= \int_0^\infty e^{tx} \cdot \frac{\beta^\alpha}{\Gamma(\alpha)} x^{\alpha-1} e^{-\beta x} \, dx$$

$$= \frac{\beta^\alpha}{\Gamma(\alpha)} \int_0^\infty x^{\alpha-1} e^{-(\beta-t)x} \, dx$$

$$= \frac{\beta^\alpha}{\Gamma(\alpha)} \left(\frac{\Gamma(\alpha)}{(\beta-t)^\alpha} \right) = \left(\frac{\beta}{\beta-t} \right)^\alpha$$

Moment Generating Function for the Gamma Distribution
Parameters α and β

$$M_X(t) = \left(\frac{\beta}{\beta-t} \right)^\alpha, \text{ for } t < \beta \qquad (9.2)$$

We can now use $M_X(t)$ to find the mean and variance of a gamma distribution. It is convenient to rewrite $M_X(t)$ as a negative power function.

$$M_X(t) = \beta^\alpha (\beta - t)^{-\alpha}$$

$$M_X'(t) = \alpha \beta^\alpha (\beta - t)^{-(\alpha+1)}$$

$$M_X''(t) = \alpha(\alpha+1)\beta^\alpha (\beta - t)^{-(\alpha+2)}$$

$$M_X'(0) = \alpha \beta^\alpha (\beta - 0)^{-(\alpha+1)} = \frac{\alpha}{\beta} = E(X)$$

$$M_X''(0) = \alpha(\alpha+1)\beta^\alpha (\beta - 0)^{-(\alpha+2)} = \frac{\alpha(\alpha+1)}{\beta^2} = E(X^2)$$

$$V(X) = E(X^2) - [E(X)]^2 = \frac{\alpha}{\beta^2}$$

We have now derived the mean and variance of the gamma distribution. Since the exponential distribution is the special case of the gamma with $\alpha = 1$, we have also found the moment generating function for the exponential distribution.

Moment Generating Function for the Exponential Distribution
Parameter β

$$M_X(t) = \frac{\beta}{\beta - t}, \quad \text{for } t < \beta \qquad (9.3)$$

9.2.3 The Normal Moment Generating Function

We will not derive this function, but will use it to derive an important property of the normal distribution.

Moment Generating Function for the Normal Distribution
Parameters μ and σ

$$M_X(t) = e^{\mu t + \frac{\sigma^2 t^2}{2}} \qquad (9.4)$$

We can now use $M_X(t)$ to find $E(X)$.

$$M'_X(t) = e^{\mu t + \frac{\sigma^2 t^2}{2}}(\mu + \sigma^2 t)$$

$$M'_X(0) = \mu$$

The reader is asked in Exercise 9-11 to find $E(X^2)$ and $V(X)$ using the moment generating function.

Suppose X has a normal distribution with mean μ and standard deviation σ, and we need to work with the transformed random variable $Y = aX + b$. Property (2) of the moment generating function enables us to find $M_Y(t)$.

$$M_{aX+b}(t) = e^{tb} \cdot M_X(at) = e^{tb} \cdot e^{\mu at + \frac{\sigma^2 (at)^2}{2}}$$

$$= e^{(a\mu+b)t + \frac{(a\sigma)^2 t^2}{2}}$$

The last expression above is the moment generating function of a normal distribution with mean $(a\mu + b)$ and standard deviation $|a|\sigma$. Thus $Y = aX + b$ must follow that distribution. We have derived the following property of normal random variables. This property was stated without proof in Section 8.4.3.

Linear Transformation of Normal Random Variables

Let X be a normal random variable with mean μ and standard deviation σ. Then $Y = aX + b$ is a normal random variable with mean $(a\mu + b)$ and standard deviation $|a|\sigma$.

The moment generating function will prove very useful in Chapter 11 when we look at sums of random variables.

9.3   The Distribution of $Y = g(X)$

9.3.1   An Example

We have already seen simple methods for finding $E[g(X)]$ and $V[g(x)]$, but the mean and variance alone are not sufficient to enable us to calculate probabilities for $Y = g(X)$. Calculation of probabilities requires knowledge of the distribution of Y. The reasoning necessary to find this distribution has already been used. It is reviewed in the next example.

Example 9.5 The monthly maintenance cost X for a machine is an exponential random variable with parameter $\beta = .01$. Next year costs will be subject to 5% inflation. Thus next year's monthly cost is $Y = 1.05X$. Find (a) $E(Y)$; (b) $P(Y \leq 100)$; (c) the cumulative distribution function $F_Y(y)$.

Solution

(a)   The given information implies that

$$E(X) = \frac{1}{\beta} = 100.$$

Then $E(Y) = 1.05E(X) = 105$. We did not need to know the distribution of Y for this calculation.

(b)   We know that the cumulative distribution function for X is

$$F_X(x) = 1 - e^{-.01x}, \, x \geq 0.$$

Some simple algebra allows us to find the desired probability for Y using the known cumulative distribution for X.

$$P(Y \leq 100) = P(1.05X \leq 100)$$

$$= P\left(X \leq \frac{100}{1.05}\right)$$

$$= F_X\left(\frac{100}{1.05}\right) = 1 - e^{-.01\left(\frac{100}{1.05}\right)} \approx .614$$

(c) We have just found $P(Y \leq 100) = F_Y(100)$. The same logic can be used to find $P(Y \leq y) = F_Y(y)$ for any value of $y \geq 0$.

$$F_Y(y) = P(Y \leq y) = P(1.05X \leq y)$$

$$= P\left(X \leq \frac{y}{1.05}\right)$$

$$= F_X\left(\frac{y}{1.05}\right) = 1 - e^{-.01\left(\frac{y}{1.05}\right)}$$

Note that the set of all possible outcomes for X is the interval $[0, \infty)$. The set of all possible outcomes for $Y = 1.05X$ is the same interval. $\square$

9.3.2 Using $F_X(x)$ to Find $F_Y(y)$ for $Y = g(X)$

The method of Example 9.5 can be used in a wide range of problems.

Example 9.6 Let X be exponential with $\beta = 3$. Find the cumulative distribution function for $Y = \sqrt{X}$.
Solution We know that $F_X(x) = 1 - e^{-3x}$.

$$F_Y(y) = P(Y \leq y) = P(\sqrt{X} \leq y)$$

$$= P(X \leq y^2)$$

$$= F_X(y^2) = 1 - e^{-3y^2}$$

The sample space for Y is the interval $[0, \infty)$. Thus $F_Y(y)$ is defined for $y \geq 0$. Note that $F_Y(y)$ is the cumulative distribution function for a Weibull random variable with $\alpha = 2$ and $\beta = 3$. $\square$

Example 9.7 Let X be exponential with $\beta = 3$. Find the cumulative distribution function for $Y = 1 - X$.

Solution We know that $S_X(x) = e^{-3x}$.

$$F_Y(y) = P(Y \le y) = P(1 - X \le y)$$

$$= P(1 - y \le X)$$

$$= S_X(1 - y) = e^{-3(1-y)}$$

The set of all possible outcomes for X is the interval $[0, \infty)$. The set of all possible outcomes for $Y = 1 - X$ is the interval $(-\infty, 1]$. *This example shows that the sample space for Y may differ from the sample space for X.* □

Finding $F_Y(y)$ gives us all the information that is needed to calculate probabilities for Y. Thus there is no real need to find the density function $f_Y(y)$. If the density function is required, it can be found by differentiating the cumulative distribution function.

$$f_Y(y) = \frac{d}{dy} F_Y(y)$$

Example 9.8 Let X be exponential with $\beta = 3$. The density function for $Y = 1 - X$ is

$$f_Y(y) = \frac{d}{dy}(e^{-3(1-y)}) = 3e^{-3(1-y)}, \text{ for } y \le 1. □$$

In each of the previous examples the function $g(x)$ was strictly increasing or strictly decreasing on the sample space interval $[0, \infty)$. Careful attention is required if $g(x)$ is not restricted in this manner.

Example 9.9 Let X have a uniform distribution on the interval $[-2, 2]$. Then for $-2 \le a \le b \le 2$,

$$P(a \le X \le b) = \frac{b - a}{4}.$$

Suppose that $Y = X^2$. The sample space for Y is the interval $[0, 4]$. For y in this interval,

$$F_Y(y) = P(Y \leq y) = P(X^2 \leq y)$$

$$= P(|X| \leq \sqrt{y})$$

$$= P(-\sqrt{y} \leq X \leq \sqrt{y})$$

$$= \frac{\sqrt{y} - (-\sqrt{y})}{4} = \frac{\sqrt{y}}{2}. \qquad \square$$

9.3.3 Finding the Density Function for $Y = g(X)$ When $g(x)$ Has an Inverse Function

Examples 9.5 through 9.7 were much simpler than Example 9.9. We will see that this is due to the fact that the function $g(x)$ was either strictly increasing or strictly decreasing on the sample space interval for X in Examples 9.5 through 9.7. For a strictly increasing or decreasing function $g(x)$, we can find an inverse function $h(y)$ defined on the sample space interval for Y. The reader should recall that if $h(y)$ is the inverse function of $g(x)$, then

$$h[g(x)] = x$$

and

$$g[h(y)] = y.$$

The inverse functions for Examples 9.5 through 9.7 are given in the following examples.

Example 9.10 In Example 9.5, $g(x) = 1.05x$, for $x \geq 0$. Then $h(y) = y/1.05$, for $y \geq 0$. $\qquad \square$

Example 9.11 In Example 9.6, $g(x) = \sqrt{x}$, for $x \geq 0$. Then $h(y) = y^2$, for $y \geq 0$. $\qquad \square$

Example 9.12 In Example 9.7, $g(x) = 1 - x$, for $x \geq 0$. Then $h(y) = 1 - y$, for $y \leq 1$. $\qquad \square$

Example 9.9 was more complicated because the function $g(x) = x^2$, for $-2 \leq x \leq 2$, did not have an inverse function. We can see why things are simpler when inverse functions are available if we look at two general cases and repeat the reasoning of our previous examples.

Case 1: $g(x)$ **is strictly increasing on the sample space for** X. Let $h(y)$ be the inverse function of $g(x)$. The function $h(y)$ will also be strictly increasing. In this case, we can find $F_Y(y)$ as follows.

$$F_Y(y) = P(Y \leq y) = P(g(X) \leq y)$$

$$= P[h(g(X)) \leq h(y)]$$

$$= P(X \leq h(y))$$

$$= F_X(h(y))$$

We can now find the density function by differentiating.

$$f_Y(y) = \frac{d}{dy} F_Y(y) = \frac{d}{dy} F_X(h(y)) = F_X'(h(y)) \cdot h'(y) = f_X(h(y)) \cdot h'(y)$$

Case 2: $g(x)$ **is strictly decreasing on the sample space for** X. Let $h(y)$ be the inverse function of $g(x)$. The function $h(y)$ will also be strictly decreasing. In this case, we can find $F_Y(y)$ as follows.

$$F_Y(y) = P(Y \leq y) = P(g(X) \leq y)$$

$$= P[h(g(X)) \geq h(y)]$$

$$= P(X \geq h(y))$$

$$= S_X(h(y))$$

We can now find the density function by differentiating.

$$f_Y(y) = \frac{d}{dy} F_Y(y) = \frac{d}{dy} S_X(h(y))$$

$$= \frac{d}{dy}(1 - F_X(h(y)))$$

$$= -F_X'(h(y)) \cdot h'(y) = -f_X(h(y)) \cdot h'(y)$$

Since $h(y)$ is decreasing, its derivative is negative. Thus the final expression in the preceding derivation is positive.

$$f_X(h(y)) \cdot (-h'(y)) = f_X(h(y)) \cdot |h'(y)|$$

The final expression above also equals $f_Y(y)$ in Case 1, since $h(y)$ is positive in Case 1. We have derived a general expression for $f_Y(y)$ which holds in either case.

Density Function for $Y = g(X)$

Let $g(x)$ be strictly increasing or strictly decreasing on the domain consisting of the sample space. Then

$$f_Y(y) = f_X(h(y)) \cdot |h'(y)|. \qquad (9.5a)$$

Example 9.13 In Example 9.6, $g(x) = \sqrt{x}$, for $x \geq 0$ and $h(y) = y^2$, for $y \geq 0$. The random variable X was exponential with $\beta = 3$ and density function $f_X(x) = 3e^{-3x}$. If $Y = \sqrt{X} = g(X)$, then

$$f_Y(y) = f_X(y^2) \cdot |2y| = 3e^{-3y^2} \cdot 2y, \text{ for } y \geq 0. \qquad \square$$

Example 9.14 In Example 9.7, $g(x) = 1 - x$, for $x \geq 0$ and $h(y) = 1 - y$, for $y \leq 1$. The random variable X was exponential with $\beta = 3$ and density function $f_X(x) = 3e^{-3x}$. If $Y = 1 - X = g(X)$, then

$$f_Y(y) = f_X(1 - y) \cdot |-1| = 3e^{-3(1-y)}, \text{ for } y \leq 1. \qquad \square$$

Some texts use a slightly different notation for this inverse function formula. Since the inverse function gives x as a function of y, we can write $x = h(y)$. Then the derivative of $h(y)$ is written as

$$h'(y) = \frac{dx}{dy}.$$

Using this notation, our rule becomes the following:

Density function for $Y = g(X)$

Let $g(x)$ be strictly increasing or strictly decreasing. Then

$$f_Y(y) = f_X(h(y)) \cdot \left| \frac{dx}{dy} \right|. \qquad (9.5b)$$

---

268   *Chapter 9*

9.4   Simulation of Continuous Distributions

9.4.1   The Inverse Cumulative Distribution Function Method

The **inverse cumulative distribution method** (also known as the inverse transformation method) is the simplest of the many methods available for simulation of continuous random variables. If X is a continuous random variable with cumulative distribution function $F(x)$, a randomly generated value of X can be obtained using the following steps:

(1)   Find the inverse function $F^{-1}(x)$ for $F(x)$.
(2)   Generate a random number u from $[0, 1)$.
(3)   The value $x = F^{-1}(u)$ is a randomly generated value of X.

This procedure requires that we find the inverse function $F^{-1}(x)$, and this may be difficult to do. However the inverse method works simply when the inverse is easy to compute. This is illustrated in the next example.

Example 9.15 Let X have the straight line density function

$$f(x) = \begin{cases} \dfrac{x}{2} & 0 \le x \le 2 \\ 0 & \text{otherwise} \end{cases}.$$

The graph of this straight-line density function is shown in the next figure.

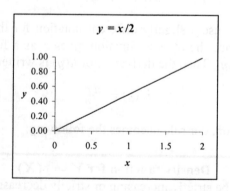

The cumulative distribution function $F(x)$ is given by

$$F(x) = \begin{cases} \frac{x^2}{4} & 0 \le x \le 2 \\ 0 & x < 0 \\ 1 & x > 2 \end{cases}.$$

$F(x)$ is strictly increasing on the interval $[0, 2]$. The inverse function is

$$F^{-1}(u) = 2\sqrt{u}, \text{ for } 0 \le u \le 1.$$

To generate values of X, we generate random numbers u from $[0, 1)$ and calculate $x = F^{-1}(u)$. The next table shows the result of generating 5 random numbers u and transforming them to values of X, $x = F^{-1}(u)$.

Trial	u	$F^{-1}(u)$
1	.15529095	0.7881395
2	.32379337	1.1380569
3	.1860507	0.8626719
4	.41523288	1.2887713
5	.21343523	0.923981

To illustrate how well this simulation method works, we generated 1000 values of X. The next figure gives a bar graph showing the percent of simulated values in subintervals of $[0, 2]$. The bar graph displays the triangular shape of the density function.

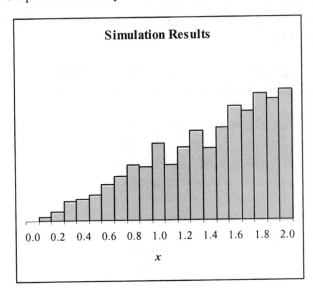

Simulation Results

x

The results on the previous page indicate that the method works fairly well, but does not show why. A look at the graph of $F(x)$ might help give an intuitive understanding of the method.

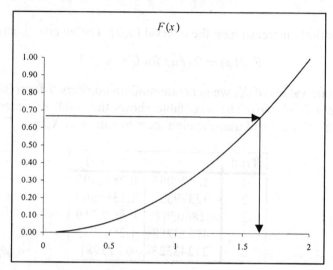

The inverse function takes us from a value selected from $[0, 1)$ (the range of F) back to a value of x in the domain of F. As we pick values at random from $[0, 1)$ on the y-axis above, the inverse procedure will convert them into random values of X on the x-axis. The proof that the procedure works is not given here. It relies on the fact that the transformed random variable $U = F(X)$ is uniform on $[0, 1)$. This is covered in Exercise 9-16.   □

9.4.2   Using the Inverse Transformation Method to Simulate an Exponential Random Variable

To simulate an exponential random variable with parameter μ, it is necessary to find the inverse of the cumulative distribution function $F(x) = 1 - e^{-\mu x}$. This is done by solving the equation $x = F(y)$ for y.

$$x = 1 - e^{-\mu y}$$

$$e^{-\mu y} = 1 - x$$

$$-\mu y = ln(1 - x)$$

$$y = -\frac{ln(1 - x)}{\mu} = F^{-1}(x)$$

In the next table we show the result of transforming 5 random numbers from $[0, 1)$ into values of the exponential random variable X with $\mu = 2$. In this case

$$F^{-1}(u) = -\frac{ln(1-u)}{2}.$$

Trial	u	$F^{-1}(u)$
1	.407381	0.261602
2	.892484	1.115058
3	.297554	0.176593
4	.485448	0.332230
5	.798462	0.800889

The graph below shows the results of 1000 trials in this simulation. The graph shows that the simulation produced values whose distribution approximated the shape of an exponential density function.

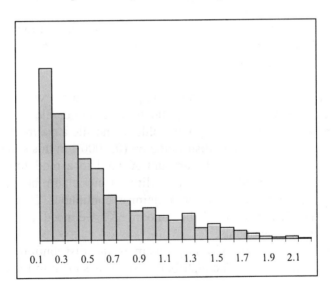

9.4.3 Simulating Other Distributions

The inverse transformation method can be applied to simulate other distributions for which $F^{-1}(x)$ is easily found. Exercises 9-17 and 9-18 ask the reader to do this for the uniform[2] and Pareto distributions. Unfortunately, some useful distributions do not have closed forms for $F(x)$ which allow a simple solution for $F^{-1}(x)$. This is true in the case of the most widely used distribution, the normal. Fortunately other methods are available. The inverse function can be approximated numerically, or entirely different methods can be used. Such work is beyond the scope of this course, but it is incorporated into computer technology that gives all of us the capability of generating values from a wide range of distributions. The spreadsheet EXCEL has inverse functions for the normal, gamma, beta and lognormal distributions. The statistics program MINITAB will generate random data from the uniform, normal, exponential, gamma, lognormal, Weibull and beta distributions.

9.5   Mixed Distributions

9.5.1   An Insurance Example

In some situations, probability distributions are a combination of discrete and continuous distributions. The next example illustrates how this may happen naturally in insurance.

Example 9.16 An insurance company has sold a warranty policy for appliance repair. 90% of the policyholders do not file a claim. 10% file a single claim. For those policyholders who file a claim, the amount paid for repair is uniformly distributed on $(0, 1000]$. In this situation, the probability distribution of the amount X paid to a randomly selected policyholder is **mixed**. The probability of no claim being filed is discrete, but the amount paid on a claim is continuous. Before we can describe the distribution of the amount X, we need to look more carefully at its components.

The discrete part of this problem is the distribution of N, the number of claims paid. The distribution of N is shown in the following table.

n	0	1
$p(n)$	.90	.10

---

[2] Note that the linear congruential generator used to produce random numbers in $[0, 1)$ is actually simulating a uniform distribution on $[0, 1)$. The inverse transformation method can be used to simulate a uniform distribution on any other interval.

The continuous distribution for claim amount applies only if we are given that a claim has been filed. This is a conditional distribution. In more formal terms

$$P(X \le x \mid N = 1) = F(x \mid N = 1) = \tfrac{x}{1000}, \text{ for } 0 < x \le 1000.$$

The insurance company needs to find the cumulative distribution function $F(x) = P(X \le x)$ for X, the amount paid to any randomly selected policyholder. This can be done in logical steps.

Case 1: $x < 0$. The amount paid cannot be negative. If $x < 0$, $P(X \le x) = F(x) = 0$.

Case 2: $x = 0$. The probability that $X = 0$ is .90, the probability that $N = 0$. Then $F(0) = P(X \le 0) = P(X = 0) = .90$.

Case 3: $0 < x \le 1000$. This case requires a probability calculation.

$$
\begin{aligned}
F(x) = P(X \le x) &= P[X = 0 \text{ or } 0 < X \le x] \\
&= P[(N = 0) \text{ or } (N = 1 \text{ and } X \le x)] \\
&= P(N = 0) + P(N = 1 \text{ and } X \le x) \\
&= P(N = 0) + P(X \le x \mid N = 1) \cdot P(N = 1) \\
&= .90 + \left(\tfrac{x}{1000}\right)(.10)
\end{aligned}
$$

Case 4: $x > 1000$. All claims are less than or equal to 1000, so $P(X \le x) = 1$.

We can now give a complete description of $F(x) = P(X \le x)$.

$$
F(x) = \begin{cases}
0 & x < 0 \\
.90 & x = 0 \\
.90 + .10\left(\tfrac{x}{1000}\right) & 0 < x \le 1000 \\
1 & x > 1000
\end{cases}
$$

The graph of $F(x)$ on the interval $[0, 1200]$ is shown below.

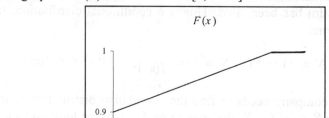

The cumulative distribution function can now be used to find probabilities for X. For example,

$$P(X \leq 500) = F(500) = .90 + .10\left(\frac{500}{1000}\right) = .95.$$

Care is necessary over the use of the relations $<$ and $\leq$ because of the mixture of discrete and continuous variables. The preceding probability is not the same as $P(0 < X \leq 500)$.

$$P(0 < X \leq 500) = F(500) - F(0) = .95 - .90 = .05 \qquad \square$$

9.5.2   The Probability Function for a Mixed Distribution

It is usually easier to derive the cumulative distribution function $F(x)$ for a mixed distribution, but problems can also be stated using a mixed probability function which is partly a discrete probability function and partly a continuous probability density function. In the next example, we find the combined probability function for the insurance problem.

Example 9.17 The probability function $p(x)$ for Example 9.16 can also be found in logical steps.

Case 1: $x < 0$. Values less than 0 are impossible, so $p(x) = 0$.

Case 2: $x = 0$. Since the probability of no claim is .90, we see that $p(0) = .90$.

Case 3: $0 < x \leq 1000$. In this case, x is a continuous random variable. For a continuous random variable, $p(x) = f(x)$ is the derivative of $F(x)$. We can find $f(x)$ for this interval by taking the derivative of the formula for $F(x)$ on this interval.

$$p(x) = f(x) = F'(x) = \frac{d}{dx}\left(.90 + .10\left(\frac{x}{1000}\right)\right) = .0001$$

Case 4: $x > 1000$. This is impossible. $p(x) = 0$.

We can summarize the probability function in the following definition by cases.

$$p(x) = \begin{cases} 0 & x < 0 \\ .90 & x = 0 \\ .0001 & 0 < x \leq 1000 \\ 0 & x > 1000 \end{cases}$$

This mixed distribution is continuous on $(0,1000]$ and is said to have a **point mass** at $x = 0$. It is graphed below, with the point mass indicated by a heavy dot.

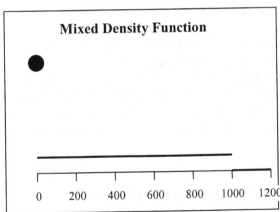

Mixed Density Function

9.5.3 The Expected Value of a Mixed Distribution

For discrete distributions, the expected value was found by summation of the probability function.

$$E(X) = \sum x \cdot p(x)$$

For continuous distributions, the expected value was found by integration of the density function.

$$E(X) = \int_{-\infty}^{\infty} x \cdot f(x) \, dx$$

For mixed distributions we can combine these ideas, sum where the random variable is discrete, and integrate where it is continuous. This is done in the next example.

Example 9.18 For the insurance example, we can use the probability function just derived.

$$E(X) = .90(0) + \int_{0}^{1000} x(.0001)dx = 50 \qquad \square$$

9.5.4   A Lifetime Example

In the next example, we will apply the reasoning used above to the lifetime of a machine part.

Example 9.19 When a new part is selected for installation, the part is first inspected. The probability that a part fails the inspection and is not used is .01. If a part passes inspection and is used, its lifetime is exponential with mean 100. Find the probability distribution of T, the lifetime of a randomly selected part.

Solution Let S be the event that a part passes inspection. Then $P(S) = .99$ and $P(\sim S) = .01$. The given exponential distribution is the conditional distribution of lifetime for a part that passes inspection. Since the mean is 100, the parameter of the exponential distribution is $\lambda = .01$.

$$P(T < t \mid S) = 1 - e^{-.01t} = F(t|S), \text{ for } t > 0$$

The cumulative distribution function $F(t) = P(T < t)$ can be found in steps, as before.

Case 1: $t < 0$. Values less than 0 are impossible, so $F(t) = 0$.

Case 2: $t = 0$. When a part fails inspection, it is not used and $T = 0$. $F(0) = P(T \leq 0) = P(T = 0) = .01$.

Case 3: $t > 0$.
$$F(t) = P(T \leq t) = P(T = 0) + P(0 < T \leq t)$$

$$= P(\sim S) + P(S \text{ and } (T \leq t))$$

$$= P(\sim S) + P(T \leq t \mid S) \cdot P(S)$$

$$= .01 + (1 - e^{-.01t}).99$$

Then $F(t)$ is given by

$$F(t) = \begin{cases} 0 & t < 0 \\ .01 & t = 0 \\ .99(1 - e^{-.01t}) & t > 0 \end{cases}.$$

The probability function is

$$p(t) = \begin{cases} 0 & t < 0 \\ .01 & t = 0 \\ .99(.01e^{-.01t}) & t > 0 \end{cases}.$$

$\square$

9.6 Two Useful Identities

In this section we will give two identities which are used in risk management applications. In each case, we will state the identity first, then give an application to illustrate its use and finish with a discussion of the derivation.

9.6.1 Using the Hazard Rate to Find the Survival Function

Let X be a random variable defined on $[0, \infty)$. If we are given the hazard rate $\lambda(x)$, we can find the survival function $S(x)$ using the identity

$$S(x) = e^{-\int_0^x \lambda(u)\,du}. \qquad (9.6)$$

Example 9.20 In Section 8.7.5, we showed that the hazard rate for a Weibull distribution with parameters α and β was

$$\lambda(x) = \alpha\beta x^{\alpha-1}.$$

Then $\int_0^x \lambda(u)\,du = \int_0^x \alpha\beta u^{\alpha-1}\,du = \beta u^\alpha\Big|_0^x = \beta x^\alpha$. The identity shows that $S(x) = e^{-\beta x^\alpha}$. $\qquad\square$

To derive this identity, recall that

$$S'(x) = \frac{d}{dx}(1 - F(x)) = -f(x).$$

By definition,

$$\lambda(x) = \frac{f(x)}{1 - F(x)} = -\frac{S'(x)}{S(x)} = -\frac{d}{dx}\ln S(x).$$

Then

$$\int_0^x \lambda(u)\,du = -\ln S(u)\Big|_0^x = -\ln S(x) + \ln 1 = -\ln S(x).$$

Thus

$$e^{-\int_0^x \lambda(u)\,du} = e^{\ln S(x)} = S(x).$$

9.6.2   Finding $E(X)$ Using $S(x)$

Let X be a random variable defined on $[0,\infty)$. If we are given the survival function $S(x) = 1 - F(x)$, we can find the expected value of X using the identity

$$E(X) = \int_0^\infty S(x)\,dx = \int_0^\infty (1 - F(x))dx. \qquad (9.7)$$

Example 9.21   In Section 8.2.4, we showed that the survival function for an exponential random variable with parameter β was

$$S(x) = e^{-\beta x},$$

for $x \geq 0$. Then

$$E(X) = \int_0^\infty e^{-\beta x}\,dx = \frac{e^{-\beta x}}{-\beta}\Big|_0^\infty = 0 - \frac{1}{-\beta} = \frac{1}{\beta}. \qquad\square$$

This identity is derived using integration by parts. The definition of $E(X)$ is

$$E(X) = \int_0^\infty x \cdot f(x)\,dx.$$

If we take

$$u = x \qquad\qquad v = -(1 - F(x))$$
$$du = dx \qquad\qquad dv = f(x)\,dx$$

we obtain

$$E(X) = -x(1 - F(x))\Big|_0^\infty + \int_0^\infty (1 - F(x))\,dx$$

$$= 0 - 0 + \int_0^\infty S(x)\,dx = \int_0^\infty S(x)\,dx.$$

In this derivation, we have made use of the fact that

$$\lim_{x\to\infty} x(1 - F(x)) = 0.$$

This requires proof:

$$\lim_{x\to\infty} x \cdot S(x) = \lim_{x\to\infty} x \int_x^\infty f(y)\,dy$$

$$= \lim_{x\to\infty} \int_x^\infty x \cdot f(y)\,dy$$

$$\leq \lim_{x\to\infty} \int_x^\infty y \cdot f(y)\,dy = 0$$

The last equality above will hold if $E(X)$ is defined, since

$$E(X) = \int_0^\infty y \cdot f(y)\,dy.$$

9.7   Exercises

9.1   Expected Value of a Function of a Random Variable

9-1.   Suppose the amount of a single loss for an insurance policy has density function $f(x) = .001e^{-.001x}$, for $x > 0$. If this policy has a $300 per claim deductible, what is the expected amount of a single claim for this policy?

9-2.   If the policy in Exercise 9-1 also has a payment cap of $1500 per claim, what is the expected amount of a single claim?

9-3.   Work Example 9.4 using the utility function $u(w) = ln(w)$. What are $E[u(W_1)]$ and $E[u(W_2)]$?

9.2   Moment Generating Functions of Continuous Random Variables

9-4.   Let X be the random variable which is uniformly distributed over the interval $[a, b]$. Find $M_X(t)$.

9-5.   Find $E(X)$ for the random variable in Exercise 9-4 using its moment generating function.

9-6.   Let X be the random variable whose density function is given by $f(x) = 2(1 - x)$, for $0 \le x \le 1$, and $f(x) = 0$ elsewhere. Find $M_X(t)$.

9-7.   Find $E(X)$ for the random variable in Exercise 9-6 using its moment generating function. (Note: the derivative of $M(t)$ is not defined at 0, but you can take the limit as t approaches 0 to find $E(X)$. This is a much more difficult way to find $E(X)$ than direct integration for this particular density function.)

9-8.   If the moment generating function of X is $\left(\dfrac{2}{2-t}\right)^5$, identify the random variable X.

9-9. If X is an exponential random variable with $\lambda = 3$, what is the moment generating function of $Y = 2X + 5$?

9-10. Let X be the random variable whose moment generating function is $e^{(t+t^2)}$. Find $E(X)$ and $V(X)$.

9-11. Let X be a normal random variable with parameters μ and σ. Use the moment generating function for X to find $E(X^2)$. Then show that $V(X) = \sigma^2$.

9.3 The Distribution of $Y = g(X)$

9-12. Let X be uniformly distributed over $[0, 1]$ and $Y = e^X$. Find (a) $F_Y(y)$; (b) $f_Y(y)$.

9-13. Let X be a random variable with density function given by $f_X(x) = 3x^{-4}$, for $x \geq 1$ (Pareto with $\alpha = 3$, $\beta = 1$), and let $Y = \ln X$. Find $F_Y(y)$.

9-14. If X is the random variable defined in Exercise 9-13 and $Y = 1/X$, find (a) $F_Y(y)$; (b) $f_Y(y)$.

9-15. The monthly maintenance cost X of a machine is an exponential random variable with unknown parameter. Studies have determined that $P(X > 100) = .64$. For a second machine the cost Y is a random variable such that $Y = 2X$. Find $P(Y > 100)$.

9.4 Simulation of Continuous Distributions

9-16. For a continuous random variable X, show that $F(X)$ is uniformly distributed over $[0, 1]$. (i.e., show $P[F(X) \leq x] = x$, for $0 \leq x \leq 1$.

For Exercises 9-17 and 9-18, use the following sequence of random numbers in $[0, 1)$.

1. .90463	6. .81008	11. .15533	16. .31239
2. .17842	7. .49660	12. .29701	17. .68995
3. .55660	8. .92602	13. .82751	18. .77787
4. .55071	9. .71729	14. .67490	19. .66928
5. .96216	10. .39443	15. .68556	20. .53100

9-17.   Let X be uniformly distributed over $[0,4]$, and use the above random numbers to simulate $F(x)$. How many of the transformed values $x = F^{-1}(u)$ are in each subinterval $[0, 1)$, $[1, 2)$, $[2, 3)$ and $[3, 4)$?

9-18.   Let X have a Pareto distribution with $\alpha = 3$ and $\beta = 3$, and use the above random numbers to simulate $F(x)$. How many of the transformed values $x = F^{-1}(u)$ are in each subinterval $[3, 4)$, $[4, 5)$, $[5, 6)$ and $[6, \infty)$.

9.5   Mixed Distributions

9-19.   For a certain type of policy, an insurance company divides its claims into two classes, minor and major. Last year 90 percent of the policyholders filed no claims, 9 percent filed minor claims, and 1 percent filed major claims. The amounts of the minor claims were uniformly distributed over $(0, 1{,}000]$, and the major claims were uniformly distributed over $(1{,}000, 10{,}000]$. Find $F(x)$, for $0 \le x \le 10{,}000$.

9-20.   Find $E(X)$ for the insurance policy in Exercise 9-19.

9-21.   An auto insurance company issues a comprehensive policy with a \$200 deductible. Last year 90 percent of the policyholders filed no claims (either no damage or damage less than the deductible). For the 10 percent who filed claims, the claim amount had a Pareto distribution with $\alpha = 3$ and $\beta = 200$. If X is the random variable of the amount paid by the insurer, what is $F(x)$, for $x \ge 0$?

9.6 Two Useful Identities

9-22. Let X be a random variable with hazard rate $\lambda(x) = \frac{2}{1+x}$, for $x \geq 0$. Find $S(x)$.

9-23. Let X be a random variable with hazard rate $\lambda(x) = \frac{1}{100-x}$, for $0 \leq x < 100$. Find $S(x)$.

9-24. Let X be the random variable defined in Exercise 9-22. Use Equation (9.7) to find $E(X)$.

9-25. Let X be a random variable whose survival function is given by $S(x) = \frac{100-x}{100}$, for $0 \leq x < 100$, and $S(x) = 0$ for $x \geq 100$. Use Equation (9.7) to find $E(X)$.

9.8 Sample Exam Problems

9-26. An insurance policy pays for a random loss X subject to a deductible of C, where $0 < C < 1$. The loss amount is modeled as a continuous random variable with density function

$$f(x) = \begin{cases} 2x & \text{for } 0 < x < 1 \\ 0 & \text{otherwise} \end{cases}$$

Given a random loss X, the probability that the insurance payment is less than 0.5 is equal to 0.64.

Calculate C.

9-27. A manufacturer's annual losses follow a distribution with density function

$$f(x) = \begin{cases} \dfrac{2.5(0.6)^{2.5}}{x^{3.5}} & \text{for } x > 0.6 \\ 0 & \text{otherwise} \end{cases}$$

To cover its losses, the manufacturer purchases an insurance policy with an annual deductible of 2.

What is the mean of the manufacturer's annual losses not paid by the insurance policy?

9-28.   An insurance policy is written to cover a loss, X, where X has a uniform distribution on [0, 1000].

At what level must a deductible be set in order for the expected payment to be 25% of what it would be with no deductible?

9-29.   A piece of equipment is being insured against early failure. The time from purchase until failure of the equipment is exponentially distributed with mean 10 years. The insurance will pay an amount x if the equipment fails during the first year, and it will pay $0.5x$ if failure occurs during the second or third year. If failure occurs after the first three years, no payment will be made.

At what level must x be set if the expected payment made under this insurance is to be 1000?

9-30.   A device that continuously measures and records seismic activity is placed in a remote region. The time, T, to failure of this device is exponentially distributed with mean 3 years. Since the device will not be monitored during its first two years of service, the time to discovery of its failure is $X = \max(T, 2)$.

Determine $E[X]$.

9-31.   An insurance policy reimburses a loss up to a benefit limit of 10. The policyholder's loss, Y, follows a distribution with density function:

$$f(y) = \begin{cases} \dfrac{2}{y^3} & y > 1 \\ 0 & \text{otherwise} \end{cases}$$

What is the expected value of the benefit paid under the insurance policy?

9-32.   The warranty on a machine specifies that it will be replaced at failure or age 4, whichever occurs first. The machine's age at failure, X, has density function

$$f(x) = \begin{cases} \dfrac{1}{5} & \text{for } 0 < x < 5 \\ 0 & \text{otherwise} \end{cases}$$

Let Y be the age of the machine at the time of replacement. Determine the variance of Y.

9-33. The owner of an automobile insures it against damage by purchasing an insurance policy with a deductible of 250. In the event that the automobile is damaged, repair costs can be modeled by a uniform random variable on the interval $(0,1500)$.

Determine the standard deviation of the insurance payment in the event that the automobile is damaged.

9-34. An insurance company sells an auto insurance policy that covers losses incurred by a policyholder, subject to a deductible of 100. Losses incurred follow an exponential distribution with mean 300.

What is the 95th percentile of actual losses that exceed the deductible?

9-35. The time, T, that a manufacturing system is out of operation has cumulative distribution function

$$F(t) = \begin{cases} 1 - \left(\dfrac{2}{t}\right)^2 & \text{for } t > 2 \\ 0 & \text{otherwise} \end{cases}$$

The resulting cost to the company is $Y = T^2$.

Determine the density function of Y, for $y > 4$.

9-36. An investment account earns an annual interest rate R that follows a uniform distribution on the interval $(0.04, 0.08)$. The value of a 10,000 initial investment in this account after one year is given by $V = 10,000e^{R}$.

Determine the cumulative distribution function, $F(v)$, of V for values of v that satisfy $0 < F(v) < 1$.

9-37. An actuary models the lifetime of a device using the random variable $Y = 10X^{.8}$, where X is an exponential random variable with mean 1 year.

Determine the probability density function $f(y)$, for $y > 0$, of the random variable Y.

9-38.   Let T denote the time in minutes for a customer service represen-
        tative to respond to 10 telephone inquiries. T is uniformly
        distributed on the interval with endpoints 8 minutes and 12
        minutes. Let R denote the average rate, in customers per minute,
        at which the representative responds to inquiries.

        Find the density function of the random variable R on the
        interval $\left(\dfrac{10}{12} \le r \le \dfrac{10}{8}\right)$.

9-39.   The monthly profit of Company I can be modeled by a continu-
        ous random variable with density function f. Company II has a
        monthly profit that is twice that of Company I.

        Determine the probability density function of the monthly profit
        of Company II.

9-40.   A random variable X has the cumulative distribution function

$$F(x) = \begin{cases} 0 & \text{for } x < 1 \\ \dfrac{x^2 - 2x + 2}{2} & \text{for } 1 \le x < 2 \\ 1 & \text{for } x \ge 2 \end{cases}$$

        Calculate the variance of X.

Chapter 10
Multivariate Distributions

10.1 Joint Distributions for Discrete Random Variables

10.1.1 The Joint Probability Function

We have already given an example of the probability distribution X for the value of a single investment asset. Most real investors own more than one asset. We will look at a simple example of an investor who owns two assets to show how things become more interesting when you have to keep track of more than one random variable.

Example 10.1 An investor owns two assets. He is interested in the value of his investments in one year. The value of the first asset in one year is a random variable X, and the value of the second asset in one year is a random variable Y. It is not enough to know the separate probability distributions. The investor must study how the two assets behave together. This requires a **joint probability distribution** for X and Y. The following table gives this information.

y x	90	100	110
0	.05	.27	.18
10	.15	.33	.02

The possible values of X are 90, 100 and 110. The possible values of Y are 0 and 10. The probabilities for all possible pairs of individual values of x and y are given in the table. For example, the probability that

$X = 90$ and $Y = 0$ is .05. The probability values in this table define a joint probability function $p(x, y)$ for X and Y, where $p(x, y)$ is the probability that $X = x$ and $Y = y$. This is written

$$p(x, y) = P(X = x, Y = y).$$

For example,

$$p(90, 0) = P(X = 90, Y = 0) = .05.$$

The information here is useful to the investor. For example, when X assumes its lowest value, Y is more likely to assume its highest value. We will discuss the use of this information further in later sections. ☐

Definition 10.1 Let X and Y be discrete random variables. The **joint probability function** for X and Y is the function

$$p(x, y) = P(X = x, Y = y).$$

Note that the sum of all the probabilities in the table in Example 10.1 is 1.00. This must hold for any joint probability function.

$$\sum_x \sum_y p(x, y) = 1 \qquad (10.1)$$

Joint probability functions for discrete random variables are often given in tables, but they may also be given by formulas.

Example 10.2 An analyst is studying the traffic accidents in two adjacent towns. The random variable X represents the number of accidents in a day in town A, and the random variable Y represents the number of accidents in a day in town B. The joint probability function for X and Y is given by

$$p(x, y) = \frac{e^{-2}}{x!y!}, \text{ for } x = 0, 1, 2, \ldots \text{ and } y = 0, 1, 2, \ldots.$$

The probability that on a given day there will be 1 accident in town A and 2 accidents in town B is

$$p(1, 2) = \frac{e^{-2}}{1!2!} \approx .068. \qquad ☐$$

The above probability function must satisfy the requirement $\sum_x \sum_y p(x,y) = 1$. If a probability function is given in a problem in this text, the reader may assume that this is true. For the above probability function, it is not hard to prove that the sum of the probabilities is 1.

$$\sum_{x=0}^{\infty}\sum_{y=0}^{\infty}\frac{e^{-2}}{x!y!} = e^{-2}\sum_{x=0}^{\infty}\left(\frac{1}{x!}\sum_{y=0}^{\infty}\frac{1}{y!}\right) = e^{-2}\sum_{x=0}^{\infty}\frac{1}{x!}(e)$$

$$= e^{-1}\sum_{x=0}^{\infty}\frac{1}{x!} = e^{-1}e = 1$$

10.1.2 Marginal Distributions for Discrete Random Variables

Once we know the joint distribution of X and Y, we can find the probabilities for individual values of X and Y. This is illustrated in the next example.

Example 10.3 The table of joint probabilities for the asset values in Example 10.1 is the following:

y \ x	90	100	110
0	.05	.27	.18
10	.15	.33	.02

The probability that X is 90 can be found by adding all joint probabilities in the first column of the table above.

$$P(X = 90) = P(X = 90, Y = 0) + P(X = 90, Y = 10)$$

$$= .05 + .15 = .20$$

The probabilities that $P(X = 100)$ and $P(X = 110)$ can be found in the same way. The probability that Y is 0 can be found by adding all the joint probabilities in the first row of the table.

$$P(Y = 0) = .05 + .27 + .18 = .50$$

The probability that Y is 10 can be found in the same way. It is efficient to display the probability function table with rows and columns added to give the individual probability distributions of X and Y.

y \ x	90	100	110	$p(y)$
0	.05	.27	.18	.50
10	.15	.33	.02	.50
$p(x)$	.20	.60	.20	

The individual distributions for the random variables X and Y are called **marginal distributions**.   □

Definition 10.2 The **marginal probability functions** of X and Y are defined by the following:

$$p_X(x) = \sum_y p(x, y) \qquad\qquad (10.2a)$$

$$p_Y(y) = \sum_x p(x, y) \qquad\qquad (10.2b)$$

Example 10.4 The joint probability function for numbers of accidents in two towns in Example 10.2 was

$$p(x, y) = \frac{e^{-2}}{x!y!}.$$

The marginal probability functions are

$$p_X(x) = \sum_{y=0}^{\infty} \frac{e^{-2}}{x!y!} = \frac{e^{-2}}{x!} \sum_{y=0}^{\infty} \frac{1}{y!} = \frac{e^{-2}}{x!} e = \frac{e^{-1}}{x!}$$

and

$$p_Y(y) = \sum_{x=0}^{\infty} \frac{e^{-2}}{x!y!} = \frac{e^{-2}}{y!} \sum_{x=0}^{\infty} \frac{1}{x!} = \frac{e^{-2}}{y!} e = \frac{e^{-1}}{y!}.$$

Each marginal distribution is Poisson with $\lambda = 1$.   □

10.1.3 Using the Marginal Distributions

Once the marginal distributions are known, we can use them to analyze the random variables X and Y separately if that is desired.

Example 10.5 For the asset value joint distribution in Examples 10.1 and 10.3,

$$P(X \geq 100) = .60 + .20 = .80$$

and

$$P(Y > 0) = .50. \qquad \square$$

Example 10.6 For the accident number joint distribution in Examples 10.2 and 10.4, both X and Y were Poisson with $\lambda = 1$. Thus

$$P(X = 2) = P(Y = 2) = \frac{e^{-1}}{2}. \qquad \square$$

In the following examples, we will calculate the mean and variance of the random variables in the last two examples. This information is important for future reference, since we will find these expectations by another method involving conditional distributions in Section 11.5.

Example 10.7 For the asset value joint distribution in Examples 10.1 and 10.3,

$$E(X) = 90(.20) + 100(.60) + 110(.20) = 100$$

and

$$E(Y) = 0(.50) + 10(.50) = 5.$$

To find variances, we first calculate the second moments.

$$E(X^2) = 90^2(.20) + 100^2(.60) + 110^2(.20) = 10,040$$

$$E(Y^2) = 0^2(.50) + 10^2(.50) = 50$$

Then

$$V(X) = 10,040 - 100^2 = 40$$

and

$$V(Y) = 50 - 5^2 = 25. \qquad \square$$

Example 10.8   For the accident number joint distribution in Examples 10.2 and 10.4, both X and Y were Poisson with $\lambda = 1$. Thus $E(X) = E(Y) = V(X) = V(Y) = 1$.   □

10.2   Joint Distributions for Continuous Random Variables

10.2.1 Review of the Single Variable Case

Probabilities for a continuous random variable X are found using a probability density function $f(x)$ with the following properties:

(i) $f(x) \geq 0$ for all x.

(ii)   The total area bounded by the graph of $y = f(x)$ and the x-axis is 1.00.

$$\int_{-\infty}^{\infty} f(x)\,dx = 1$$

(iii) $P(a \leq X \leq b)$ is given by the area under $y = f(x)$ between $x = a$ and $x = b$.

$$P(a \leq X \leq b) = \int_{a}^{b} f(x)\,dx$$

It is important to review these properties, since the joint probability density function will be defined in a similar manner.

10.2.2 The Joint Probability Density Function
for Two Continuous Random Variables

Probabilities for a pair of continuous random variables X and Y must be found using a continuous real-valued function of two variables $f(x,y)$. A function of two variables will define a surface in three dimensions. Probabilities will be calculated as volumes under this surface, and double integrals will be used in this calculation.

Definition 10.3 The **joint probability density function** for two continuous random variables X and Y is a continuous, real-valued function $f(x, y)$ satisfying the following properties:

(i) $f(x, y) \geq 0$ for all x, y.

(ii) The total volume bounded by the graph of $z = f(x, y)$ and the x-y plane is 1.00.

$$\int_{-\infty}^{\infty} \int_{-\infty}^{\infty} f(x, y) \, dx \, dy = 1 \qquad (10.3)$$

(iii) $P(a \leq X \leq b, c \leq Y \leq d)$ is given by the volume between the surface $z = f(x, y)$ and the region in the x-y plane bounded by $x = a$, $x = b$, $y = c$ and $y = d$.

$$P(a \leq X \leq b, c \leq Y \leq d) = \int_{a}^{b} \int_{c}^{d} f(x, y) \, dy \, dx \qquad (10.4)$$

Example 10.9 A company is studying the amount of sick leave taken by its employees. The company allows a maximum of 100 hours of paid sick leave in a year. The random variable X represents the leave time taken by a randomly selected employee last year. The random variable Y represents the leave time taken by the same employee this year. Each random variable is measured in hundreds of hours, e.g., $X = .50$ means that the employee took 50 hours last year. Thus X and Y assume values in the interval $[0, 1]$. The joint probability density function for X and Y is

$$f(x, y) = 2 - 1.2x - .8y, \text{ for } 0 \leq x \leq 1, 0 \leq y \leq 1.$$

The surface is shown in the next figure.

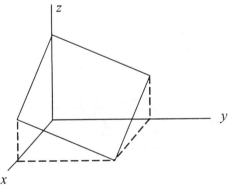

We will first verify that the total volume bounded by the surface and the
x-y plane is 1.

$$\int_0^1 \int_0^1 (2 - 1.2x - .8y)\, dx\, dy = \int_0^1 (2x - .6x^2 - .8xy)\Big|_{x=0}^{1} dy$$

$$= \int_0^1 (1.4 - .8y)\, dy = 1$$

To illustrate a basic probability calculation, we will find the probability
that $X \geq .50$ and $Y \geq .50$. In the notation used in property (iii) of
Definition 10.3, we need to find

$$P(.50 \leq X \leq 1.0, .50 \leq Y \leq 1.0) = \int_{.5}^1 \int_{.5}^1 f(x, y)\, dy\, dx$$

$$= \int_{.5}^1 \int_{.5}^1 (2 - 1.2x - .8y)\, dy\, dx$$

$$= \int_{.5}^1 (2y - 1.2xy - .4y^2)\Big|_{y=.5}^{1} dx$$

$$= \int_{.5}^1 (.7 - .6x)\, dx = .125.$$

The volume represented by this calculation is shown in the next figure.

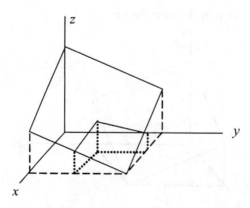

The region of integration for this probability calculation is the region in the x-y plane defined by $R = \{(x, y) | .50 \le x \le 1 \text{ and } .50 \le y \le 1\}$. It is often helpful to include a separate figure for the region of integration. This is given below.

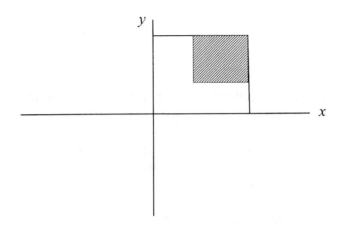

In this example, the random variables X and Y were limited to the interval $[0, 1]$. The next example gives random variables which assume values in $[0, \infty)$. $\square$

Example 10.10 In Example 10.2, an analyst was studying the traffic accidents in two adjacent towns, A and B. That example gave the joint distribution of X and Y, the discrete random variables for the number of accidents in the two towns. In this example we look at the continuous random variables S and T, the time between accidents in towns A and B, respectively. The joint density function of S and T is

$$f(s, t) = e^{-(s+t)}, \text{ for } s \ge 0 \text{ and } t \ge 0.$$

We will first check that the total volume under the surface is 1.00.

$$\int_0^\infty \int_0^\infty e^{-(s+t)} ds\, dt = \int_0^\infty e^{-t}(-e^{-s})\Big|_{s=0}^\infty dt = \int_0^\infty e^{-t}(1)\, dt = 1$$

The density function can now be used to calculate probabilities. For example, the probability that $S \le 1$ and $T \le 2$ is given by the following:

$$P(0 \leq S \leq 1, 0 \leq T \leq 2) = \int_0^2 \int_0^1 e^{-(s+t)} ds\, dt$$

$$= \int_0^2 e^{-t}(-e^{-s})\Big|_{s=0}^1 dt$$

$$= \int_0^2 e^{-t}(1 - e^{-1})dt$$

$$= (1 - e^{-1})(1 - e^{-2}) \approx .547 \qquad \square$$

10.2.3 Marginal Distributions for Continuous Random Variables

In Section 10.1.2, we found the discrete marginal distribution $p_X(x)$ by keeping the value of x fixed and adding the values of $p(x, y)$ for all y. Similarly, $p_Y(y)$ was found by fixing y and adding over x values. These marginal probability functions are given by Equations (10.2a) and (10.2b).

For continuous functions, the addition is performed continuously by integration. Thus the marginal distributions for a continuous joint distribution are defined by integrating over x or y instead of summing over x or y.

Definition 10.4 Let $f(x, y)$ be the joint density function for the continuous random variables X and Y. Then the **marginal density functions** of X and Y are defined by the following:

$$f_X(x) = \int_{-\infty}^{\infty} f(x, y)\, dy \qquad (10.5a)$$

$$f_Y(y) = \int_{-\infty}^{\infty} f(x, y)\, dx \qquad (10.5b)$$

The probability distributions of X and Y are referred to as the **marginal distributions** of X and Y.

Example 10.11 For the sick leave random variables of Example 10.9, the joint density function was $f(x, y) = 2 - 1.2x - .8y$, for $0 \leq x \leq 1, 0 \leq y \leq 1$. The marginal density functions are

$$f_X(x) = \int_0^1 (2 - 1.2x - .8y)\, dy = (2y - 1.2xy - .4y^2)\Big|_0^1 = 1.6 - 1.2x$$

and

$$f_Y(y) = \int_0^1 (2 - 1.2x - .8y)\, dx = (2x - .6x^2 - .8xy)\Big|_0^1 = 1.4 - .8y.$$

□

Example 10.12 For the joint distribution of waiting times for accidents in Example 10.10, the joint probability density function was $f(s,t) = e^{-(s+t)}$, for $s \geq 0$ and $t \geq 0$. The marginal density functions are

$$f_S(s) = \int_{-\infty}^{\infty} f(s,t)\, dt = \int_0^{\infty} e^{-(s+t)}\, dt = e^{-s} \int_0^{\infty} e^{-t}\, dt = e^{-s}$$

and

$$f_T(t) = \int_{-\infty}^{\infty} f(s,t)\, ds = \int_0^{\infty} e^{-(s+t)}\, ds = e^{-t} \int_0^{\infty} e^{-s}\, ds = e^{-t}.$$

The marginal distributions of S and T are exponential with $\lambda = 1$. □

10.2.4 Using Continuous Marginal Distributions

We can now use the continuous marginal distributions to study X and Y separately.

Example 10.13 Let X be the number of sick leave hours last year and Y the number of sick leave hours this year from Example 10.9. We showed in Example 10.11 that

$$f_X(x) = 1.6 - 1.2x, \text{ for } 0 \leq x \leq 1$$

and

$$f_Y(y) = 1.4 - 8y, \text{ for } 0 \leq y \leq 1.$$

We can now calculate probabilities of interest.

$$P(X > .50) = \int_{.5}^1 (1.6 - 1.2x)\, dx = .35$$

$$P(Y > .50) = \int_{.5}^1 (1.4 - .8y)\, dy = .40$$

For each year the above probability is the probability that the sick leave exceeds 50 hours. This probability has increased from last year to this year. We can see the same type of increase if we calculate expected values.

$$E(X) = \int_0^1 x \cdot f_X(x)\, dx = \int_0^1 (1.6x - 1.2x^2)\, dx = .40$$

$$E(Y) = \int_0^1 y \cdot f_Y(y)\, dy = \int_0^1 (1.4y - .8y^2)\, dy = .4\dot{3}$$

The mean number of sick leave hours has increased from 40 to 43.3̇. □

Example 10.14 Let S and T be the accident waiting times in Example 10.12. The marginal distributions of S and T each have an exponential distribution with $\lambda = 1$. Thus $E(S) = E(T) = 1$ and $P(S > 1) = P(T > 1) = e^{-1}$.   □

10.2.5 More General Joint Probability Calculations

In the previous examples, we have only used the joint density function to find the probability that X and Y lie within a rectangular region in the x-y plane.

$$P(a \leq X \leq b, c \leq Y \leq d) = \int_a^b \int_c^d f(x, y)\, dy\, dx$$

Integration of the joint density function can be used to find the probability that X and Y lie within a more general region R of the x-y plane, such as a triangle or a circle. We will not prove this, but will use this fact in applied problems. The general probability integral statement is

$$P((X, Y) \in R) = \int\int_R f(x, y)\, dx\, dy.$$

The next example is typical of the kind of probability calculation which requires integration over a more general region.

Example 10.15 Let X be the sick leave hours last year and Y the sick leave hours this year as given in Example 10.9. Suppose we wish to find the probability that an individual's sick leave hours are greater this year than last year. This is $P(Y > X)$. Recall that X and Y assume only non-zero values in the rectangular region of the x-y plane, where $0 \le x \le 1$ and $0 \le y \le 1$. The region R where $Y > X$ is the triangular half of that rectangle pictured below.

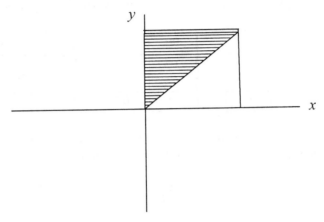

To find $P(Y > X)$ we must integrate the density function over that region.

$$P\big((X,Y) \in R\big) = \iint_R f(x,y)\, dx\, dy$$

$$= \int_0^1 \int_0^y (2 - 1.2x - .8y)\, dx\, dy$$

$$= \int_0^1 (2x - .6x^2 - .8xy)\big|_{x=0}^{y}\, dy$$

$$= \int_0^1 (2y - 1.4y^2)\, dy \ = \ \frac{1.6}{3} \ = \ .5\dot{3}$$

The probability that the number of sick leave hours for an employee increases over the two years is .53.   □

10.3 Conditional Distributions

10.3.1 Discrete Conditional Distributions

We will illustrate conditional distributions by returning to our previous examples.

Example 10.16 The joint probability function for the two assets in Examples 10.1 and 10.3 is given below (with marginals included).

y ⟍ x	90	100	110	$p_Y(y)$
0	.05	.27	.18	.50
10	.15	.33	.02	.50
$p_X(x)$	.20	.60	.20	

Suppose we are given that $Y = 0$. Then we can compute conditional probabilities for X based on this information.

$$P(X = 90|Y = 0) = \frac{P(X = 90, Y = 0)}{P(Y = 0)} = \frac{p(90, 0)}{p_Y(0)} = \frac{.05}{.50} = .10$$

$$P(X = 100|Y = 0) = \frac{p(100, 0)}{p_Y(0)} = \frac{.27}{.50} = .54$$

$$P(X = 110|Y = 0) = \frac{p(110, 0)}{p_Y(0)} = \frac{.18}{.50} = .36$$

These values give a complete probability function $p(x|Y = 0)$ for X, given the information that $Y = 0$.

x	90	100	110
$p(x|0)$	.10	.54	.36

In this calculation, the conditional probabilities were obtained by dividing each joint probability in the first row of the table above by the marginal probability at the end of the first row. A similar procedure could be used for the second row to obtain the conditional distribution for X given that $Y = 10$.

x	90	100	110
$p(x\|10)$	.30	.66	.04

The two conditional distributions show that there is a useful relation between X and Y. When Y is low ($Y = 0$), then X has a greater probability of assuming higher values; when Y is high ($Y = 10$), then X has a greater probability of assuming lower values. Thus X and Y tend to offset the risk of the other. □

The calculation technique used here is summarized in the following definition.

Definition 10.5 The **conditional probability function** of X, given that $Y = y$, is given by

$$P(X = x|Y = y) = p(x|y) = \frac{p(x, y)}{p_Y(y)}.$$

Similarly, the conditional probability function of Y, given that $X = x$, is given by

$$P(Y = y|X = x) = p(y|x) = \frac{p(x, y)}{p_X(x)}.$$

Example 10.17 The conditional probability function of Y, given that $X = 90$, is given by

$$P(Y = 0|X = 90) = \frac{p(90, 0)}{p_X(90)} = \frac{.05}{.20} = .25$$

and

$$P(Y = 10|X = 90) = \frac{p(90, 10)}{p_X(90)} = \frac{.15}{.20} = .75. \qquad □$$

Example 10.18 In Example 10.2, the joint probability function for X and Y (the numbers of accidents in two towns) was given by

$$p(x, y) = \frac{e^{-2}}{x!y!}, \text{ for } x = 0, 1, 2, \dots \text{ and } y = 0, 1, 2, \dots.$$

In Example 10.4 we showed that the marginal probability functions were Poisson with $\lambda = 1$.

$$p_X(x) = \frac{e^{-1}}{x!} \qquad p_Y(y) = \frac{e^{-1}}{y!}$$

This enables us to compute conditional probability functions.

$$p(x|y) = \frac{p(x,y)}{p_Y(y)} = \frac{\frac{e^{-2}}{x!y!}}{\frac{e^{-1}}{y!}} = \frac{e^{-1}}{x!}$$

Thus the conditional distribution of X, given $Y = y$, is also Poisson with $\lambda = 1$. The conditional distribution of Y, given $X = x$, is also Poisson.

$$p(y|x) = \frac{e^{-1}}{y!} \qquad \square$$

10.3.2 Continuous Conditional Distributions

Conditional distribution functions for two continuous random variables X and Y are defined using the pattern established for discrete random variables.

Definition 10.6 Let X and Y be continuous random variables with joint density function $f(x,y)$. The **conditional density function** for X, given that $Y = y$, is given by

$$f(x|Y = y) = f(x|y) = \frac{f(x,y)}{f_Y(y)}.$$

Similarly, the conditional density for Y, given that $X = x$, is given by

$$f(y|X = x) = f(y|x) = \frac{f(x,y)}{f_X(x)}.$$

Example 10.19 Let X be the sick leave hours last year and Y the sick leave hours this year from Example 10.9. The joint density and marginal density functions are

$$f(x,y) = 2 - 1.2x - .8y, \text{ for } 0 \le x \le 1, 0 \le y \le 1,$$

$$f_X(x) = 1.6 - 1.2x, \text{ for } 0 \le x \le 1,$$

and

$$f_Y(y) = 1.4 - 0.8y, \text{ for } 0 \le y \le 1.$$

Using Definition 10.6, we can calculate the conditional densities.

$$f(x|y) = \frac{f(x,y)}{f_Y(y)} = \frac{2 - 1.2x - .8y}{1.4 - .8y}, \text{ for } 0 \le x \le 1$$

$$f(y|x) = \frac{f(x,y)}{f_X(x)} = \frac{2 - 1.2x - .8y}{1.6 - 1.2x}, \text{ for } 0 \le y \le 1$$

This enables us to calculate probabilities of interest. Suppose an individual had $X = .10$ (10 hours of sick leave last year). Then his conditional density for Y (the hours of sick leave this year) is

$$f(y|.10) = \frac{2 - 1.2(.10) - .8y}{1.6 - 1.2(.10)} = \frac{1.88 - .8y}{1.48}, \text{ for } 0 \le y \le 1.$$

The probability that this individual has less than 40 hours of sick leave next year is $P(Y < .40 | X = .10)$.

$$P(Y < .40 | X = .10) = \int_0^{.40} \left(\frac{1.88 - .8y}{1.48} \right) dy \approx .465 \qquad \square$$

Example 10.20 For the joint distribution of waiting times for accidents in Example 10.10, the joint probability density function and marginal density functions were

$$f(s,t) = e^{-(s+t)}, \text{ for } s \ge 0, t \ge 0,$$

$$f_S(s) = e^{-s}, \text{ for } s \ge 0,$$

and

$$f_T(t) = e^{-t}, \text{ for } t \ge 0.$$

The conditional densities are identical with the marginal densities.

$$f(s|t) = \frac{f(s,t)}{f_T(t)} = \frac{e^{-(s+t)}}{e^{-t}} = e^{-s}, \text{ for } s \ge 0$$

$$f(t|s) = \frac{f(s,t)}{f_S(s)} = \frac{e^{-(s+t)}}{e^{-s}} = e^{-t}, \text{ for } t \ge 0 \qquad \square$$

10.3.3 Conditional Expected Value

Once the conditional distribution is known, we can compute conditional expectations. For discrete random variables we have the following:

$$E(Y|X = x) = \sum_y y \cdot p(y|x) \qquad (10.6a)$$

$$E(X|Y = y) = \sum_x x \cdot p(x|y) \qquad (10.6b)$$

Example 10.21 Let X and Y be the asset value random variables of Example 10.1. The conditional distribution of X, given that $Y = 0$, was found in Example 10.16.

x	90	100	110
$p(x|0)$	.10	.54	.36

The conditional expected value of X, given that $Y = 0$, is

$$E(X|Y = 0) = 90(.10) + 100(.54) + 110(.36) = 102.60. \qquad \square$$

When X and Y are continuous, the conditional expected values are found by integration, rather than summation.

$$E(Y|X = x) = \int_{-\infty}^{\infty} y \cdot f(y|x) \, dy \qquad (10.7a)$$

$$E(X|Y = y) = \int_{-\infty}^{\infty} x \cdot f(x|y) \, dx \qquad (10.7b)$$

Example 10.22 Let X be the sick leave hours last year and Y the sick leave hours this year from Example 10.9. The conditional density function of Y, given $X = .10$, is

$$f(y|.10) = \frac{1.88 - .8y}{1.48}, \text{ for } 0 \le y \le 1.$$

The conditional expected value, given that $X = .10$, is found by using Equation (10.7a).

$$E(Y|X = .10) = \int_{-\infty}^{\infty} y \cdot f(y|.10) \, dy = \int_{0}^{1} y \left(\frac{1.88 - .8y}{1.48} \right) dy \approx .455$$

$\square$

Conditional variances can also be defined. There are some interesting applications of conditional expected values and variances. These will be discussed in Section 11.5.

10.4 Independence for Random Variables

10.4.1 Independence for Discrete Random Variables

We have already discussed independence of events. When two events A and B are independent, then $P(A \cap B) = P(A) \cdot P(B)$. The definition of independence for two discrete random variables relies on this multiplication rule. If the events $X = x$ and $Y = y$ are independent, then $P(X = x \text{ and } Y = y) = P(X = x) \cdot P(Y = y)$.

Definition 10.7 Two discrete random variables X and Y are **independent** if

$$p(x, y) = p_X(x) \cdot p_Y(y),$$

for all pairs of outcomes (x, y).

Example 10.23 A gambler is betting that a fair coin will come up heads when it is tossed. If the coin comes up heads, he gets \$1; otherwise he must pay \$1. He bets on two consecutive tosses. X is the amount won or paid on the first toss, and Y is the corresponding amount for the second toss. The joint distribution for X and Y is given below with marginal distributions.

y \ x	-1	1	$p_Y(y)$
-1	.25	.25	.50
1	.25	.25	.50
$p_X(x)$	.50	.50	

The values of $p(x,y)$ in this table were constructed using the multiplication rule, since we know that successive coin tosses are independent. Definition 10.7 is satisfied, and X and Y are independent random variables.

In this betting example, joint distribution functions were constructed by the multiplication rule because the events involved were known to be independent. We can also look at joint distributions which have already been constructed and use the definition to check for independence.   □

Example 10.24 The joint probability function for the two assets in Examples 10.1 and 10.3 is given below (with marginals included).

y \ x	90	100	110	$p_Y(y)$
0	.05	.27	.18	.50
10	.15	.33	.02	.50
$p_X(x)$	.20	.60	.20	

Note that $p(90,0) = .05$ and $p_X(90) \cdot p_Y(0) = .20(.50) = .10$. The random variables X and Y are *not* independent.   □

Example 10.25 In Example 10.2, the joint probability function and marginals for X and Y (the numbers of accidents in two towns) were

$$p(x,y) = \frac{e^{-2}}{x!y!}, \text{ for } x = 0,1,2,\dots \text{ and } y = 0,1,2,\dots,$$

$$p_X(x) = \frac{e^{-1}}{x!},$$

and

$$p_Y(y) = \frac{e^{-1}}{y!}.$$

In this case, $p(x,y) = p_X(x) \cdot p_Y(y)$, and X and Y are independent. (This is probably a reasonable assumption to make about numbers of accidents in two different towns.)   □

In Example 10.18 we found the conditional distributions for the independent accident numbers X and Y. We showed that these conditional distributions were the same as the marginal distributions. This is an identity that holds in general for independent random variables X and Y.

Conditional Discrete Distributions for Independent X and Y

$$p(x|y) = p_X(x) \qquad\qquad (10.8a)$$

$$p(y|x) = p_Y(y) \qquad\qquad (10.8b)$$

This follows directly from the definitions of independence and the conditional distribution.

$$p(x|y) = \frac{p(x,y)}{p_Y(y)} \underset{independence}{=} \frac{p_X(x) \cdot p_Y(y)}{p_Y(y)} = p_X(x)$$

10.4.2 Independence for Continuous Random Variables

The definition of independence for continuous random variables is the natural modification of the definition for the discrete case.

Definition 10.8 Two continuous random variables X and Y are **independent** if

$$f(x,y) = f_X(x) \cdot f_Y(y),$$

for all pairs (x, y).

Example 10.26 Let X be the sick leave hours last year and Y the sick leave hours this year from Example 10.9. The joint density and marginal density functions are

$$f(x,y) = 2 - 1.2x - .8y, \text{ for } 0 \le x \le 1, 0 \le y \le 1,$$

$$f_X(x) = 1.6 - 1.2x, \text{ for } 0 \le x \le 1,$$

and

$$f_Y(y) = 1.4 - 0.8y, \text{ for } 0 \le y \le 1.$$

X and Y are *not* independent, since $f(x,y) \ne f_X(x) \cdot f_Y(y)$. $\qquad\square$

Example 10.27 For the joint distribution of waiting times for accidents in Example 10.10, the joint probability density function and marginal density functions were

$$f(s,t) = e^{-(s+t)}, \quad \text{for} \quad s \geq 0, t \geq 0,$$

$$f_S(s) = e^{-s}, \quad \text{for} \quad s \geq 0,$$

and

$$f_T(t) = e^{-t}, \quad \text{for} \quad t \geq 0.$$

In this case $f(s,t) = f_S(s) \cdot f_T(t)$ and S and T are independent. (This is also a reasonable assumption to make about time between accidents in two different towns.)   □

As in the discrete case, the conditional distributions for independent random variables X and Y are the same as their marginal distributions.

Conditional Continuous Distributions for Independent X and Y

$$f(x|y) = f_X(x) \qquad (10.9a)$$

$$f(y|x) = f_Y(y) \qquad (10.9b)$$

10.5 The Multinomial Distribution

In this chapter we have studied bivariate distributions. In many cases there are more than two variables and we have a true **multivariate distribution.** We will illustrate this by looking at the widely used **multinomial distribution.**

The multinomial distribution will remind you of the binomial distribution, and the binomial distribution is a special case of it. Before starting, we will review the partition counting formula –formula 2.10 of Chapter 2.

Counting Partitions

The number of partitions of n objects into k distinct groups of size $n_1, n_2, ..., n_k$ is given by

$$\binom{n}{n_1, n_2, ..., n_k} = \frac{n!}{n_1! \, n_2! \cdots n_k!}.$$

Suppose that a random experiment has k mutually exclusive outcomes $E_1, ..., E_k$, with $P(E_i) = p_i$. Suppose that you repeat this experiment in n independent trials. Let X_i be the number of times that the outcome E_i occurs in the n trials. Then

$$P(X_1 = n_1 \,\&\, X_2 = n_2 \,\&\, \cdots \,\&\, X_k = n_k)$$

$$= \binom{n}{n_1, n_2, ..., n_k} p_1^{n_1} p_2^{n_2} \cdots p_k^{n_k}$$

Example 10.28 You are spinning a spinner that can land on three colors – red, blue and yellow. For this spinner $P(red) = .4$, $P(blue) = .35$, and $P(yellow) = .25$, you spin the spinner 10 times. What is the probability that you spin red five times, blue three times and yellow two times?

Solution There are $k = 3$ mutually exclusive outcomes. Let X_1, X_2 and X_3 be the number of times the spinner comes up red, blue, and yellow respectively. Then $p_1 = P(X_1) = .4$, $p_2 = P(X_2) = .35$, and $p_3 = P(X_3) = .25$. We need to find

$$P(X_1 = 5 \,\&\, X_2 = 3 \,\&\, X_3 = 2) = \binom{10}{5, 3, 2} .4^5 .35^3 .25^2$$

$$= 2520(.4^5 .35^3 .25^2)$$

$$= .069.$$

The sample exam problem 10-37 uses the multinomial distribution.

310

Chapter 10

10.6   Exercises

10.1   Joint Distributions for Discrete Random Variables

10-1. Let $p(x,y) = (xy + y)/27$, for $x = 1,2,3$ and $y = 1,2$, be the joint probability for the random variables X and Y. Construct a table of the joint probabilities of X and Y and the marginal probabilities of X and Y.

10-2. A company has 5 CPA's, 3 actuaries, and 2 economists. Two of these 10 professionals are selected at random to prepare a report. Let X be the random variable for the number of CPA's chosen and let Y be the random variable for the number of actuaries chosen. Construct a table of the joint probabilities for X and Y and the marginal probabilities of X and Y.

10-3. For the random variables in Exercise 10-1, find $E(X)$ and $E(Y)$.

10-4. For the random variables in Exercise 10-2, find $E(X)$ and $E(Y)$.

10-5. For the random variables in Exercise 10-2, find $V(X)$ and $V(Y)$.

10.2   Joint Distributions for Continuous Random Variables

10-6. Show that the function $f(x,y) = \frac{1}{4} + \frac{x}{2} + \frac{y}{2} + xy$, for $0 \le x \le 1$ and $0 \le y \le 1$, is a joint probability density function. Find $P(0 \le X \le .50, .50 \le Y \le 1)$.

10-7. For the joint density function in Exercise 10-6, find (a) $f_X(x)$; (b) $f_Y(y)$.

10-8. Let $f(x,y) = 2x^2 + 3y$, for $0 \le y \le x \le 1$. Find (a) $f_X(x)$; (b) $f_Y(y)$.

10-9. For the joint density function in Exercise 10-8, use the marginal distributions to find (a) $P(X > .50)$; (b) $P(Y > .50)$.

10-10. For the joint density function in Exercise 10-6, find $E(X)$.

10-11. For the joint density function in Exercise 10-6, find $P(X > Y)$.

10-12. For the joint density function in Exercise 10-8, find $E(X)$ and $E(Y)$.

10-13. An auto insurance company separates its comprehensive claims into two parts: losses due to glass breakage and losses due to other damage. If X is the random variable for losses due to glass breakage and Y the random variable for other damage, $f(x, y) = (30 - x - y)/1875$, for $0 \leq x \leq 5, 0 \leq y \leq 25$, where x and y are in hundreds of dollars. Find $P(X \geq 4, Y \geq 20)$.

10-14. For the random variables in Exercise 10-13, find (a) $f_X(x)$; (b) $f_Y(y)$.

10-15. For the random variables in Exercise 10-13, find $E(X)$ and $E(Y)$.

10.3   Conditional Distributions

Exercises 10-16, 10-17 and 10-18 refer to Exercise 10-1.

10-16. Find $P(X|Y = 1)$.

10-17. Find $P(Y|X = 1)$.

10-18. Find $E(X|Y = 1)$.

10-19. For the joint density function in Exercise 10-6, find $f(x \mid y)$.

10-20. For the joint density function in Exercise 10-8, find $f(y \mid x)$.

10-21. For the conditional density function in Exercise 10-20, find (a) $f(y \mid .50)$; (b) $E(Y \mid X = .50)$.

10-22. If $f(x, y) = 6x$, for $0 < x < y < 1$ and 0 elsewhere, find (a) $f_Y(y)$; (b) $f(x \mid y)$; (c) $E(X \mid Y = y)$; (d) $E(X \mid Y = .50)$.

10.4   Independence for Random Variables

10-23. Determine if the random variables in Exercise 10-1 are dependent or independent.

10-24. Determine if the random variables in Exercise 10-2 are dependent or independent.

10-25. Determine if the random variables in Exercise 10-6 are dependent or independent.

10-26. Determine if the random variables in Exercise 10-8 are dependent or independent.

10.7   Sample Actuarial Examination Problems

10-27. A doctor is studying the relationship between blood pressure and heartbeat abnormalities in her patients. She tests a random sample of her patients and notes their blood pressures (high, low, or normal) and their heartbeats (regular or irregular). She finds that:

(i)   14% have high blood pressure.

(ii) 22% have low blood pressure.

(iii) 15% have an irregular heartbeat.

(iv) Of those with an irregular heartbeat, one-third have high blood pressure.

(v)   Of those with normal blood pressure, one-eighth have an irregular heartbeat.

What portion of the patients selected have a regular heartbeat and low blood pressure?

10-28. A large pool of adults earning their first driver's license includes 50% low-risk drivers, 30% moderate-risk drivers, and 20% high-risk drivers. Because these drivers have no prior driving record, an insurance company considers each driver to be randomly selected from the pool. This month, the insurance company writes 4 new policies for adults earning their first driver's license.

What is the probability that these 4 will contain at least two more high-risk drivers than low-risk drivers?

10-29. A device runs until either of two components fails, at which point the device stops running. The joint density function of the lifetimes of the two components, both measured in hours, is

$$f(x,y) = \frac{x+y}{8} \quad \text{for} \quad 0 < x < 2 \quad \text{and} \quad 0 < y < 2$$

What is the probability that the device fails during its first hour of operation?

10-30. A device runs until either of two components fails, at which point the device stops running. The joint density function of the lifetimes of the two components, both measured in hours, is

$$f(x,y) = \frac{x+y}{27} \quad \text{for} \quad 0 < x < 3 \quad \text{and} \quad 0 < y < 3$$

Calculate the probability that the device fails during its first hour of operation.

10-31. A device contains two components. The device fails if either component fails. The joint density function of the lifetimes of the components, measured in hours, is $f(s,t)$, where $0 < s < 1$ and $0 < t < 1$.

Express the probability that the device fails during the first half hour of operation as a double integral.

10-32. The future lifetimes (in months) of two components of a machine have the following joint density function:

$$f(x,y) = \begin{cases} \frac{6}{125,000}(50-x-y) & \text{for} \quad 0 < x < 50-y < 50 \\ 0 & \text{otherwise} \end{cases}$$

What is the probability that both components are still functioning 20 months from now? Express your answer as a double integral, but do not evaluate it.

10-33. An insurance company sells two types of auto insurance policies: Basic and Deluxe. The time until the next Basic Policy claim is an exponential random variable with mean two days. The time until the next Deluxe Policy claim is an independent exponential random variable with mean three days.

What is the probability that the next claim will be a Deluxe Policy claim?

10-34. Two insurers provide bids on an insurance policy to a large company. The bids must be between 2000 and 2200. The company decides to accept the lower bid if the two bids differ by 20 or more. Otherwise, the company will consider the two bids further.

Assume that the two bids are independent and are both uniformly distributed on the interval from 2000 to 2200.

Determine the probability that the company considers the two bids further.

10-35. A car dealership sells 0, 1, or 2 luxury cars on any day. When selling a car, the dealer also tries to persuade the customer to buy an extended warranty for the car.

Let X denote the number of luxury cars sold in a given day, and let Y denote the number of extended warranties sold.

$$P(X = 0, Y = 0) = 1/6$$

$$P(X = 1, Y = 0) = 1/12$$

$$P(X = 1, Y = 1) = 1/6$$

$$P(X = 2, Y = 0) = 1/12$$

$$P(X = 2, Y = 1) = 1/3$$

$$P(X = 2, Y = 2) = 1/6$$

What is the variance of X?

10-36. Let X and Y be continuous random variables with joint density function

$$f(x,y) = \begin{cases} 24xy & \text{for } 0 < x < 1 \text{ and } 0 < y < 1-x \\ 0 & \text{otherwise.} \end{cases}$$

Find $P\left(Y < X \mid X = \dfrac{1}{3}\right)$

10-37. Once a fire is reported to a fire insurance company, the company makes an initial estimate, X, of the amount it will pay to the claimant for the fire loss. When the claim is finally settled, the company pays an amount, Y, to the claimant. The company has determined that X and Y have the joint density function

$$f(x,y) = \frac{2}{x^2(x-1)} y^{-(2x-1)/(x-1)}, \quad x > 1, y > 1.$$

Given that the initial claim estimated by the company is 2, determine the probability that the final settlement amount is between 1 and 3.

10-38. A company offers a basic life insurance policy to its employees, as well as a supplemental life insurance policy. To purchase the supplemental policy, an employee must first purchase the basic policy.

Let X denote the proportion of employees who purchase the basic policy, and Y the proportion of employees who purchase the supplemental policy. Let X and Y have the joint density function $f(x,y) = 2(x+y)$ on the region where the density is positive.

Given that 10% of the employees buy the basic policy, what is the probability that fewer than 5% buy the supplemental policy?

10-39. Two life insurance policies, each with a death benefit of 10,000 and a one-time premium of 500, are sold to a couple, one for each person. The policies will expire at the end of the tenth year. The probability that only the wife will survive at least ten years is 0.025, the probability that only the husband will survive at least ten years is 0.01, and the probability that both of them will survive at least ten years is 0.96.

What is the expected excess of premiums over claims, given that the husband survives at least ten years?

10-40. A diagnostic test for the presence of a disease has two possible outcomes: 1 for disease present and 0 for disease not present. Let X denote the disease state of a patient, and let Y denote the outcome of the diagnostic test. The joint probability function of X and Y is given by:

$$P(X = 0, \, Y = 0) = 0.800$$

$$P(X = 1, \, Y = 0) = 0.050$$

$$P(X = 0, \, Y = 1) = 0.025$$

$$P(X = 1, \, Y = 1) = 0.125$$

Calculate $Var(Y \mid X = 1)$.

10-41. The stock prices of two companies at the end of any given year are modeled with random variables X and Y that follow a distribution with joint density function

$$f(x,y) = \begin{cases} 2x & \text{for} \quad 0 < x < 1 \quad \text{and} \quad x < y < x+1 \\ 0 & \text{otherwise} \end{cases}$$

What is the conditional variance of Y given that $X = x$?

10-42. An actuary determines that the annual numbers of tornadoes in counties P and Q are jointly distributed as follows:

Annual number in Q / Annual number in P	0	1	2	3
0	0.12	0.06	0.05	0.02
1	0.13	0.15	0.12	0.03
2	0.05	0.15	0.10	0.02

Calculate the conditional variance of the annual number of tornadoes in *county Q, given that there are no tornadoes in county P.*

10-43. A company is reviewing tornado damage claims under a farm insurance policy. Let X be the portion of a claim representing damage to the house and let Y be the portion of the same claim representing damage to the rest of the property. The joint density function of X and Y is

$$f(x,y) = \begin{cases} 6[1-(x+y)] & \text{for } x>0, y>0 \text{ and } x+y<1 \\ 0 & \text{otherwise} \end{cases}$$

Determine the probability that the portion of a claim representing damage to the house is less than 0.2.

10-44. Let X and Y be continuous random variables with joint density function

$$f(x,y) = \begin{cases} 15y & \text{for } x^2 \le y \le x \\ 0 & \text{otherwise} \end{cases}$$

Find g, the marginal density function of Y.

10-45. An auto insurance policy will pay for damage to both the policyholder's car and the other driver's car in the event that the policyholder is responsible for an accident. The size of the payment for damage to the policyholder's car, X, has a marginal density function of 1 for $0 < x < 1$. Given $X = x$, the size of the payment for damage to the other driver's car, Y, has conditional density of 1 for $x < y < x+1$.

If the policyholder is responsible for an accident, what is the probability that the payment for damage to the other driver's car will be greater than 0.500?

10-46. An insurance policy is written to cover a loss X where X has density function

$$f(x) = \begin{cases} \frac{3x^2}{8} & \text{for} \quad 0 \le x \le 2 \\ 0 & \text{otherwise} \end{cases}$$

The time (in hours) to process a claim of size x, where $0 \le x \le 2$, is uniformly distributed on the interval from x to $2x$.

Calculate the probability that a randomly chosen claim on this policy is processed in three hours or more.

10-47. Let X represent the age of an insured automobile involved in an accident. Let Y represent the length of time the owner has insured the automobile at the time of the accident.

X and Y have joint probability density function

$$f(x,y) = \begin{cases} \frac{1}{64}(10 - xy^2) & \text{for} \quad 2 \le x \le 10 \quad \text{and} \quad 0 \le y \le 1 \\ 0 & \text{otherwise} \end{cases}.$$

Calculate the expected age of an insured automobile involved in an accident.

10-48. A device contains two circuits. The second circuit is a backup for the first, so the second is used only when the first has failed. The device fails when and only when the second circuit fails.

Let X and Y be the times at which the first and second circuits fail, respectively. X and Y have joint probability density function.

$$f(x,y) = \begin{cases} 6e^{-x}e^{-2y} & \text{for } 0 < x < y < \infty \\ 0 & \text{otherwise} \end{cases}$$

What is the expected time at which the device fails?

10-49. A study of automobile accidents produced the following data:

An automobile from one of the model years 1997, 1998, and 1999 was involved in an accident.

Model	Proportion of All Vehicles	Probability of Involvement in an Accident
1997	0.16	0.05
1998	0.18	0.02
1999	0.20	0.03
Other	0.46	0.04

Determine the probability that the model year of this automobile is 1997.

Chapter 11
Applying Multivariate Distributions

11.1 Distributions of Functions of Two Random Variables

11.1.1 Functions of X and Y

Many practical applications require the study of a function of two or more random variables. For example, if an investor owns two assets with values X and Y, the function $g(X, Y) = X + Y$ is the random variable that gives the total value of his two assets.

In this text, we will focus on four important functions: $X + Y$, XY, $minimum(X, Y)$, and $maximum(X, Y)$. The reader should be aware that a more general theory can be developed for a wider class of functions $g(X, Y)$, but that theory will not be developed in this text.

11.1.2 The Sum of Two Discrete Random Variables

Example 11.1 We return to the two asset random variables X and Y in Example 10.1.

y \ x	90	100	110
0	.05	.27	.18
10	.15	.33	.02

Probabilities for the sum $S = X + Y$ can be found by direct inspection. For example, $X + Y = 90$ can occur only if $x = 90$ and $y = 0$.

$$P(X + Y = 90) = p(90, 0) = .05$$

$X + Y$ assumes a value of 100 for the two outcome pairs $(100, 0)$ and $(90, 10)$.

$$P(X + Y = 100) = p(100, 0) + p(90, 10) = .27 + .15 = .42$$

Similarly,

$$P(X + Y = 110) = p(110, 0) + p(100, 10) = .18 + .33 = .51$$

and

$$P(X + Y = 120) = p(110, 10) = .02.$$

We have now found the entire distribution of $S = X + Y$.

s	90	100	110	120
$p(s)$	.05	.42	.51	.02

□

The technique we used to find $p(s)$ was simply to add up all values of $p(x, y)$ for which $x + y = s$. Another way to say this is that we added all joint probability values of the form $p(x, s - x)$. This is stated symbolically as

$$p(s) = \sum_x p(x, s - x). \tag{11.1}$$

11.1.3 The Sum of Independent Discrete Random Variables

When the two random variables X and Y are independent, then we have $p(x, s - x) = p_X(x) \cdot p_Y(s - x)$. In this case Equation (11.1) assumes a form that is convenient for calculation.

Probability Function for $S = X + Y$
(X and Y are Independent)

$$p_S(s) = \sum_x p_X(x) \cdot p_Y(s - x) \tag{11.2}$$

Example 11.2 An insurance company has two clients. The random variables representing the number of claims filed by each client are X and Y. X and Y are independent, and each has the same probability distribution.

x	0	1	2	y
$p_X(x)$	1/2	1/4	1/4	$p_Y(y)$

We can find the distribution for $S = X + Y$ using Equation 11.2.

$$P(S = 0) = p_S(0) = p_X(0) \cdot p_Y(0) = \frac{1}{2} \cdot \frac{1}{2} = \frac{1}{4}$$

$$p_S(1) = p_X(0) \cdot p_Y(1) + p_X(1) \cdot p_Y(0) = \frac{1}{2} \cdot \frac{1}{4} + \frac{1}{4} \cdot \frac{1}{2} = \frac{1}{4}$$

$$p_S(2) = p_X(0) \cdot p_Y(2) + p_X(2) \cdot p_Y(0) + p_X(1) \cdot p_Y(1)$$
$$= \frac{1}{2} \cdot \frac{1}{4} + \frac{1}{4} \cdot \frac{1}{2} + \frac{1}{4} \cdot \frac{1}{4} = \frac{5}{16}$$

$$p_S(3) = p_X(1) \cdot p_Y(2) + p_X(2) \cdot p_Y(1)$$
$$= \frac{1}{4} \cdot \frac{1}{4} + \frac{1}{4} \cdot \frac{1}{4} = \frac{1}{8}$$

$$p_S(4) = p_X(2) \cdot p_Y(2) = \frac{1}{4} \cdot \frac{1}{4} = \frac{1}{16}$$

The distribution of S is given by the following:

s	0	1	2	3	4
$p_S(s)$	1/4	1/4	5/16	1/8	1/16

The above calculation (based on Equation 11.2) is referred to as finding the **convolution** of the two independent random variables X and Y. We will return to convolutions when we look at the sum of independent continuous random variables. $\square$

11.1.4 The Sum of Continuous Random Variables

Finding probabilities for $X + Y$ is a bit more complicated in the continuous case, since summation is replaced by integration.

Example 11.3 Let X be the sick leave hours last year and Y the sick leave hours this year in Example 10.9. The joint density function is

$$f(x,y) = 2 - 1.2x - .8y, \text{ for } 0 \le x \le 1, 0 \le y \le 1.$$

Let $S = X + Y$ be the total sick leave hours for both years. We will calculate the probability that $S = X + Y \le .50$. (This is actually a single value of the cumulative distribution function of the random variable S, since $P(S \le .50) = F_S(.50)$). The points (x, y) where the random variable $X + Y$ is less than or equal to .50 are in the region R in the x-y plane satisfying the inequalities $x + y \le .50$, for $0 \le x \le 1$, $0 \le y \le 1$. If we integrate the density function $f(x, y)$ over this region, we will find the desired probability.

$$P(X + Y \le .50) = \iint_R f(x,y)\, dx\, dy$$

The region R is shown in the following figure.

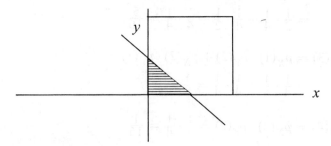

We can now evaluate the double integral.

$$P(X + Y \le .50) = \int_0^{.50} \int_0^{.50-y} (2 - 1.2x - .8y)\, dx\, dy$$

$$= \int_0^{.50} (2x - .6x^2 - .8xy)\Big|_{x=0}^{.50-y}\, dy$$

$$= \int_0^{.50} (.2y^2 - 1.8y + .85)\, dy = .20833 \qquad \square$$

Example 11.3 required a fair amount of work to find a single value of $F_S(s)$. However, the pattern of the last calculation will apply to the task of finding $F_S(s)$ for $0 \le s \le 1$. The region of integration changes to require a different integral for $F_S(s)$ for $1 < s \le 2$. This reasoning is developed in Exercise 11-4.

11.1.5 The Sum of Independent Continuous Random Variables

In the preceding example, the two random variables X and Y were not independent. In many applications, the random variables which are being added are independent. Fortunately, calculations are simpler if X and Y are independent. The simplification results from the use of a convolution rule. For two independent discrete random variables, the convolution rule was

$$p(s) = \sum_x p_X(x) \cdot p_Y(s - x).$$

The same reasoning with summation replaced by integration leads to the continuous convolution principle.

Density Function for $S = X + Y$
(X and Y Independent)

$$f_S(s) = \int_{-\infty}^{\infty} f_X(x) \cdot f_Y(s - x) \, dx \qquad (11.3)$$

Example 11.4 In Example 10.10, we looked at the waiting times S and T between accidents in two towns. For notational simplicity, we will use the variable names X and Y instead of S and T in this example. The probability density function and marginal density functions are

$$f(x, y) = e^{-(x+y)}, \text{ for } x \geq 0, y \geq 0,$$

$$f_X(x) = e^{-x}, \text{ for } x \geq 0,$$

and

$$f_Y(y) = e^{-y}, \text{ for } y \geq 0.$$

In Example 10.27, we showed that X and Y are independent. Thus we can use Equation 11.3 to find the density function of $S = X + Y$.

$$f_S(s) = \int_{-\infty}^{\infty} f_X(x) \cdot f_Y(s - x) \, dx = \int_0^s e^{-x} e^{-(s-x)} dx$$

$$= e^{-s} \int_0^s 1 \, dx = s e^{-s}$$

Note the limits on the second integral above. The random variables X, Y, and S are all non-negative. Thus $x \geq 0$, $y = s - x \geq 0$, and $s \geq x \geq 0$.

The two independent random variables X and Y were exponential with parameter $\beta = 1$. The sum $S = X + Y$ is a gamma random variable with parameters $\alpha = 2$ and $\beta = 1$. In Section 8.3.3 we stated (without proof) that the sum of n independent exponential random variables with parameter β has a gamma distribution with parameters $\alpha = n$ and β. We have just derived a special case of that result.   □

The distribution of $X + Y$ could also be found by evaluating the cumulative probability $P(S \leq s) = F_S(s)$ as a double integral.

$$P(X + Y \leq s) = \int \int_R f(x, y) \, dx \, dy$$

The reader is asked to do this in Exercise 11-5. The convolution approach is simpler, and is widely used. The reader should be aware that in some examples the limits of integration in Equation 11.3 become tricky. In the following sections, we will look at even simpler ways to obtain information about $X + Y$.

11.1.6 The Minimum of Two Independent Exponential Random Variables

For most of this section we have concentrated on the function $g(X, Y) = X + Y$. To illustrate that distribution functions can be found for other functions of X and Y, we will now look at the minimum function $min(X, Y)$ for independent exponential random variables X and Y. We first need to review basic properties of the exponential random variable. An exponential random variable X with parameter β has the following cumulative and survival functions:

$$F(t) = P(X \leq t) = 1 - e^{-\beta t}$$

$$S(t) = P(X > t) = e^{-\beta t}$$

Suppose that X and Y are exponential with parameters β and λ, respectively, and let M denote the random variable $min(X,Y)$. We will find the survival function for M.

$$S_M(t) = P(min(X,Y) > t) \quad = \quad P(X > t \text{ and } Y > t)$$

$$\underset{independence}{=} P(X > t) \cdot P(Y > t)$$

$$= \quad e^{-\beta t}e^{-\lambda t} = e^{-(\beta+\lambda)t}$$

The function $e^{-(\beta+\lambda)t}$ is the survival function $S(t)$ for an exponential distribution with parameter $\beta+\lambda$. Thus M must have that distribution.

Minimum of Independent Exponential Random Variables
(X and Y Independent with Parameters β and λ)

$M = min(X,Y)$ is exponential with parameter $\beta+\lambda$

Example 11.5 We return to X and Y, the independent waiting times for accidents in Example 11.4. X and Y have exponential distributions with parameters $\beta = 1$ and $\lambda = 1$, respectively. Then $M = min(X,Y)$ has an exponential distribution with parameter $\beta + \lambda = 2$. This can be interpreted in a natural way. In each of two separate towns, we are waiting for the first accident in a process where the average number of accidents is 1 per month. When we study the accidents for both towns, we are waiting for the first accident in a process where the average number of accidents is a total of 2 per month. □

11.1.7 The Minimum and Maximum of any Two Independent Random Variables

Suppose that X and Y are two independent random variables. Recall that the survival function of a random variable X is defined by

$$S_X(t) = P(X > T) = 1 - F_X(t)$$

The general reasoning for analyzing $Min = min(X < Y)$ follows the argument we used for the minimum of two independent exponential random variables.

$$S_{Min}(t) = P\big(min(X,Y) > t\big) = P(X > t \,\&\, Y > t)$$
$$\underset{independence}{=} P(X > t) \cdot P(Y > t) = S_X(t)S_Y(t)$$

The method of analysis for $Max = max(X,Y)$ is very similar.

$$F_{Max}(t) = P(max(X,Y) \le t) = P(X \le t \,\&\, Y \le t)$$
$$\underset{independence}{=} P(X \le t) \cdot P(Y \le t) = F_X(t)F_Y(t)$$

The next example shows that once we use the previous identities to get $F_{Max}(t)$ or $S_{Min}(t)$,, we can find density functions and expected values for the maximum and the minimum.

Example 11.6 For a uniform random variable X on $[0,100]$,

$$F_X(x) = \frac{x}{100} \quad \text{and} \quad S_X(x) = 1 - \frac{x}{100} = \frac{100 - x}{100}.$$

Suppose X and Y are independent uniform random variables on $[0,100]$. Then

$$S_{Min}(t) = P(min(X,Y) > t) = S_X(t)S_Y(t) = \frac{(100 - t)^2}{10,000}$$

$$F_{Min}(t) = 1 - \frac{(100 - t)^2}{10,000}$$

$$F_{Max}(t) = P(max(X,Y) \le t) = F_X(t)F_Y(t) = \frac{t^2}{10,000}$$

Taking derivatives, we can find the density functions for $min(X,Y)$ and $max(X,Y)$

$$f_{Min}(t) = \frac{-2(100-t)}{10,000} = \frac{100 - t}{5,000} \quad f_{Max}(t) = \frac{t}{5,000}$$

$$E[min(X,Y)] = \int_0^{100} t \frac{100-t}{5,000} dt = \frac{100t^2}{10,000} - \frac{t^3}{15,000} \Big|_0^{100} = 33.\overline{3}$$

$$E[max(X,Y)] = \int_0^{100} t \frac{t}{5000} dt = \frac{t^3}{15,000} \Big|_0^{100} = 66.\overline{6} \qquad \square$$

This method can easily be extended to more than two independent random variables, as the next example shows.

Example 11.7 Let X,Y and Z be three independent exponential random variables with mean 100. Find $P(max(X,Y,Z) \le 50)$.

Solution Each of the random variables has density function and cumulative distribution function

$$f(x) = \left(\frac{1}{100}\right)e^{-x/100} = .01e^{-.01x} \qquad F(x) = 1 - e^{-.01x}$$

Using the same reasoning used for two random variables, we see that

$$P(max(X,Y,Z) \le 50) = P(X \le 50 \ \& \ Y \le 50 \ \& \ Z \le 50)$$
$$\underset{independence}{=} F_X(50) F_Y(50) F_Z(50)$$
$$= (1 - e^{-.01(50)})^3$$
$$= .061 \qquad \square$$

11.2 Expected Values of Functions of Random Variables

11.2.1 Finding $E[g(X,Y)]$

We have seen that finding the distribution of $g(X,Y)$ can require a fair amount of work for a function as simple as $g(X,Y) = X+Y$. However, the expected value of $g(X,Y)$ can be found without first finding the distribution of $g(X,Y)$. This is due to the following theorem which is stated without proof.

Theorem 11.1 Let X and Y be random variables and let $g(x, y)$ be a function of two variables.

(a)   If X and Y are discrete with joint probability function $p(x, y)$,

$$E[g(X, Y)] = \sum_x \sum_y g(x, y) \cdot p(x, y).$$

(b)   If X and Y are continuous with joint density $f(x, y)$,

$$E[g(X, Y)] = \int_{-\infty}^{\infty} \int_{-\infty}^{\infty} g(x, y) \cdot f(x, y)\, dx\, dy.$$

11.2.2 Finding $E(X + Y)$

We will begin with an example to illustrate the application of the preceding theorem with $g(x, y) = x + y$.

Example 11.8 We return to the two asset random variables X and Y in Example 10.1.

y \ x	90	100	110
0	.05	.27	.18
10	.15	.33	.02

The theorem says that

$$E(X + Y) = \sum_x \sum_y (x + y) \cdot p(x, y)$$

$$= (0+90)(.05) + (0+100)(.27) + (0+110)(.18)$$
$$+ (10+90)(.15) + (10+100)(.33) + (10+110)(.02)$$

$$= 105.$$

We were not required to find the probability function for $S = X + Y$. The theorem allows us to work directly with the joint distribution function. We can check our answer here, since we have already found the probability function for S.

s	90	100	110	120
$p(s)$	.05	.42	.51	.02

Then $E(S) = 90(.05) + 100(.42) + 110(.51) + 120(.02) = 105.$ □

A very useful result becomes apparent if we look at the random variables X and Y in the last example separately. We have previously shown that $E(X) = 100$ and $E(Y) = 5$. Thus

$$105 = E(X + Y) = E(X) + E(Y).$$

This useful result always holds. If X and Y are discrete,

$$E(X + Y) = \sum_x \sum_y (x + y) \cdot p(x, y)$$

$$= \sum_x \sum_y x \cdot p(x, y) + \sum_y \sum_x y \cdot p(x, y)$$

$$= \sum_x x \sum_y p(x, y) + \sum_y y \sum_x p(x, y)$$

$$= \sum_x x \cdot p_X(x) + \sum_y y \cdot p_Y(y)$$

$$= E(X) + E(Y).$$

A similar proof is used for continuous random variables, with summation replaced by integration. This is left for Exercise 11-9.

Expected Value of a Sum of Two Random Variables

$$E(X + Y) = E(X) + E(Y) \qquad\qquad (11.4)$$

Example 11.9 Let X be the sick leave hours last year and Y the sick leave hours this year from Example 10.9. We have shown in Example 10.13 that $E(X) = .40$ and $E(Y) = .4\dot{3}$. Then

$$E(X + Y) = .40 + .4\dot{3} = .8\dot{3}. \qquad\qquad \square$$

11.2.3 The Expected Value of XY

We have just shown that the expected value of a sum is the sum of the expected values. Products of random variables are not so simple; the expected value of XY does *not* always equal the product of the expected values. This is shown in the next example.

Example 11.10 We return again to the two asset random variables X and Y in Example 10.1.

y x	90	100	110
0	.05	.27	.18
10	.15	.33	.02

Using the expected value theorem with $g(x, y) = xy$,

$$E(XY) = \sum_x \sum_y (x\,y) \cdot p(x, y).$$

$$= (0 \cdot 90)(.05) + (0 \cdot 100)(.27) + (0 \cdot 110)(.18)$$
$$+ (10 \cdot 90)(.15) + (10 \cdot 100)(.33) + (10 \cdot 110)(.02)$$

$$= 487.$$

Note that

$$E(X) \cdot E(Y) = 100(5) = 500.$$

In this case, $E(XY) \neq E(X) \cdot E(Y)$. ☐

In the special case where X and Y are independent, it is true that $E(XY) = E(X) \cdot E(Y)$. If X and Y are discrete and independent,

$$E(X) \cdot E(Y) = \left(\sum_x x \cdot p_X(x) \right) \left(\sum_y y \cdot p_Y(y) \right)$$

$$= \sum_x \sum_y xy \cdot p_X(x) \cdot p_Y(y)$$

$$= \sum_x \sum_y xy \cdot p(x, y)$$

$$= E(XY).$$

A similar proof applies for independent continuous random variables.

Expected Value of XY
(X and Y Independent)
$E(XY) = E(X) \cdot E(Y)$ (11.5)

Note: a) The identity in (11.5) may fail to hold if X and Y are not independent. b) There are examples of random variables X and Y which are not independent but satisfy (11.5). See problem 11-19.

Example 11.11 The random variables X and Y in Example 11.2 represented the number of claims filed by two insured clients. X and Y were independent, and each had the same probability distribution.

x	0	1	2	y
$p_X(x)$	1/2	1/4	1/4	$p_Y(y)$

Each random variable also had the same expected value.

$$E(X) = 0\left(\tfrac{1}{2}\right) + 1\left(\tfrac{1}{4}\right) + 2\left(\tfrac{1}{4}\right) = \tfrac{3}{4} = E(Y)$$

By Equation (11.5),

$$E(XY) = E(X) \cdot E(Y) = \left(\tfrac{3}{4}\right)\left(\tfrac{3}{4}\right) = \tfrac{9}{16}. \qquad \square$$

In Exercise 11-10, the reader is asked to find $E(XY)$ directly and verify the last answer.

Example 11.12 X and Y, the waiting times for accidents in Example 11.4, were independent exponential distributions with parameters $\beta = 1$ and $\lambda = 1$.

$$E(X) = \tfrac{1}{\beta} = 1 = \tfrac{1}{\lambda} = E(Y)$$

By Equation (11.5),

$$E(XY) = E(X) \cdot E(Y) = 1. \qquad \square$$

It is important to be able to calculate $E(XY)$ directly when X and Y are not known to be independent. We have already done this for the discrete case in Example 11.10. The following example illustrates the calculation for the continuous case.

Example 11.13 Let X be the sick leave hours last year and Y the sick leave hours this year from Example 10.9. The joint density function is

$$f(x,y) = 2 - 1.2x - .8y, \text{ for } 0 \le x \le 1, 0 \le y \le 1.$$

We will calculate $E(XY)$ by integration, using part (b) of Theorem 11.1.

$$E(XY) = \int_0^1 \int_0^1 xy(2 - 1.2x - .8y)\, dx\, dy$$

$$= \int_0^1 (x^2 y - .4x^3 y - .4x^2 y^2)\Big|_{x=0}^{1}\, dy$$

$$= \int_0^1 (-.4y^2 + .6y)dy = \tfrac{1}{6}$$

The reader should note that $E(X) \cdot E(Y) = .4(.4\dot{3}) = .17\dot{3} \neq E(XY)$.

$\square$

11.2.4 The Covariance of X and Y

The covariance is an extremely useful expected value with many applications. It is a key component of the formula for $V(X+Y)$, and it is used in measuring association between random variables.

Definition 11.1 Let X and Y be random variables. The **covariance** of X and Y is defined by

$$Cov(X, Y) = E[(X - \mu_X)(Y - \mu_Y)].$$

Example 11.14 For the two asset random variables X and Y in Example 10.1, $E(X) = \mu_X = 100$ and $E(Y) = \mu_Y = 5$. The joint distribution table is as follows:

y \ x	90	100	110
0	.05	.27	.18
10	.15	.33	.02

We will calculate $Cov(X, Y)$ directly from the definition.

$$Cov(X, Y) = E[(X - \mu_X)(Y - \mu_Y)]$$

$$= (90-100)(0-5)(.05)$$
$$+ (100-100)(0-5)(.27)$$
$$+ (110-100)(0-5)(.18)$$
$$+ (90-100)(10-5)(.15)$$
$$+ (100-100)(10-5)(.33)$$
$$+ (110-100)(10-5)(.02)$$

$$= 50(.05)$$
$$+ 0(.27)$$
$$+ -50(.18)$$
$$+ -50(.15)$$
$$+ 0(.33)$$
$$+ 50(.02)$$

$$= 2.5$$
$$+ 0$$
$$+ -9$$
$$+ -7.5$$
$$+ 0$$
$$+ 1$$

$$= -13 \qquad \square$$

The sign of the covariance is determined by the relationship between the random variables X and Y. In our example above, the random variables X and Y are said to be **negatively associated**, since higher values of X tend to occur simultaneously with lower values of Y. The covariance was negative for these negatively associated random variables because the negative terms in the covariance had more influence on the sum than the positive terms. (The negative terms are shaded for emphasis.) Note that an individual term in the covariance is negative when $(x - \mu_X)$ and $(y - \mu_Y)$ are of opposite sign and positive when $(x - \mu_X)$ and $(y - \mu_Y)$ have the same sign. Thus the negative terms occur when the realized value of X is above the mean and the value of Y is simultaneously below the mean or vice versa, i.e., when higher values of X are paired with lower values of Y or vice versa.

Paired random variables such as the height and weight of an individual are said to be **positively associated,** because higher values of both tend to occur for the same individuals and lower values do the same. For positively associated random variables, the covariance will be positive. The study of measures of association is really a topic for a statistics course, but it is useful to have some idea of the meaning that is attached to the covariance in this course. Positive covariance implies some positive association, and negative covariance implies some negative association.

We calculated the covariance directly from the definition in the last example in order to give an intuitive interpretation. There is another way to calculate the covariance.

$$Cov(X,Y) = E[(X - \mu_X)(Y - \mu_Y)]$$
$$= E(XY - \mu_Y X - \mu_X Y + \mu_X \cdot \mu_Y)$$
$$= E(XY) - \mu_Y \cdot E(X) - \mu_X \cdot E(Y) + \mu_X \cdot \mu_Y$$
$$= E(XY) - \mu_X \cdot \mu_Y$$

Alternative Calculation of Covariance

$$Cov(X,Y) = E(XY) - E(X) \cdot E(Y) \qquad (11.6)$$

Example 11.15 For the two asset random variables X and Y in Example 10.1, $E(X) = \mu_X = 100$ and $E(Y) = \mu_Y = 5$. In Example 11.10 we showed that $E(XY) = 487$. Then Equation (11.6) shows that

$$Cov(X,Y) = E(XY) - E(X) \cdot E(Y) = 487 - (100)(5) = -13.$$
□

Example 11.16 Let X be the sick leave hours last year and Y the sick leave hours this year from Example 10.9. In Example 11.13 we showed that $E(XY) = \frac{1}{6}$ and $E(X) \cdot E(Y) = .173$. Then Equation (11.6) shows that

$$Cov(X,Y) = .166 - .173 = -.0066.$$
□

We know from Equation (11.5) that when X and Y are independent, $E(XY) = E(X) \cdot E(Y)$. This means that $Cov(X,Y)$ will be zero.

> ### Covariance of XY
> ### (X and Y Independent)
>
> $$Cov(X,Y) = 0$$

Example 11.17 X and Y, the waiting times for accidents in Example 11.4, were independent exponential distributions with parameters $\beta = 1$ and $\lambda = 1$. Then $Cov(X,Y) = 0$.   □

11.2.5 The Variance of $X + Y$

The covariance is of special interest because it can be used in a simple formula for the variance of the sum of two random variables.

> ### Variance of $X + Y$
>
> $$V(X+Y) = V(X)+V(Y)+2 \cdot Cov(X,Y) \qquad (11.7)$$

The derivation is straightforward.

$$
\begin{aligned}
V(X+Y) &= E[(X+Y)^2] - (E(X+Y))^2 \\
&= E(X^2 + 2XY + Y^2) - (\mu_X + \mu_Y)^2 \\
&= E(X^2) + 2E(XY) + E(Y^2) - (\mu_X^2 + 2\mu_X \cdot \mu_Y + \mu_Y^2) \\
&= E(X^2) - \mu_X^2 + E(Y^2) - \mu_Y^2 + 2(E(XY) - \mu_X \cdot \mu_Y) \\
&= V(X) + V(Y) + 2 \cdot Cov(X,Y)
\end{aligned}
$$

The calculations in our previous examples will now enable us to calculate $V(X+Y)$ without finding the distribution of $X + Y$.

Example 11.18 The joint probability function for the two assets in Examples 10.1 and 10.3 is given below (with marginals included).

y \ x	90	100	110	$p_Y(y)$
0	.05	.27	.18	.50
10	.15	.33	.02	.50
$p_X(x)$	.20	.60	.20	

We have already found that $E(X) = 100$, $V(X) = 40$, $E(Y) = 5$ and $V(Y) = 25$. In Example 11.15, we found that $Cov(X,Y) = -13$. Thus

$$V(X+Y) = V(X) + V(Y) + 2 \cdot Cov(X,Y) = 40 + 25 - 2(13) = 39.$$

We can proceed in the same way if X and Y are continuous.   □

Example 11.19 Let X be the sick leave hours last year and Y the sick leave hours this year from Example 10.9. The joint density and marginal density functions are

$$f(x,y) = 2 - 1.2x - .8y, \text{ for } 0 \le x \le 1, 0 \le y \le 1,$$

$$f_X(x) = 1.6 - 1.2x, \text{ for } 0 \le x \le 1,$$

and

$$f_Y(y) = 1.4 - 0.8y, \text{ for } 0 \le y \le 1.$$

We have already found that $E(X) = .40$ and $E(Y) = .4\dot{3}$. Using the marginal density functions,

$$E(X^2) = \int_0^1 x^2(1.6 - 1.2x)\, dx = .23\dot{3},$$

$$E(Y^2) = \int_0^1 y^2(1.4 - 0.8y)\, dy = .26\dot{6},$$

$$V(X) = .23\dot{3} - .40^2 = .073\dot{3},$$

and

$$V(Y) = .26\dot{6} - .43\dot{3}^2 = .078\dot{8}.$$

In Example 11.16, we found that $Cov(X,Y) = -.006\dot{6}$. Thus

$$V(X+Y) = V(X) + V(Y) + 2 \cdot Cov(X,Y) = .138\dot{8}. \qquad □$$

In the special case where the random variables X and Y are independent, $Cov(X,Y) = 0$. This leads to a nice result for independent random variables.

Variance of $X + Y$
(X and Y Independent)

$$V(X+Y) = V(X) + V(Y) \qquad (11.8)$$

Example 11.20 X and Y, the waiting times for accidents in Example 11.4, were independent exponential distributions with parameters $\beta = 1$ and $\lambda = 1$. Then

$$V(X) = \frac{1}{\beta^2} = 1 = \frac{1}{\lambda^2} = V(Y).$$

Equation (11.8) shows that

$$V(X + Y) = V(X) + V(Y) = 2. \qquad \square$$

11.2.6 Useful Properties of Covariance

The covariance has a number of useful properties. Five of these are given below with derivations.

(1) $Cov(X, Y) = Cov(Y, X)$

$$E[(X - \mu_X)(Y - \mu_Y)] = E[(Y - \mu_Y)(X - \mu_X)]$$

(2) $Cov(X, X) = V(X)$

$$\begin{aligned}
Cov(X, X) &= E[(X - \mu_X)(X - \mu_X)] \\
&= E[(X - \mu_X)^2] \\
&= V(X)
\end{aligned}$$

(3) If k is a constant random variable, then $Cov(X, k) = 0$.

Since k is constant, $E(k) = k$. Then

$$Cov(X, k) = E[(X - \mu_X)(k - k)] = E[0] = 0.$$

(4) $Cov(aX, bY) = ab \cdot Cov(X, Y)$

Since $E(aX) = a \cdot \mu_X$ and $E(bY) = b \cdot \mu_Y$, then

$$\begin{aligned}
Cov(aX, bY) &= E[(aX - a \cdot \mu_X)(bY - b \cdot \mu_Y)] \\
&= ab \cdot E[(X - \mu_X)(Y - \mu_Y)] \\
&= ab \cdot Cov(X, Y).
\end{aligned}$$

(5) $Cov(X, Y + Z) = Cov(X, Y) + Cov(X, Z)$
Since $E(Y + Z) = E(Y) + E(Z) = \mu_Y + \mu_Z$, then

$$Cov(X, Y+Z) = E[(X - \mu_X)(Y + Z - (\mu_Y + \mu_Z)]$$
$$= E[(X - \mu_X)((Y - \mu_Y) + (Z - \mu_Z))]$$
$$= E[(X - \mu_X)(Y - \mu_Y)]$$
$$+ E[(X - \mu_X)(Z - \mu_Z)]$$
$$= Cov(X, Y) + Cov(X, Z).$$

11.2.7 The Correlation Coefficient

The correlation coefficient is used in statistics to measure the level of association between two random variables X and Y. A detailed analysis of the correlation coefficient and its properties can be found in any mathematical statistics text. The correlation coefficient is defined using the covariance. We have already observed that the sign of the covariance is detemined by the association between X and Y.

Definition 11.2 Let X and Y be random variables. The **correlation coefficient** between X and Y is defined by

$$\rho_{XY} = \frac{Cov(X, Y)}{\sigma_X \sigma_Y} = \frac{Cov(X, Y)}{\sqrt{V(X) \cdot V(Y)}}.$$

Although we will not prove all of the properties of ρ_{XY} discussed in this section, it is a simple matter to derive the value of ρ_{XY} when X and Y are linearly related, i.e., $Y = aX + b$.

$$\rho_{XY} = \frac{Cov(X, aX + b)}{\sigma_X \sigma_{aX+b}} = \frac{Cov(X, aX) + Cov(X, b)}{\sigma_X(|a|\sigma_X)}$$

$$= \frac{a \cdot V(X) + 0}{|a|(\sigma_X)^2} = \frac{a}{|a|} = \begin{cases} 1 & a > 0 \\ -1 & a < 0 \end{cases}$$

Thus when X and Y are linearly related, the correlation coefficient is 1 when the slope of the straight line is positive, and -1 when the slope is negative. The following properties can also be shown.

(a) If $\rho_{XY} = 1$, then $Y = aX + b$ with $a > 0$.
(b) If $\rho_{XY} = -1$, then $Y = aX + b$ with $a < 0$.[2]

Thus we can simply look at the correlation coefficient and determine that there is a positive linear relationship between X and Y if $\rho_{XY} = 1$ or a negative relationship between X and Y if $\rho_{XY} = -1$.

To see what might happen when X and Y are not linearly related, we will look at the extreme case in which X and Y are independent and have no systematic relationship. When X and Y are independent, then $Cov(X,Y) = 0$. Thus

$$\rho_{XY} = \frac{Cov(X,Y)}{\sigma_X \sigma_Y} = \underset{independence}{} \frac{0}{\sigma_X \sigma_Y} = 0.$$

Clearly $\rho_{XY} = 0$ whenever $Cov(X,Y) = 0$. (There are examples of random variables X and Y which are not independent but still satisfy $Cov(X,Y) = 0$. One is given in Exercise 11-19.)

It can be shown that

$$-1 \le \rho_{XY} \le 1,$$

for any random variables X and Y. We display the possible values of ρ_{XY} and their verbal interpretations on the following diagram.

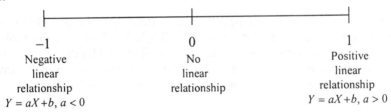

The possible values of ρ_{XY} lie on a continuum between -1 and 1. Values of ρ_{XY} close to ± 1 are interpreted as an indication of a high level of linear association between X and Y. Values of ρ_{XY} near 0 are interpreted as implying little or no linear relationship between X and Y.

In the following examples, we will find ρ_{XY} for random variables presented earlier in this chapter.

[2] More advanced texts would say that $Y = aX + b$ with probability 1. This is done to include more complicated random variables which are beyond the scope of this text.

Example 11.21 Let X and Y be the two asset random variables defined in Example 10.1. We have shown that $V(X) = 40$, $V(Y) = 25$ and $Cov(X, Y) = -13$.

$$\rho_{XY} = \frac{-13}{\sqrt{40(25)}} = -.411 \qquad \qquad \square$$

Example 11.22 Let X and Y be the sick leave hour random variables defined in Example 10.9. We have shown that $V(X) = .07\dot{3}$, $V(Y) = .07\dot{8}$, and $Cov(X, Y) = -.006\dot{6}$.

$$\rho_{XY} = \frac{-.006\dot{6}}{\sqrt{.07\dot{3}(.07\dot{8})}} \approx -.088 \qquad \qquad \square$$

Although both of the correlation coefficients above are closer to 0 than to 1, the implied association, however small, may be of some use. We have already noted that the relationship between the two assets X and Y may be useful in reducing risk. In practical situations, the interpretation of the correlation coefficient can be subtle. As we have mentioned previously, this is discussed more extensively in statistics texts.

11.2.8 The Bivariate Normal Distribution

There is a multivariate analogue of the normal distribution. This is important in advanced statistics, and we will briefly illustrate it by looking at the two variable multivariate normal distribution. The density function looks complicated at first glance. Two random variables X and Y have a **bivariate normal distribution** if their join density is of the form

$$f(x, y) = \frac{1}{2\pi\sigma_1\sigma_2\sqrt{1-\rho^2}} e^{\frac{-1}{2(1-\rho^2)}\left[\left(\frac{x-\mu_1}{\sigma_1}\right)^2 - 2\rho\left(\frac{x-\mu_1}{\sigma_1}\right)\left(\frac{y-\mu_2}{\sigma_2}\right) + \left(\frac{y-\mu_2}{\sigma_2}\right)^2\right]}$$

X and Y are also referred to as **jointly normally distributed**.

We will not look at the bivariate normal in depth, but it is nice to note here that:

a) The marginal distribution of X is normal with mean μ_1 and standard deviation σ_1.
b) The marginal distribution of Y is normal with mean μ_2 and standard deviation σ_2.
c) The correlation coefficient between X and Y is ρ.

11.3 Moment Generating Functions for Sums of Independent Random Variables; Joint Moment Generating Functions

11.3.1 The General Principle

If X and Y are independent random variables, we can conclude that the random variables e^{tX} and e^{tY} used in the definition of the moment generating function are also independent. This gives a nice simplification for the moment generating function of $X + Y$.

$$\begin{aligned} M_{X+Y}(t) = E(e^{t(X+Y)}) &= E(e^{tX} \cdot e^{tY}) \\ &\underset{independence}{=} E(e^{tX}) \cdot E(e^{tY}) = M_X(t) \cdot M_Y(t) \end{aligned}$$

Moment Generating Function of $X+Y$
(X and Y Independent)

$$M_{X+Y}(t) = M_X(t) \cdot M_Y(t) \qquad (11.9)$$

This leads to a number of nice results about sums of random variables.

11.3.2 The Sum of Independent Poisson Random Variables

The moment generating function of a Poisson random variable X with parameter λ is
$$M_X(t) = e^{\lambda(e^t - 1)}.$$

If Y is Poisson with parameter β and Y is independent of X, the moment generating function of $X + Y$ is given by

$$M_{X+Y}(t) = M_X(t) \cdot M_Y(t) = e^{\lambda(e^t-1)} \cdot e^{\beta(e^t-1)} = e^{(\lambda+\beta)(e^t-1)}.$$

The final expression is the moment generating function of a Poisson random variable with parameter $(\lambda + \beta)$.

> If X and Y are independent Poisson random variables with parameters λ and β, then $X + Y$ is Poisson with parameter $(\lambda + \beta)$.

Example 11.23 In Example 10.2, the joint probability function and marginal probability functions for X and Y (the numbers of accidents in two towns) were

$$p(x, y) = \frac{e^{-2}}{x!y!}, \text{ for } x = 0, 1, 2, \ldots \text{ and } y = 0, 1, 2, \ldots,$$

and

$$p_X(x) = \frac{e^{-1}}{x!},$$

$$p_Y(y) = \frac{e^{-1}}{y!}.$$

In this case, $p(x, y) = p_X(x) \cdot p_Y(y)$ and X and Y are independent Poisson random variables with $\lambda = 1$. Thus $X + Y$ is a Poisson random variable with $\lambda = 2$.   □

11.3.3 The Sum of Independent and Identically Distributed Geometric Random Variables

The moment generating function of a geometric random variable with success probability p is

$$M_X(t) = \frac{p}{1 - qe^t}.$$

If Y is also geometric with success probability p, then Y has the same distribution as X. In this case X and Y are said to be **identically distributed**. If Y is independent of X, the moment generating function of $X + Y$ is given by

$$M_{X+Y}(t) = M_X(t) \cdot M_Y(t) = \left(\frac{p}{1 - qe^t}\right)^2.$$

This is the moment generating function of a negative binomial distribution with success probability p and $r = 2$.

> The sum of two independent and identically distributed geometric random variables with success probability p has a negative binomial distribution with the same p and $r = 2$.

This is consistent with our interpretation of the geometric and negative binomial distributions. The geometric random variable represents the number of failures before the first success in a series of independent trials. The sum of two independent geometric random variables would give the total number of failures before the second success which is represented by a negative binomial random variable with $r = 2$.

11.3.4 The Sum of Independent Normal Random Variables

The moment generating function of a normal random variable with mean μ and variance σ^2 is

$$M_X(t) = e^{\mu t + \frac{\sigma^2 t^2}{2}}.$$

If Y is normal with mean ν and variance τ^2 and Y is independent of X, then the moment generating function of $X + Y$ will be

$$M_{X+Y}(t) = M_X(t) \cdot M_Y(t) = e^{\mu t + \frac{\sigma^2 t^2}{2}} \cdot e^{\nu t + \frac{\tau^2 t^2}{2}} = e^{(\mu+\nu)t + \frac{(\sigma^2 + \tau^2)t^2}{2}}.$$

The final expression is the moment generating function of a normal random variable with mean $\mu + \nu$ and variance $\sigma^2 + \tau^2$.

> If X and Y are independent normal random variables with respective means μ and ν and respective variances σ^2 and τ^2, then $X + Y$ is normal with mean $\mu + \nu$ and variance $\sigma^2 + \tau^2$.

11.3.5 The Sum of Independent and Identically Distributed Exponential Random Variables

The moment generating function of an exponential random variable with parameter β is

$$M_x(t) = \frac{\beta}{\beta - t}.$$

If Y is an identically distributed exponential random variable with parameter β and Y is independent of X, the moment generating function of $X + Y$ is given by

$$M_{X+Y}(t) = M_X(t) \cdot M_Y(t) = \left(\frac{\beta}{\beta - t}\right)^2.$$

The final expression is the moment generating function of a gamma random variable with parameters $\alpha = 2$ and β.

If X and Y are independent and identically distributed exponential random variables with parameter β, then $X + Y$ is a gamma random variable with parameters $\alpha = 2$ and β.

Example 11.24 In Example 11.4 we looked at X and Y, the independent waiting times between accidents in two towns. X and Y were independent and identically distributed exponential random variables with $\beta = 1$. In Example 11.4 we used convolutions to find the distribution of $X + Y$, and showed that $X + Y$ was a gamma random variable with $\alpha = 2$ and $\beta = 1$. The moment generating function result above confirms this conclusion without requiring the work of convolution integrals. □

It is very important to keep in mind that these results rely upon the assumption of independence. The situation is much more complex when the random variables X and Y are not independent.

11.3.6 Joint Moment Generating Functions

In the one variable case, the moment generating function is defined by $M_X(t) = E[e^{tX}]$. In the bivariate case the joint moment generating function for X and Y is defined similarly as

$$M_{X,Y}(s,t) = E[e^{sX+tY}].$$

We will illustrate this with a simple discrete example. Let the joint distribution for X and Y be given by the table below.

	x	1	2	$p_Y(y)$
y				
3		.2	.3	.5
6		.4	.1	.5
$p_X(x)$		.6	.4	

For this distribution

$$M_{X,Y}(s,t) = E[e^{sX+tY}]$$
$$= .2e^{s+3t} + .3e^{2s+3t}$$
$$+ .4e^{s+6t} + .1e^{2s+6t}$$

Recall that in the single variable case we can use derivatives of the moment generating function to find moments of X using the relationship $M_X^{(n)}(0) = E(X^n)$.

In the bivariate case we can use partial derivatives of the joint moment generating function to get the expected values of mixed moments involving powers of both X and Y. The key relationship is

$$E[X^j Y^k] = \frac{\partial^{j+k} M_{X,Y}}{\partial s^j \partial t^k}(0,0).$$

We will illustrate this in our example by using the joint moment generating function to find

$$E[XY] = \frac{\partial^2 M_{X,Y}}{\partial s \partial t}(0,0)$$

$$\frac{\partial M_{X,Y}}{\partial t} = .2(3)e^{s+3t} + .3(3)e^{2s+3t} + .4(6)e^{s+6t} + .1(6)e^{2s+6t}$$

$$\frac{\partial^2 M_{X,Y}}{\partial s \partial t} = .2(1)(3)e^{s+3t} + .3(2)(3)e^{2s+3t}$$
$$+ .4(1)(6)e^{s+6t} + .1(2)(6)e^{2s+6t}$$

$$E[XY] = \frac{\partial^2 M_{X,Y}}{\partial s \partial t}(0,0)$$
$$= .2(1)(3) + .3(2)(3) + .4(1)(6) + .1(2)(6) = 6$$

You can check this result by calculating $E(XY)$ directly.

Note that we can use the joint moment generating function to get the individual moment generating functions of X and Y.

$$M_{X,Y}(s,0) = E(e^{sX+0Y}) = E(e^{sX}) = M_X(s)$$

$$M_{X,Y}(0,t) = E(e^{0X+tY}) = E(e^{tY}) = M_Y(t)$$

When X and Y are independent, the joint moment generating function is easy to find.

$$M_{X,Y}(s,t) \underset{X,Y\ independent}{=} M_X(s)M_Y(t)$$

11.4   The Sum of More Than Two Random Variables

11.4.1 Extending the Results of Section 11.3

The basic results of Section 11.3 can be extended for more than two random variables by the same technique of multiplication of moment generating functions. The results and some examples are given below without repeating the proof.

> If $X_1, X_2, ..., X_n$ are independent Poisson random variables with parameters $\lambda_1, \lambda_2, ..., \lambda_n$, then $X_1 + X_2 + \cdots + X_n$ is Poisson with parameter $\lambda_1, \lambda_2 + \cdots + \lambda_n$.

Example 11.25 A company has three independent customer service locations. Calls come in to the three locations at average rates of 5, 7 and 8 per minute. The number of calls per minute at each location is a Poisson random variable. Then the total number of calls at all three locations is a Poisson random variable with $\lambda = 5+7+8 = 20$.

> The sum of n independent and identically distributed geometric random variables with success probability p is a negative binomial random variable with the same p and $r = n$.

Example 11.26 Four marksmen aim at a target. Each marksman hits the target with probability $p = .70$ on each individual shot. Individual shots are independent, and the marksmen are independent of each other. Each fires until the first hit is made. For each marksman, the number of misses before the first hit is a geometric random variable with $p = .70$. The total number of misses for all four is a negative binomial random variable with $p = .70$ and $r = 4$. $\square$

If X_1, X_2, ..., X_n are independent normal random variables with respective means μ_1, μ_2, ..., μ_n and respective variances σ_1^2, σ_2^2, ..., σ_n^2, then the sum $X_1 + X_2 + \cdots + X_n$ is normal with mean $\mu_1 + \mu_2 + \cdots + \mu_n$ and variance $\sigma_1^2 + \sigma_2^2 + \cdots + \sigma_n^2$.

Example 11.27 Three salesmen have variable annual incomes with means of fifty-five thousand, seventy thousand, and one hundred thousand dollars per year, respectively. The variance of income is $10,000 for each, and the incomes are independent normal random variables. Then the total income of the three salesmen is a normal random variable with a mean of $\mu = 55,000 + 70,000 + 100,000 = \$225,000$ and a variance of $3(10,000) = \$30,000$. $\square$

If X_1, X_2, ..., X_n are independent and identically distributed exponential random variables with parameter β, then the sum $X_1 + X_2 + \cdots + X_n$ is a gamma random variable with parameters $\alpha = n$ and β.

Example 11.28 The waiting time for the next customer at a service station is exponential with an average waiting time of 2 minutes. Since $E(X) = 1/\beta$, the exponential parameter β is $\frac{1}{2}$. Waiting times for successive customers are independent and identically distributed. Then the total waiting time for the fifth customer is a gamma random variable with parameters $\alpha = 5$ and $\beta = \frac{1}{2}$. $\square$

11.4.2 The Mean and Variance of $X + Y + Z$

In this section we will find the mean and variance of the sum of three random variables. This will enable us to see the pattern of the general result for the sum of n random variables. The results are based on use of the formulas for the sum of two random variables.

$$E[(X + (Y+Z)] = E(X) + E(Y+Z) = E(X) + E(Y) + E(Z)$$

$$\begin{aligned}
V[(X + (Y+Z)] &= V(X) + V(Y+Z) + 2 \cdot Cov(X, Y+Z) \\
&= V(X) + [V(Y) + V(Z) + 2 \cdot Cov(Y, Z)] \\
&\quad + 2 \cdot Cov(X, Y) + 2 \cdot Cov(X, Z)
\end{aligned}$$

Mean and Variance of $X + Y + Z$

$$E(X + Y+Z) = E(X) + E(Y) + E(Z)$$

$$\begin{aligned}
V(X + Y + Z) &= V(X) + V(Y) + V(Z) \\
&\quad + 2[Cov(X,Y) + Cov(X,Z) + Cov(Y,Z)]
\end{aligned}$$

Example 11.29 Let X, Y and Z be random variables with mean 20 and variance 3, and $Cov(X,Y) = Cov(X,Z) = Cov(Y,Z) = 1$.

$$E(X + Y + Z) = 20 + 20 + 20 = 60$$

$$V(X + Y + Z) = 3 + 3 + 3 + 2[1+1+1] = 15 \qquad \square$$

The general pattern is now easy to see. The expected value of a sum of random variables is the sum of their expected values. The variance of a sum of random variables is the sum of their variances plus twice the sum of their covariances.

Mean and Variance of $X_1 + X_2 + \cdots + X_n$

$$E\left(\sum_{i=1}^{n} X_i\right) = \sum_{i=1}^{n} E(X_i)$$

$$V\left(\sum_{i=1}^{n} X_i\right) = \sum_{i=1}^{n} V(X_i) + 2\sum_{i<j} Cov(X_i, X_j)$$

If all the random variables X_1, X_2, ..., X_n are independent, then all covariance terms are 0. Then the variance of the sum is the sum of the variances.

$$V\left(\sum_{i=1}^{n} X_i\right) \underset{independence}{=} \sum_{i=1}^{n} V(X_i)$$

11.4.3 The Sum of a Large Number of Independent and Identically Distributed Random Variables

In Section 8.4.4, we looked at an insurance company which had 1000 policies. The company was willing to assume that all of the policies were independent, and that each policy loss amount had the same (non-normal) distribution with

$$E(X) = \frac{1000}{3} \quad \text{and} \quad V(X) = \frac{500{,}000}{9}.$$

Then the company was really responsible for 1000 random variables, X_1, X_2, ..., X_{1000}. The total claim loss S for the company was the sum of the losses on all the individual policies, $S = X_1 + X_2 + \cdots + X_{1000}$. S was shown to be approximately normal (even though the individual policies X_i were not) using the Central Limit Theorem.

Central Limit Theorem Let X_1, X_2, ..., X_n be independent random variables all of which have the same probability distribution and thus the same mean μ and variance σ^2. If n is large, the sum

$$S = X_1 + X_2 + \cdots + X_n$$

will be approximately normal with mean $n\mu$ and variance $n\sigma^2$.

This theorem was stated without proof. The mean and variance of S can now be derived.

$$\begin{aligned}
E(S) &= E(X_1 + X_2 + \cdots + X_n) \\
&= E(X_1) + E(X_2) + \cdots + E(X_n) \\
&= n\mu \\
V(S) &= V(X_1 + X_2 + \cdots + X_n) \\
&\underset{independence}{=} V(X_1) + V(X_2) + \cdots + V(X_n) \\
&= n\sigma^2
\end{aligned}$$

This result enabled us to see that for the insurance company

$$E(S) = 1000 \cdot \frac{1000}{3}$$

and

$$V(S) = 1000 \cdot \frac{500,000}{9}.$$

It is more difficult to show that S must be normal, and we will not prove that here. (One way to prove normality is based on moment generating functions.) However, it is important to remember the result for application. In many practical examples, the random variable being considered is the sum of a large number of independent random variables and probabilities can be easily found as they were in Section 8.4.4.

11.5 Double Expectation Theorems

11.5.1 Conditional Expectations

In this section we will return to the conditional expectations which were discussed in Section 10.3.3. We will use the joint probability function for two assets as our key example.

Example 11.30 The joint distribution of two assets was given with its marginal distributions in Example 10.3.

y $\quad x$	90	100	110	$p_Y(y)$
0	.05	.27	.18	.50
10	.15	.33	.02	.50
$p_X(x)$	.20	.60	.20	

In Example 10.7 we found that $E(X) = 100$ and $E(Y) = 5$. In Example 10.16, we calculated the conditional distribution for X given the information that $Y = 0$ by dividing each element of the top row of the preceding table by $p_Y(0) = .50$. This gave us the conditional distribution.

x	90	100	110
$p(x\|0)$	.10	.54	.36

The conditional distribution was used to find the conditional expectation.

$$E(X|Y = 0) = 90(.10) + 100(.54) + 110(.36) = 102.60$$

We can repeat these steps to find the conditional distribution of X and the conditional expected value of X given that $Y = 10$.

x	90	100	110
$p(x|10)$	.30	.66	.04

$$E(X|Y = 10) = 90(.30) + 100(.66) + 110(.04) = 97.4$$

Up to this point, all of the material in this example has been review work. The new insight in this example comes from the observation that the two conditional expectations we have just calculated are values of a new random variable which depends on Y. We might see this more clearly if we create a probability table.

y	0	10
$p_Y(y)$	.50	.50
$E(X|Y = y)$	102.6	97.4

The numerical quantity $E(X|Y = y)$ depends on the chance event that either $Y = 0$ or $Y = 10$ occurs. We can find the expected value of this new random variable in the usual way.

$$E[E(X|Y)] = .50(102.6) + .50(97.4) = 100 = E(X)$$

The above equality holds for any two random variables X and Y. ☐

Double Expectation Theorem for Expected Value

$$E[E(X|Y)] = E(X)$$

$$E[E(Y|X)] = E(Y)$$

We will not give a proof. The reader will be asked to verify that $E[E(Y|X)] = E(Y)$ for the two asset example in Exercise 11-26. The identity is very useful in applications in which only conditional expectations are given.

Example 11.31 The probability that a claim is filed on an insurance policy is .10. Only one claim may be filed. When a claim is filed, the expected claim amount is $1000. (Claim amounts may vary.) A policyholder is picked at random. Find the expected amount of claim paid to that policyholder.

Solution Note that the expected amount paid to the randomly selected policyholder is not $1000; only 10% of the policyholders actually file claims. To solve this problem we need to identify random variables X and Y for the double expectation theorem. First, let Y be the number of claims filed by a policyholder. The probability function of Y is shown in the following table:

y	0	1
$p_Y(y)$	.90	.10

Let X be the amount of claim paid. We are not given the joint distribution of X and Y, but we are given (in words) the value of $E(X|Y = 1)$. It is the expected amount of $1000 paid if a claim is filed. If no claim is filed, the amount paid is $0, so that is the value of $E(X|Y = 0)$. Thus

$$E(X|Y = 0) = 0 \text{ and } E(X|Y = 1) = 1000.$$

The average claim amount paid to *any* policyholder is

$$E[E(X|Y)] = .90(0) + .10(1000) = 100 = E(X). \qquad \square$$

11.5.2 Conditional Variances

Since the expected value of X is the expected value of the conditional means $E(X|Y)$, the reader might expect the variance of X to be the expected value of conditional variances. However, the situation is a bit more complicated. We will illustrate it by continuing our analysis of the two asset distribution.

Example 11.32 In Example 10.7 we found that $V(X) = 40$ and $V(Y) = 25$. To find conditional variances for X, we will first find $E(X^2|Y = y)$ and use the identity

$$V(X|Y = y) = E(X^2|Y = y) - (E(X|Y = y))^2.$$

When $Y = 0$, we have the following conditional distribution:

x	90	100	110
$p(x\vert 0)$	.10	.54	.36

Then $E(X^2\vert Y = 0) = 90^2(.10) + 100^2(.54) + 110^2(.36) = 10{,}566$ and $V(X\vert Y = 0) = 10{,}566 - 102.6^2 = 39.24$. When $Y = 10$, we have the following conditional distribution:

x	90	100	110
$p(x\vert 10)$	.30	.66	.04

Then $E(X^2\vert Y = 10) = 90^2(.30) + 100^2(.66) + 110^2(.04) = 9514$ and $V(X\vert Y = 10) = 9514 - 97.4^2 = 27.24$. The conditional variance $V(X\vert Y)$ is also a random variable. A probability table for it is given below.

y	0	10
$p_Y(y)$	.50	.50
$V(X\vert Y = y)$	39.24	27.24

We can find the expected value of $V(X\vert Y)$ from the information in the table.

$$E[V(X\vert Y)] = 39.24(.50) + 27.24(.50) = 33.24$$

Note that $E[V(X\vert Y)]$ does not equal the value of $V(X) = 40$. It is short by an amount of $40 - 33.24 = 6.76$. However, we can account for the remaining 6.76. It is the variance of the values of the random variable $E(X\vert Y)$. We repeat the table for this random variable below.

y	0	10
$p_Y(y)$	.50	.50
$E(X\vert Y = y)$	102.6	97.4

The expected value of $E(X\vert Y)$ was $\mu = 100$. Then the variance of $E(X\vert Y)$ is

$$V[E(X\vert Y)] = (102.6-100)^2(.50) + (97.4-100)^2(.50) = 6.76.$$

Now we have two expressions whose sum is the variance of X.

$$V(X) = 40 = 33.24 + 6.76 = E[V(X|Y)] + V[E(X|Y)]$$

This identity always holds. □

Double Expectation Theorem for Variance

$$V(X) = E[V(X|Y)] + V[E(X|Y)]$$

$$V(Y) = E[V(Y|X)] + V[E(Y|X)]$$

We will not give a proof of this identity. The reader will be asked to verify that $V(Y) = E[V(Y|X)] + V[E(Y|X)]$ for the two asset example in Exercise 11-30. As we have already seen, this identity is useful in situations where conditional means and variances are given without additional information about the distribution.

Example 11.33 We return to the insurance Example 11.31. In that example we were given the information that the probability of a claim being filed by a policyholder is .10 and the expected amount of an individual claim (given that a claim is filed) is $1000. Suppose we are given that the variance of claim amount (given that a claim is filed) is $100. Find the variance of claim amount for a randomly selected policyholder.

Solution We have already identified the random variables involved. Y is the number of claims filed by a randomly selected policyholder, and X is the amount of claim paid to that policyholder. We have already found that $E(X) = 100$. To find $V(X)$ we need to find the two components: (a) $E[V(X|Y)]$ and (b) $V[E(X|Y)]$.

(a) Given that a claim is filed, the variance of claim amount is 100. Thus $V(X|Y = 1) = 100$. If no claim is filed, the claim amount is the constant 0, so $V(X|Y = 0) = 0$. Then

$$E[V(X|Y)] = .90(0) + .10(100) = 10.$$

(b) The mean of the random variable $E(X|Y)$ is $E(X) = 100$. Thus the variance is

$$V[E(X|Y)] = (E(X|0)-100)^2(.90) + (E(X|1)-100)^2(.10)$$
$$= (0-100)^2(.90) + (1000-100)^2(.10)$$
$$= 100^2(.90) + 900^2(.10) = 90,000.$$

We can now find $V(X)$.

$$V(X) = E[V(X|Y)] + V[E(X|Y)]$$
$$= 10 + 90,000 = 90,010 \qquad \square$$

The student who has studied statistics may have seen the variance identity before. In the above example, the expected value $E[V(X|Y)]$ is the mean of the variances within each of the two categories $Y = 0$ (no claim filed) and $Y = 1$ (1 claim filed). It is often referred to as the variance *within* groups. The term $V[E(X|Y)]$ is the variance of the means of the two groups and is referred to as the variance *between* groups.

11.6 Applying the Double Expectation Theorem; The Compound Poisson Distribution

11.6.1 The Total Claim Amount for an Insurance Company: An Example of the Compound Poisson Distribution

In previous chapters we have looked at insurance claims in two different ways. Using discrete distributions, we found the probability of the number of claims that might be experienced. The number of claims experienced is called the **claim frequency**. Using continuous distributions, we found the probability of the amount of a single claim. The amount of a claim is called the **claim severity**. The insurance company's total experience depends on the combination of frequency and severity. This is illustrated in the next example.

Example 11.34 Claims come in to an insurance office at an average rate of 3 per day. The number of claims in a day is a Poisson random variable N with mean $\lambda = 3$. Claim amounts X are independent of N and independent of other claim amounts. All claim amounts have the same distribution. The ith claim X_i is uniformly distributed on the interval $[0, 1000]$. The experience in one series of five days is given in the next table.

Day	Number of claims N	Amount X_1	Amount X_2	Amount X_3	Amount X_4	Total S
1	2	628	864			1492
2	2	322	947			1269
3	4	640	559	457	322	1978
4	3	184	447	144		775
5	3	448	523	620		1591

The variable of real importance to the company is the total amount of claims that must be paid out. This random variable is denoted by S in the table above. Note that the number of claims on different days varies, so that the number of summands in the total varies from day to day. We can write total claims as

$$S = X_1 + X_2 + \cdots + X_N.$$

S is a sum of a random number of random variables. It is referred to as a **compound Poisson random variable** because the number of claims N has a Poisson distribution. $\qquad\qquad\qquad\qquad\qquad\qquad\qquad\qquad\qquad$ □

11.6.2 The Mean and Variance of a Compound Poisson Random Variable

The double expectation theorems can be used to find the mean and variance of a compound Poisson distribution. We will leave the derivation for Section 11.6.3. First we will give the mean and variance formulas and show how to use them in Example 11.34. There is one notation to discuss first. Since the claim amounts X_i are identically distributed, they are all copies of the same random variable X and all have the same mean $E(X)$ and variance $V(X)$.

Compound Poisson Random Variable
N Poisson, with parameter λ
$X = X_i$ independent and identically distributed
$$S = X_1 + X_2 + \cdots + X_N$$

$$E(S) = E(N) \cdot E(X) = \lambda \cdot E(X)$$
$$V(S) = \lambda \cdot E(X^2) = \lambda[V(X) + (E(X))^2]$$

Example 11.35 For the insurance company in Example 11.34, the number of claims N was Poisson with parameter $\lambda = 3 = E(N)$. The claim amount X was uniform on $[0, 1000]$. Thus

$$E(X) = 500$$

and

$$V(X) = \frac{1000^2}{12}.$$

The above formulas immediately show that

$$E(S) = 3(500) = 1500$$

and

$$V(S) = 3\left[\frac{1000^2}{12} + 500^2\right] = 1,000,000.$$

There is a very natural intuitive interpretation for $E(S)$. We expect an average of 3 claims with an average amount of 500. The expected total is 3(500). $\square$

Example 11.36 A large insurance company has claims occur at a rate of 1000 per month. The number of claims N is assumed to be Poisson with $\lambda = 1000$. Claim amounts X are assumed to be independent and identically distributed, with $E(X) = 800$ and $V(X) = 10,000$. Then S, the total amount of all claims in a month, has a compound Poisson distribution with

$$E(S) = 1000(800) = 800,000$$

and

$$V(S) = 1000[10,000 + 800^2] = 650,000,000. \qquad \square$$

11.6.3 Derivation of the Mean and Variance Formulas

We will begin by looking at some conditional expectations which will come up in the double expectation calculation. Recall that

$$S = X_1 + X_2 + \cdots + X_N.$$

Then $E(S|N)$ can be written as a sum

$$E(S|N) = E(X_1 + X_2 + \cdots + X_N \,|\, N)$$
$$= E(X_1) + E(X_2) + \cdots + E(X_N) = N \cdot E(X).$$

Since the claim amounts are independent, the variance of the sum is the sum of the variances.

$$V(S|N) = V(X_1 + X_2 + \cdots + X_N |N)$$
$$= V(X_1) + V(X_2) + \cdots + V(X_N) = N \cdot V(X)$$

Now we have all necessary information to use the double expectation theorems.

$$E(S) = E[E(S|N)] = E[N \cdot E(X)] = E(X) \cdot E(N) = \lambda \cdot E(X)$$

$$V(S) = E[V(S|N)] + V[E(S|N)]$$
$$= E[N \cdot V(X)] + V[N \cdot E(X)]$$
$$= V(X) \cdot E(N) + (E(X))^2 \cdot V(N)$$
$$= \lambda \cdot V(X) + \lambda \cdot (E(X))^2$$
$$= \lambda \cdot E(X^2)$$

11.6.4 Finding Probabilities for the Compound Poisson S by a Normal Approximation

The mean and variance formulas in the preceding sections are useful, but in insurance risk management it is important to be able to find probabilities for the compound Poisson S as well as the mean and variance. Methods for this have been developed, and the actuarial student can find them in Chapter 12 of Bowers et al. [2]. Those methods will not be covered in this text. However, there is a special case in which probabilities for S can be approximated by a normal distribution with the same mean and variance. This is the case in which the Poisson mean λ is very large.

> **Normal Approximation to the Compound Poisson for Large λ**
>
> If $S = X_1 + X_2 + \cdots + X_N$ has a compound Poisson distribution, then the distribution of S approaches a normal distribution with mean $\lambda \cdot E(X)$ and variance $\lambda \cdot E(X^2)$ as $\lambda \to \infty$.

We will not give a proof here. (The interested reader is referred to Bowers et al. [2], page 386.) The next example shows how it can be applied for an insurance company with a large claim rate λ.

Example 11.37 In Example 11.36 we looked at an insurance company with the large claim rate $\lambda = 1000$. We showed that the compound Poisson claim total S had mean $E(S) = 800,000$ and variance $V(S) = 650,000,000$. Thus the standard deviation of S is $\sqrt{650,000,000} \approx 25,495$. Suppose the company has $850,000 available to pay claims and wants to know the probability that this will be enough to pay all claims that come in. This is the probability $P(S \leq 850,000)$. We can find it using the normal approximation above.

$$P(S \leq 850,000) = P\left(Z \leq \frac{850,000 - 800,000}{25,495}\right)$$

$$= P(Z \leq 1.96) = .9750 \qquad \square$$

11.7 Exercises

11.1 Distributions of Functions of Two Random Variables

11-1. Let $p(x,y)$ be the joint probability function of Exercise 10-1, and let $S = X + Y$. Find the probability function $p_S(s)$.

11-2. Let $f(x,y) = \frac{4(1-xy)}{3}$, for $0 \leq x \leq 1$, $0 \leq y \leq 1$. Find $P(X+Y \leq 1)$.

11-3. Let X and Y be independent random variables with marginal distribution functions $f_X(x) = 2e^{-2x}$, for $x \geq 0$, and $f_Y(y) = 3e^{-3y}$, for $y \geq 0$, and let $S = X + Y$. Find $f_S(s)$.

11-4. For the joint density function given in Example 11.3, find $P(X+Y \leq 1.5)$. Hint: Find $P(X+Y > 1.5)$ first.

11-5. Let $f(x,y)$ be the joint density function given in Example 11.4, and let $S = X + Y$. Use a double integral to find $F_S(s)$, take the derivative of this to get $f_S(s)$, and compare with Example 11.4.

11-6. Let X and Y be the independent random variables in Exercise 10-6. Find $P(min(X,Y) > t)$, for $0 < t < 1$. Note: X and Y are *not* exponential random variables.

11.2   Expected Values of Functions of Random Variables

11-7.   For the random variables in Exercise 10-1, find $E(X+Y)$ using the joint probabilities in the table. Then find $E(X+Y)$ using the function $p_S(s)$ found in Exercise 11-1. Show that each of these is equal to $E(X)+E(Y)$, as found in Exercise 10-3.

11-8.   Let $f(x,y) = \dfrac{4(1-xy)}{3}$, for $0 \le x \le 1$ and $0 \le y \le 1$, as in Exercise 11-2. Find $E(X+Y)$ using the joint density function. Show that this is equal to $E(X)+E(Y)$.

11-9.   Prove that $E(X+Y) = E(X)+E(Y)$ for continuous random variables.

11-10.   For the random variables in Example 11.11, find $E(XY)$ directly.

11-11.   For the random variables in Exercise 11-8, find (a) $E(XY)$; (b) $E(X) \cdot E(Y)$; (c) $Cov(X,Y)$.

11-12.   For the random variables in Exercise 11-8, find (a) $V(X)$; (b) $V(Y)$; (c) $V(X+Y)$.

11-13.   For the random variables in Exercise 10-1, find $V(X+Y)$.

11-14.   Let X and Y be random variables whose joint probability distribution and marginal distributions are given below.

y \ x	1	2	$p_Y(y)$
1	.15	.25	.40
2	.35	.25	.60
$p_X(x)$	.50	.50	

Find (a) $E(X)$; (b) $E(Y)$; (c) $V(X)$; (d) $V(Y)$; (e) $Cov(X,Y)$; (f) $V(X+Y)$.

11-15.   Let X and Y be the random variables in Exercise 10-22 with joint density function $f(x,y) = 6x$, for $0 < x < y < 1$, and $f(x,y) = 0$ elsewhere. Find (a) $V(X)$; (b) $V(Y)$; (c) $E(XY)$; (d) $V(X+Y)$.

11-16. For the random variables given in Exercise 11-14, find the correlation coefficient.

11-17. For the random variables given in Exercise 11-15, find the correlation coefficient.

11-18. Let X and Y be random variables with joint density function $f(x,y) = x + y$, for $0 \le x \le 1$ and $0 \le y \le 1$, and $f(x,y) = 0$ elsewhere. Find the correlation coefficient.

11-19. Let X and Y be random variables whose joint density function is $f(x,y) = \dfrac{3(x^2 + y^2)}{8}$, for $-1 \le x \le 1$ and $-1 \le y \le 1$, and $f(x,y) = 0$ elsewhere.
   (a) Find $f_X(x)$ and $f_Y(y)$, and show that X and Y are not independent.
   (b) Find $E(X)$, $E(Y)$, $E(XY)$ and $Cov(X,Y)$.

11.3 Moment Generating Functions for Sums of Independent Random Variables

11-20. Let X and Y be independent random variables with joint probability function $f(x,y) = x(y + 1)/15$, for $x = 1,2$ and $y = 1,2$. Find $M_{X+Y}(t)$.

11-21. Let X and Y be independent random variables, each uniformly distributed over $[0,2]$. Find $M_{X+Y}(t)$.

11.4 The Sum of More Than Two Random Variables

11-22. The random variable S representing the sum of n fair dice is the sum of n independent random variables, X_i, $i = 1,2,\ldots,n$, where X_i represents the number of dots on the toss of the ith die. Find $E(S)$ and $V(S)$.

11-23. Let X_1, X_2, X_3 and X_4 be random variables such that for each i, $V(X_i) = 13/162$, and for $i \ne j$, $Cov(X_i, X_j) = -1/81$. Find $V(X_1 + X_2 + X_3 + X_4)$.

11-24. Let $S = X_1 + X_2 + \cdots + X_{10}$ be the sum of random variables such that $V(S) = 500/9$, $V(X_i) = 25/3$ for each i, and all covariances, for $i \neq j$, are the same. Find $Cov(X_i, X_j)$.

11-25. Let $S = X_1 + X_2 + \cdots + X_{500}$, where the X_i are independent and identically distributed with mean .50 and variance .25. Use the Central Limit Theorem to find $P(235 \leq S \leq 265)$.

11.5 Double Expectation Theorems

Exercises 11-26 through 11-30 refer to the random variables and distributions in Examples 11.30 and 11.32.

11-26. Find (a) $E(Y|X = 90)$; (b) $E(Y|X = 100)$; (c) $E(Y|X = 110)$.

11-27. Find $E[E(Y|X)]$.

11-28. Find (a) $V(Y|X = 90)$; (b) $V(Y|X = 100)$; (c) $V(Y|X = 110)$.

11-29. Find $E[V(Y|X)]$.

11-30. Find $V[E(Y|X)]$, and verify the identity

$$E[V(Y|X)] + V[E(Y|X)] = V(Y).$$

11-31. The probability that a claim is filed on an insurance policy is .07, and at most one claim is filed in a year. Claim amounts are for either $500, $1000 or $2000. Given that a claim is filed, the distribution of claim amounts is $P(500) = .60$, $P(1000) = .30$ and $P(2000) = .10$. Find the variance of the claim amount paid to a randomly selected policyholder. (Recall that some policyholders do not file a claim and are paid nothing.)

Exercises 11-32 through 11-36 refer to the random variables in Exercise 10-24, whose joint density function is $f(x, y) = 6x$, for $0 < x < y < 1$, and $f(x, y) = 0$ elsewhere.

11-32. Find (a) $f_X(x)$; (b) $E(X)$; (c) $V(X)$.

11-33. Find $E[E(X|Y)]$. (This should be equal to $E(X)$.)

11-34. Find $V(X|Y = y)$.

11-35. Find $E[V(X|Y)]$.

11-36. Find $V[E(X|Y)]$. Verify that $E[V(X|Y)] + V[E(X|Y)] = V(X)$.

11.6 Applying the Double Expectation Theorem; The Compound Poisson Distribution

11-37. The number of claims received by an insurance company in a month is a Poisson random variable with $\lambda = 20$. The claim amounts are independent of each other, and each is uniformly distributed over $[0, 500]$. S is the random variable for the total amount of claims paid. Find (a) $E(S)$; (b) $V(S)$.

11-38. Let the claim amounts in Exercise 11-37 have a lognormal distribution, whose underlying normal distribution has $\mu = 5$ and $\sigma = .40$. Find (a) $E(S)$; (b)$V(S)$.

Use the normal approximation to the compound Poisson distribution in Exercises 11-39 and 11-40.

11-39. The number of claims received in a year by an insurance company is a Poisson random variable with $\lambda = 500$. The claim amounts are independent and uniformly distributed over $[0, 500]$. If the company has \$140,000 available to pay claims, what is the probability that it will have enough to pay all the claims that come in?

11-40. The number of claims received in a year by an insurance company is a Poisson random variable with $\lambda = 500$. The claim amount distribution has mean $E(X) = 600$ and variance $V(X) = 12,000$. What is the minimum amount the company would need so that it would have a .95 probability of being able to pay all claims? (Use the fact that $F_Z(1.645) \approx .95$.)

11.8   Sample Actuarial Examination Problems

11-41. An insurance company determines that N, the number of claims received in a week, is a random variable with $P[N=n] = \frac{1}{2^{n+1}}$, where $n \geq 0$. The company also determines that the number of claims received in a given week is independent of the number of claims received in any other week.

Determine the probability that exactly seven claims will be received during a given two-week period.

11-42. A company agrees to accept the highest of four sealed bids on a property. The four bids are regarded as four independent random variables with common cumulative distribution function
$$F(x) = \frac{1}{2}(1 + \sin \pi x) \quad \text{for} \quad \frac{3}{2} \leq x \leq \frac{5}{2}$$
Which of the following represents the expected value of the accepted bid?

(A) $\pi \int_{3/2}^{5/2} x \cos \pi x \, dx$ (D) $\frac{1}{4}\pi \int_{3/2}^{5/2} \cos \pi x (1 + \sin \pi x)^3 \, dx$

(B) $\frac{1}{16} \int_{3/2}^{5/2} (1 + \sin \pi x)^4 \, dx$ (E) $\frac{1}{4}\pi \int_{3/2}^{5/2} x \cos \pi x (1 + \sin \pi x)^3 \, dx$

(C) $\frac{1}{16} \int_{3/2}^{5/2} x (1 + \sin \pi x)^4 \, dx$

11.43. Claim amounts for wind damage to insured homes are independent random variables with common density function
$$f(x) = \begin{cases} \dfrac{3}{x^4} & \text{for } x > 1 \\ 0 & \text{otherwise} \end{cases}$$
where x is the amount of a claim in thousands.

Suppose 3 such claims will be made. What is the expected value of the largest of the three claims?

11-44. An insurance company insures a large number of drivers. Let X be the random variable representing the company's losses under collision insurance, and let Y represent the company's losses under liability insurance. X and Y have joint density function

$$f(x) = \begin{cases} \dfrac{2x+2-y}{4} & \text{for } 0 < x < 1 \text{ and } 0 < y < 2 \\ 0 & \text{otherwise} \end{cases}$$

What is the probability that the total loss is at least 1?

11-45. A family buys two policies from the same insurance company. Losses under the two policies are independent and have continuous uniform distributions on the interval from 0 to 10. One policy has a deductible of 1 and the other has a deductible of 2. The family experiences exactly one loss under each policy.

Calculate the probability that the total benefit paid to the family does not exceed 5.

11-46. Let T_1 be the time between a car accident and reporting a claim to the insurance company. Let T_2 be the time between the report of the claim and payment of the claim. The joint density function of T_1 and T_2, $f(t_1, t_2)$, is constant over the region $0 < t_1 < 6$, $0 < t_2 < 6$, $t_1 + t_2 < 10$, and zero otherwise.

Determine $E[T_1 + T_2]$, the expected time between a car accident and payment of the claim.

11-47. Let T_1 and T_2 represent the lifetimes in hours of two linked components in an electronic device. The joint density function for T_1 and T_2 is uniform over the region defined by $0 \le t_1 \le t_2 \le L$ where L is a positive constant.

Determine the expected value of the sum of the squares of T_1 and T_2.

11-48. In a small metropolitan area, annual losses due to storm, fire, and theft are assumed to be independent, exponentially distributed random variables with respective means 1.0, 1.5, and 2.4.

Determine the probability that the maximum of these losses exceeds 3.

11-49. A company offers earthquake insurance. Annual premiums are modeled by an exponential random variable with mean 2. Annual claims are modeled by an exponential random variable with mean 1. Premiums and claims are independent.

Let X denote the ratio of claims to premiums.

What is the density function of X?

11-50. Let X and Y be the number of hours that a randomly selected person watches movies and sporting events, respectively, during a three-month period. The following information is known about X and Y:

$$E(X) = 50 \quad Var(X) = 50 \quad E(Y) = 20$$
$$Var(Y) = 30 \quad Cov(X,Y) = 10$$

One hundred people are randomly selected and observed for these three months. Let T be the total number of hours that these one hundred people watch movies or sporting events during this three-month period.

Approximate the value of $P(T < 7100)$.

11-51. The profit for a new product is given by $Z = 3X - Y - 5$. X and Y are independent random variables with $Var(X) = 1$ and $Var(Y) = 2$. What is the variance of Z?

11-52. A company has two electric generators. The time until failure for each generator follows an exponential distribution with mean 10. The company will begin using the second generator immediately after the first one fails.

What is the variance of the total time that the generators produce electricity?

11-53. A joint density function is given by

$$f(x,y) = \begin{cases} kx & \text{for } 0 < x < 1, \ 0 < y < 1 \\ 0 & \text{otherwise} \end{cases}$$

where k is a constant. What is $Cov(X,Y)$?

11-54. Let X and Y be continuous random variables with joint density function

$$f(x,y) = \begin{cases} \frac{8}{3}xy & \text{for } 0 \le x \le 1, \ x \le y \le 2x \\ 0 & \text{otherwise} \end{cases}$$

Calculate the covariance of X and Y.

11-55. Let X and Y denote the values of two stocks at the end of a five-year period. X is uniformly distributed on the interval $(0,12)$. Given $X = x$, Y is uniformly distributed on the interval $(0,x)$.

Determine $Cov(X,Y)$ according to this model.

11-56.   An actuary determines that the claim size for a certain class of
         accidents is a random variable, X, with moment generating
         function

$$M_X(t) = \frac{1}{(1-2500t)^4} .$$

Determine the standard deviation of the claim size for this class
of accidents.

11-57.   A company insures homes in three cities, J, K, and L. Since
         sufficient distance separates the cities, it is reasonable to assume
         that the losses occurring in these cities are independent.

The moment generating functions for the loss distributions of the
cities are:

$$M_J(t) = (1-2t)^{-3} \qquad M_K(t) = (1-2t)^{-2.5} \qquad M_L(t) = (1-2t)^{-4.5}$$

Let X represent the combined losses from the three cities.
Calculate $E(X^3)$

11-58.   An insurance policy pays a total medical benefit consisting of
         two parts for each claim.

Let X represent the part of the benefit that is paid to the surgeon,
and let Y represent the part that is paid to the hospital. The
variance of X is 5000, the variance of Y is 10,000, and the
variance of the total benefit, $X+Y$, is 17,000.

Due to increasing medical costs, the company that issues the
policy decides to increase X by a flat amount of 100 per claim
and to increase Y by 10% per claim.

Calculate the variance of the total benefit after these revisions
have been made.

11-59. Let X denote the size of a surgical claim and let Y denote the size of the associated hospital claim. An actuary is using a model in which $E(X) = 5$, $E(X^2) = 27.4$, $E(Y) = 7$, $E(Y^2) = 51.4$, and $Var(X+Y) = 8$.

Let $C_1 = X + Y$ denote the size of the combined claims before the application of a 20% surcharge on the hospital portion of the claim, and let C_2 denote the size of the combined claims after the application of that surcharge.

Calculate $Cov(C_1, C_2)$.

11-60. Claims filed under auto insurance policies follow a normal distribution with mean 19,400 and standard deviation 5,000.

What is the probability that the average of 25 randomly selected claims exceeds 20,000?

11-61. A company manufactures a brand of light bulb with a lifetime in months that is normally distributed with mean 3 and variance 1. A consumer buys a number of these bulbs with the intention of replacing them successively as they burn out. The light bulbs have independent lifetimes.

What is the smallest number of bulbs to be purchased so that the succession of light bulbs produces light for at least 40 months with probability at least 0.9772?

11-62. An insurance company sells a one-year automobile policy with a deductible of 2.

The probability that the insured will incur a loss is .05. If there is a loss, the probability of a loss of amount N is K/N, for $N = 1,...,5$ and K a constant. These are the only possible loss amounts and no more than one loss can occur.

Determine the net premium for this policy.

11-63. An auto insurance company insures an automobile worth 15,000
        for one year under a policy with a 1,000 deductible. During the
        policy year there is a .04 chance of partial damage to the car and
        a .02 chance of a total loss of the car. If there is partial damage to
        the car, the amount X of damage (in thousands) follows a
        distribution with density function

$$f(x) = \begin{cases} .5003e^{-x/2} & \text{for } 0 < x < 15 \\ 0 & \text{otherwise} \end{cases}$$

What is the expected claim payment?

Chapter 12
Stochastic Processes

12.1 Simulation Examples

In many situations it is important to study a series of random events over time. Insurance companies accumulate a series of claims over time. Investors see their holdings increase or decrease over time as the stock market or interest rates fluctuate. These processes in which random events affect variables over time are called **stochastic processes**. In this section we will give a number of examples of stochastic processes. Each example will contain simulation results designed to give the reader an intuitive understanding of the process.

12.1.1 Gambler's Ruin Problem

We return to the gambling roots of probability for our first example.

Example 12.1 Two gamblers, A and B, are betting on tosses of a fair coin. The two gamblers have four coins between them: A has 3 coins and B has 1. On each play, one of the players tosses one of his coins and calls heads or tails while the coin is in the air. If his call is correct, he gets a coin from the other player. Otherwise, he loses his coin to the other player. The players continue the game until one player has all the coins.

Solution Intuitively, it seems that A would be more likely to end up with all the coins, since A starts with more coins. We can test this hypothesis experimentally with a computer simulation. The probability that A wins on any single toss is $P(H) = P(T) = .50$. We can simulate tosses of the coin by generating a random number in $[0, 1)$ and giving A a loss if the number is in $[0, .5)$ and a win if the number is in $[.5, 1)$. The result of one simulation of the game is shown below.

Play	Random Number	A has
Begin		3
1	0.007510	2
2	0.126708	1
3	0.614643	2
4	0.621189	3
5	0.913130	4

In this game, A had two losses in a row but was able to recover with three wins in a row to get all 4 coins. It is less likely that A will lose, but that is possible. The next simulation shows a series of plays in which B ended up with all 4 coins and A with none.

Play	Random Number	A has
Begin		3
1	0.425238	2
2	0.971694	3
3	0.217407	2
4	0.362054	1
5	0.942864	2
6	0.076474	1
7	0.262251	0

Any time this game is played, one player will eventually get all of the coins. The process is random in any single game, but if a large number of such games is played, an interesting pattern emerges. We used the computer to play this game to completion 100 times. In that series of simulations, Player A won 75 times and Player B won 25 times. It appears that the player who starts with 75% of the coins has a 75% probability of winning all the money, but our simulation only tells us that this *might* be true; it does not tell us that this *must* be true. We repeated the experiment of 100 plays a number of times, and found that in each sequence of plays the number of wins for A was near (but not exactly equal to) 75. In Section 12.2 we will develop some theory to prove that $P(\text{A wins all coins}) = .75$.

This problem is called the **gambler's ruin problem** because one of the gamblers will always lose all of his money. Theory can be developed to show that if A starts with a coins and B starts with b coins, then

$$P(\text{A wins all coins}) = \frac{a}{a+b}.$$

For example, when A has 10,000,000 coins and B has 200, the probability that A wins all of the coins and B leaves with nothing is

$$\frac{10,000,000}{10,000,200} \approx .99998.$$

This is useful to remember when you are B entering a casino. □

12.1.2 Fund Switching

Example 12.2 Employees in a pension plan have their money invested in one of two funds which we will call Fund 0 and Fund 1. Each month they are allowed to switch to the other fund if they feel that it may perform better. For investors in Fund 0, the probability of staying in Fund 0 is .55 and the probability of moving to Fund 1 is .45. For investors in Fund 1, the probability of a switch to Fund 0 is .30 and the probability of staying in Fund 1 is .70. We can summarize this in the following table of probabilities.

Start in \ End in	0	1
0	.55	.45
1	.30	.70

We can simulate the progress of a single employee over time as follows:

(a) Generate a random number from $[0, 1)$.
(b) If the employee is in Fund 0 now, keep the employee in Fund 0 if the random number is in $[0, .55)$. Otherwise switch the employee to Fund 1.
(c) If the employee is in Fund 1 now, switch the employee to Fund 0 if the random number is in $[0, .30)$. Otherwise keep the employee in Fund 1.

The result of one such simulation for 6 months gave the following results for an employee starting in Fund 1:

Month	Random Number	Fund
Start		1
1	0.232	0
2	0.099	0
3	0.768	1
4	0.773	1
5	0.427	1
6	0.101	0

As with the gambler's ruin example, there is a long-run pattern to be found. We simulated this process for 100 months at a time, and found that a typical employee was in Fund 1 approximately 60% of the time. We will be able to use theory in Section 12.2 to prove that this must happen.   □

12.1.3 A Compound Poisson Process

The crucial process for an insurance company is to observe the frequency and severity of claims day by day. On each day a random number of claims for random amounts comes in. The company must manage the risk of its total claims S over time. If the number of claims N is Poisson, and the claim amounts X are independent of each other and of N, then S follows a compound Poisson distribution. We have already given a simulation example for such a process in Chapter 11. In Example 11.34 the number of claims in a day was a Poisson random variable N with mean $\lambda = 3$. Claim amounts X were independent, as required. The ith claim X_i was uniformly distributed on the interval $[0, 1000]$. The experience in one series of five days was the following:

Day	Number of claims N	Amount X_1	Amount X_2	Amount X_3	Amount X_4	Total S
1	2	628	864			1492
2	2	322	947			1269
3	4	640	559	457	322	1978
4	3	184	447	144		775
5	3	448	523	620		1591

This is only one simulation of the process for a short number of days. Theory can also be used here to develop useful patterns for risk management, but that theory will not be studied in this text.

12.1.4 A Continuous Process: Simulating Exponential Waiting Times

All of the previous stochastic processes were recorded for discrete time periods. The plays or months were indexed using the positive integers $1, 2, 3, \ldots$. Other stochastic processes occur in continuous time. For example, the exact waiting time for the next accident at an intersection can be any real number. The reader might recall that the waiting time T for the next accident at an intersection can be modeled using an exponential random variable. This is illustrated in the next example.

Example 12.3 The waiting time T (in months) between accidents at an intersection is exponential with $\lambda = 2$. We can simulate values of this random variable using the inverse transformation method from Section 9.5.2. The following table contains the result of a simulation of the waiting time for the next 5 accidents at the intersection.

Trial	Random u	$F^{-1}(u)$ Time to Next Accident	Total Time
1	0.391842	0.248660	
2	0.603216	0.462181	0.710841
3	0.094226	0.049483	0.760324
4	0.092443	0.048499	0.808823
5	0.489792	0.336468	1.145291

The first accident occurred at time .24866 and the second accident occurred .462181 time units later, at a total time of .710841. These results are in continuous time. □

The reader might note that the first 4 accidents occurred before one time unit (month) had been completed. Thus the random number of accidents in one month was $N = 4$ accidents. In this exponential simulation, we have simulated one value of the Poisson random variable N which gives the number of accidents in a month. One method for simulating the Poisson random variable is based on using exponential simulations in this way.

12.1.5 Simulation and Theory

We have provided simulations here to illustrate the basic intuitions behind simple stochastic processes. The processes studied here could have been analyzed without simulation, since there are theorems to determine their long-term behavior. We will illustrate the theory used on random walks and fund switching in Section 12.2. The reader can find additional useful theoretical results for Poisson processes in other texts. However, simulation plays a very important role in modern stochastic analyses. The processes given here are very basic, but in many other practical examples the stochastic processes are so complex that exact theoretical results are not available and simulation is the only way to seek long term patterns.

12.2   Finite Markov Chains

12.2.1 Examples

The first two examples in Section 12.1 were examples of finite Markov chains. We will return to Example 12.1 to illustrate the basic properties of a finite Markov chain.

Example 12.4 In the gambler's ruin example, two gamblers bet on successive coin tosses. The two gamblers have exactly 4 coins between them. On each toss, the probability that a gambler wins or loses a coin is .50. The gamblers play until one has all the coins. At the end of each play, there are only 5 possibilities for a gambler: he may have 0, 1, 2, 3, or 4 coins. The number of coins the gambler has is referred to as his **state** in the process. In other words, if the gambler has exactly i coins, he is said to be in State i. The process is called finite because the number of states is finite. If the gambler is in State 2, there is a .50 probability of moving to State 3 and a .50 probability of moving to State 1. The probability of moving to any other state is 0, since only one coin is won or lost on each play. It is helpful to have a general notation for the probability of moving from one state to another. The probability of moving from State i to State j on a single toss is called a **transition probability** and is written as p_{ij}. In our example, $p_{23} = .50$, $p_{21} = .50$, $p_{24} = 0$, $p_{22} = 0$, and $p_{01} = 0$.

The last probability is of special interest. Once you are in State 0, you have lost all your money and play stops. The probability of going to any other state is 0. In this process, the States 0 and 4 are called **absorbing states**, because once you reach them the game ends and the probability of leaving the state is 0. Since there are only finitely many states, we can display all the transition probabilities in a table. This is done for the gambler's ruin process in the next table. The beginning states are displayed in the left column, the ending states in the first row, and the probabilities in the body of the table.

Beginning state \ Ending state	0	1	2	3	4
0	1	0	0	0	0
1	.5	0	.5	0	0
2	0	.5	0	.5	0
3	0	0	.5	0	.5
4	0	0	0	0	1

It is simpler to write the transition probabilities p_{ij} in matrix form, without including the states. The resulting matrix is called the **transition matrix P**. For our gambler's ruin example, the transition matrix is

$$P = \begin{bmatrix} 1 & 0 & 0 & 0 & 0 \\ .5 & 0 & .5 & 0 & 0 \\ 0 & .5 & 0 & .5 & 0 \\ 0 & 0 & .5 & 0 & .5 \\ 0 & 0 & 0 & 0 & 1 \end{bmatrix}.$$

A key feature of the gambler's ruin process is the fact that the gambler's next state depends only on his last state and not on any previous states. If the gambler is in State 2, he will move to State 3 on the next play with probability .50. This does not depend in any way on the fact that he may have been in State 1 or State 3 a few plays before. The probability of moving from State i to State j in the next play depends only on being in State i now, and thus can be written simply as p_{ij}. ☐

In general, a **finite Markov chain** is a stochastic process in which there are only a finite number of states $s_0, s_1, s_2, \ldots, s_n$. The probability of moving from State i to State j in one step of the process is written as p_{ij}, and depends only on the present State i, not on any prior state. The matrix $\mathbf{P} = [p_{ij}]$ is the transition matrix of the process. Our next example is taken from the fund switching process of Example 12.2.

Example 12.5 Members of a pension plan may invest their pension savings in either Fund 0 or Fund 1. There are only two states, 0 and 1. Each month members may switch funds if they wish. The probabilities of switching remain constant from month to month. The probability of switching from 0 to 1 is $p_{01} = .45$. The probability of switching from 1 to 0 is $p_{10} = .30$. The transition matrix for this process is

$$\mathbf{P} = \begin{bmatrix} .55 & .45 \\ .30 & .70 \end{bmatrix}.$$

This process is different from the gambler's ruin process. There are no absorbing states. It is possible to go from any state to any other.   □

The use of constant transition probabilities for fund switching may not be completely realistic. It is difficult to accept the assumption that the transition probability p_{ij} is the same for every step of the fund-switching process and does not change over time. Investor behavior is influenced by a number of factors which may change over time. It is also likely that investor behavior is influenced by past history, so that the probability of a switch may depend on what happened two months ago as well as the present state. We will use this process to illustrate the mathematics of Markov chains in the next section, but it is important to remember that results will change if the probabilities p_{ij} change over time instead of remaining constant.

12.2.2 Probability Calculations for Markov Processes

Example 12.6 Suppose the pension plan in Example 12.5 started at time 0 with 50% of its employees in Fund 0 and 50% of its employees in Fund 1. We would like to know the percent of employees in each fund at the end of the first month. In probability language, the probabilities of an employee being in Fund 0 or Fund 1 at time 0 are each .50, and we would like to find the probability that an employee is in either fund at time 1. To analyze this, we will use the notation

$$p_i^{(k)} = \text{the probability of being in State } i \text{ at time } k.$$

We are given that

$$p_0^{(0)} = .50$$

and

$$p_1^{(0)} = .50.$$

We need to find $p_0^{(1)}$ and $p_1^{(1)}$. We can find $p_0^{(1)}$ using basic rules of probability from Chapter 2.

$$p_0^{(1)} = P(\text{An employee is in Fund 0 at time 1})$$

$$= P(\text{The employee started in Fund 0 and did not switch})$$
$$+ P(\text{The employee started in Fund 1 and switched to Fund 0})$$

$$= P(\text{Stay in Fund 0} \mid \text{Start in Fund 0}) \times P(\text{Start in Fund 0})$$
$$+ P(\text{Switch to Fund 0} \mid \text{Start in Fund 1}) \times P(\text{Start in Fund 1})$$

$$= p_{00} \cdot p_0^{(0)} + p_{10} \cdot p_1^{(0)}$$

$$= .55(.50) + .30(.50) = .425$$

We can find $p_1^{(1)}$ in a similar manner.

$$p_1^{(1)} = p_{01} \cdot p_0^{(0)} + p_{11} \cdot p_1^{(0)} = .45(.50) + .70(.50) = .575$$

This sequence of calculations can be written much more simply using the transition matrix **P**. Note that

$$\left[p_0^{(0)}, p_1^{(0)} \right] \mathbf{P} = [.50 \ .50] \begin{bmatrix} .55 & .45 \\ .30 & .70 \end{bmatrix}$$

$$= [.50(.55) + .50(.30), \quad .50(.45) + .50(.70)]$$

$$= [.425, .575] = \left[p_0^{(1)}, p_1^{(1)} \right].$$

We can calculate the probabilities of being in States 0 or 1 at time 1 using matrix multiplication. □

In the preceding calculation, we have shown that we can use multiplication by $\mathbf{P}$ to move from the probability distribution of funds at time 0 to the probability distribution at time 1.

$$\left[p_0^{(0)}, p_1^{(0)}\right] \mathbf{P} = \left[p_0^{(1)}, p_1^{(1)}\right]$$

The same reasoning can be used to show that we can move from the distribution at any time i to the distribution at the next time $i + 1$ using multiplication by $\mathbf{P}$.

$$\left[p_0^{(i)}, p_1^{(i)}\right] \mathbf{P} = \left[p_0^{(i+1)}, p_1^{(i+1)}\right]$$

This gives us a simple way to find the probability distribution of funds at any point in time.

$$\left[p_0^{(1)}, p_1^{(1)}\right] = \left[p_0^{(0)}, p_1^{(0)}\right] \mathbf{P}$$

$$\left[p_0^{(2)}, p_1^{(2)}\right] = \left[p_0^{(1)}, p_1^{(1)}\right] \mathbf{P} = \left[p_0^{(0)}, p_1^{(0)}\right] \mathbf{P}^2$$

$$\left[p_0^{(3)}, p_1^{(3)}\right] = \left[p_0^{(2)}, p_1^{(2)}\right] \mathbf{P} = \left[p_0^{(0)}, p_1^{(0)}\right] \mathbf{P}^3$$

In general, if we are given the probability of being in each fund at time 0, we can find the probability distribution for the two funds at time n using the identity

$$\left[p_0^{(n)}, p_1^{(n)}\right] = \left[p_0^{(0)}, p_1^{(0)}\right] \mathbf{P}^n.$$

On the following page are the first 7 powers of the transition matrix for fund switching, along with the distributions for the first 7 months starting at [.50, .50].

n	$\mathbf{P}^n$	$\left[p_0^{(n)} \quad p_1^{(n)} \right]$
0		[0.5000 0.5000]
1	$\begin{bmatrix} 0.5500 & 0.4500 \\ 0.3000 & 0.7000 \end{bmatrix}$	[0.4250 0.5750]
2	$\begin{bmatrix} 0.4375 & 0.5625 \\ 0.3750 & 0.6250 \end{bmatrix}$	[0.4063 0.5938]
3	$\begin{bmatrix} 0.4094 & 0.5906 \\ 0.3938 & 0.6063 \end{bmatrix}$	[0.4016 0.5984]
4	$\begin{bmatrix} 0.4023 & 0.5977 \\ 0.3984 & 0.6016 \end{bmatrix}$	[0.4004 0.5996]
5	$\begin{bmatrix} 0.4006 & 0.5994 \\ 0.3996 & 0.6004 \end{bmatrix}$	[0.4001 0.5999]
6	$\begin{bmatrix} 0.4001 & 0.5999 \\ 0.3999 & 0.6001 \end{bmatrix}$	[0.4000 0.6000]
7	$\begin{bmatrix} 0.4000 & 0.6000 \\ 0.4000 & 0.6000 \end{bmatrix}$	[0.4000 0.6000]

This calculation shows us that even though the pension plan started with 50% of the employees in each fund, the distribution of employees appears to be stabilizing with 40% in Fund 0 and 60% in Fund 1. In Section 12.3 we will show that there will eventually be 40% of all employees in Fund 0 and 60% in Fund 1, no matter what the starting distribution is.

The matrix multiplication procedure works for any finite Markov process. If the states are $s_0, s_1, s_2, \ldots, s_k$, the probability distribution at time i is the row vector

$$\mathbf{p}^{(i)} = [p_0^{(i)}, p_1^{(i)}, \ldots, p_k^{(i)}].$$

If **P** is the transition matrix for the process, then we can move from the probability distribution at time i to the probability distribution at time $i + 1$ using the identity

$$\mathbf{p}^{(i+1)} = \mathbf{p}^{(i)}\mathbf{P} .$$

The probability distribution at time n is related to the initial probability distribution $\mathbf{p}^{(0)}$ by the identity

$$\mathbf{p}^{(n)} = \mathbf{p}^{(0)}\mathbf{P}^n.$$

Example 12.7   For the gambler's ruin example with 4 coins between the two gamblers, the transition matrix was

$$\mathbf{P} = \begin{bmatrix} 1 & 0 & 0 & 0 & 0 \\ .5 & 0 & .5 & 0 & 0 \\ 0 & .5 & 0 & .5 & 0 \\ 0 & 0 & .5 & 0 & .5 \\ 0 & 0 & 0 & 0 & 1 \end{bmatrix}.$$

Suppose a gambler starts with 1 coin. His initial probability distribution at time 0 is given by the row vector

$$\mathbf{p}^{(0)} = [0, 1, 0, 0, 0].$$

His probability distribution at time 1 is given by

$$\mathbf{p}^{(1)} = \mathbf{p}^{(0)}\mathbf{P} = [.5, 0, .5, 0, 0].$$

We can observe what happens to this gambler in the long run by looking at $\mathbf{p}^{(n)} = \mathbf{p}^{(0)}\mathbf{P}^n$ for larger values of n. Such calculations are a problem when done by hand, but calculators such as the TI-83 will do them easily. Below are the results for $n = 12$. The matrix $\mathbf{P}^{12}$ is given next with all entries rounded to three places.

$$\begin{bmatrix} 1.000 & 0.000 & 0.000 & 0.000 & 0.000 \\ 0.742 & 0.008 & 0.000 & 0.008 & 0.242 \\ 0.492 & 0.000 & 0.016 & 0.000 & 0.492 \\ 0.242 & 0.008 & 0.000 & 0.008 & 0.742 \\ 0.000 & 0.000 & 0.000 & 0.000 & 1.000 \end{bmatrix}$$

The probability distribution for the gambler after 12 plays is the row vector

$$[.742, .008, .000, .008, .242].$$

We will show in Section 12.4 that the long-term probability distribution for a gambler starting with one out of 4 coins is $[.75, 0, 0, 0, .25]$. □

12.3 Regular Markov Processes

12.3.1 Basic Properties

We return to the analysis of fund switching in Example 12.6 to illustrate the basic properties of regular finite Markov chains. The transition matrix for that process was

$$P = \begin{bmatrix} .55 & .45 \\ .30 & .70 \end{bmatrix}.$$

Note that all the entries in P are positive. A stochastic process is called **regular** if, for some n, all entries in P^n are positive. Thus the fund-switching process above is regular with $n = 1$. An important consequence of this definition is that for a regular process it is always possible to move from State i to State j in exactly n steps for any choice of i and j. Note that the gamblers ruin process is not regular. If you have lost all your money and are in State 0, it is not possible to move to any other state.

We can describe the long-term behavior of regular finite Markov processes by looking at the limit of P^n as n approaches infinity. We observed in Example 12.6 that the matrix P^n rapidly approached a limiting matrix L. The matrices P^6 and P^7 were

$$\begin{bmatrix} 0.4001 & 0.5999 \\ 0.3999 & 0.6001 \end{bmatrix}$$

and

$$\begin{bmatrix} 0.4000 & 0.6000 \\ 0.4000 & 0.6000 \end{bmatrix} = \mathbf{L}.$$

Note that the limiting matrix $\mathbf{L}$ had identical rows. It can be proved that this happens for any regular finite Markov chain.

Limit of $\mathbf{P}^n$ for a Regular Finite Markov Chain

If $\mathbf{P}$ is the transition matrix of a regular finite Markov process, then the powers $\mathbf{P}^n$ converge to a limiting matrix $\mathbf{L}$.

$$\lim_{n \to \infty} \mathbf{P}^n = \mathbf{L}$$

The rows of $\mathbf{L}$ are all equal to the same row vector $\boldsymbol{\ell}$.

In our example of fund switching, the limiting matrix $\mathbf{L}$ was

$$\mathbf{L} = \begin{bmatrix} .4 & .6 \\ .4 & .6 \end{bmatrix},$$

and the common row vector was $\boldsymbol{\ell} = [.4 \quad .6]$. In that example, the distribution of employees was shown to approach $\boldsymbol{\ell}$ over time. This will happen no matter what the distribution of employees is at time 0. If the initial distribution is $\left[p_0^{(0)}, p_1^{(0)} \right]$, then the limiting distribution is

$$\lim_{n \to \infty} \left[p_0^{(0)}, p_1^{(0)} \right] \mathbf{P}^n = \left[p_0^{(0)}, p_1^{(0)} \right] \lim_{n \to \infty} \mathbf{P}^n$$

$$= \left[p_0^{(0)}, p_1^{(0)} \right] \begin{bmatrix} .4 & .6 \\ .4 & .6 \end{bmatrix}$$

$$= [.4p_0^{(0)} + .4p_1^{(0)}, \quad .6p_0^{(0)} + .6p_1^{(0)}]$$

$$= [.4, \quad .6].$$

Note that the limiting distribution is given by the common row vector $\boldsymbol{\ell}$ of $\mathbf{L}$, and that $\mathbf{p}^{(0)}\mathbf{L} = \boldsymbol{\ell}$. This, too, holds for every regular finite Markov chain.

Limiting Distribution for a Regular Finite Markov Chain

For any regular finite Markov chain, $\mathbf{p}^{(0)}\mathbf{L} = \boldsymbol{\ell}$ no matter what initial distribution $\mathbf{p}^{(0)}$ is chosen. The limiting probability distribution is given by the common row vector $\boldsymbol{\ell}$ of the limiting matrix $\mathbf{L}$.

12.3.2 Finding the Limiting Matrix of a Regular Finite Markov Chain

The vector $\boldsymbol{\ell}$ can be found using a simple system of equations. The system is based on the observation that $\boldsymbol{\ell}\mathbf{P} = \boldsymbol{\ell}$. Intuitively, this equation tells us that once we have reached the limiting distribution, future steps of the process leave us there. A derivation of the equation $\boldsymbol{\ell}\mathbf{P} = \boldsymbol{\ell}$ is outlined in Exercise 12-12. We will use this equation to find the limiting distribution of the fund-switching process in the next example.

Example 12.8 If we write the unknown vector $\boldsymbol{\ell}$ for the fund-switching process as $[x, y]$, the equation $\boldsymbol{\ell}\mathbf{P} = \boldsymbol{\ell}$ becomes

$$[x, \ y]\begin{bmatrix} .55 & .45 \\ .30 & .70 \end{bmatrix} = [x, \ y].$$

This reduces to the following system of equations:

$$.55x + .30y = x$$
$$.45x + .70y = y$$

This, in turn, reduces to the following linear homogeneous system:

$$-.45x + .30y = 0$$
$$.45x - .30y = 0$$

This system has infinitely many solutions, but we are looking for the solution which is a probability distribution, so that it satisfies the condition $x + y = 1$. Thus we solve the following system:

$$-.45x + .30y = 0$$
$$.45x - .30y = 0$$
$$x + y = 1$$

The solution of this system is $x = .40$ and $y = .60$. Thus we have demonstrated that $\ell = [.40, .60]$. This procedure works in general. $\square$

Finding the Limiting Distribution for a Regular Finite Markov Chain

For any regular finite Markov chain, we can find the common row vector $\ell = [x_1, x_2, \ldots, x_n]$ of the limiting matrix $\mathbf{L}$ by solving the system of $n+1$ linear equations given by

$$[x_1, x_2, \ldots, x_n]\mathbf{P} = [x_1, x_2, \ldots, x_n]$$

and

$$x_1 + x_2 + \cdots + x_n = 1.$$

Example 12.9   Another pension plan gives its employees the choice of three funds: Fund 0, Fund 1 and Fund 2. Participants are permitted to change funds at the end of each month. The transition matrix for the fund-switching process is given by

$$\mathbf{P} = \begin{bmatrix} .2 & .5 & .3 \\ .3 & .6 & .1 \\ .2 & .3 & .5 \end{bmatrix}.$$

Then the limiting distribution $\ell = [x, y, z]$ can be found by solving the following system:

$$[x, y, z]\begin{bmatrix} .2 & .5 & .3 \\ .3 & .6 & .1 \\ .2 & .3 & .5 \end{bmatrix} = [x, y, z]$$

$$x + y + z = 1$$

This leads to the following system of equations:

$$-.8x + .3y + .2z = 0$$
$$.5x - .4y + .3z = 0$$
$$.3x + .1y - .5z = 0$$
$$x + y + z = 1$$

The solution is $x = .25$, $y = .50$ and $z = .25$. In the long run, the pension plan will have 25% of employees in Fund 0, 50% in Fund 1, and 25% in Fund 2. This solution can be checked by evaluating powers of the transition matrix. The TI-83 (with rounding set to three places) gives

$$\mathbf{P}^6 = \begin{bmatrix} .250 & .500 & .250 \\ .250 & .501 & .249 \\ .250 & .499 & .251 \end{bmatrix}$$

and

$$\mathbf{P}^7 = \begin{bmatrix} .250 & .500 & .250 \\ .250 & .500 & .250 \\ .250 & .500 & .250 \end{bmatrix}.$$

Thus this switching process should be very close to its limit in 6 or 7 months. □

12.4 Absorbing Markov Chains

12.4.1 Another Gambler's Ruin Example

The gambler's ruin process in Example 12.7 did not follow the patterns observed in Section 12.3, since it was not a regular process. It was not possible to get from any state to any other, since it was impossible to leave an absorbing state. However, the gambler's ruin process had a long-term pattern of another kind. In the next example we will look at a simpler gambler's ruin problem (with three coins instead of four) to illustrate the basic properties of absorbing Markov chains.

Example 12.10   Two gamblers start with a total of 3 coins between them. As before, they bet on coin tosses until one player has all the coins. In this case, the table of states and probabilities is as follows:

Beginning state Ending state	0	1	2	3
0	1	0	0	0
1	.5	0	.5	0
2	0	.5	0	.5
3	0	0	0	1

The transition matrix is

$$\mathbf{P} = \begin{bmatrix} 1 & 0 & 0 & 0 \\ .5 & 0 & .5 & 0 \\ 0 & .5 & 0 & .5 \\ 0 & 0 & 0 & 1 \end{bmatrix}.$$

This chain is called an **absorbing Markov chain** because it is possible to go from any state to an absorbing state. If we take powers of the matrix $\mathbf{P}$, we will see a long-term pattern develop. For example, the TI-83 calculator gives the result (with rounding to 3 places)

$$\mathbf{P}^{20} = \begin{bmatrix} 1.000 & .000 & .000 & .000 \\ .667 & .000 & .000 & .333 \\ .333 & .000 & .000 & .667 \\ .000 & .000 & .000 & 1.000 \end{bmatrix}.$$

This seems to imply the intuitive results that one player will eventually win all the coins, and the player with 2 out of 3 coins will win all the coins with a probability of 2/3.   □

12.4.2 Probabilities of Absorption

The statement that one player will eventually win all the coins in this process is equivalent to the statement that the probability of the absorbing chain eventually reaching an absorbing state is 1. We will not prove this, but it is true.

> The probability that an absorbing Markov chain will eventually reach an absorbing state is 1.

The major task is to find the exact probability of eventually ending up in each absorbing state. In order to do this, it helps to rewrite the table for the process with the absorbing states first. For the three-coin gambler's ruin, the table changes to the following table.

Beginning state ⟍ Ending state	0	3	1	2
0	1	0	0	0
3	0	1	0	0
1	.5	0	0	.5
2	0	.5	.5	0

Now the transition matrix is written differently. The reader must remember that the order of states has changed.

$$\mathbf{P} = \begin{bmatrix} 1 & 0 & 0 & 0 \\ 0 & 1 & 0 & 0 \\ .5 & 0 & 0 & .5 \\ 0 & .5 & .5 & 0 \end{bmatrix}$$

This matrix can be partitioned into four distinct parts in a natural way.

$$\left[\begin{array}{cc|cc} 1 & 0 & 0 & 0 \\ 0 & 1 & 0 & 0 \\ \hline .5 & 0 & 0 & .5 \\ 0 & .5 & .5 & 0 \end{array} \right]$$

The matrix in the upper left corner is denoted by $\mathbf{I}$; it shows that the probability of staying in each absorbing state is 1 and the probability of leaving is 0. The matrix in the lower left corner is denoted by $\mathbf{R}$; it gives the probabilities of going in one step from each non-absorbing state to each absorbing state. If we use the transition probability notation,

$$\mathbf{R} = \begin{bmatrix} p_{10} & p_{13} \\ p_{20} & p_{23} \end{bmatrix} = \begin{bmatrix} .5 & 0 \\ 0 & .5 \end{bmatrix}.$$

The matrix in the lower right corner is denoted by $\mathbf{Q}$; it shows the one-step probabilities of moving between the non-absorbing states.

$$\mathbf{Q} = \begin{bmatrix} p_{11} & p_{12} \\ p_{21} & p_{22} \end{bmatrix} = \begin{bmatrix} 0 & .5 \\ .5 & 0 \end{bmatrix}$$

When the transition matrix is arranged this way it is said to be in **standard form**. We could write this schematically as

$$\left[\begin{array}{c|c} \mathbf{I} & \mathbf{0} \\ \hline \mathbf{R} & \mathbf{Q} \end{array} \right].$$

We will use the matrices introduced above to solve for the probabilities of ending up in each absorbing state. One absorption probability we need to find is

a_{ij} = the probability of eventually being absorbed in the absorbing State j, from a start in the non-absorbing State i.

In this problem, there are four such unknown probabilities: a_{10}, a_{20}, a_{13}, and a_{23}. We can write four equations in these four unknowns by setting up some basic probability relationships. The first unknown is

a_{10} = the probability of eventually being absorbed in State 0, from a start in the non-absorbing State 1.

There are three ways to start in State 1 and eventually be absorbed in State 0. They are given below with their probabilities.

P(move from State 1 to State 0 in one step) = p_{10}

P(move from State 1 to State 1 in one step *and* eventually reach State 0)
$$= p_{11}a_{10}$$

P(move from State 1 to State 2 in one step and eventually reach State 0)
$$= p_{12}a_{20}$$

The desired a_{10} is the sum of these three probabilities.

$$a_{10} = p_{10} + p_{11}a_{10} + p_{12}a_{20} = .5 + 0a_{10} + .5a_{20}$$

We can reason similarly to obtain three more linear equations.

$$a_{20} = p_{20} + p_{21}a_{10} + p_{22}a_{20} = 0 + .5a_{10} + 0a_{20}$$

$$a_{13} = p_{13} + p_{11}a_{13} + p_{12}a_{23} = 0 + 0a_{13} + .5a_{23}$$

$$a_{23} = p_{23} + p_{21}a_{13} + p_{22}a_{23} = .5 + .5a_{13} + 0a_{23}$$

We now have a system of four equations in four unknowns which can be solved for the absorption probabilities. The matrix notation introduced in this section can make this task considerably easier. The four simultaneous equations are equivalent to the single matrix equation

$$\begin{bmatrix} a_{10} & a_{13} \\ a_{20} & a_{23} \end{bmatrix} = \begin{bmatrix} p_{10} & p_{13} \\ p_{20} & p_{23} \end{bmatrix} + \begin{bmatrix} p_{11} & p_{12} \\ p_{21} & p_{22} \end{bmatrix} \begin{bmatrix} a_{10} & a_{13} \\ a_{20} & a_{23} \end{bmatrix}.$$

If we write **A** for the unknown matrix of absorption probabilities, this matrix equation is

$$\mathbf{A} = \mathbf{R} + \mathbf{QA}.$$

We can then solve this equation for **A**.

$$\mathbf{A} - \mathbf{QA} = \mathbf{R}$$

$$(\mathbf{I} - \mathbf{Q})\mathbf{A} = \mathbf{R}$$

$$\mathbf{A} = (\mathbf{I} - \mathbf{Q})^{-1}\mathbf{R}$$

For our three-coin gambler's ruin problem, the values of the necessary matrices are

$$\mathbf{R} = \begin{bmatrix} .5 & 0 \\ 0 & .5 \end{bmatrix},$$

$$\mathbf{Q} = \begin{bmatrix} 0 & .5 \\ .5 & 0 \end{bmatrix},$$

and

$$\mathbf{I} - \mathbf{Q} = \begin{bmatrix} 1 & -.5 \\ -.5 & 1 \end{bmatrix}.$$

Then

$$(I - Q)^{-1} = \begin{bmatrix} \frac{4}{3} & \frac{2}{3} \\ \frac{2}{3} & \frac{4}{3} \end{bmatrix}.$$

We find that the matrix of absorption probabilities is

$$A = (I - Q)^{-1}R = \begin{bmatrix} \frac{4}{3} & \frac{2}{3} \\ \frac{2}{3} & \frac{4}{3} \end{bmatrix} \begin{bmatrix} .5 & 0 \\ 0 & .5 \end{bmatrix} = \begin{bmatrix} \frac{2}{3} & \frac{1}{3} \\ \frac{1}{3} & \frac{2}{3} \end{bmatrix}.$$

The top row of the matrix A shows that $a_{10} = \frac{2}{3}$ and $a_{13} = \frac{1}{3}$. A gambler with one coin will end up with no coins with probability $\frac{2}{3}$, and all three coins with probability $\frac{1}{3}$, as predicted. The second row of the matrix can be interpreted similarly. Another item of interest is the expected number of times a gambler will be in each non-absorbing state if he starts in a particular non-absorbing state.

n_{ij} = the expected number of visits (before absorption) to non-absorbing State j, from a start in the non-absorbing State i.

In the three-coin gambler's ruin problem, we would like to find the entries in the matrix

$$N = \begin{bmatrix} n_{11} & n_{12} \\ n_{21} & n_{22} \end{bmatrix}.$$

It can also be shown that

$$N = (I - Q)^{-1}.$$

Thus in the three-coin gambler's ruin problem,

$$N = (I - Q)^{-1} = \begin{bmatrix} \frac{4}{3} & \frac{2}{3} \\ \frac{2}{3} & \frac{4}{3} \end{bmatrix}.$$

For a gambler with one coin, the expected number of visits to State 1 is 4/3 (including a count of 1 for the start in State 1 and an expected value of 1/3 subsequent visits before absorption), and the expected number of visits to State 2 before absorption is 2/3. The game will end fairly soon.

We have examined these matrix results for a simple gambler's ruin chain, but the same reasoning can be used to show that they apply to any absorbing finite Markov chain.

Absorbing Finite Markov Chains

The transition matrix can always be written in the form

$$\left[\begin{array}{c|c} \mathbf{I} & \mathbf{0} \\ \hline \mathbf{R} & \mathbf{Q} \end{array}\right].$$

The matrix of absorption probabilities is given by

$$\mathbf{A} = (\mathbf{I} - \mathbf{Q})^{-1}\mathbf{R}.$$

The entries of the matrix

$$(\mathbf{I} - \mathbf{Q})^{-1} = \mathbf{N}$$

give the expected number of visits to non-absorbing State j from a start in non-absorbing State i.

In the next example, we will apply this theory to the gambler's ruin problem in which the two gamblers have a total of four coins.

Example 12.11 The four-coin process has standard form matrix

$$\mathbf{P} = \begin{bmatrix} 1 & 0 & 0 & 0 & 0 \\ 0 & 1 & 0 & 0 & 0 \\ .5 & 0 & 0 & .5 & 0 \\ 0 & 0 & .5 & 0 & .5 \\ 0 & .5 & 0 & .5 & 0 \end{bmatrix}.$$

The matrices needed to find $\mathbf{N}$ and $\mathbf{A}$ are

$$\mathbf{R} = \begin{bmatrix} .5 & 0 \\ 0 & 0 \\ 0 & .5 \end{bmatrix}$$

and

$$\mathbf{Q} = \begin{bmatrix} 0 & .5 & 0 \\ .5 & 0 & .5 \\ 0 & .5 & 0 \end{bmatrix}.$$

We then calculate the following:

$$(\mathbf{I} - \mathbf{Q}) = \begin{bmatrix} 1 & -.5 & 0 \\ -.5 & 1 & -.5 \\ 0 & -.5 & 1 \end{bmatrix}$$

$$\mathbf{N} = (\mathbf{I} - \mathbf{Q})^{-1} = \begin{bmatrix} 1.5 & 1 & .5 \\ 1 & 2 & 1 \\ .5 & 1 & 1.5 \end{bmatrix}$$

$$\mathbf{A} = (\mathbf{I} - \mathbf{Q})^{-1}\mathbf{R} = \mathbf{NR} = \begin{bmatrix} 1.5 & 1 & .5 \\ 1 & 2 & 1 \\ .5 & 1 & 1.5 \end{bmatrix} \begin{bmatrix} .5 & 0 \\ 0 & 0 \\ 0 & .5 \end{bmatrix} = \begin{bmatrix} .75 & .25 \\ .50 & .50 \\ .25 & .75 \end{bmatrix}$$

These absorption probabilities are those we suspected on the basis of our matrix power calculations. For example, a gambler who starts with one coin has a .75 probability of absorption in State 0 (losing all his coins) and a .25 probability of absorption in State 4 (winning all four coins.) □

12.5   Further Study of Stochastic Processes

The material in this chapter was included to show the reader that theory can be developed to study the long-term behavior of stochastic processes. Much further study and additional coursework is needed to learn the wide range of additional theory that can be used in financial risk management. For example, the reader who has had a course in the theory of interest can get a nice introduction to the stochastic theory of interest rates by reading Chapter 6 of Broverman [3]. Hopefully the end of this text has served only as a beginning.

12.6   Exercises

12.1   Simulation Examples

For Exercises 12-1 through 12-3, use the following sequence of random numbers.

1. .57230	6. .82496	11. .02480	16. .78322
2. .85472	7. .52184	12. .99954	17. .00067
3. .37282	8. .49837	13. .81708	18. .24844
4. .77133	9. .76729	14. .90535	19. .14118
5. .20525	10. .50986	15. .76227	20. .47417

12-1.   For the two gamblers in Example 12.1, suppose A has 3 coins and B has 5 coins, and the game is played as described in the example. Use the random numbers given above to simulate the game. Which player would win the game, and how many coin tosses were needed to decide the winner?

12-2.   For an employee in the pension plan in Example 12.2, the probabilities for staying in a fund or switching funds are given in the following table.

End in Start in	0	1
0	.65	.35
1	.25	.75

Use the decision-making process for switching funds described in the example and the random numbers given above to simulate the progress of an employee who is initially in Fund 0. How many times in the next 20 months would he switch to, or stay in, Fund 1?

12-3.   Suppose the waiting time in months between accidents at an intersection is exponential with $\lambda = 3$. Use the method in Example 12.3 and the random numbers given above to simulate the time between accidents. How many accidents occur in each of the first three months at this intersection?

12.2   Finite Markov Chains

12-4.   For members in a pension plan, the transition matrix of probabilities of switching funds is

$$\mathbf{P} = \begin{bmatrix} .65 & .35 \\ .25 & .75 \end{bmatrix}.$$

If the initial probability distribution is $\mathbf{p}^{(0)} = [.50, .50]$, find (a) $\mathbf{p}^{(1)}$; (b) $\mathbf{p}^{(2)}$.

12-5.   The transition matrix for a Markov process with 2 states is

$$\mathbf{P} = \begin{bmatrix} .72 & .28 \\ .36 & .64 \end{bmatrix},$$

and the initial probability distribution is $\mathbf{p}^{(0)} = [.40, .60]$. Find (a) $\mathbf{p}^{(1)}$; (b) $\mathbf{p}^{(2)}$.

12-6.   The transition matrix for a Markov process with 3 states is

$$\mathbf{P} = \begin{bmatrix} .4 & .2 & .4 \\ .2 & .5 & .3 \\ .1 & .3 & .6 \end{bmatrix},$$

and the initial probability distribution is $\mathbf{p}^{(0)} = [.30, .30, .40]$. Find $\mathbf{p}^{(1)}$.

12-7.   A mutual fund investor has the choice of a stock fund (Fund 0), a bond fund (Fund 1), and a money market fund (Fund 2). At the end of each quarter she can move her money from fund to fund. The probability that she stays in Fund 0 is .60, in Fund 1, .50, and in Fund 2, .40. If she switches funds, she will move to each of the other funds with equal probability. If she starts with all of her money in the stock fund, what is the probability distribution after two quarters?

12.3   Regular Markov Processes

12-8.   For the transition matrix in Exercise 12-4, find the limiting distribution.

12-9.   What is the limiting distribution for the Markov process in Exercise 12-5?

12-10. What is the limiting distribution for the Markov process in Exercise 12-6?

12-11. What is the limiting distribution for the investor in Exercise 12-7?

12-12. Prove that if $\mathbf{P}$ is the transition matrix of a regular finite Markov process and $\boldsymbol{\ell}$ is its limiting distribution, then $\boldsymbol{\ell}\mathbf{P} = \boldsymbol{\ell}$. Hint: Write $\boldsymbol{\ell}\mathbf{P}^n = (\boldsymbol{\ell}\mathbf{P}^{n-1})\mathbf{P}$ and take the limit of both sides.

12.4   Absorbing Markov Chains

12-13. In the gambler's ruin example, suppose the game is rigged so that the probability that A wins is 1/3 and the probability that B wins is 2/3. Let the states represent the number of coins that A has at any time, and let the total number of coins between both players be 3.
   (a)   Find the matrix $\mathbf{N}$.
   (b)   Find the matrix $\mathbf{A}$.
   (c)   If A starts with 2 coins, what is the probability that he will lose (end in State 0)?

12-14. Let the gamblers in Exercise 12-13 start with 4 coins between them.
   (a)   Find the matrix $\mathbf{N}$.
   (b)   Find the matrix $\mathbf{A}$.
   (c)   If A starts with 2 coins, what is the probability that he will lose?

12.3   Regular Markov Processes

12-8   For the transition matrix in Exercise 12-4 find the limiting distribution.

12-9   What is the limiting distribution for the Markov process in Exercise 12-5?

12-10   What is the limiting distribution for the Markov process in Exercise 12-6.

12-11   What is the limiting distribution for the process in Exercise 12-7?

12-12   Prove that if P is the transition matrix of a regular finite Markov process and z is its limiting distribution, then $zP = z$. Hint: Write $zP^n = zP^{n-1}P$ and take the limit of both sides.

12.4   Absorbing Markov Chains

12-13   In the gambler's ruin example, suppose the game is rigged so that the probability that A wins is 1/3 and the probability that B wins is 2/3. Let the states represent the number of coins that A has at any time, and let the total number of coins between both players be 3.
    (a)   Find the matrix N.
    (b)   Find the matrix A.
    (c)   If A starts with 2 coins, what is the probability that he will lose (end in State 0)?

12-14   For the gamblers in Exercise 12-13 start with 4 coins between them.
    (a)   Find the matrix N.
    (b)   Find the matrix A.
    (c)   If A starts with 2 coins, what is the probability that he will lose?

Appendix A

Values of the Cumulative Distribution Function for the Standard Normal Random Variable Z

z	0.00	0.01	0.02	0.03	0.04	0.05	0.06	0.07	0.08	0.09
0.0	0.5000	0.5040	0.5080	0.5120	0.5160	0.5199	0.5239	0.5279	0.5319	0.5359
0.1	0.5398	0.5438	0.5478	0.5517	0.5557	0.5596	0.5636	0.5675	0.5714	0.5753
0.2	0.5793	0.5832	0.5871	0.5910	0.5948	0.5987	0.6026	0.6064	0.6103	0.6141
0.3	0.6179	0.6217	0.6255	0.6293	0.6331	0.6368	0.6406	0.6443	0.6480	0.6517
0.4	0.6554	0.6591	0.6628	0.6664	0.6700	0.6736	0.6772	0.6808	0.6844	0.6879
0.5	0.6915	0.6950	0.6985	0.7019	0.7054	0.7088	0.7123	0.7157	0.7190	0.7224
0.6	0.7257	0.7291	0.7324	0.7357	0.7389	0.7422	0.7454	0.7486	0.7517	0.7549
0.7	0.7580	0.7611	0.7642	0.7673	0.7704	0.7734	0.7764	0.7794	0.7823	0.7852
0.8	0.7881	0.7910	0.7939	0.7967	0.7995	0.8023	0.8051	0.8078	0.8106	0.8133
0.9	0.8159	0.8186	0.8212	0.8238	0.8264	0.8289	0.8315	0.8340	0.8365	0.8389
1.0	0.8413	0.8438	0.8461	0.8485	0.8508	0.8531	0.8554	0.8577	0.8599	0.8621
1.1	0.8643	0.8665	0.8686	0.8708	0.8729	0.8749	0.8770	0.8790	0.8810	0.8830
1.2	0.8849	0.8869	0.8888	0.8907	0.8925	0.8944	0.8962	0.8980	0.8997	0.9015
1.3	0.9032	0.9049	0.9066	0.9082	0.9099	0.9115	0.9131	0.9147	0.9162	0.9177
1.4	0.9192	0.9207	0.9222	0.9236	0.9251	0.9265	0.9279	0.9292	0.9306	0.9319
1.5	0.9332	0.9345	0.9357	0.9370	0.9382	0.9394	0.9406	0.9418	0.9429	0.9441
1.6	0.9452	0.9463	0.9474	0.9484	0.9495	0.9505	0.9515	0.9525	0.9535	0.9545
1.7	0.9554	0.9564	0.9573	0.9582	0.9591	0.9599	0.9608	0.9616	0.9625	0.9633
1.8	0.9641	0.9649	0.9656	0.9664	0.9671	0.9678	0.9686	0.9693	0.9699	0.9706
1.9	0.9713	0.9719	0.9726	0.9732	0.9738	0.9744	0.9750	0.9756	0.9761	0.9767
2.0	0.9772	0.9778	0.9783	0.9788	0.9793	0.9798	0.9803	0.9808	0.9812	0.9817
2.1	0.9821	0.9826	0.9830	0.9834	0.9838	0.9842	0.9846	0.9850	0.9854	0.9857
2.2	0.9861	0.9864	0.9868	0.9871	0.9875	0.9878	0.9881	0.9884	0.9887	0.9890
2.3	0.9893	0.9896	0.9898	0.9901	0.9904	0.9906	0.9909	0.9911	0.9913	0.9916
2.4	0.9918	0.9920	0.9922	0.9925	0.9927	0.9929	0.9931	0.9932	0.9934	0.9936
2.5	0.9938	0.9940	0.9941	0.9943	0.9945	0.9946	0.9948	0.9949	0.9951	0.9952
2.6	0.9953	0.9955	0.9956	0.9957	0.9959	0.9960	0.9961	0.9962	0.9963	0.9964
2.7	0.9965	0.9966	0.9967	0.9968	0.9969	0.9970	0.9971	0.9972	0.9973	0.9974
2.8	0.9974	0.9975	0.9976	0.9977	0.9977	0.9978	0.9979	0.9979	0.9980	0.9981
2.9	0.9981	0.9982	0.9982	0.9983	0.9984	0.9984	0.9985	0.9985	0.9986	0.9986
3.0	0.9987	0.9987	0.9987	0.9988	0.9988	0.9989	0.9989	0.9989	0.9990	0.9990
3.1	0.9990	0.9991	0.9991	0.9991	0.9992	0.9992	0.9992	0.9992	0.9993	0.9993
3.2	0.9993	0.9993	0.9994	0.9994	0.9994	0.9994	0.9994	0.9995	0.9995	0.9995

Second Decimal Place in z

	Second Decimal Place in z									
z	0.09	0.08	0.07	0.06	0.05	0.04	0.03	0.02	0.01	0.00
-3.2	0.0005	0.0005	0.0005	0.0006	0.0006	0.0006	0.0006	0.0006	0.0007	0.0007
-3.1	0.0007	0.0007	0.0008	0.0008	0.0008	0.0008	0.0009	0.0009	0.0009	0.0010
-3.0	0.0010	0.0010	0.0011	0.0011	0.0011	0.0012	0.0012	0.0013	0.0013	0.0013
-2.9	0.0014	0.0014	0.0015	0.0015	0.0016	0.0016	0.0017	0.0018	0.0018	0.0019
-2.8	0.0019	0.0020	0.0021	0.0021	0.0022	0.0023	0.0023	0.0024	0.0025	0.0026
-2.7	0.0026	0.0027	0.0028	0.0029	0.0030	0.0031	0.0032	0.0033	0.0034	0.0035
-2.6	0.0036	0.0037	0.0038	0.0039	0.0040	0.0041	0.0043	0.0044	0.0045	0.0047
-2.5	0.0048	0.0049	0.0051	0.0052	0.0054	0.0055	0.0057	0.0059	0.0060	0.0062
-2.4	0.0064	0.0066	0.0068	0.0069	0.0071	0.0073	0.0075	0.0078	0.0080	0.0082
-2.3	0.0084	0.0087	0.0089	0.0091	0.0094	0.0096	0.0099	0.0102	0.0104	0.0107
-2.2	0.0110	0.0113	0.0116	0.0119	0.0122	0.0125	0.0129	0.0132	0.0136	0.0139
-2.1	0.0143	0.0146	0.0150	0.0154	0.0158	0.0162	0.0166	0.0170	0.0174	0.0179
-2.0	0.0183	0.0188	0.0192	0.0197	0.0202	0.0207	0.0212	0.0217	0.0222	0.0228
-1.9	0.0233	0.0239	0.0244	0.0250	0.0256	0.0262	0.0268	0.0274	0.0281	0.0287
-1.8	0.0294	0.0301	0.0307	0.0314	0.0322	0.0329	0.0336	0.0344	0.0351	0.0359
-1.7	0.0367	0.0375	0.0384	0.0392	0.0401	0.0409	0.0418	0.0427	0.0436	0.0446
-1.6	0.0455	0.0465	0.0475	0.0485	0.0495	0.0505	0.0516	0.0526	0.0537	0.0548
-1.5	0.0559	0.0571	0.0582	0.0594	0.0606	0.0618	0.0630	0.0643	0.0655	0.0668
-1.4	0.0681	0.0694	0.0708	0.0721	0.0735	0.0749	0.0764	0.0778	0.0793	0.0808
-1.3	0.0823	0.0838	0.0853	0.0869	0.0885	0.0901	0.0918	0.0934	0.0951	0.0968
-1.2	0.0985	0.1003	0.1020	0.1038	0.1056	0.1075	0.1093	0.1112	0.1131	0.1151
-1.1	0.1170	0.1190	0.1210	0.1230	0.1251	0.1271	0.1292	0.1314	0.1335	0.1357
-1.0	0.1379	0.1401	0.1423	0.1446	0.1469	0.1492	0.1515	0.1539	0.1562	0.1587
-0.9	0.1611	0.1635	0.1660	0.1685	0.1711	0.1736	0.1762	0.1788	0.1814	0.1841
-0.8	0.1867	0.1894	0.1922	0.1949	0.1977	0.2005	0.2033	0.2061	0.2090	0.2119
-0.7	0.2148	0.2177	0.2206	0.2236	0.2266	0.2296	0.2327	0.2358	0.2389	0.2420
-0.6	0.2451	0.2483	0.2514	0.2546	0.2578	0.2611	0.2643	0.2676	0.2709	0.2743
-0.5	0.2776	0.2810	0.2843	0.2877	0.2912	0.2946	0.2981	0.3015	0.3050	0.3085
-0.4	0.3121	0.3156	0.3192	0.3228	0.3264	0.3300	0.3336	0.3372	0.3409	0.3446
-0.3	0.3483	0.3520	0.3557	0.3594	0.3632	0.3669	0.3707	0.3745	0.3783	0.3821
-0.2	0.3859	0.3897	0.3936	0.3974	0.4013	0.4052	0.4090	0.4129	0.4168	0.4207
-0.1	0.4247	0.4286	0.4325	0.4364	0.4404	0.4443	0.4483	0.4522	0.4562	0.4602
0.0	0.4641	0.4681	0.4721	0.4761	0.4801	0.4840	0.4880	0.4920	0.4960	0.5000

Discrete Distributions

Distribution	Probability Function Parameters	Mean	Variance	Moment Generating Function
Binomial	$\binom{n}{k}p^k q^{n-k}$, $k=0,\ldots,n$ $0\le p\le 1$, $q=1-p$	np	npq	$(q+pe^t)^n$
Hypergeometric	$\dfrac{\binom{N-r}{n-k}\binom{r}{k}}{\binom{N}{n}}$, $k=0,\ldots,n$ $r\ge n$	$n\left(\frac{r}{N}\right)$	$n\left(\frac{r}{N}\right)\left(1-\frac{r}{N}\right)\left(\frac{N-n}{N-1}\right)$	
Poisson	$\dfrac{e^{-\lambda}\lambda^k}{k!}$, $k=0,1,\ldots$ $\lambda>0$	λ	λ	$e^{\lambda(e^t-1)}$
Geometric	$q^k p$, $k=0,1,\ldots$ $0\le p\le 1$, $q=1-p$	$\dfrac{q}{p}$	$\dfrac{q}{p^2}$	$\dfrac{p}{1-qe^t}$
Negative Binomial	$\binom{r+k-1}{r-1}q^k p^r$, $k=0,1,\ldots$ $0\le p<1$, $q=1-p$	$\dfrac{rq}{p}$	$\dfrac{rq}{p^2}$	$\left(\dfrac{p}{1-qe^t}\right)^r$
Discrete Uniform on $1,\ldots,n$	$\dfrac{1}{n}$, $k=1,\ldots,n$	$\dfrac{n+1}{2}$	$\dfrac{n^2-1}{12}$	$\dfrac{e^t(1-e^{nt})}{n(1-e^t)}$, for $t\ne 0$

Continuous Distributions

Distribution	Probability Density Function; Parameters	Mean	Variance	Moment Generating Function
Uniform	$\dfrac{1}{b-a}$, $a \le x \le b$	$\dfrac{a+b}{2}$	$\dfrac{(b-a)^2}{12}$	$\dfrac{e^{bt}-e^{at}}{(b-a)t}$, $t \ne 0$
Exponential	$\lambda e^{-\lambda t}$, $t \ge 0; \lambda > 0$	$\dfrac{1}{\lambda}$	$\dfrac{1}{\lambda^2}$	$\left(\dfrac{\lambda}{\lambda-t}\right)$, $t < \lambda$
Gamma	$\dfrac{\beta^\alpha}{\Gamma(\alpha)}x^{\alpha-1}e^{-\beta x}$, $x \ge 0; \alpha,\beta > 0$	$\dfrac{\alpha}{\beta}$	$\dfrac{\alpha}{\beta^2}$	$\left(\dfrac{\beta}{\beta-t}\right)^\alpha$, $t < \beta$
Normal	$\dfrac{1}{\sqrt{2\pi}\sigma}e^{-\frac{(x-\mu)^2}{2\sigma^2}}$, $-\infty < x < \infty; \sigma > 0$	μ	σ^2	$e^{\mu t + \frac{\sigma^2 t^2}{2}}$
Lognormal	$\dfrac{1}{\sigma y\sqrt{2\pi}}e^{-\frac{1}{2}\left(\frac{\ln y-\mu}{\sigma}\right)^2}$, $y > 0; \sigma > 0$	$e^{\mu+\frac{\sigma^2}{2}}$	$e^{2\mu+\sigma^2}(e^{\sigma^2}-1)$	
Pareto	$\dfrac{\alpha}{\beta}\left(\dfrac{\beta}{x}\right)^{\alpha+1}$, $x \ge \beta > 0; \alpha > 2$	$\dfrac{\alpha\beta}{\alpha-1}$	$\dfrac{\alpha\beta^2}{\alpha-2}-\left(\dfrac{\alpha\beta}{\alpha-1}\right)^2$	
Weibull	$\alpha\beta x^{\alpha-1}e^{-\beta x^\alpha}$, $x \ge 0; \alpha,\beta > 0$	$\dfrac{\Gamma\left(1+\frac{1}{\alpha}\right)}{\beta^{\frac{1}{\alpha}}}$	$\dfrac{1}{\beta^{\frac{2}{\alpha}}}\left[\Gamma\left(1+\dfrac{2}{\alpha}\right)-\Gamma\left(1+\dfrac{1}{\alpha}\right)^2\right]$	
Beta	$\dfrac{\Gamma(\alpha+\beta)}{\Gamma(\alpha)\cdot\Gamma(\beta)}x^{\alpha-1}(1-x)^{\beta-1}$, $0 < x < 1$; $\alpha,\beta > 0$	$\dfrac{\alpha}{\alpha+\beta}$	$\dfrac{\alpha\beta}{(\alpha+\beta)^2(\alpha+\beta+1)}$	

Answers to the Exercises

CHAPTER 2

2-1.   KH, QH, JH, KD, QD, JD

2-2.   (a) $S = \{x|x > 0 \text{ and } x \text{ rational}\}$
        (b) $E = \{x| \, 1,000 < x < 1,000,000 \text{ and } x \text{ rational}\}$

2-3.   (a) $S = \{1, 2, 3, \ldots, 25\}$ (b) $E = \{1, 3, 5, \ldots, 25\}$

2-4. $(1, 1),(1, 2),(1, 3),(1, 4),(1, 5),(1, 6),(2, 1),(2, 2),(2, 3),(2, 4),(2, 5),(2, 6),$
        $(3, 1),(3, 2),(3, 3),(3, 4),(3, 5),(3, 6),(4, 1),(4, 2),(4, 3),(4, 4),(4, 5),(4, 6),$
        $(5, 1),(5, 2),(5, 3),(5, 4),(5, 5),(5, 6),(6, 1),(6, 2),(6, 3),(6, 4),(6, 5),(6, 6)$

2-5.   (a) 6 (b) 5 (c) 2 (d) 8

2-6.   BBB, BBG, BGB, BGG, GBB, GBG, GGB,GGG

2-7. $\sim E = \{2, 4, 6, \ldots, 24\}$

2-8.   KC, QC, JC

2-9. $A \cup B = \{x|1,000 < x < 500,000 \text{ and } x \text{ rational}\}$,
        $A \cap B = \{x|50,000 < x < 100,000 \text{ and } x \text{ rational}\}$

2-10. $(H, 3)$, $(H, 4)$, $(H, 5)$, $(H, 6)$

2-11. $E \cup F$
        $= \{(1, 5),(2, 4),(3, 3),(4, 2),(5, 1),(1, 1),(2, 2),(4, 4),(5, 5),(6, 6)\}$
        $E \cap F = \{(3, 3)\}$

2-12. $E = \{GGG, GGB, GBG, GBB\}$, $F = \{GBG, GBB, BBG, BBB\}$,
        $E \cup F = \{GGG, GGB, GBG, GBB, BBG, BBB\}$,
        $E \cap F = \{GBG, GBB\}$

2-15.   (a)   "You are not taking either a mathematics course or an
              economics course" is equivalent to "you are not taking a
              mathematics course *and* you are not taking an econo-
              mics course."
        (b)   "You are not taking both a mathematics course and an
              economics course" is equivalent to "you are either not
              taking a mathematics course or you are not taking an
              economics course."

2-16.   46

2-17.   92

2-18.   25

2-19.   92

2-20.   61

2-21.   (a) 11 (b) 17 (c) 44 (d) 50

2-22.   12

2-23.   360

2-24.   1568

2-25.   208

2-27.   1296; 360

2-28.   8,000,000;   483,840

2-29.   3,991,680

2-30.   5040

2-31. 24,360

2-32. 17,280

2-33. 10,080

2-34. 4,060

2-35. 2,598,960

2-36. (a) 1,287 (b) 5,148 (c) 144

2-37. 1,756,755

2-38. 146,107,962

2-39. 34,650

2-40. 27,720

2-41. 1,680

2-42. 280

2-43. $16s^4 - 32s^3t + 24s^2t^2 - 8st^3 + t^4$

2-44. $-48,384$

2-47. 880

CHAPTER 3

3-1. 3/8

3-2. 7/8

3-3. (a) 3/16 (b) 9/16

3-4. $47/68 \approx .6912$

3-5. (a) 1/6 (b) 1/18 (c) 1/6

3-6. $17/78 \approx .2179$

3-7.   (a) 1/30 (b) 1/2 (c) 1/5

3-8.   (a) .5729 (b) .0651

3-9.   .0079

3-10.   .6271

3-11.   .6501

3-12. $31/33 \approx .9394$

3-13.   .0014

3-14.   .0475

3-15.   (a) 1:5 (b) 17:1

3-16. $\dfrac{b}{a+b}$

3-19.   .459

3-20.   .54

3-21.   (a) .721 (b) .183

3-22.   .16

3-23.   .1817

3-24.   .6493

3-25.   .8125

3-26.   (a) .0588 (b) .5588 (c) .3824

3-27.   3/7

3-28.   1/2

3-29.   .0859

3-32. (A, C)

3-33.   Dependent

3-34.   (a) .63   (b) .33

3-35.   .8574

3-36.   .2696

3-37.   No

3-38.   (a) 29%   (b) .2759

3-39.   5/9

3-40.   (a) .7059   (b) .7273

3-41.   .1905

3-42.   (a) .5581   (b) .0175

3-43.   1/4

3-44.   .6087

3-45.   .2442

3-46.   .05

3-47.   .60

3-48.   .256

3-49.   .48

3-50.   .52

3-51.   .33

3-52.   .40

3-53.   2/5

3-54.   .173

3-55.   4

3-56.   .467

3-57.   1/2

3-58.   .53

3-59.   .657

3-60.   .0141

3-61.   .2922

3-62.   .21955

3-63.   .40

3-64.   .42

CHAPTER 4

4-1.

Number of heads (x)	0	1	2	3
$p(x)$	1/8	3/8	3/8	1/8

4-2. $p(x) = 1/10 \quad x = 0, 1, \ldots, 9$

4-3. $p(x) = (1/6)(5/6)^x \quad x = 0, 1, 2, \ldots$
       $F(x) = 1 - (5/6)^{x+1} \quad x = 0, 1, 2, \ldots$

4-4.

x	$p(x)$	$F(x)$
2	1/36	1/36
3	1/18	1/12
4	1/12	1/6
5	1/9	5/18
6	5/36	5/12
7	1/6	7/12
8	5/36	13/18
9	1/9	5/6
10	1/12	11/12
11	1/18	35/36
12	1/36	1

4-5.   7

4-6. $267/108 \approx 2.47$

4-7. $114; $114

4-8. $1190

4-10.   5

4-11.   Modes are 1 and 2

4-12. $210/36 \approx 5.8333$

4-13.   3,427.84

4-15.   (a) .75   (b) .9444

4-16. $\mu = .276; \quad \sigma = .53587$

4-17. $\bar{x} = 3.64; \quad s = 1.9667$

4-18.   45%

4-19.   374.4

4-20.   984.58

CHAPTER 5

5-1.   (a) 0.2461   (b) 0.05469

5-2.   (a) 0.2907   (b) 0.5155

5-3.   0.00217

5-4.   (a) 0.1858   (b) $\mu = 20$; $\sigma^2 = 19.6$

5-5.   Loss of $14

5-6.   (a) .0898   (b) .8670

5-7.   5,000; 4,500

5-8.   (a) .1754   (b) .2581   (c) .8416

5-9.   .9945

5-11. $2/9 \approx .2222$

5-12.   .3709

5-13.   (a) .2448   (b) 3

5-14.   (a) 8.1   (b) 3.199

5-15.   3.25, 1.864

5-16.   (a) .3293   (b) .1219

5-17.   (a) .2231   (b) .3347   (c) .2510

5-18.   1,900

5-19.   (a) .244   (b) .9747   (c) 244

5-20.   (a) .0719   (b) .8913

5-23.   .0372

5-24.   (a) .0791   (b) .0374

5-25. $E(X) = 12; \quad V(X) = 156$

5-26. (a) .0783 (b) .0347

5-27. (a) .0751 (b) 15

5-28. (a) .0404 (b) 24 (20 failures and 4 successes)

5-29. $E(X) = 25; \quad V(X) = 150$

5-30. .0375

5-31. 40 (32 failures and 8 successes)

5-32. (a) .0437 (b) 34

5-34. $\mu = \$13,000; \quad \sigma = \$7,211.10$

5-36. .92452

5-37. .469

5-38. .0955

5-39 2

5-40 7,231

5-41. .04

CHAPTER 6

6-1. (a) 250 (b) 0.6 (c) 1.06

6-2. 5.8333

6-3. $E[u(W_1)] = 8.289; \quad E[u(W_2)] = 8.926$

6-9. (b) $E(X) = (n + 1)/2; \quad V(X) = (n^2 - 1)/12$

6-10. $M_X(t) = .42 + .30e^t + .17e^{2t} + .11e^{3t}$;
       $E(X) = .97$; $E(X^2) = 1.97$

6-12. $e^{4t}(.4 + .6e^{3t})^8$

6-13. Negative binomial with $p = .7$ and $r = 5$

6-14. 1, 4, 15, 2, 13, 0, 11, 14, 9, 12, 7, 10, 5, 8, 3

6-15. 7

6-16. 2, 3, 2, 2

6-17. 698.9

6-18. $\frac{19}{27} + \frac{8}{27}e^t$

CHAPTER 7

7-1. (b) $F(X) = 0$ for $x < 0$, $.75x^2 + .25x$ for $0 \le x \le 1$, and 1 for
      $x > 1$ (c) $P(0 \le X \le 1/2) = .3125$; $P(1/4 \le X \le 3/4) = .50$

7-2. (a) 6 (b) .6936

7-3. .75

7-4. (a) $2/\pi$ (b) 1/2

7-5. .4343; 2/3; .8471

7-6. (a) .4055; .6419 (b) $ln2$

7-7. .20; .4940

7-8. .625; .0677

7-9. 0.3

7-12. .46875

7-13.   93.06

7-14.   1/2

7-15.   28/15

7-16.   1/9

7-17.   .57813

CHAPTER 8

8-2.   50;   833.33

8-3.   1/6

8-4.   (a) 3/10 (b) 1/12

8-5.   (a) 42.5; 18.75   (b) 44 minutes

8-7.   (a) 70;   300   (b) .7167

8-8.   (a) .3818 (b) .1455

8-9.   (a) .4512 (b) .1653

8-10. $\frac{1}{\lambda} \cdot ln\, 2$

8-11.   (a) .5654 (b) .1889

8-12. $\frac{1}{b-t}$

8-13.   (a) .4821 (b) .4541

8-15.   (a) .0111 (b) .2063

8-16.   1.9179; 9.2420

8-19.   (a) .1535 (b) .3679

8-22.   1.20;   .48

8-23.   1.50;   .1875

8-24. $\alpha = 12$; $\beta = 2/3$

8-25.   (a) $1 - e^{-3x}(3x+1)$ (b) .9988   (c) .1818

8-26.   3270

8-27.   (a) .8155   (b) .4238   (c) .6826   (d) .0990

8-28.   (a) 0.93   (b) -1.90 (c) -1.35 (d) 0.97   (e) 1.645   (f) 1.96

8-29. $1 - \alpha$; $2\alpha - 1$

8-30.   .8272 (Table),   .82689 (TI-83)

8-31.   .9793 (Table),   .97939 (TI-83)

8-32.   (a) .9270 (Table), .92698 (TI-83)
        (b) .9711 (Using Table answer in binomial probability),
             .97104 (using TI-83 answer)

8-33.   (a) .7881 (Table), .78815(TI-83)
        (b) .4895 (Using Table answer in binomial probability),
             .48957 (using TI-83 answer)

8-34.   .5244 (Table),   .524304 (TI-83)

8-35.   3.5

8-36. $E(Y) = 160.77$; $V(Y) = 4{,}484.96$

8-37.   .6684 (Table), .6691 (TI-83)

8-38.   .1335 (Table), .1330 (TI-83)

8-39. e^{μ}

8-40. (a) .2776(Table), .276668(TI-83)
       (b) .1788(Table), .178096(TI-83)

8-41. $\mu = 7.7498;$ $\sigma = .3853$

8-43. (a) 5.6 (b) 5.9733 (c) 4.8761 (d) .22054

8-44. (a) 700 (b) 200 (c) 93,333.33

8-45. (a) $(1/2)\pi^{1/2}$ (b) $(3/4)\pi^{1/2}$ (c) $(15/8)\pi^{1/2}$

8-46. (a) .2007 (b) .1666

8-47. $10.5x^2$

8-48. (a) .4737 (b) .0613 (c) .66389

8-50. $315x^3(1 - x)^{1/2}/32$

8-51. 105

8-52. .60; .04

8-53. .3125

8-54. .47178

8-56. .42045

8-57. .1915

8-58. 10,256

8-59. .4348

8-60   173.3

8-61. .123

8-62. .8185

8-63.   .1587

8-64.   .9887

8-65.   .7698

8-66.   6,342,547.5

CHAPTER 9

9-1.   740.82

9-2.   575.52

9-3. $E[u(W_1)] = 2.3009;\quad E[u(W_2)] = 2.2574$

9-4. $(e^{bt} - e^{at})/[t(b - a)]$ if $t \neq 0$, 1 if $t = 0$.

9-5. $(b + a)/2$

9-6. $(2e^t - 2t - 2)/t^2$ if $t \neq 0$, 1 if $t = 0$

9-7.   1/3

9-8.   Gamma with $\alpha = 5$ and $\beta = 2$

9-9. $e^{5t}[3/(3 - 2t)]$

9-10. $E(X) = 1;\quad V(X) = 2$

9-11. $E(X^2) = \mu^2 + \sigma^2$

9-12.   (a) $ln\, y$ (b) $1/y$ (both on $[1, e]$)

9-13. $1 - e^{-3y}$, for $y \geq 0$

9-14.   (a) y^3 (b) $3y^2$, for $0 < y \leq 1$

9-15.   .80

9-17.   2, 4, 8, 6

9-18.   9, 6, 2, 3

9-19. $F(0) = .90$
$F(x) = .90 + .09x/1000$, for $0 < x \leq 1000$
$F(x) = .99 + .01(x-1000)/9000$, for $1000 < x \leq 10,000$

9-20.   100

9-21. $F(0) = .90$
$F(x) = .90 + .10[1 - (200/(x+200))^3]$, for $x > 0$

9-22. $\dfrac{1}{(1 + x)^2}$, $x \geq 0$

9-23. $\dfrac{100 - x}{100}$, $0 \leq x < 100$

9-24.   1

9-25.   50

9-26.   .3

9-27.   .93427

9-28.   500

9-29.   5644.30

9-30. $2 + 3e^{-2/3}$

9-31.   1.9

9-32.   1.7067

9-33.   403.436

9-34.   998.72

9-35. $\dfrac{4}{y^2}$

9-36. $25\left[\ln\left(\frac{v}{10,000}\right) - .04\right]$

9-37. $.125e^{-(.10y)^{1.25}}(.1y)^{.25}$

9-38. $\frac{5}{2r^2}$

9-39. $f_X\left(\frac{y}{2}\right)\left[\frac{1}{2}\right]$

9-40. $\frac{5}{36}$

CHAPTER 10

10-1.

y \ x	1	2	3	p(y)
1	2/27	1/9	4/27	1/3
2	4/27	2/9	8/27	2/3
p(x)	2/9	1/3	4/9	

10-2.

y \ x	0	1	2	p(y)
0	1/45	10/45	10/45	21/45
1	6/45	15/45	0	21/45
2	3/45	0	0	3/45
p(x)	10/45	25/45	10/45	

10-3. $E(X) = 20/9; \quad E(Y) = 5/3$

10-4. $E(X) = 1; \quad E(Y) = 3/5$

10-5. $V(X) = 4/9; \quad V(Y) = 28/75$

10-6.   15/64

10-7.   (a) $1/2 + x, \ 0 \le x \le 1$ (b) $1/2 + y, \ 0 \le y \le 1$

10-8.   (a) $2x^3 + (3/2)x^2, 0 \le x \le 1$
       (b) $2/3 + 3y - (2/3)y^3 - 3y^2, \ 0 \le y \le 1$

10-9. (a) 29/32 (b) 41/96

10-10. 7/12

10-11. 1/2

10-12. $E(X) = 31/40;\quad E(Y) = 9/20$

10-13. 1/125

10-14. (a) $(35 - 2x)/150, 0 \le x \le 5$ (b) $(55 - 2y)/750, 0 \le y \le 25$

10-15. $E(X) = 85/36;\quad E(Y) = 325/36$

10-16.

x	1	2	3
$p(x\|1)$	2/9	1/3	4/9

10-17.

y	1	2
$p(y\|1)$	1/3	2/3

10-18. 20/9

10-19. $1/2 + x,\ 0 \le x \le 1$

10-20. $(2x^2 + 3y)/(2x^3 + ((3/2)x^2)),\ \ 0 < y \le x \le 1$

10-21. (a) $4/5 + (24/5)y,\ 0 \le y \le 1/2$ (b) 3/10

10-22. (a) $3y^2, 0 < y < 1$ (b) $2x/y^2, 0 < x < y < 1$ (c) $2y/3$

(d) 1/3

10-23. Independent

10-24. Dependent

10-25. Independent

10-26. Dependent

10-27. 20%

10-28. .0488

10-29. .625

10-30. .41

10-31. $\displaystyle\int_{0}^{0.5}\int_{0.5}^{1} f(s,t)\,ds\,dt + \int_{0}^{1}\int_{0}^{0.5} f(s,t)\,ds\,dt$

10-32. $\displaystyle\frac{6}{125,000}\int_{20}^{30}\int_{20}^{50-x}(50-x-y)\,dy\,dx$

10.33. 2/5

10-34. .19

10-35. .576

10-36. 1/4

10-37. 8/9

10-38. .4167

10-39. 896.91

10-40. .204

10-41. 1/12

10-42. .9856

10-43. .488

10-44. $15y^{3/2}(1-y^{1/2})$

10-45. 7/8

10-46. .172

10-47. 5.78

10.48. .833

10-49. .45474

CHAPTER 11

11-1.

s	2	3	4	5
$p_S(s)$	2/27	7/27	10/27	8/27

11-2. 11/18

11-3. $6(e^{-2s} - e^{-3s})$

11-4. .95833

11-5. $F_S(s) = 1 - e^{-s}(1+s)$

11-6. $(1 - t/2 - t^2/2)^2$

11-7. $E(X + Y) = 35/9 = 20/9 + 15/9 = E(X) + E(Y)$

11-8. $E(X + Y) = 8/9; \quad E(X) = E(Y) = 4/9$

11-11. (a) 5/27 (b) 16/81 (c) $-1/81$

11-12. (a) 13/162 (b) 13/162 (c) 11/81

11-13. 68/81

11-14. (a) 1.5 (b) 1.6 (c) .25 (d) .24 (e) $-.05$ (f) .39

11-15. (a) 1/20 (b) 3/80 (c) 2/5 (d) 11/80

11-16. $-.2041$

11-17. .5774

11-18. $-\frac{1}{11}$

11-19. (a) $f_X(x) = \frac{1}{4} + \frac{3}{4}x^2,\ f_Y(y) = \frac{1}{4} + \frac{3}{4}y^2,$
$f_X(x) \cdot f_Y(y) \neq f(x,y)$

(b) $E(X) = E(Y) = E(XY) = Cov(X,Y) = 0$

11-20. $(2e^{2t} + 7e^{3t} + 6e^{4t})/15$

11-21. $[(e^{2t} - 1)^2/(4t^2)]$

11-22. $E(S) = n(7/2);\quad V(S) = n(35/12)$

11-23. 14/81

11-24. $-25/81$

11-25. .8198 (Table),   .82029 (TI-83)

11-26. (a) 7.5   (b) 5.5   (c) 1

11-27. 5

11-28. (a) 18.75   (b) 24.75   (c) 9

11-29. 20.4

11-30. 4.6

11-31. 56,364

11-32. (a) $6x(1 - x)$, for $0 < x < 1$ (b) 1/2   (c) 1/20

11-33. 1/2

11-34. $y^2/18$

11-35. 1/30

11-36. 1/60

11-37. (a) 5000   (b) 1,666,666.67

11-38. (a) 3215.48   (b) 606,665.15

11-39. .9898(Table),   .98993(TI-83)

11-40. 322,434.81

11-41. 1/64

11-42. $\dfrac{1}{4}\pi \displaystyle\int_{3/2}^{5/2} x \cos \pi x (1 + \sin \pi x)^3 \, dx$

11-43. 2025

11-44. .71

11-45. .295

11-46. 5.72

11-47. $\dfrac{2L^2}{3}$

11-48. .414

11-49. $\dfrac{2}{(2x+1)^2}$ for $x > 0$

11-50. .8413

11-51. 11

11-52. 200

11-53. 0

11-54. .041

11-55. 6

11-56. 5,000

11-57. 10,560

11-58. 19,300

11-59. 8.80

11-60. .2743

11-61. 16

11-62 .03139

11-63. 328

CHAPTER 12

12-1.   A would win in 13 tosses

12-2.   13

12-3.   2, 3, 3

12-4.   (a) [.45, .55] (b) [.43, .57]

12-5.   (a) [.504, .496] (b) [.54144, .45856]

12-6.   [.22, .33, .45]

12-7.   [.47, .28, .25]

12-8.   [5/12, 7/12]

12-9.   [9/16, 7/16]

12-10. [11/57, 20/57, 26/57]

12-11. [15/37, 12/37, 10/37]

12-13. (a) $\begin{bmatrix} 9/7 & 3/7 \\ 6/7 & 9/7 \end{bmatrix}$ (b) $\begin{bmatrix} 6/7 & 1/7 \\ 4/7 & 3/7 \end{bmatrix}$ (c) 4/7

12-14. (a) $\begin{bmatrix} 7/5 & 3/5 & 1/5 \\ 6/5 & 9/5 & 3/5 \\ 4/5 & 6/5 & 7/5 \end{bmatrix}$ (b) $\begin{bmatrix} 14/15 & 1/15 \\ 4/5 & 1/5 \\ 8/15 & 7/15 \end{bmatrix}$ (c) 4/5

Bibliography

[1]   Bodie, Z., A. Kane and A. Marcus, *Investments* (Sixth Edition).
        New York: Richard D. Irwin, 2005.

[2]   Bowers, N. et al., *Actuarial Mathematics* (Second Edition).
        Schaumburg: Society of Actuaries, 1997.

[3]   Broverman, S., *Mathematics of Investment and Credit* (Third
        Edition). Winsted: Actex Publications, 2004.

[4]   Herzog, T., *Introduction to Credibility Theory* (Third Edition).
        Winsted: Actex Publications, 1999.

[5]   Hogg, R. and A. Craig, *Introduction to Mathematical Statistics*
        (Sixth Edition). New York: McMillan, 2004.

[6]   Hossack, I., J. Pollard and B. Zehnwirth, *Introductory Statistics
        with Applications in General Insurance* (Second Edition).
        Cambridge: Cambridge University Press, 1999.

[7]   Hull, J., *Options, Futures and Other Derivatives* (Sixth Edition).
        Upper Saddle River: Prentice-Hall, 2003.

[8]   Klugman, S., H. Panjer and G. Willmot, *Loss Models: From
        Data to Decisions* (Second Edition). New York: John Wiley &
        Sons, 2004.

[9]   London, D., *Survival Models and Their Estimation* (Third
        Edition). Winsted: Actex Publications, 1997.

[10]   Meyer, P., *Introductory Probability and Statistical Applications* (Second Edition). Reading: Addison-Wesley, 1976.

[11]   Markowitz, H., "Portfolio Selection," Journal of Finance, 7:   77-91 (March 1952).

[12]   Mood, A., F. Graybill and D. Boes, *Introduction to the Theory of Statistics* (Third Edition). New York: McGraw-Hill, 1974.

[13]   Panjer, H., "AIDS: Survival Analysis of Persons Testing HIV+," *TSA* XL (1988), 517.

[14]   Panjer, H. (editor), *Financial Economics*.   Schaumburg: The Actuarial Foundation, 1998.

[15]   Ross, S., *Introduction to Probability Models* (Eighth Edition). San Diego: Academic Press, 2003.

[16]   Sheaffer, R., *Introduction to Probability and Its Applications* (Second Edition). Duxbury Press, 1995.

[17]   United States Bureau of the Census, *Statistical Abstract of the United States*, 125th Edition. Washington D.C., 2006.

[18]   Weiss, N., *Introductory Statistics* (Seventh Edition). Reading: Addison-Wesley, 2005.

Index